BOOK OF ANONYMITY

Before you start to read this book, take this moment to think about making a donation to punctum books, an independent non-profit press,

@ https://punctumbooks.com/support

If you're reading the e-book, you can click on the image below to go directly to our donations site.

Any amount, no matter the size, is appreciated and will help us to keep our ship of fools afloat. Contributions from dedicated readers will also help us to keep our commons open and to cultivate new work that can't find a welcoming port elsewhere. Our adventure is not possible without your support.
Vive la Open Access.

Hieronymus Bosch, *Ship of Fools* (1490–1500)

BOOK OF ANONYMITY

An edited collection

p. punctumbooks

Preface

Writing Anonymity

The Book of Anonymity gathers contributions by more than forty writers, academics, and artists. Published in the tradition of author-less texts, the volume is edited by the Anon Collective. Contributions are published partially anonymously, too. Withholding author identities affects writing and reading, adding a reflexive layer to the collection, raising broader questions about anonymity, and thus providing one way into the subject. In place of a foreword, we share our thoughts on writing anonymously as one reading guide to this volume. We also supply a how-to guide for citing the book and its anonymous contributions.

Writing anonymously amplifies well-established questions of authorship and readership: who gets to speak, with what authority, from what position; who is foregrounded and who is marginalized; what constitutes a writing subject and what brings a reader, a public into being? Rarely framed in terms of anonymity, these questions nevertheless have been interrogated at length, in Foucauldian critiques of authorship, the writing culture debates of the late 1980s, or feminist scholarship, for example. That the body of literature on the death of the author is attributed to particular authors perhaps demonstrates how resilient notions of authorship are. Such writing and reading questions evoked by notions of authorship have lost none of their relevance. On the contrary, the digitalization of textual-visual production, the algorithmic aggregation and segregation of knowledge publics, the relentless competition and self-branding of individualized knowledge producers, coupled with techniques for securing and defying attribution have intensified the stakes. Copyrights and intellectual property, the battle for open access, the grip of evaluation regimes, whistleblowers, fake news: there is no lack of evidence that the relations between authors and texts, knowledge producers and their products, are highly contested, much debated, and embedded in open-ended processes of change.

Editing and contributing anonymously constitute experiments in anonymity that speak to the aggressive valuation regimes shaping contemporary artistic and academic knowledge productions alike. This is not to discount the usefulness of attribution, but to trouble the ease with which labor and imagination are dissected, measured, and attached to the nexus of person, value, and knowledge. To name, in the words of one Deleuzian (oh, no, we just did it again) contribution to this volume, is to "define people, things, as individuals, to mark them, hold them, hierarchize them, to press them into service and turn them into value"[1]. Another contribution advocates and questions whether an ethics of anonymity can engender the kind of care that individualized practices arguably strive for yet undermine.[2] Not all contributions speak to such concerns directly. Still, all consider what is at stake in the im/possibilities of anonymous expression, at a time of thick digital traces, data aggregation, and data mining. Editing and contributing anonymously are practical commitments to one of the red threads crisscrossing this book.

The absence of author names does not necessarily do away with authors. Withholding author names, at least in this context, does not give us no-authors, but gives us unidentified, or yet to be identified, authors. Far from making authors disappear, the absence of author names renders authorship more powerfully present. The argument that anonymity can be understood as a particular patterning of absences and presences, we develop further in the introduction. Here, we simply note that removing

[1] See "Speak Their Endless Names," this volume, 424.

[2] See "Longing for a Selfless Self and Other Ambivalences of Anonymity," this volume, 401.

names can also enforce the notion of author that it seemingly undermines.

Obviously, more is missing than just names: without names, making sense through attribution becomes harder. You do not know whether you know us from other circumstances, be it personal encounters or by reading other stuff we have written. Without our names, you rely on implicit markers of our gender, class, or attachments to this or that language. Citation cartels and other means of distinction are disrupted. There is no straightforward way of googling us, and therefore you can only guess our professions, our institutional and disciplinary affiliations, or status. Titles and texts are all you have, to establish what interests you, or to judge what is justified, or trustworthy.

The Book of Anonymity consists of texts and visuals from contributors whom we, the editors, know—either through collaborative projects, conferences and workshops, or through their work in art, social and cultural sciences, or open-data activism. Most contributors are well known in their respective fields; some speak from "emerging" positions, while others still live in the contemporary reality of being established yet precarious. The writing-we of this editorial introduction is that of the Google Docs–mediated Anon Collective: five people; two social anthropologists, one sociologist, one designer, and one curator; two women and three men. While the editing collective is German-ish, the authors of this volume come from a more extensive array, including artists from France, the UK, Germany, and Iran as well as criminologists, art theorists, computer scientists, philosophers, political scientists, and scholars of media and culture from all over Europe and the United States. Now, you know quite a bit about the bunch behind this volume. Still, you do not know who has done what. Within this anonymity set, we remain unidentified but not unknown, leaving you free to guess what is written by an artist or an academic, by someone "prominent" and perhaps comfortably safe or someone "emerging" and probably struggling. This might leave you to concentrate more, or differently, on the content — unless the opposite occurs, and you spend your time guessing.

This book, however, must be taken into account to be fair to those who struggle to make their labor count. With this in mind, we choose to proceed in a way that highlights tensions between authorship and anonymity, while still allowing attribution and referencing for individual contributions. In terms of citation, this means that the book and book chapters will be referenced like this:

> BOOK: Anon Collective, ed. *Book of Anonymity*. Earth: punctum books, 2020.
>
> CHAPTERS: Individual contributions are referenced with full author names and chapter titles, except for "Longing for a Selfless Self," whose author chooses to remain fully anonymous.

The authors, to summarize, are only partially anonymous because they can be identified in the back of the book, where we provide an overview of contributors and a citation how-to for each contribution (page 481). This is a concession to people's dependence on contemporary knowledge regimes, but it also speaks to the temporality of anonymity more broadly. At a time when the possibilities for data storage continue to increase, data are always subject to future computation, pattern recognition, cross-linking, and thus potential identification. Anonymity, under these conditions, is often temporary, fragile, and incomplete. Returning to the notion of a reading guide, we note that anonymity's temporal fragility helps to maintain the tense space in which absences and presences play out. Anonymity's play of absences and presences, and its temporal vulnerability then, is a feature of our writing experiment and a guiding theme of this book.

> —The Anon Collective, Earth, Internet, June 2, 2020

CITATION GUIDE
The author is dead, and this *Book of Anonymity* is written in the tradition of author-less text. Yet, bound up in regimes of accountability, we are providing a citation guide on page 481, complying with conventions of authorship.

FREE COLOUR
The *Book of Anonymity* is printed in black and white, to keep it affordable. A full-colour PDF version of the book is available at punctum books for free download.

Keywords
Anonymity, Data Security, Surveillance, Personhood,
Privacy, Art-Science Collaboration, Digital Cultures

Subject Codes
COM079010 COMPUTERS / Human-Computer Interaction (HCI)
COM079000 COMPUTERS / Social Aspects
SOC000000 SOCIAL SCIENCE / General
SOC010000 SOCIAL SCIENCE / Feminism & Feminist Theory
SOC071000 SOCIAL SCIENCE / Technology Studies

Edited by Anon Collective

All contributions to this volume are published pseudo-anonymously.
Aiming to highlight tensions between authorship and anonymity while still
allowing attribution, we provide an overview of contributors and
a citation how-to for each contribution in the
back of this book (page 481).

Book of Anonymity. Copyright © 2020 by the editors and authors.
This work carries a Creative Commons BY-NC-SA 4.0 International
license, which means that you are free to copy and redistribute the
material in any medium or format, and you may also remix, transform and
build upon the material, as long as you clearly attribute the
work to the authors (but not in a way that suggests the authors or
punctum books endorses you and your work), you do not use this work for
commercial gain in any form whatsoever, and that for any remixing
and transformation, you distribute your rebuild under the same license.
http://creativecommons.org/licenses/by-nc-sa/4.0/. Normal citations
in academic and other forms of literature, are, of course,
possible in any case.

This book has been made possible with the generous support of
the Volkswagen Foundation (project number VW89490).

VolkswagenStiftung

First published in 2021 by punctum books,
Earth, Milky Way. www.punctumbooks.com

ISBN 978-1-953035-30-1 (print)
ISBN 978-1-953035-31-8 (ePDF)
DOI: https://www.doi.org/10.21983/P3.0315.1.00
LCCN 2020951163

Book design: Dicey Studios

6   Preface

Section A   **INTRO**

16   Toward a Kaleidoscopic Understanding
      of Anonymity

35   Artistic Research on Anonymity

Section B   **RECONFIGURATION**

70   Anonymity and Transgression: Caste,
      Social Reform, and Blood Donation in India

88   Anonymity: The Politicisation of a Concept

110   USAE

116   Big Data's End Run around Anonymity
      and Consent

142   A List of Famous Artists Who Used
      to Be Invigilators

151   Anonymity as Everyday Phenomenon
      and as a Topic of Research

167   Anonymity on Demand: The Great Offshore

Section C — ASSAULT

- 188 — DNA Works!
  Merging Genetics and the Digital Realm

- 210 — Sanitary Policy and the Policy of Anonymity:
  Observations on a Game on Endocrine Disruptors

- 226 — Where Do the Data Live?
  Anonymity and Neighborhood Networks

- 255 — Fraught Platform Governmentality:
  Anonymity, Content Moderation, and Regulatory Strategies over Yik Yak

- 275 — Anonymity: Obsolescence and Desire

- 286 — Policing Normality: Police Work, Anonymity, and a Sociology of the Mundane

Section D — WEAPON

- 294 — Amazonian Flesh: How to Hang in Trees during Strike?

- 306 — Proximity, Distance, and State Powers:
  Policing Practices and the Regulation of Anonymity

- 326 — Dual Reality:
  (Un)Observed Magic in the Workplace

336   A Provisional Manifesto for Invigilator-Friendly Artworks, or Your Artwork Is an Invigilator's Labor Conditions: Informally Sourced from Security Guards at an Art Gallery in Central London

340   Care or Control?
Police, Youth, and Mutual Anonymity

346   She Remembers

Section E   **DELIGHT**

356   Collective Pleasures of Anonymity:
From Public Restrooms to 4chan and Chatroulette

379   Transformella Malor Ikeae:
InnerCity Ikeality [4.4.6.11]

394   Authenticity

401   Longing for a Selfless Self and other Ambivalences of Anonymity: A Personal Account

424   Speak their Endless Names

433   Bitcoin Anonymous? Of Trust in Code and Paper

447   Anonymity Workshop

466   List of Figures
470   List of Artworks
471   Contributors
481   Citation Guide
486   Acknowledgments

A
INTRO

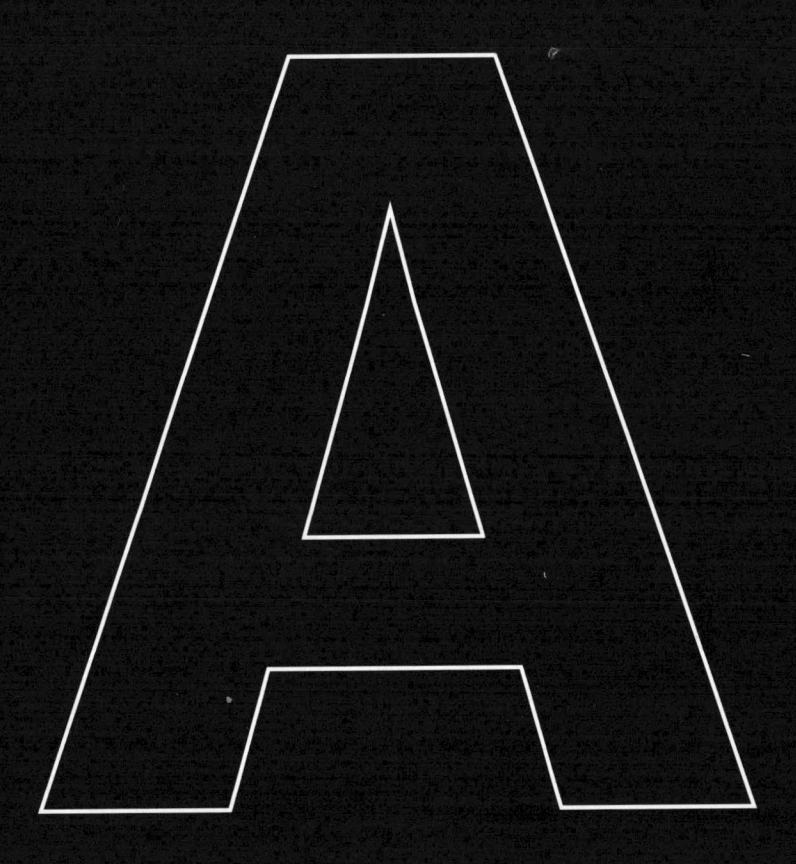

Toward a Kaleidoscopic Understanding of Anonymity

I've been through the desert on a horse with no name.
It felt good to be out of the rain.
In the desert you can't remember your name,
'Cause there ain't no one for to give you no pain.
La la, la, la, la la la, la la la, la.
—Dewey Bunnell, "Horse with No Name"

Let's start an anonymous club,
we can sit close in the dark.
Come round to mine,
we can swap clothes and drink wine all night....
Let's start an anonymous club,
I'll make us name badges with question marks.
—Courtney Barnett, "Anonymous Club"

Anonymity, in Dewey Bunell's song, evokes a lonely rider. High "on a horse with no name," a.k.a. cocaine, the rider is part of an imaginary, where anonymity grants freedom from social control and norms. In tension with the romantic image of a free life, accountable to no one, stand other experiences with anonymity. Unaccountability can be the breeding ground for racism, for example, or for genocidal crimes. Anonymity can also be an inherent part of such crimes, enabling further violence toward those who are robbed of their name, rights, and protections. The freedom granted by anonymity is deeply problematic. But freedom is not the only thing that anonymity has to offer. In Courtney Barnett's "Anonymous Club," we might, if we believe the song, encounter more caring forms of togetherness, unconstrained by name badges. Anonymity can take many forms, ranging from coked-up riders all the way to hyperlocal, technologically delinked but socially intensively connected utopias.

Forgetting your name on a nameless horse and creating an anonymity club by drawing the curtains and changing the name badges have one thing in common, though: in an age of thick digital traces, ubiquitous surveillance technologies, and biometrical identification, they appear increasingly fantastical. Deserts today no longer grant much anonymity. Drones inhabit desert skies, movements in the sand are tracked via GPS, and humans in a connected society are evermore surrounded by identification technologies. All understandings of anonymity that do not take into account the ubiquity of technologies of surveillance and identification are bound to be naïve. But conceptualizing anonymity merely as a set of technologies and techniques has come to a dead end, too: its inevitable consequence is that anonymity is increasingly impossible, because it cannot be ensured anymore by technologies alone. Yet, that, too, would be an incomplete story. While anonymity is technically becoming increasingly impossible, we also see sociotechnical practices on the rise that generate and make accessible a multitude of partial, temporarily restricted forms of anonymity in transformation. It therefore seems to be much more accurate to view the present moment as a "less *and* more of anonymity" at the same time, a moment in which anonymity becomes simultaneously impossible *and* amplified.

With this in mind, this collection aims to expand understandings of anonymity beyond technological frames while acknowledging their importance. Establishing a broader understanding of anonymity, which includes practices and relations, is crucial because it widens the cast of characters, providing the condition for a broader participation in the current reconfiguration of anonymity. Exploring multiple forms of anonymity, and reconceptualizing anonymity theoretically, can open new pathways for the technologies and techniques with which we can achieve it. But how do we reconceptualize anonymity? Our starting point is that anonymity is more than a set of increasingly ineffective techniques for preventing identification, or a fantasy of being unknown or unreachable. Anonymity has to be understood as a mode of knowing and being, indeed as a social form with a very distinct character. Anonymity, however fragile and temporary, often but not necessarily entails specific techniques; sometimes it happens by as a side effect. Whether or not it happens intentionally, anonymity can always be understood as a mode. And more often than not, being anonymous opens up potentialities or the possibility for things to be otherwise—further states, affects, practices, publics, and so on—which can then be tied to even further bigger goals, all the way to the elements of the famous slogan that was inscribed on the uniforms of the revolutionary Gardes Nationale in 1790: liberté (as in the case of anonymous speech), egalité (anonymous peer reviewing), and fraternité (anonymous encounters and collectivities). On the other hand, postcolonial approaches dealing with totalitarian forms of governance have shown us that anonymity can also open possibilities for genocide or hate speech. The question of what ethics might spring from such an understanding of anonymity remains critical.

This book has therefore not only a theoretical but also a political motivation. Broadening the understanding of anonymity beyond more or less effective techniques opens a path for broader participation. Understanding anonymity as a mode of being leads us into a more relational conception of anonymity and allows us to account for partial forms of anonymity, which might be easier to achieve under conditions of radically unequal power distribution. Thinking of anonymity as a mode of being and knowing also alerts us to its potentialities and consequences, asking, once more, questions about equality, freedom, collectivity, and their entanglements with power, exclusion, privilege, and aggression. If we want to grasp and shape the profound reconfigurations that anonymity undergoes, we need to do all this at once.[1]

On Method: The *Book of Anonymity* as Kaleidoscope

The research collaboration that led to this book included a diverse group of scholars, activists, and artists. Complex phenomena, like the reconfiguration of anonymity and related notions of privacy and transparency, cannot be sufficiently understood from within any one discipline. Anthropology, sociology, and cultural and media studies scholars brought case studies of anonymity and theoretical-analytical consideration to the table. Activists shared their experiences and analysis of working with, for, or against practices and theories of anonymity, while keeping visible what is at stake. Artists contributed interventions that challenged notions of where anonymity can be found, and how it can be achieved and maintained, offering new insight into the surprising shapes anonymity can take and enable. Like many schemes bringing together various disciplines, we sought ways of working that would allow new relations to form across

[1] Of course, our analytical and empirical work builds on the work and insights of a rich body of scholarship. The following references provided crucial conceptional input for our understanding of anonymity: Georg Simmel, "The Metropolis and Mental Life," in *Georg Simmel on Individuality and Social Forms*, ed. Donald. N. Levine (1903; Chicago: Chicago University Press, 1971); Kathleen. A. Wallace, "Anonymity," *Ethics and Information Technology* 1 (1999): 23–35; Gary T. Marx, "What's in a Name? Some Reflections on the Sociology of Anonymity," *Information Society* 15, no. 2 (1999): 99–112;
Martin Rost, "Über die Funktionalität von Anonymität für die bürgerliche Gesellschaft," in *Anonymität im Internet*, ed. H. Bäumler and A. von Mutius (Wiesbaden: Vieweg Verlag, 2003);
Monica Konrad, *Nameless Relations: Anonymity, Melanesia and Reproductive Gift Exchange between British Ova Donors and Recipients* (New York: Berghahn Books, 2005);
Julie Ponesse, "Navigating the Unknown: Towards a Positive Conception of Anonymity," *Southern Journal of Philosophy* 51, no. 3 (2013): 320–44;
and Julie Ponesse, "The Ties that Blind: Conceptualizing Anonymity." *Journal of Social Philosophy* 45, no. 3 (2014): 304–22.
Key texts for the conceptualization of anonymity and technology are furthermore Helen Nissenbaum, "The Meaning of Anonymity in an Information Age," *Information Society* 15 (1999): 141–44;
Ian Kerr, Carole Lucock, and Valerie Steeves, *Lessons from the Identity Trail: Anonymity, Pseudonymity and Identity in a Networked Society* (New York: Oxford University Press, 2009);

disciplines and forms of working, without doing away with disciplinary boundaries. The way we combine these approaches takes the form of a kaleidoscope.

Most people will be familiar with the kaleidoscope from their childhood: usually a tube, with a small viewing hole on one end and a (concave) lens on the other. Two or more mirrors are angled toward another along the length of the tube. Anything seen through the device will be reflected over and over again, creating an abundance of kaleidoscopic arrangements. Small pieces of loose colored glass are commonly added in front of the lens, creating the characteristic patterns, optical effects that have not failed to fascinate since the early nineteenth century, when the inventor David Brewster patented a new optical instrument called "'The Kaleidoscope' for exhibiting and creating beautiful forms and patterns of great use in all the ornamental arts."[2] Brewster was an established member of British scientific circles and played a substantial role in the development of experimental optics. The kaleidoscope was a byproduct of his scientific experiments, and it is telling that he considered it most suitable to the "ornamental arts," that unlike a science aiming for universal validity, the tool had good use for methods that would yield an "infinity of patterns." Brewster's patent, filed in 1815, seems to suggest that the infinity of patterns is the realm of art, not science. But notions of science as a field of uncontested methods and singular universal truth claims appear anachronistic today.

As a working metaphor, the kaleidoscope helped us to establish and maintain a conceptual space in editing this book and running the wider research project, where disciplines encounter one another in shifting relations while remaining distinct, yet establishing common patterns at certain points in time. The kaleidoscope helps us to relate different patterns to another without flattening them in two ways: First, our use of the kaleidoscope draws on a search for (scientific) ways of working

Andreas Pfitzmann and Marit Hansen, "Terminology for Talking about Privacy by Data Minimization: Anonymity, Unlinkability, Undetectability, Unobservability, Pseudonymity, and Identity Management," Technische Universität Dresden, August 10, 2010;
Carolin Wiedemann, "Irrepresentable Collectivity: Anonymous and the Technologies of the Common," in *World of the News*, ed. Geoff Cox and Christian U. Andersen, (Aarhus: Transmediale/Digital Aesthetics Research Centre, Aarhus University, 2012);
Finn Brunton and Helen Nissenbaum, *Obfuscation* (Cambridge, MA: MIT Press, 2015);
Gabriella Coleman, *Hacker, Hoaxer, Whistleblower, Spy: The Many Faces of Anonymous* (Brooklyn, NY: Verso, 2014); and Shoshana Zuboff, *The Age of Surveillance Capitalism: The Fight for a Human Future at the New Frontier of Power* (New York: Public Affairs/Hachette, 2019);
and important case studies are provided by Catarina Frois, *The Anonymous Society: Identity, Transformation and Anonymity in 12 Steps* (Cambridge: Cambridge Scholars, 2009);
Stefan Hirschauer, "Editorial Judgments: A Praxeology of 'Voting' in Peer Review," *Social Studies of Science* 40 (2010): 71–103;
Craig Scott, *Anonymous Agencies, Backstreet Businesses, and Covert Collectives: Rethinking Organizations in the 21st Century* (Palo Alto, CA: Stanford University Press, 2013);
and Maren Klotz, *(K)information: Gamete Donation and Kinship Knowledge in Germany and Britain*. Frankfurt: Campus Verlag, 2014). Some members of the editorial collective of this book were also members of the editorial

together that can hold and appreciate situated, diverse understandings of knowledge practices and methods. It helped us to build, imagine, and work in joint endeavors without merging the fundamentally different approaches of art and science (and also the fundamental differences between the artists, activist, and scientists) in all-too-close forms. "No Convergence!" was a slogan of our project as we tried to protect and even intensify a heterogeneity of practices, staying "kaleidoscopic" to each other. We had no intention of becoming "synthesized," or "more homogenous," or "mixed up." Working alongside each other, we aimed to shed new light on each other's work, refracting and diffracting as we went on, respecting different practices while "doing difference together" in good faith.[3] Kaleidoscopic objectivity refers to an assemblage of heterogeneous forms of knowledge in which each refracts and sheds light on the other in specific ways. Similar to Kenneth Burke's idea of the "creative principle of apposition," it can be understood as a collaborative strategy that modifies and enlarges "viewpoints that would otherwise be determined by the less supple oppositional strategies."[4]

During the editing of this book, the kaleidoscope gained a second meaning: we now concentrate less on the process of working together and more on what kinds of analysis and insights emerge from this work. To stay in the metaphor, we shuffle the artistic and scholarly contributions, looking through the kaleidoscope, documenting the new images that are emerging. In contrast to the ubiquitous practices of curating, assembling, remediating, or cutting and pasting, "staying kaleidoscopic" for us meant addressing anonymity as a partial, complex phenomena via multiple readings of the volume. The limitations and predicaments of the editorial collective form part of the kaleidoscopic optics of this book. The kaleidoscope helped us to articulate some of the book's shifting patterns. Here, colors that mix but do not merge, and patterns that form but are not set in stone, correspond to the constellations formed by

collective of a special issue, which includes not only further contributions inspired by a similar approach, but also, in its introduction, a more detailed literature review: Götz Bachmann, Michi Knecht, and Andreas Wittel, "The Social Productivity of Anonymity," special issue, *ephemera: Theory and Politics in Organization*, 17, no. 2 (2017).

[2] David Brewster's 1817 *A Treatise on the Kaleidoscope* (Edinburgh: Archibald Constable), 2.

[3] Helen Verran and Michael Christie, "Doing Difference Together—Towards a Dialogue with Aboriginal Knowledge Authorities through an Australian Comparative Empirical Philosophical Inquiry," *Culture and Dialogue* 1, no. 2 (2011): 21–36.

[4] Mark C. Lang, "Tending to the Imagination: Perspective and Incongruity in William Carlos Williams and Kenneth Burke" (paper presented at the Modern Language Association Conference, Toronto, December 1997).

the contributions to this book. We can see different orders emerging in this abundance. The way patterns have recursive elements mirrors how we can see similar patterns emerge within and between contributions. And, most importantly, the kaleidoscope allows different patterns to take a "provisional gestalt," a pattern centered on a center, forming together one way anonymity can be understood and analyzed, one turn at a time.

Both applications of the kaleidoscopic metaphor draw on feminist scholarship's sustained critique of modern scientific knowledge claims as disembodied, disinterested, and universally valid. The scientific gaze, seemingly cast from nowhere, the argument goes, is always situated, coming from particular positions. Visual knowledge metaphors, such as transparency, obscure the situatedness of knowledge practices, and thus establish some knowledge claims as objective and universal while dismissing others as partial and subjective. Faced with such metaphors that have frequently produced mutually exclusive and seemingly clear-cut dichotomies, and questioning the power-knowledge they manifest, feminist scholars have adopted and developed visual metaphors, such as refraction and diffraction, that make visible that tools are never transparent in any straightforward sense.[5] Methods and devices, in this way of thinking, do not depict the world as it is but, participate in rendering some versions of the world real, inevitably at the expense of others. The sciences that feminist scholars such as Karen Barad, Donna Haraway, or Helen Verran advocate for no longer "explain away difference in the here and now by relocating it to an ideal realm."[6] Grasping modes of knowledge production, objects, and practices while holding them together in their difference is an ambition that also informs our use of the kaleidoscope.[7] Training the kaleidoscope on anonymity, we now aim to illuminate what its optics contribute to studies of anonymity specifically.

[5] The search for optical devices that make other forms of knowledge imaginable led Karen Barad to Nils Bohr's studies of refraction, which imply that tools do not merely depict but shape reality. With a background in both natural sciences and feminist scholarship, Donna Haraway and Karen Barad have problematized the notion of reflection, instead offering diffracting and diffraction as a model to rethink the coming together and continuous co-evolving of different practices, entities, and relations; Donna Haraway, *Modest-Witness@Second-Millennium, FemaleMan-Meets-OncoMouse: Feminism and Technosciences* (New York: Routledge, 1997); and Karen Barad, "Diffracting Diffraction: Cutting Together-Apart," *Parallax* 20, no. 3 (2014): 168–87. Barad redefines diffracting—in classical optics a practice of breaking apart—as an intra-action that "cuts together-apart" (ibid., 168) and highlights not the opposition between refracting and diffracting but their overlaps, or parallels, in which both participate in "difference attentive" modes of reconfiguration (ibid.) Not always linked back to this empirical origin, the terms *refraction* and *diffraction* have come to signify the reality-making capacity of knowledge devices more widely.

[6] Helen Verran. "Working with Those Who Think Otherwise," *Common Knowledge* 20, no. 3 (2014): 527–39.

[7] Kim and Mike Fortun's project PECE (Platform for Experimental, Collaborative Ethnography) can be understood as an attempt to operationalize ways to work kaleidoscopically with larger collectives. We learned the productivity of "kaleidoscopic objectivity" from them. See

A Kaleidoscopic Understanding of Anonymity

The kaleidoscopic approach of the book offers seven understandings of anonymity, three of which we have already introduced in the initial passages of this introduction. There, we argue that first, anonymity can be understood as a *catalogue of anonymity techniques*. This includes both technologies (narrowly defined as devices) and techniques in the wider sense, meaning technologies in practice and practices of anonymizing that do not rely on devices, such as, for example, not naming a person. This understanding of anonymity looks primarily at how anonymity is *produced*. Read with such a focus on techniques, the collated case studies, think pieces, and artworks present strikingly diverse ways for gaining, maintaining, or undermining anonymity, ranging from the mundane to the magical. But as crucial as this understanding of anonymity is, we also argue that such a pattern, especially if it focuses on technologies alone, is not enough.

Our next gaze into the kaleidoscope are focused on outcomes: that is what gets produced, which, in turn, has two elements. On the one hand, anonymity itself can be understood as a particular *mode of being and knowing*. It is, indeed, a social form that entails different states and relations. Read as an *index of different states of anonymity*, the contributions in this book paint a complex picture of the meanings and practical implications attached to being anonymous. The third pattern is structured around anonymity's potential. By this we mean that anonymity can manifest, cause, or afford desirable or undesirable consequences. This also includes potential futures, some of them directly achievable, others more utopian or dystopian. Many contributions of the book add to *an archive of anonymity's potentialities*, often by evoking alternative configurations of the world.

Building on these opening observations, we add a fourth kaleidoscopic understanding of anonymity as a regime.

Kim Fortun, "About," PECE, July 2015; and Kim Fortun and Mike Fortun, "What's So Funny about PECE, TAF and Data Sharing?," in *Collaborative Anthropology Today: A Collection of Exceptions*, ed. Dominic Boyer and George Marcus (Ithaca, NY: Cornell University Press, forthcoming).

Analogous to Collier and Lakoff's concept of "regimes of living," the notion of "regime" here means an emerging assemblage or configuration, a "manner, method, or system of rule or government, including principles of reasoning, valuation and practice, that have a provisional coherence and consistency."[8] Assuming that anonymity is deeply historical, with its shapes and meanings in flux, and just as deeply tied to specific cultural notions and conditions, we assert that there is no one stable form of anonymity-as-such. Thinking in terms of regimes reminds us that anonymity is specific to particular situations as well as being historically, culturally, and socially specific. Regimes of anonymity, in other words, place anonymity in broader social and cultural relations, and thus within ever-changing and situation-specific yet also situation-transcending social, technical, regulatory, and normative contexts. Read as *accounts of regimes of anonymity*, the contributions point to the relationality of anonymity and the underlying unequal distributions of power and the force and potential violence implied in many anonymity practices.

[8] Stephen J. Collier and Andrew Lakoff. "On Regimes of Living," in *Global Assemblages. Technology, Politics, and Ethics as Anthropological Problems*, ed. Aihwa Ong and Stephen J. Collier. (Malden, MA, Oxford, and Victoria: Blackwell, 2005): 22–39.

Our fifth turn of the kaleidoscope follows up from the insight that anonymity sometimes simply occurs, such as when one experiences anonymity in a foreign town, but more often it is produced. Such occurrence, or production, of anonymity is increasingly difficult to maintain for us, as citizens of a connected world. IP addresses give us away; we present our facial features and retina patterns to cameras tied to databases, which are analyzed by sophisticated algorithms that often stem out of processes of machine learning. Leaving DNA, we are recognizable long after we have passed. Our gait gives us away, and so does the modulation of our voice. The specifics of our vocabulary and that of our keyboard typing are recognizable. We leave data traces, which can be aggregated, cross-referenced, and analyzed at any future point. We might not know if, when, and how our data are used, nor do we know by whom and for what ends. What will become of our data in the future is even harder to anticipate, but by now, we are no longer innocent. We question if anonymity can be reliable, and rightly so, because anonymity more than ever is a fragile, temporal achievement, always at risk of reversal. Summarizing, we can say that anonymity is indeed the production or occurrence of an absence of identification, but this absence of identification is often partial, situational, fragile, and temporal. Anonymity's absence of identification is often not simply a binary state but situated in the gray areas of practice. Read like this, the manifold case studies and artworks in this book constitute a *mapping of anonymity's gray areas*.

A sixth turn of the kaleidoscope brings anonymity's relationship to absence into focus. Anonymity's absence is peculiar: it is an absence of identification that allows and produces something. We have already established (in the third turn, to be precise) that this "something" is a range of possibilities, from the freedom of the lone rider all the way to the collectivity of the anonymous club. But how does this come about? How can anonymity act if it is defined primarily as an absence? In art and typography, negative space denotes the (often) white space that surrounds characters and figures on the page. Much of typography's theory and practice is dedicated to negative space as a condition of legibility. Rhetoric, too, knows that intentional silence magnifies the word. In music, active silence refers to breaks in the composition that are timed so that silence becomes audible. The proximity of musical figures shapes music's active silences. It is a relational effect, and it can be understood not by focusing simply on what is there and what is not, but only if we attend to the relational field of absences and presences.[9] Returning to the example of the nameless author, the power of the absent name can only be fathomed if we attend to textual conventions and their institutional histories. Like music's active silence, and typography's white space, anonymity brings into experience what usually goes unnoticed, namely the powerful, constituting presence of that which is absent.

The notion that active silence is a constituent of music is analog to the notion that the absence of identification constitutes anonymity. Drawing on the significance that musical composition grants active silence, we suggest that anonymity issues something we might call *active absence*. Crucially, the notion of active absence introduces the question of what is made present: what kinds of objects, subjects, publics, or ethics are obscured or brought into being in the absence of certain identifiers? The empirical cases in this volume suggest that the absence of certain identifiers can supercharge the meaning of, for example, the unknown name, or open a space in which new constellations can be articulated that were previously unthinkable—read from this perspective, the contributions form a *compendium of anonymity's active absences*.

The seventh turn of the kaleidoscope emphasizes notions of figuration, foregrounding anonymity as a relational achievement. Anonymity is never just the anonymous. The simplest relational understanding of anonymity considers two positions: the anonymizer and the anonymized. Even when the anonymous and the anonymizer are one person, we already have two positions. Computer science models of anonymity include a third position, the rather martially named attacker, a position we might, in avoidance of militaristic language, want to think of as the potential identifier. This has the counterintuitive yet important consequence that anonymity exists only in relation to potential acts, actors, and techniques of identification. The NSA and the CIA, Facebook's clear name policy, and the more than a dozen sensors that Apple or Samsung have built into their smartphones are thus inherent parts of the larger complex that is anonymity. They not only disable anonymity but also produce new sites for its reemergence. On an analytical level, we thus arrive at a *triadic social figure*, consisting of the anonymous, the identifier, and the anonymizer. Anonymity here necessitates relations between the anonymous, the anonymizer, and the attacker/identifier.

9 How absence and presence mutually constitute each other is a question with multiple genealogies. Theoretically, we here draw on science and technology studies, and the work on absence/presence developed by Keith Hetherington and John Law and Vicky Singleton; see Hetherington, "Second-handedness: Consumption, Disposal, and Absent Presence," *Environment and Planning D* 22, no. 1 (2004): 157–73; and Law and Singleton, "Object Lessons," working paper, July 2, 2004. Noma Bar's ingenious works illustrate the power of negative space, and Elizabeth Hellmuth Margulis is insightful on silence in musical composition; see Bar, *Negative Space* (New York: Mark Batty, 2009); and Elizabeth Margulis, "Moved by Nothing: Listening to Musical Silence," *Journal of Music Theory* 51 (2007): 245–76.

Anonymity, understood as a social figure, asserts agency. Like other triadic social figures (the promise or the gift, for example), anonymity's agency exceeds those who evoke it. Anonymity changes the conditions for actions, enabling desirable and undesirable practices, contributing to the shape that organizations take, modifying collectivities and social behavior. We should also remember, however, that such a preference for a triadic figuration of anonymity should remain grounded empirically, insofar as models and practices of anonymity frequently evoke the three positions that it describes. Our argument therefore does not automatically imply that anonymity is *essentially* triadic. Quite the contrary, relational figurations of anonymity necessarily oppose essential readings of anonymity. So while triadic figurations of anonymity might have traction in practice, we should not forget that figuration is used in feminist and postcolonial scholarship as an inclusive term designed to multiply and extend the cast of characters, by, for example, including nonhuman actors.[10] As an *inventory of anonymity's figurations*, this volume is an invitation to consider what figurations anonymity takes, and how these shape practices, subject positions, and institutions.

[10] For a recent use of the term in science and technology studies, see Claudia Castañeda, *Figurations: Child, Bodies, Worlds* (Durham, NC: Duke University Press, 2003). For an earlier conceptualization of figuration, see Norbert Elias, *What Is Sociology?* (London: Hutchinson, 1978).

Contributions

This book gathers artworks and academic essays, as well as more experimental texts. Contributions are presented in five sections – (A) Introductions, (B) Reconfigurations, (C) Assaults, (D) Weapons, and (E) Delights.

Section A: Introductions
The book opens with this introduction and the essay "Artistic Research on Anonymity," which addresses the collaboration between artists and academics that shaped many of the contributions and this book.

Section B: Reconfigurations
The second section collates more conceptually oriented

contributions that speak to questions about the ongoing profound transformation of anonymity's techniques, modes, potentialities, regimes, gray areas, and figurations. What can count as anonymous still? How might it be defined? What does this mean in different contexts? Why does it still matter? "Anonymity and Transgression," the opening contribution, draws on blood donation practices in India, showing how anonymously donated blood can figure blood as a kind of universal humanist substance that promises to transcend racial and class distinctions. The second essay in this section, "Anonymity: The Politicization of a Concept," provides an account of the recent politicization of anonymity, arguing that it has started to gain serious momentum only in the wake of the digital turn. *USAE* is the first artwork in this section. Returning to academic territory, "Big Data's End Run around Anonymity and Consent" argues that under the conditions of big data, anonymity has the potential to undermine privacy. "Famous Artists Who Used to Be Invigilators" collects more or less well-known artists who at some point in their careers worked as anonymous invigilators in art galleries and museums. As an artwork, it raises the question of how this seemingly menial, anonymous labor shaped the artists' work, or not, a question that is explored in different ways in the piece's companion work, "A Provisional Manifesto for Invigilator-Friendly Artworks," which can be found in section D. "Anonymity as an Everyday Phenomenon and as a Topic of Research" offers a conceptual exploration of anonymity, drawing on German classical sociology and critical theory. Section B closes with the artistic essay "Anonymity on Demand." Based on research on the financial offshore industry, the authors argue that anonymity has become a class-based service, available only to the rich.

Section C: Assaults

The third section gathers contributions describing anonymity under threat, investigating changes in the regimes of anonymity so dramatic that some observers are declaring the "end of anonymity."[11] "DNA Works!," the opening contribution, introduces us to stories of donor-conceived persons in the UK and Germany who now live with the possibilities of DNA testing and mostly proprietary DNA databases. "Sanitary Police and the Politics of Anonymity" offers observations on an artistic intervention that takes the form of a game. The game invites players to question how endocrine disruptors, substances that interfere with hormonal systems, emerge out of the anonymity of invisible substances and become established social agents. "Where Do the Data Live?" looks at the strange mix of anonymity and identification characteristic of both real-world and data neighborhoods. The question of how anonymity and forms of community go together is taken up in "Fraught Platform Governmentality." The essay investigates content moderation and regulatory practices aimed at governing abusive user behavior at the now defunct digital platform Yik Yak, which allowed users to remain anonymous. "Anonymity—Obsolescence and Desire" introduces nine artworks in image and text. From the "stoical nonpresence" of CCTV cameras, to rocks that cast a local network broadcasting survival guides when heated, to the public destruction of data storage, the works raise questions about the aesthetics, circulation, durability, and life of data and of data practices. "Policing Normality" takes us to urban streets and neighborhoods, following plain clothes police officers and the question of how unmarked police negotiate the intertwined politics of visibility, identification, and categorization.

[11] Zygmunt Bauman, "Is This the End of Anonymity?" *The Guardian*, June 28, 2011.

Section D: Weapons

The essays in the fourth section consider anonymity as a political tool of control and subversion, weaponized by both those in power and those in apparent resistance. The first two essays in this section demonstrate that anonymity can be strategically employed for very different purposes. "Amazonian Flesh" is an artistic exploration, staking out possibilities and conditions for anonymous labor strikes in highly automated, computer-driven and computer-controlled work environments such as

Amazon logistics centers. "Proximity, Distance, and State Powers" contrasts the notion of the anonymous state with empirical accounts of anonymity in policing practices, suggesting that anonymity can be understood as a relational effect that sheds light on the mutual figuration of state and citizen. "Dual Reality," a collaboration between an artist and a scholar, contrasts ethnographic accounts of working as a computer programmer with experiences of working as a gallery invigilator. In both cases anonymity takes place in plain sight, with people pursuing largely invisible work while performing the work that they are actually paid to do. "A Provisional Manifesto for Invigilator-Friendly Artworks" offers a guide for artists to create works friendly to the people, often artists, working as guards in galleries. "Care and Control?" takes us back to the urban police force, this time to observe how mutual anonymity enables, obstructs, and problematizes the relationship between youth protection officers and their youthful subjects. Officers, the author argues, mix anonymizing and deanonymizing techniques to stabilize relationships of both care and control. Section D concludes with "She Remembers." This artistic photo essay shows one of the sites where Iranian security forces buried their victims in unmarked graves. It portrays a space heavy with traumatic absences but also of memory and community for the friends and families of the deceased.

Section E: Delights

This volume's final section is devoted to the gratifications of anonymity. The essay "Collective Pleasures of Anonymity" takes us on a tour, from public restrooms to 4chan and Chatroulette. Anonymous mass publicness, the author argues, can bring about a pleasurable and potential liberating experience of self loss. "Authenticity" suggests that considering anonymity and authenticity as diametrically opposed concepts prevents us from understanding that the productive tension between those two terms coconstitutes their meaning. "Longing for a Selfless Self and Other Ambivalences of Anonymity" reflects on anonymous collectivity as a strategy against corrosive individualism, based on fieldwork in anonymous self-help groups. Linking her insights to scholarly practice, the author asks what anonymous collectivity could bring to scientific production. In the artwork *Transformella Malor Ikeae*, an avatar arising from a complex architecture of temporary identities acts as our tour guide on a trip to downtown IKEA to investigate the anonymous furnishings and symbolic territories of normality production of our late capitalist interiors. Back from IKEA, "Speak Their Endless Names" offers a textual meditation on the relationship between naming and anonymity. "Bitcoin Anonymous?" is a practical guide to purchasing, owning, and spending Bitcoins anonymously. It demonstrates that Bitcoin's anonymity is not afforded by the infrastructure in a straightforward sense but requires the skillful forging of connections and disconnections. The book ends with "Anonymity Workshop," a report on a series of experiments in art pedagogy that took place at the L'École nationale supérieure des Arts Décoratifs (EnsAD) in Paris. The author's tentative conclusion resonates with the notion that the dissolution of the self might allow for more collaborative forms of inquiry and accountability.

Above we outline seven kaleidoscopic readings of anonymity, suggesting that this book can be read as (1) a catalog of anonymity techniques, (2) an index of different states of anonymity, (3) an archive of anonymity's potentialities, (4) a collection of accounts of regimes of anonymity, (5) a mapping of anonymity's gray areas, (6) a compendium of anonymity's active absences, and (7) a triadic social figure. This necessarily incomplete list not only suggests several possible paths through this volume, but also constitutes the introduction's central claim: the complex, relational, and at times magical technosocial phenomenon of anonymity requires a multifaceted analysis, shifting with its moving target—it asks for a kaleidoscopic understanding.

Bibliography

Bachmann, Götz, Michi Knecht, and Andreas Wittel. "The Social Productivity of Anonymity," special issue, *ephemera: Theory and Politics in Organization*, 17, no. 2 (2017).

Bakke, Gretchen, and Marina Peterson, eds. *Between Matter and Method: Encounters in Anthropology and Art*. London: Bloomsbury, 2017.

Bar, Noma. *Negative Space*. New York: Mark Batty, 2009.

Barad, Karen. *Meeting the Universe Halfway: Quantum Physics and the Entanglement of Matter and Meaning*. Durham, NC: Duke University Press, 2007.

Barad, Karen. "Diffracting Diffraction: Cutting Together-Apart." *Parallax* 20, no. 3 (2014): 168–87.

Bauman, Zygmunt. "Is This the End of Anonymity?" *The Guardian*, June 28, 2011.

Brewster, David. *A Treatise on the Kaleidoscope*. Edinburgh: Archibald Constable, 1817. https://archive.org/details/b29295440.

Brunton, Finn, and Helen Nissenbaum. *Obfuscation*. Cambridge, MA: MIT Press, 2015.

Castañeda, Claudia. *Figurations: Child, Bodies, Worlds*. Durham, NC: Duke University Press, 2003.

Coleman, Gabriella. *Hacker, Hoaxer, Whistleblower, Spy: The Many Faces of Anonymous*. Brooklyn, NY: Verso, 2014.

Collier, Stephen J., and Andrew Lakoff. "On Regimes of Living". In *Global Assemblages. Technology, Politics, and Ethics as Anthropological Problems*, edited by Aihwa Ong and Stephen J. Collier. Malden, MA, Oxford, and Victoria: Blackwell, (2005): 22–39.

Elias, Norbert. *What Is Sociology?* London: Hutchinson, 1978.

Fortun, Kim, and Mike Fortun. "What's So Funny about PECE, TAF and Data Sharing?" In *Collaborative Anthropology Today: A Collection of Exceptions*, edited by Dominic Boyer and George Marcus. Ithaca, NY: Cornell University Press, forthcoming.

Frois, Catarina. *The Anonymous Society: Identity, Transformation and Anonymity in 12 Steps*. Cambridge: Cambridge Scholars, 2009.

Geertz, Evelien, and Iris van der Tuin. "Diffraction & Reading Diffractively". In *New Materialism Almanac (2016), https://newmaterialism.eu/almanac/d/diffraction.html*.

Haraway, Donna. *Modest_Witness@Second_Millennium, FemaleMan_Meets_OncoMouse: Feminism and Technosciences*. New York: Routledge, 1997.

Hetherington, Keith. "Secondhandedness: Consumption, Disposal, and Absent Presence." *Environment and Planning D* 22, no. 1 (2004): 157–73.

Hirschauer, Stefan. "Editorial Judgments: A Praxeology of 'Voting' in Peer Review." *Social Studies of Science* 40 (2010): 71–103.

Kerr, Ian, Carole Lucock, and Valerie Steeves, eds. *Lessons from the Identity Trail: Anonymity, Pseudonymity and Identity in a Networked Society*. New York: Oxford University Press, 2009.

Klotz, Maren. *(K)information: Gamete Donation and Kinship Knowledge in Germany and Britain*. Frankfurt: Campus Verlag, 2014.

Konrad, Monica. *Nameless Relations: Anonymity, Melanesia and Reproductive Gift Exchange between British Ova Donors and Recipients*. New York: Berghahn Books, 2005.

Lang, Mark C. "Tending to the Imagination: Perspective and Incongruity in William Carlos Williams and Kenneth Burke." Paper presented at the Modern Language Association Conference, Toronto, December 1997. https://www.kbjournal.org/long_tending.

Law, John, and Vicky Singleton. "Object Lessons." Working paper, July 2, 2004. http://www.heterogeneities.net/publications/LawSingleton2004ObjectLessons.pdf.

Margulis, Elizabeth. "Moved by Nothing: Listening to Musical Silence." *Journal of Music Theory* 51 (2007): 245–76. https://doi.org/10.1215/00222909-2009-003.

Marx, Gary. T. "What's in a Name? Some Reflections on the Sociology of Anonymity." *Information Society* 15, no. 2 (1999): 99–112.

Nissenbaum, Helen. "The Meaning of Anonymity in an Information Age." *Information Society* 15 (1999): 141–44.

Pfitzmann, Andreas and Marit Hansen. "A Terminology for Talking about Privacy by Data Minimization: Anonymity, Unlinkability, Undetectability, Unobservability, Pseudonymity, and Identity Management." Technische Universität Dresden, August 10, 2010. https://dud.inf.tu-dresden.de/literatur/Anon_Terminology_v0.34.pdf.

Ponesse, Julie. "Navigating the Unknown: Towards a Positive Conception of Anonymity." *Southern Journal of Philosophy* 51, no. 3 (2013): 320–44.

Ponesse, Julie. "The Ties That Blind: Conceptualizing Anonymity." *Journal of Social Philosophy* 45, no. 3 (2014): 304–22.

Rost, Martin. "Über die Funktionalität von Anonymität für die bürgerliche

Gesellschaft." In *Anonymität im Internet*, edited by H. Bäumler and A. von Mutius, 62–74. Wiesbaden: Vieweg-Verlag, 2003.

Scott, Craig. *Anonymous Agencies, Backstreet Businesses, and Covert Collectives: Rethinking Organizations in the 21st Century*. Palo Alto, CA: Stanford University Press, 2013.

Simmel, Georg. "The Metropolis and Mental Life." In *Georg Simmel on Individuality and Social Forms*, edited by Donald N. Levine, 324–39. 1903. Chicago: Chicago University Press, 1971.

Verran, Helen. "Working with Those who Think Otherwise". In *Common Knowledge* 20, no. 3 (2014): 527–39.

Verran, Helen, and Michael Christie. "Doing Difference Together— Towards a Dialogue with Aboriginal Knowledge Authorities through an Australian Comparative Empirical Philosophical Inquiry." *Culture and Dialogue* 1, no. 2 (2011): 21–36.

Wallace, Kathleen A. "Anonymity." *Ethics and Information Technology* 1 (1999): 23–35.

Wiedemann, Carolin "Irrepresentable Collectivity: Anonymous and the Technologies of the Common." In *World of the News*, edited by Geoff Cox and Christian U. Andersen, 1–32. Aarhus, Denmark: Transmediale/Digital Aesthetics Research Centre, Aarhus University, 2012.

Zuboff, Shoshana. *The Age of Surveillance Capitalism: The Fight for a Human Future at the New Frontier of Power*. New York: Public Affairs/ Hachette, 2019.

Artistic Research on Anonymity

Introduction

How can we grasp the current transformation of anonymity, the ways it is understood and practiced?[1] This was the question that stood at the beginning of the interdisciplinary research project Reconfiguring Anonymity (RCA), first initiated in 2014 by several social and cultural scientists from the universities in Bremen, Hamburg, and Lüneburg.[2] The aim of the project was to examine how regimes of anonymity emerge in contemporary hybrid online and offline worlds, as well as how they are modified, evaluated, defended, or abolished. Collectively, the project participants approached these questions through ethnographic methodologies and artistic research. In this chapter, we reflect on the project's interdisciplinary approach, contrasting and evaluating the different methods, ontologies, and epistemologies. More specifically, we present and analyze the artistic research program of the interdisciplinary research project. We do this from the perspective of the lead researchers and curators of the artistic program. Our work encompassed conceptualizing the artistic research component, selecting and accompanying the artists, and preparing the exhibition and

[1] The scholarship on anonymity is widespread and dispersed. For recent attempts at overviews, see Andreas Wittel, Götz Bachmann, and Michi Knecht, eds., "The Social Productivity of Anonymity," special issue, *ephemera* 17, no. 2 (2017). Two essays that have sought to structure the discursive field and that have informed the RCA project discussed here are Julie Ponesse, "Navigating the Unknown: Towards a Positive Conception of Anonymity," *Southern Journal of Philosophy* 51, no. 3 (2013): 320–44; and Thorsten Thiel, "Anonymität und der digitale Strukturwandel der Öffentlichkeit," *Zeitschrift für Menschenrechte* 10, no. 1 (2016): 9–24.

[2] The project Reconfiguring Anonymity: Contemporary Forms of Reciprocity, Identifiability and Accountability in Transformation (RCA) was conducted from 2015 to 2019 and funded by the German Volkswagen Foundation through its program Key Issues in Science and Society.

artistic contributions to the closing events, which took place in October 2018 at the arts center Kampnagel in Hamburg.[3]

The main focus of our common research was on ways in which anonymity regimes reconfigure individuality and personhood, sociality and collectivity, property and practices of sharing, as well as reciprocity, responsibility, and identifiability. The aim of the project was to generate new knowledge about anonymity, especially through ethnographic case studies and in collaboration with artists, digital activists, and technicians, and then to retheorize anonymity on this basis. The research group consisted of artists as well as scholars of ethnology, cultural anthropology, digital culture, media studies, criminalistics, surveillance research, and art history. This interdisciplinary approach to the project, specifically bringing in artists, was motivated by how art-based research can provide modes of knowledge production that frequently opens up unexpected dimensions, ruptures assumptions, and queers routines. Art offers methodologies and forms of observation and intervention that can complement social science methodologies but that are also unique in their deliberately undisciplined, often nonutilitarian and alogical, approaches to social structures and phenomena. In art's tendency toward both unorthodoxy and representation, it can act as an important interface in the dialogue between science and society.

Overall, our approaches to the critical investigation of regimes of anonymity were conceptual (including evaluating the existing literature on and definitions of anonymity), ethnographic (based on participant observation and the gradual evolution of research questions), and artistic (including the context of previous works by the participating artists, experimental and idiosyncratic methodologies, and the importance of the production of a "work"—or something to present—at the concluding event).

RCA brought together researchers from ethnography, sociology, media studies, art, and art history from Bremen University, Hamburg University, and Leuphana University of Lüneburg. Reconfiguring Anonymity website, accessed December 7, 2018, www.reconfiguring-anonymity.net.

[3] For examples from an extensive bibliography on curatorial practice, see Beatrice von Bismarck, Jörn Schafaff, and Thomas Weski, eds., *Cultures of the Curatorial* (Berlin: Sternberg, 2012); Jens Hoffmann, *(Curating) From A to Z* (Zurich: JRP/Ringier, 2014); and Paul O'Neill, *The Culture of Curating and the Curating of Culture(s)* (Cambridge, MA: MIT Press, 2012).

Reconfiguring Anonymity consisted of five projects: four mainly ethnographic projects, and one that focused on artistic research. The aim of the latter was to establish a dialogue between artistic research on anonymity and the other, social scientific projects. Methodological considerations played a crucial role in the framing of this interdisciplinary encounter: What aspects of anonymity can be addressed through artistic inquiries? Does the semiautonomous field of artistic research allow access to everyday interactions that remain closed to ethnographic methods? How can the structure of certain forms of anonymity be explored through experimental situations? And more generally, can the experimental methods of artistic research contribute to an interdisciplinary study of anonymity as a social phenomenon helping to create an expanded understanding of what anonymity means in contemporary societies? The goal was to identify particular artistic strategies of speculation, unconventional forms of action and interaction, and analytical and practical methods and tools for "hacking" virtual and social identity systems, institutional practices, and systems of social, legal, and technical exclusion.

Through its interdisciplinary approach, Reconfiguring Anonymity sought to contribute to the development of critical awareness as well as social and political competency in dealing with issues of anonymity.

Art projects and exhibitions can provide, besides the individual experiences of exhibition visitors, a special public interface for presenting issues of anonymity in the sociologically particular field of contemporary art, as well as, importantly, occasions for critical reflection and debate in the public sphere through reviews in mass media and other forms of public debate. They create experimental and exceptional situations and thus provide poignant occasions for reflection on the technical, social, and aesthetic dimensions of the ethnographic projects, as well as on their methodologies and assumptions, by offering idiosyncratic scenarios that fundamentally put such dimensions, their logics and regimes, to the test.

For conceptual and practical reasons, we decided to work with a small number of artists (or collectives) over the full three-year period of the RCA project, and to bring in some additional artistic positions at a later stage, especially for the final presentation and exhibition at the end of the project period. Part and parcel of any such long-term curatorial process is that the parameters shift and change over time. In this chapter, we take a retrospective view and reflect only on readjustments and shifts when they seem particularly relevant for the overall argument. In general, we want to argue for the productivity of artistic research in developing a new, refined, and critical understanding of social issues such as anonymity. Here, the RCA project is our case study, but we hope to contribute to a discussion that looks at the role of artistic research in a broader and more general perspective.

Fig. 1 Kampnagel Piazza, Hamburg (October 2018), with installation "Forgot your password? (Hamburg)" (bottom left), and banner created by participating artist collective (center left)

Artists Researching Anonymity

The artists who were initially invited in 2015 to participate in the RCA project were Aram Bartholl, Heath Bunting, Parastou Forouhar, and the group knowbotiq (Christian Hübler and Yvonne Wilhelm). Important general criteria for their selection were that these artists had dealt with issues relating to anonymity in previous works; that in their artistic practice, research methods play an important role; and that they were open to participate in a dialogical and cooperative interdisciplinary research trajectory like that envisioned for the RCA project. Another aspect of the overall selection was a certain level of differentiation in working methods and thematic approaches taken by the various artists.

The cooperation over the following three years consisted mainly of a series of workshop sessions, during which conceptual concerns were shared as well as preliminary research results. A symposium halfway through the project drew into the process several additional researchers and artists who were also working on the topic of anonymity. Finally, toward the end of the project period, in 2018, a conference and exhibition event was organized at Kampnagel Hamburg, under the title of *A=ANONYM*, to present the results of the individual artistic and scientific research projects and to discuss the findings of the overall project in a public forum. While the conference program, with keynote lectures, panel discussions, and workshops, took place in the semiformal space of one of the "industrial" theater halls, the exhibition of artworks was distributed across the large Kampnagel foyer. Here, each piece could be installed in a specific spatial context that, at least in most cases, contributed to the efficacy of the works and placed them at the intersection of the RCA closing event and the regular program proceedings at Kampnagel, with its hundreds of visitors for the daily live performance acts.

In the following section, we use the conceptual framework of the Reconfiguring Anonymity research project to provide an overview of the role of the artists in the research process and discuss their contributions to the closing event. We first introduce them with their previous work and the specific projects they realized in the RCA context.

The works of Berlin-based German artist Aram Bartholl deal with phenomena of digital culture at the intersections of physical and virtual spaces. Bartholl's works often mimic carefully crafted "ready-mades," which seem to add something to the digitally enhanced everyday

Fig. 2 "Is this you in the video?"; installation view (2018, Kampnagel Piazza, Hamburg)

environments, and which, so it seems, could easily have been there even without the artist's intervention. The notion of anonymity has played an important role in many of Bartholl's projects, including the anonymous public and offline data storage points of *Dead Drops* (2010–12), and the DIY workshop production of the Guy Fawkes masks that became iconic for the Anonymous online hacker community—only in Bartholl's version, *How to Vacuum Form* (2012), these masks are made of transparent plastic and thus reveal more of the "masked" face than they hide.[4] Similarly, Bartholl's two contributions to the exhibition at Kampnagel pointed to the ambivalence of surveillance and privacy systems: the installation *Is This You in the Video?* placed a surveillance camera that seemed to track the movements of passersby in the forecourt of the Kampnagel building; the absence of a display, though, suggested that the recorded images might not be more than junk information, so that any concern about this particular surveillance system might be unnecessary. A second work, *Forgot Your Password? (Hamburg)*, reflected on the widespread online availability of stolen personal passwords, those illusionary markers of privacy and data protection.

Since in the context of digital culture, with which Bartholl and others engage, anonymity is often seen as a positive value that protects and enables, it seemed important for the RCA project to also include an artist for whom anonymity would quite explicitly have a negative connotation. This was distinctly the case for the Iranian German artist Parastou Forouhar, who in her graphic and installation-based work frequently addresses aspects of physical and psychological violence in human relations.[5] Forouhar combines this approach with a visual language reminiscent of Islamic graphic aesthetics. In her images, the facelessness of the victims of torture and violence appears as an aspect of their submission. Moreover, the repetitive ornamental patterns camouflage the presence of guns, knives, and other instruments of torture, together with those of the human figures, metaphorically occluding the precarious status of the individual in settings of structural violence.

The preparatory conversations for the RCA project made it clear that Forouhar would act as an important advocate of such an expanded perspective on anonymity that does not so much celebrate but decry its social and psychological effects. She "gave a face" to this problematic side of anonymity in a film about a deserted area on the outskirts of Tehran, called Khavaran,

[4] See Domenico Quaranta, ed., *Aram Bartholl: The Speed Book* (Berlin: Gestalten Verlag, 2012); and Aram Bartholl's website, accessed December 7, 2018, www.arambartholl.com.

[5] See Parastou Forouhar's website, accessed December 7, 2018, www.parastou-forouhar.de.

where murdered dissidents to the regime of the Islamic revolution were buried in the 1980s.[6] To date, it remains unknown who was buried here and where exactly. The dispersion and anonymization of these graves were intended to exterminate not only the individuals but also the memory of them. In the film *Sie erinnert sich* (She remembers), Forouhar and a friend visit one of these sites, where relatives of the deceased make the place their own by carefully marking it with pebbles, scattering flowers, enunciating memories, and singing songs together, thus countering, if only symbolically, the attempted elimination.

The British artist Heath Bunting, in the context of his *Status Project* (2004–14), has dealt with the construction and deconstruction of identities through administrative and institutional structures for more than a decade.[7] Such constructions of identity appear as the flipside, and thus a conceptual complement, to the notion and construction of anonymity. Based on his more recent research on the principle of anonymous corporations, Bunting prepared a series of eight diagrams that describe—in a highly formalized, abstracted manner—the requirements for a fictitious collective, the *Woody*

[6] See also "Sie erinnert sich" in this publication, containing photographs of Kharavan, made secretly by the artist during her visits to the location.

[7] See *The Status Project* website, accessed December 7, 2018, http://status.irational.org.

Fig. 3 "woody bay survival group" (series of posters); installation view (2018, Kampnagel, west wing, Hamburg)

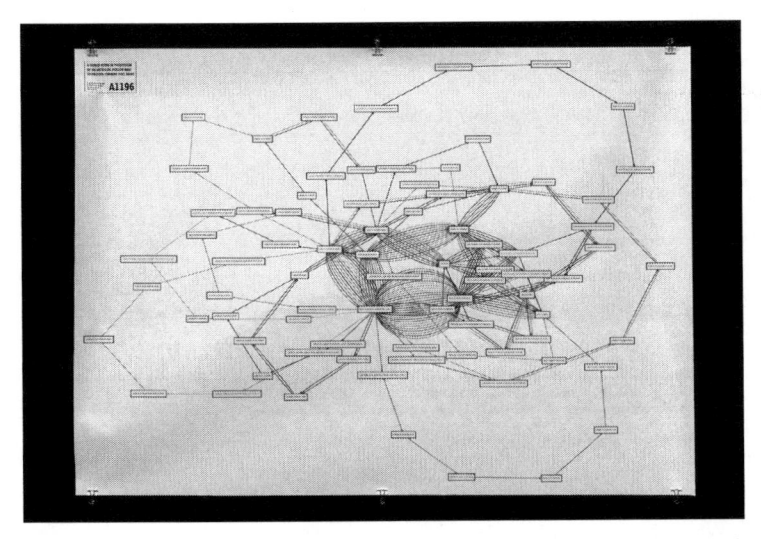

Fig. 4 "woody bay survival group" (series of posters, detail); installation view (2018, Kampnagel, west wing, Hamburg)

Bay Survival Group, to live anonymously in a remote spot on the west coast of England, a rural niche in a world that seems to have almost done away with anonymity altogether. The project explores ways of withdrawing from the all-encompassing digital identity regimes and the social consequences of such a withdrawal. The underlying reflection on the radical disengagement from normative and state structures is also the basis for Bunting's contribution to the present volume, in which the letters USAE signify the desire to unmask the imperialist dimension of the global political, economic, and military order. Bunting's strategy of unhinging achieved knowledge patterns by means of questions and the introduction of apocryphal knowledge into the RCA working meetings had the important effect of probing the methodological foundations and orthodoxies on which our discussions on anonymity relied.

The German artist Johannes Paul Raether has, over the past decade, developed a series of fictitious characters that he calls "Avataras," hybrid and queer personae that Raether performs in collective live situations in public spaces, as well as in gallery exhibitions.[8] One of the main themes of Raether's research is reproductive technologies

[8] For the branching of Raether's Avataras in what he terms "Identitecture," see his website, accessed December 7, 2018, www.johannespaulraether.net.

and their potential for bringing forth new forms of social relations. Raether's contribution to the art program presented at Kampnagel was a new version of his Avatara and "SelfSister" performance *Transformalor [Transformella malor ikeae]*, an identity through which Raether deals with questions of the self, belonging, and potentially new formations of kin made possible through reproductive technologies. The project reflects on

Fig. 5 + 6 Performance "Transformalor [Transformella malor 4.4.6.11.]"; part of the A=ANONYM program (2018, IKEA Hamburg City, Hamburg)

Fig. 7 Performance "Transformalor [Transformella malor 4.4.6.11.]" part of the A=ANONYM program (2018, Große Bergstraße, Altona, near IKEA Hamburg City, Hamburg)

unknown origins and an anonymous descent that may deprive a person of—or free them from—the possibilities of identifying with known biological ancestors and "family" histories. Staged as a hypothetical positive take on the developments of a biodigital capitalism, the performance took a group of around forty participants to an inner-city branch of the IKEA store in Hamburg. Infiltrated by *Transformalor* and its temporary repro-communal tribe, the performance investigated this corporate space as a symbolic territory of the production of social norms and normalities.

The Zurich-based group knowbotiq (consisting of Austrian artist Christian Hübler and German artist Yvonne Wilhelm), in their engagement with the sociotechnical aspects of digital culture, have moved away from a more technoculturally oriented perspective, which they held in the 1990s, toward questions of presence, visibility, and agency of the human body and of labor under the conditions of a digital and global economy. In 2009, knowbotiq developed the figurative concept of *MacGhillie*, a human figure masked by a traditional military camouflage suit,

Fig. 8 + 9 + 10 "Amazonian Flesh, how to hang in trees during strike"; installation view (detail) (2018, Kampnagel, "Meisterbude"/main foyer, Hamburg)

A — INTRO
Artistic Research on Anonymity

which in public presentations was offered to members of the audience, who could temporarily wear the suit and thus become the anonymous and somewhat amorphous figure of *MacGhillie*.[9] More recently, this trajectory of research brought the group to study the regimes of labor and the subjection of laboring human bodies in logistics and distribution centers like those of the company Amazon. Their installation *Amazonian Flesh, How to Hang in Trees during Strike* was presented in the former supervision booth of the Kampnagel factory, offering speculative interfaces for a subversive communication between human laborers and algorithmic bots, as well as the vision of a free space of idleness that might exist beyond the matrices and techniques of optimization and value creation.[10] The investigation of anonymity here shifted from assertive discourses around subject positions and social relations toward the more ambivalent field of human-machine interaction, where software bots and logistics workers are both faceless nonpersonae, and where anonymity is not so much a social desire or drama but a technical given.

[9] See Andreas Broeckmann and knowbotic research, eds., *Opaque Presence: Manual of Latent Invisibilities* (Zurich: Diaphanes / Edition Jardins des Pilotes, 2010); and knowbotiq + krcf, accessed December 7, 2018, www.knowbotiq.net.

[10] See also "Amazonian Flesh: How to Hang in Trees during Strike?" in this publication, containing excerpts from text mantras by speculative Amazon bots, which were translated into a sonic environment for the installation *Amazonian Flesh, How to Hang in Trees during Strike* at the Kampnagel exhibition.

Fig. 11 "Amazonian Flesh, how to hang in trees during strike"; installation view (detail) (2018, Kampnagel, "Meisterbude"/main foyer, Hamburg)

Fig. 12 "Towards an Art History of Art Gallery Security Guards"; installation view (2018, Kampnagel, "the artist studio"/main foyer, Hamburg)

In May 2017, about halfway through the project, the British artist Simon Farid was invited to join the symposium organized to include external researchers and artists already working on anonymity-related themes without being part of the RCA project group. Farid consequently stayed with the project until the end. In his artistic work, Farid deals with the work of invigilators in contemporary art galleries.[11] Working as an invigilator and organizing several clandestine activities with some colleagues in the past, Farid now used the opportunity of the RCA project to develop research and presentation methods that would also make it possible to show some of this fragile work in public. For the Kampnagel event, Farid designed an exhibition and information booth that presented his research about other artists who have worked as gallery guards over the past decades, combined with a series of photos that show Farid visiting and viewing works of these artists—photos deliberately taken from the perspective of a potential gallery guard—and speculating about the possible impact that this form of labor may have had on the history of contemporary art.[12]

[11] See Simon Farid's website, accessed December 7, 2018, www.simonfarid.com.

[12] See also "Towards an Art History of Art Gallery Guards" in this book, the listing of famous artists who used to work as gallery security guards or other (anonymous) security personnel in art institutions, as well as the "Provisional Manifesto for Invigilator-Friendly Artworks."

A — INTRO
Artistic Research on Anonymity

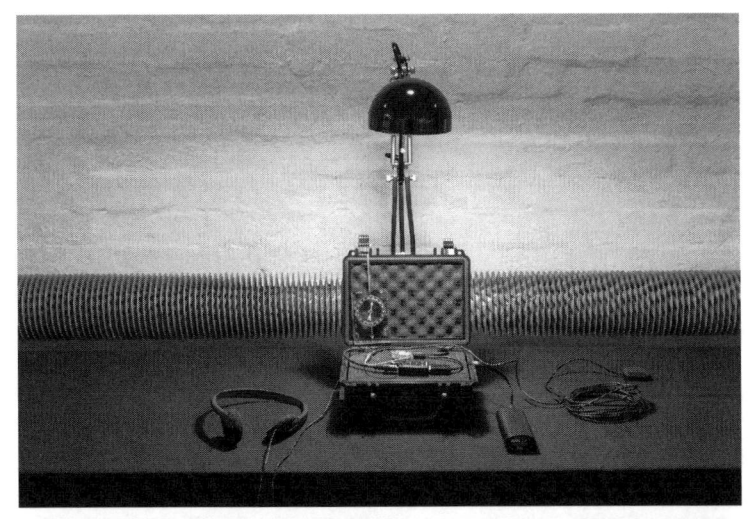

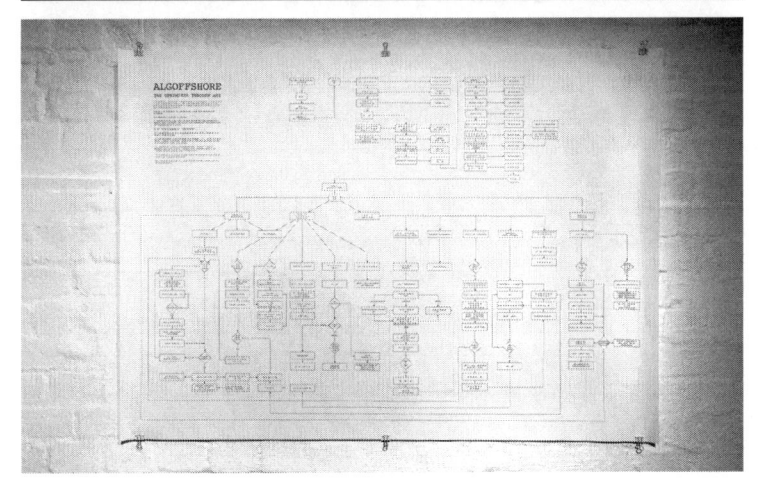

Fig. 13 + 14 "The Great Offshore"
Fig. 15 "Algoffshore"; installation view (detail) (2018, Kampnagel, main foyer, Hamburg)

To connect more directly to the broader Kampnagel audience, we asked the French artist collective RYBN.ORG to design, based on their long-term project *The Great Offshore*, an installation and workshop that would have "popular" aspects in two respects: first, through the choice of the topic (e. g., the illegal offshore financial trade, as it has become widely known through the publication of the Panama Papers in 2016), and then through the realization of a workshop that would involve members of the general audience more directly in the artist group's research.[13] Over the past decade, RYBN.ORG has gathered detailed knowledge about the effects and affects of anonymity created through the architectures and uses of specific algorithms in online financial trading software. This technical infrastructure, as well as related laws and regulations, support the creation and inner workings of financial tax havens through anonymity created and provided by the software. Moreover, the algorithms act as anonymous and increasingly "intelligent" agents.[14] The exchange during the days of the conference and exhibition showed how in the zones of resonance between the artists' work and that of the scientists researching software companies and digital service applications, anonymity becomes visible as a relation that is constructed under very specific temporal, technical, and juridical conditions.

The last artistic position brought into the art program's constellation at Kampnagel was that of the French artist group Bureau d'études, known for cartographies and particularly detailed maps of political, social, and economic systems, revealing and suggesting complex relations and constellations of global allegiance and dependency that normally remain invisible.[15] The work of Bureau d'études touched on many issues discussed in the overall RCA project, even without having focused explicitly on anonymity, and the artists were consequently invited to take part in the program presented at Kampnagel, with a workshop based on their current research on bio- and chemo-politics, focusing

[13] See the RYBN.ORG website, accessed December 7, 2018, www.rybn.org.

[14] See also "Anonymity on Demand" in this publication.

[15] See the Bureau d'études website, accessed December 7, 2018, www.bureaudetudes.org.

on synthetic molecular substances as anonymous agents affecting the health and bodily integrity of living beings. To deal with this topic, the artists are developing a game that is to be played in groups, intended to serve as a starting point for the participants to reflect on the economic and legal structures, regulations, and politics that define, name, and identify—or anonymize—political agents.[16]

16 See also "Sanitary Police and the Politics of Anonymity: Observations on a Game about Endocrine Disruptors" in this publication.

Fig. 16 + 17 Workshop "Chemopolitics. A collective game about endocrine disruptors"; part of the A=ANONYM program (2018, Kampnagel, Hamburg)

Doing Research in Artistic Practice

While there is a boom of research-oriented artistic practices fueled and institutionalized by grants, fellowships, and Ph.D. programs, the notion of "artistic research" continues to be controversial. While the activity of researching is usually accepted as one that can be carried out by anyone and that does not necessarily have to be connected to a professional environment, the noun "research" is often associated with science. The assumption is that research proper can only be conducted under the standardized and methodical conditions offered by scientific disciplines, whether in the natural and social sciences or in the humanities. It remains a matter of debate whether "research" can happen outside such contexts. In the case of the arts, an additional point of dispute is what might differentiate artistic "research" from other artistic practices, equally geared at exploring, scrutinizing, testing, and seeking insight into the world. Whether and how the term "research" as it is used in the sciences can be applied to artistic practices thus remains an open question.[17] Advocates of a strong notion of artistic research argue that scientific research and all other processes of knowledge production are never completely transparent and objective but always to some degree based on intuition, creativity, or practices of experimentation characterized by "implicit knowledge."[18] At the same time, "doing science" is defined by a value and justification system of result-oriented, classification-based, systematic, reproducible, and falsifiable working methods. Such criteria may become relevant for artists, but only if their research is inspired especially by the natural sciences. It is therefore important to differentiate between "artistic research," on the one hand, and projects taking place under the labels "art+science," "sci/art," "artsci," and so forth, on the other; the latter refer specifically to artistic practices that seek inspiration from scientific innovations and research, or from historic scientific experiments, leading artists to develop scientific experiments of their own.[19] What we want

[17] Examples from an extensive bibliography on artistic research include Jens Badura, Selma Dubach, and Anke Haarmann, eds., *Künstlerische Forschung: Ein Handbuch* (Zurich: Diaphanes, 2015); Michael Biggs and Henrik Karlsson, eds., *The Routledge Companion to Research in the Arts* (London: Routledge, 2011); Elke Bippus, ed., *Kunst des Forschens: Praxis eines ästhetischen Denkens* (Zurich: Diaphanes, 2009); Henk Borgdorff, *The Conflict of the Faculties: Perspectives on Artistic Research and Academia* (Leiden: Leiden University Press, 2012); Michael Schwab, ed., *Experimental Systems: Future Knowledge in Artistic Research* (Leuven: Leuven University Press, 2013); and "Artistic Research," special issue, *Texte zur Kunst* 20, no. 82 (2011).

[18] See Karen van den Berg and Stephan Schmidt-Wulffen, "The Politics of Artistic Knowledge at Universities," in *Artistic Research in Applied Arts*, ed. Harald Gruber, Gabriele Schmid, Peter Sinapius, and Rosemarie Tüpker (Berlin: HPB University Press, 2015), 159–76; and Hans-Jörg Rheinberger, "On the Art of Exploring the Unknown," in *Say It Isn't So: Naturwissenschaften im Visier der Kunst/Art Trains Its Sights on the Natural Sciences*, ed. Peter Friese, Guido Boulboullé, and Susanne Witzgall (Bremen: Kehrer Verlag, 2007), 82–90.

[19] See Theresa Schubert and Andrew Adamatzky, eds., *Experiencing the Unconventional: Science in Art* (Hackensack, NJ: World Scientific, 2015); and Arthur I. Miller, *Colliding Worlds: How Cutting-Edge Science Is Redefining Contemporary Art* (New York: Norton, 2014).

to discuss and look at here, though, is a more general understanding of "artistic research," which more or less systematically and experimentally explores societal issues that, importantly, are relevant beyond the art field.

Looking more closely at this terminology and how "research" might be done by artists, the questions at the core of the debate seem to be: What is the aesthetic dimension of thought, knowledge, and research? And how can artistic practice make this aesthetic dimension of any research practice fruitful for other disciplines and fields of knowledge production? What is the role of the artist as researcher in and for contemporary art, science, and society? The challenge for artists in the particular field of anonymity research is to develop ways in which the possibilities and implications of social and technological change can be addressed, used, appropriated, and critically engaged with from an artistic perspective. To approach questions that are not readily addressed by the research and development contexts that produce these technologies, artists instead make use of the potentials inherent to speculative and disruptive creative practices for the production of new forms of experiential knowledge. The difficulties of discussing such nonscientific approaches and methods to research arise mainly at a linguistic level, when it comes to verbally capturing such nonverbal practices through a scientific vocabulary, led by the need to describe, explain, and evaluate the artistic work and its processes. The current debate and discourse around the notion of "artistic research" aims at developing an appropriate vocabulary by reevaluating and refining definitions and terminologies, in terms of differentiating artistic from scientific research, as well as highlighting their points of intersection, and in terms of finding and developing nuanced articulations for the processes, methods, and logics of artistic research. In an attempt to create a manual to art as research, the German artist, author, and researcher Florian Dombois has established ten criteria that delineate the contested areas related to the notion of artistic research.[20] He confronts the linguistic hurdles of verbally capturing such nonverbal practices by drawing lines between three consecutive manifestations: "cognizance" gained in the research process, which manifests through its communicability; the "research result" taking shape as the work of art; and the produced "knowledge" that results from this research process and that is contained in the presentation of the work's form and expression developed and chosen by the artist. Dombois's method of breaking down the individual steps of the process can denote qualities and functions of these different steps within the artistic research process. Yet his analysis still leaves the question of how the methods of artistic research and the knowledge they produce help us to understand the aesthetic dimension of artistic thought, knowledge, and research.

[20] Florian Dombois, "Kunst als Forschung: Ein Versuch, sich selbst eine Anleitung zu entwerfen," in *Hochschule der Künste Bern HKB 2006*, ed. HKB/HEAB (Bern: Hochschule der Künste Bern, 2006), 21–29.

Fig. 18 Presentaion and discussion of works with RCA research team members (2017, Steyerberg, Lower Saxony)

In Christoph Schenker's text on artistic forms of knowledge, "Wissensformen der Kunst" (2015), the Swiss art theorist describes artistic work as a way of inventing and experimenting with new terms and notions.

He argues that art is a means to search for new ways of thinking and to put normative or normalized behaviors to the test; it therefore always takes shape as a practice of differentiation (Unterscheidungsverhalten) tested against specific terms, notions, or behaviors. While the concepts and notions put to the test do not necessarily have clear equivalents in the language of words, they are always anchored and established in the structures of perception, and in specific societies or cultures. Schenker emphasizes that, as a researcher, the artist's frame of reference for testing and exploring dissociations and differences goes beyond the limitations of artistic contexts and always involves or reflects other forms and disciplines of knowledge, as well as contexts of life. He proposes to think of artistic research as a way of creating new terms and notions to experiment with, and to reflect about the implications they could have on ways of living and on belief systems.[21]

The process of such artistic experimentation being as important as the results, artistic research practices invite a high level of exchange and sharing of expertise across different disciplines and fields of knowledge. As outlined in one of the ten clauses established by Dombois's manual: once the artist articulates and defines a specific research interest and question, overlappings and intersections with those of researchers in other fields and disciplines appear, and therefore possibilities to network and collaborate also appear. Guided by the logic of a common topic, "research communities" can form and enable deeper, more complex and encompassing structures of evaluation.[22]

Analyzing and describing the different practices and approaches the artists applied within the specific context of the RCA project gave us the opportunity to observe and analyze the productivity of artistic research for developing a new, refined, and critical understanding of social issues, such as anonymity, based on concrete examples of the processes and dynamics experienced

[21] Christoph Schenker, "Wissensformen der Kunst," in Badura, Dubach, and Haarmann, *Künstlerische Forschung: Ein Handbuch*, 105–10.

[22] Dombois, "Kunst als Forschung," 24.

within such an interdisciplinary project. What kinds of reflections and knowledge about anonymity would the artistic projects contribute?

Motivated by our need to describe those processes and dynamics, as well as the motivations and potentials of concrete practices and projects by the invited artists to various audiences, institutions, and collaborators, we developed and implemented another set of concepts, which crystallized in the group's internal discussions and external communication and helped to conceptualize the aesthetics of knowledge and research.

Three Concepts in Artistic Research and Knowledge Production

A main concern in the RCA project's interdisciplinary communication was to find a way of describing the relation between the different methods that artists and scientists use, as well as to clarify in what ways their combination could be made productive, without one methodology compromising the other.

Looking at the array of techniques and methods of doing research among the different disciplines, which together multiply the perspectives on both the overall topic and single aspects, the German ethnologist and project lead of one of the ethnographic subprojects, Michi Knecht, proposed the notion of *kaleidoscopic knowledge production* to describe the relation and interaction between disciplines: multilayered, multidisciplinary forms and fields of knowledge in different compositions and overlapping constellations, offering different perspectives and insights that are recomposed and rearranged like the images in a kaleidoscope, changing with every turn of the cylinder.[23] The term attempts to convey the complex set of actions, reactions, and interactions of attractions, affinities, or incompatibilities that occur in interdisciplinary and differentiated research

[23] Michi Knecht, in conversation with the authors, 2016.

communities brought together by a common interest and topic. Kaleidoscopic knowledge production points to the diverse constellations that, in a comparison of artistic and scientific research, the German composer, film director, and cofounder of the Society for Artistic Research in Germany, Julian Klein, describes like this: "Not everything that is regarded as art must therefore be unscientific, and not everything that is regarded as science must be unartistic.… The artistic and scientific content of objects, processes, and events can be mixed independently of each other and in ever-changing dosages."[24]

Not always do mutual influences become apparent directly in different group constellations, interactions, and exchanges, nor even necessarily over a longer period. What we could observe during the research process of the RCA project were often rather indirect yet discernable dynamics caused specifically by the disruptive and transformative forces that appear in the confrontation of methodologically different approaches and different perspectives to the same topic. The embodied ways of thinking and engaging that characterize, for instance, the performance practice of Johannes Paul Raether,

[24] Julian Klein, "Was ist künstlerische Forschung?" "Auditive Perspektiven," special issue, *kunsttexte* 2 (2011): 2 (translated from German by the authors).

Fig. 19 Workshop "KILLYOURPHONE.COM" with RCA research team members

or Parastou Forouhar's use of her own body, identity, personal history, and culture, as well as the sometimes humorous, always critical approaches to sociotechnical structures and systems in Aram Bartholl's, Heath Bunting's, knowbotiq's, Simon Farid's, RYBN.ORG's, or Bureau d'Études artistic practices strongly influenced the exchanges with other researchers, and the resulting discussions shed light on orthodoxies, motivations, and restrictions in the work of each different actor, of artists as well as scientists.

While the metaphor of the kaleidoscope is helpful to describe the interdisciplinary interaction that introduces new perspectives and the integration of yet undefined knowledge, it does not articulate the processes and dynamics in this exchange between different knowledge practices. Yet, the idea of colorful shards and flinders in a kaleidoscope rolling through the cylinder, breaking the light in different ways as they overlap and reflect, led us to further adopt the notion of *diffraction*, which was introduced into the critical discourse on science and knowledge by feminist thinkers and philosophers of science Donna Haraway and Karen Barad. A term from optics and classical physics, diffraction originally described a phenomenon that occurs when waves (of light, sound, electromagnetic radiation, etc.) encounter the edge of an obstacle and are slightly bent, resulting in the waves proceeding in a different direction and causing a blur at the edge of the shadow of the obstacle. Haraway first employed the term figuratively to denote a critical and difference-attentive mode of consciousness in relation to thought, difference, and alterity. She contrasted diffraction to the notion of reflexivity, which in her eyes "only displaces the same elsewhere, leading to concerns about copy and original and the search for the authentic and really real."[25] Instead, "Diffraction does not produce 'the same' displaced, as reflection and refraction do. Diffraction is a mapping of interference, not of replication, reflection, or reproduction. A diffraction pattern does not map where differences appear,

[25] Donna J. Haraway, *Modest_Witness@Second_Millennium.FemaleMan_Meets_OncoMouse: Feminism and Technoscience* (New York: Routledge, 1997), 16; and Karen Barad, *Meeting the Universe Halfway: Quantum Physics and the Entanglement of Matter and Meaning* (Durham, NC: Duke University Press, 2007), 72.

but rather maps where the effects of difference appear."[26] These effects of difference lie at the core of what we want to refer to here as *difference-attentive kaleidoscopic knowledge*. Works like Heath Bunting's hypercomplex diagrams, for example, map the construction of identity and the juridical organization of social relations. Hardly readable in an analytical sense, their exaggerated complexity offers a clear, intuitive, and diffractional insight into the structural fragility of anonymous relations. Also Aram Bartholl's artistic strategy highlights the effects of epistemological diffraction: it extrapolates from the potentials of technologies, based on an informed critique of their functionality, and invents speculative applications and experimental scenarios in which these potentials become visible as transformations of the meanings of the technologies in their social contexts. They make it necessary to rethink and critique anonymity in relation to the very sociotechnical structures that constitute its predominant contemporary frames of reference.

[26] Donna J. Haraway, "The Promises of Monsters: A Regenerative Politics for Inappropriate/d Others," in *Cultural Studies*, ed. Lawrence Grossberg, Cary Nelson, and Paula Treichler (New York: Routledge, 1992), 300.

But what exactly are the spaces where such knowledge is being produced, and where it appears in the encounter between different disciplines and research methods? The concept of diffraction refers to the processes and dynamics taking place in this exchange between different knowledge practices, and it can be complemented with the notion of *zones of resonance* to highlight the areas or points of encounter and intersection between the disciplines and practices. Borrowed from an essay by filmmaker and anthropologist Rachel Thompson, published in the context of her reflections about the intersections of artistic practice and anthropological endeavors, the concept of zones of resonance became a third useful instrument for describing and reflecting on our interdisciplinary research cooperation. The concept of zones of resonance does not intend to demarcate "clear boundaries or the dimensions of common terrain," or methods to borrow from, but rather proposes "strategies of suggestion, insinuation, and montage,

Fig. 20 Banner created for the A=ANONYM exhibition; installation view (2018, Kampnagel, main foyer, Hamburg)

so as to configure a space of possible resonance between these two inquisitive endeavors, a zone where neighboring objects might oscillate in sympathetic vibration"—a resonance that can be conceived both in a physical and in a metaphorical way, as the following examples illustrate.[27]

27 Rachel Thompson, "Labyrinth of Linkages— Cinema, Anthropology, and the Essayistic Impulse," in *Between Matter and Method*, ed. by Gretchen Bakke and Marina Peterson (London: Bloomsbury Academic, 2017), 1–20.

The artist Johannes Paul Raether was first brought into the meetings of the RCA project because he happened to be a visiting artist at Leuphana University's Leuphana Arts Program. It quickly turned out that his interests resonated not only with the project's general deconstructive approach to identity but also and in particular with the research of the ethnographers Michi Knecht and Amelie Baumann on anonymous gamete donations. An ongoing dialogue was forged between them, leading Raether to join the RCA working meetings on several occasions.

Another, even more striking case of resonance created among artistic and scientific perspectives on anonymity was triggered by artist Simon Farid's research about the social spaces in which anonymous relations are constituted and performed. His project became the basis of a lively exchange between him and the ethnographers and media scholars Götz Bachmann, Paula Bialski, and Randi Heinrichs, based on their respective interest in forms of anonymity at the workplace and their effects on the individual behavior and social relations of the workers. To study these, Bialski, and Heinrichs conduct ethnographic research by engaging with software and application developers working for commercial companies in Berlin and Hamburg. In contrast, Farid's artistic practice is informed by working as a gallery guard, so that for him, labor relation, research, and artistic performative practice are inseparably entangled. Despite the differences of the addressed work environments and respective tasks (in Farid's case, a museum for contemporary art; for Bialski, and Heinrichs, software and digital service companies), both investigated how a worker is affected by, reacts to, or rejects different forms of imposed or provided anonymity. Here, the resonance between the different approaches became most manifest through observations and reflections made during the presentations in the conference program at Kampnagel and, even more importantly, during the discussion of Farid's work in the space of the art installation. Talking about how Farid had, in his photographs, staged the worker's perspective aesthetically and more generally in relation to the previously presented ethnographic research, Bachmann pointed out how Farid's visual and conceptual approach provided an alternative passage, and an alternative logic, showing how one project (be it scientific or artistic) could be read and interpreted through the logic of the other, opening up new spaces of reflection for both.

The RCA artistic research projects thus introduced novel conceptual perspectives and methodological approaches to the research topic of anonymity: highlighting the performative aspects of anonymity (Farid, knowbotiq), problematizing the question of visibility and invisibility (Bartholl, Forouhar), crossing the topic of anonymity with the structures and politics of collectivities and corpo-

Fig. 21 Artist talk and discussion with the audience as part of the A=ANONYM conference program (2018, Kampnagel, "the artist studio"/main foyer, Hamburg)

rations (Bunting, RYBN, Bureau d'études), and extrapolating alternative readings of the social and psychological effects of anonymity (Raether, Farid). As Schenker argues in his take on artistic research, these new terms and notions made it possible and necessary for all participating researchers to rethink their own perspective on anonymity, and to experiment—conceptually or practically—with such alternative notions and methodical approaches. The artistic projects exemplify the necessity of approaching any instance of knowledge about anonymity as a form of kaleidoscopic knowledge that occurs and diffracts in zones of resonance.

Spaces of Encounter

The discussion of artistic research methods observed in our case study has drawn on the concepts of kaleidoscopic knowledge production, diffraction, and zones of resonance, with the aim of developing a conceptual framework for describing the aesthetics of knowledge production in this particular field. All three concepts use perceptual and spatial metaphors to describe the interaction between practices and their understanding

Fig. 22 Workshop of the Reconfiguring Anonymity team, Leuphana University, Lüneburg, January 2016.

in research contexts. We therefore want to conclude this text with a more explicit analysis of the spatial and practical conditions in which these research practices and communication processes have taken place, hoping to show that those concepts are to be taken not only metaphorically, but also quite literally as descriptions for spatial interactions.

The microphysics of communication are determined in part by individual styles and habits of correspondence, of presentation and dialogue, that each of the participants brings to the cooperation. The encounters during the RCA working meetings were structured through a mix of written papers, lectures, artist presentations, seminar-style dialogues, and joint workshop-style practices, the latter having been proposed and introduced particularly by some of the participating artists. In the preparations for the retreat meeting in autumn 2017, the curators made space in the schedule for such open formats, which were not preconfigured in advance and which replaced the habits of consecutive speaking by more polylogical and performative forms of interaction.

Equally important was the arrangement of the spaces in which these encounters took place. What are the grounds and, quite literally, the territories and institutional spaces in which interdisciplinary communication takes place? Institutional routines tend to bring artists into academic spaces, rather than scientists into artist studios, exhibition spaces, or other, hybrid or public spaces, where artistic practices usually unfold.[28] Most of the working meetings of the RCA project took place in university seminar rooms, where people usually sit on chairs that are placed at a set of tables, looking at one another and conducting a consecutive conversation. The egalitarian, horizontal structure of such spaces, with their temporal and behavioral routines, may be useful for certain purposes, but it can also prove problematic or a hindrance for an exchange between subject positions that are "eccentric" and "exceptional," counterproductively homogenizing the exchange. On several occasions, when the group discussions were shifted from the academic conference and seminar setting to the art exhibition space—whether improvised or more formal—this shift significantly changed the type of engagement between the participants. This was particularly true in the aforementioned workshop with Parastou Forouhar, and in the situation created during the "labor" panel in Simon Farid's installation for the A=ANONYM exhibition. In both cases, the artistically induced discussion on visibility and social interaction brought up reflections about possible further perspectives in scientific research.

A similar productive interference occurred in the encounter between artist Johannes Paul Raether and ethnographers Michi Knecht and Amelie Baumann, with their rather different takes on and interests in the legal, societal, and individual implications of reproductive technologies. Their exchange about what questions were most relevant for both sides, and what the possible answers would imply for the others, became fruitful for their conversations, enriched by the sharing of reference texts as well as other research materials. Together they decided to create a loop of engagement with each other's materials and approaches. Raether's Avatara performance

[28] See also Karen van den Berg, "Ungefährliche Experimente—Das Studio als Labor," *Zeitschrift für Ästhetik und Allgemeine Kunstwissenschaft* 57 (2012): 307–20.

Transformalor [Transformella malor ikeae] in Hamburg was based on accounts that Baumann had collected during her research from people who had been conceived with anonymously donated gametes. In turn, Knecht and Baumann participated in this performance as though it were a research trip, taking field notes that contributed to their ongoing ethnographic research, thus interlacing the different roles of the artist (as agent, research commissioner, and object of study) and of the scientists (as art audience and ethnographers). These transgressions proved particularly productive because these actors did not meet for the first time but knew each other and had engaged with each other's work repeatedly over the previous years.

An important spatial dimension of the collaborative experience of the RCA project was, finally, marked by the physical spaces of Kampnagel Hamburg, where the closing event took place. They constituted a physical environment and platform of encounter that provided neither a typical and easy-to-use "white cube"-like situation (as usually found in institutions presenting and displaying works of visual art), nor a typical environment for academic conferences. Kampnagel confronted everyone involved with unusual circumstances: the artists and the curators for installing and planning the displays of the artworks, and the scientists for planning the conference as an exchange at eye level with the artistic approaches, as well as for considering an audience with potentially diverse backgrounds. The physical and intellectual environment provided by Kampnagel was a logical consequence and extension of the spaces of encounter tested during the course of the project. It provided a context for yet further attempts to actively blur the lines between conference settings and installations, between formal and contemplative situations of presentation, allowing zones of resonance and shadowy areas of diffraction to appear and to activate changes in the attitudes and forms of exchange.

Bibliography

Bachmann, Götz, Michi Knecht, and Andreas Wittel. "The Social Productivity of Anonymity," special issue, *ephemera: Theory and Politics in Organization*, 17, no. 2 (2017).

Badura, Jens, Selma Dubach, Anke Haarmann, Dieter Mersch, Anton Rey, Christoph Schenker, and Germán Toro Pérez, eds. *Künstlerische Forschung. Ein Handbuch*. Zurich: Diaphanes, 2015.

Barad, Karen. *Meeting the Universe Halfway: Quantum Physics and the Entanglement of Matter and Meaning*. Durham, NC: Duke University Press, 2007.

Berg, Karen van den. "Ungefährliche Experimente—Das Studio als Labor," *Zeitschrift für Ästhetik und Allgemeine Kunstwissenschaft*, 57 (2012): 307–20.

Berg, Karen van den, and Stephan Schmidt-Wulffen. "The Politics of Artistic Knowledge at Universities." In *Artistic Research in Applied Arts*, edited by Harald Gruber, Gabriele Schmid, Peter Sinapius, and Rosemarie Tüpker, 159–76. Berlin: HPB University Press, 2015.

Biggs, Michael, Henrik Karlsson, and Stiftelsen Riksbankens Jubileumsfond, eds. *The Routledge Companion to Research in the Arts*. London: Routledge, 2010.

Bippus, Elke, ed. *Kunst des Forschens: Praxis eines ästhetischen Denkens*. Zurich: Diaphanes, 2009.

Bismarck, Beatrice von, Jörn Schafaff, and Thomas Weski. eds. *Cultures of the Curatorial*. Berlin: Sternberg Press, 2012.

Borgdorff, Henk. *The Conflict of the Faculties: Perspectives on Artistic Research and Academia*. Leiden: Leiden University Press, 2012.

Broeckmann, Andreas, and knowbotic research. *Opaque Presence: Manual of Latent Invisibilities*. Zurich: Diaphanes / Edition Jardins des Pilotes, 2010.

Dombois, Florian. "Kunst als Forschung. Ein Versuch, sich selbst eine Anleitung zu entwerfen." *Hochschule der Künste Bern HKB* (2006): 21–29.

Haraway, Donna. "The Promises of Monsters: A Regenerative Politics for Inappropriate/d Others." In *Cultural Studies*, edited by Lawrence Grossberg, Cary Nelson, and Paula Treichler, 295–337. New York: Routledge, 1992.

Haraway, Donna. *Modest-Witness@Second-Millennium, FemaleMan-Meets-OncoMouse: Feminism and Technosciences*. New York: Routledge, 1997.

Hoffmann, Jens. *Jens Hoffmann: (Curating) From A to Z*. Zurich: JRP|Ringier, 2014.

Klein, Julian. "Was ist künstlerische Forschung?" *kunsttexte.de – E-Journal für Kunst- und Bildgeschichte* no. 2 (2011). https://edoc.hu-berlin.de/bitstream/handle/18452/7501/klein.pdf.

Miller, Arthur. *Colliding Worlds: How Cutting-Edge Science Is Redefining Contemporary Art*. New York: Norton, 2014.

O'Neill, Paul. *The Culture of Curating and the Curating of Culture(s)*. Cambridge, MA: MIT Press, 2012.

Ponesse, Julie. "Navigating the Unknown: Towards a Positive Conception of Anonymity." *Southern Journal of Philosophy* 51, no. 3 (2013): 320–44.

Quaranta, Domenico. ed. *Aram Bartholl: The Speed Book*. Berlin: Gestalten, 2012.

Rheinberger, Hans-Jörg. "On the Art of Exploring the Unknown". In *Say it isn't so. Naturwissenschaften im Visier der Kunst/Art Trains Its Sights on the Natural Sciences*, edited by Peter Friese, Guido Boulboullé, and Susanne Witzgall. Bremen: Kehrer Verlag (2007): 82–90.

Schenker, Christoph. "Wissensformen der Kunst." In *Künstlerische Forschung. Ein Handbuch*, edited by Jens Badura, Selma Dubach, Anke Haarmann, Dieter Mersch, Anton Rey, Christoph Schenker, and Germán Toro Pérez, 105–10. Zurich: Diaphanes 2015.

Schubert, Theresa, and Andrew Adamatzky, eds. *Experiencing the Unconventional: Science in Art*. Hackensack, NJ: World Scientific, 2015.

Schwab, Michael, ed. *Experimental Systems: Future Knowledge in Artistic Research*. Leuven: Leuven University Press, 2013.

Thiel, Thorsten. "Anonymität und der digitale Strukturwandel der Öffentlichkeit." *Zeitschrift für Menschenrechte* 10, no. 1 (2016): 9–24.

Thompson, Rachel. "Labyrinth of Linkages — Cinema, Anthropology, and the Essayistic Impulse." In *Between Matter and Method*, edited by Gretchen Bakke and Marina Peterson, 1–20. London: Bloomsbury Academic, 2017.

B

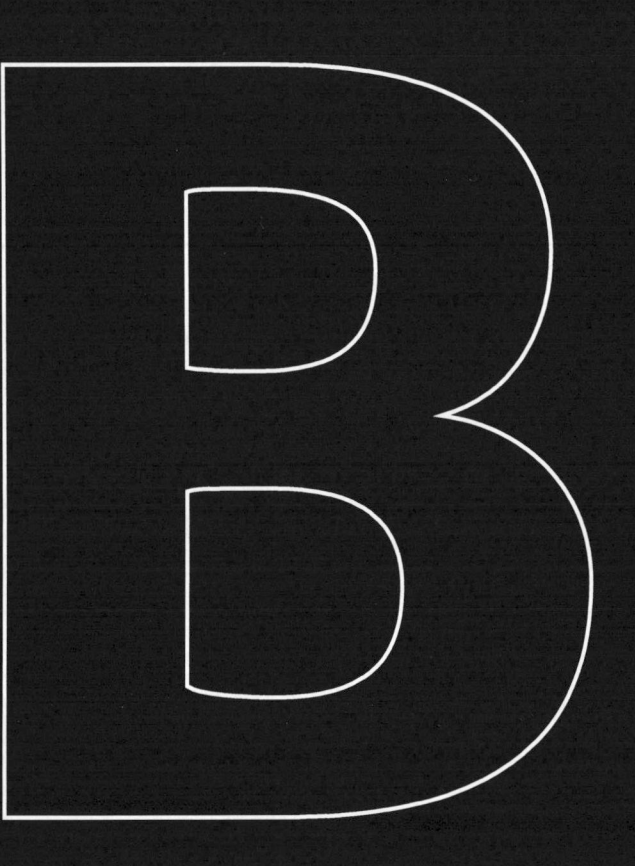

RECONFIGURATION

Anonymity and Transgression
Caste, Social Reform, and Blood Donation in India

Introduction

This chapter investigates critical social processes that come into view when we focus our attention on anonymity as a particular feature of voluntary blood donation in India. Anthropological theorizations of gift exchange have established the centrality of giving and receiving in maintaining and disrupting social ties. Gifts are always more than the transfer of objects and wealth; rather, they reveal how social bonds are conceptualized as weak or stable and the reflexive acts that strengthen or weaken these bonds. In such practices of exchange, whether the gift is made anonymously or in personalized terms crucially inflects its meaning and force. With blood donation as a mode of transfer, this is particularly the case, and even more so in India, where the anonymity of the transaction allows blood-banking professionals and donors alike to produce conceptions of the practice as a desired mode of "progressive transgression." Through the giving of blood, these actors claim to transgress modes of community distinction (namely, caste, religion) that are frequently themselves figured in terms of blood. In this way, and precisely because of its anonymous nature, voluntary blood donation becomes charged with humanistic and nationalist significance: "spilling over" narrow community distinctions, wider national and human collectivities can be imagined and even—the hope is—brought into existence. The anonymity of voluntary blood donation thus allows for what we might call a transcategorial impulse, with ideologues of the Indian blood-banking world depicting the transgressions of the practice as prefiguring and foreshadowing a transcategorial future that it simultaneously helps to bring into being—a prefigurative politics of anonymous blood donation.[1] This is significant because many prior analyses have equated anonymity with anomie and atomization. In contrast we show that rather than disabling integrative narratives, anonymity enables blood donations to cross social boundaries. Specifically, we elaborate imaginative spaces of transgression and traversal that are produced (rather than foreclosed) by the non-availability of knowledge about to whom one gives and from whom one receives—a characteristic of voluntary blood donation. Yet at the same time, we argue in a consideration of artificial blood that anonymity may also lead to these utopic visions breaking down. Anonymity, our material suggests, is not reducible to either utopic or disintegrative narratives and

[1] Graeber explains that prefigurative politics means "making one's means as far as possible identical with one's ends," acting in the present to create forms of relationality "that at least approximate those that might exist in the kind of society we'd like to bring about." David Graeber, "Anthropology and the Rise of the Professional-Managerial Class," HAU 4, no. 3 (2014): 85.

experiences; rather, it possesses powerful potentials either way.

For much of India's late-colonial and postcolonial history, biomedical blood donation took place in the form of "replacement," with relatives of recipients asked to replace (in advance) the blood they require, most often as a condition of treatment of their family member. One donated blood *for* (if not directly *to*) a known person. In the latter half of the twentieth century, this convention ran afoul of the now globally established policy orthodoxy that the safety of donated blood is greater when derived from voluntary unpaid donors in an anonymous system of procurement. This orthodoxy—associated with the influential British policy analyst Richard Titmuss—is supported and maintained by international arbiters of health policy and funding: the World Health Organization and the Red Cross both subscribe to Titmuss's dictum that voluntary anonymous blood donation provides the safest blood for transfusion.[2] Recognizing this accepted view, India's Supreme Court banned paid donation from January 1998 and demanded the phasing out of replacement donation, directing the government instead to encourage anonymous voluntary donation.[3] Despite the many campaigns to outmode it, however, replacement donation still accounts for more than 50 percent of all donated blood in India. To redress this, blood professionals (blood bank officials, organizers of donation camps, civil society organizers, and public health experts) seek to bring existing sociocultural concepts of gift giving, virtue, service, kinship, and nationalism into alignment with the public health commitment to anonymity.

At present, replacement donation is not illegal and remains the dominant collection mode, despite the order stipulating that it should be phased out. There is no central blood collection agency, and little cooperation between blood banks.[4] Statistics concerning the relative prevalence of different modes of blood collection are unreliable. And in a statistical sleight of hand, the govern-

[2] Richard Morris Titmuss, *The Gift Relationship: From Human Blood to Social Policy* (London: Allen and Unwin, 1970).

[3] Ostensibly very different forms of blood donation, the relationship between paid and replacement forms is in fact complex: paid donation, though illegal, still takes place under the sign of replacement. Relatives of those requiring a transfusion—perhaps too afraid themselves to donate—often pay "professionals" to act as relatives in their place. Moreover, and strictly speaking, paid donation is just as anonymous as voluntary blood donation, with donors and recipients separated by the mediating entity of the blood bank. Paid donation, however, cannot conjure wider imagined collectivities in the same way as voluntary donation because in the former case one is donating explicitly for one's self-interest (for cash) and moreover in a manner that potentially endangers transfusion recipients (that is, the incentive that payment gives donors to conceal information that would, if truthfully revealed, disqualify them from donating; infection rates are higher in remunerated forms of donation).

[4] Tim J. Bray and K. Prabhakar, "Blood Policy and Transfusion Practice—India," *Tropical Medicine & International Health* 7, no. 6 (2002): 477–78.

ment recently began categorizing replacement donations as voluntary donations, generating thoroughly misleading headlines such as "Voluntary Blood Donation Hits 80% Mark." Yet, despite much-reported setbacks, various nefarious practices, and definitional tangles, there *has* been a renewed emphasis by the state and the medical establishment on promoting anonymous voluntary blood donation. Further, this reformed modality of blood donation is made congruent with several other social reformist agendas. For in this reformed (voluntary, anonymous) mode, one no longer knows but may *imagine* one's recipients. This widening aligns blood donation with the idea of service and sacrifice for broader imagined communities — the nation, the abstract entity of "society" and of a "family" larger than immediate kin and caste fellows.

The point we want to emphasize here is that anonymity plays a crucial structuring role in this transitive moment in blood donation practices in India, creating an imaginative space for novel ideational maneuvers and moving beyond narrow community distinctions. Our work here builds on and develops Monica Konrad's conceptualization of anonymity in her work on the British system of ova donation.[5] As Konrad describes it, anonymity as a social practice is not limiting or obscuring but revelatory and productive because it allows donors to take "effective action from out of the uncertain knowledge set up by the conditions of anonymity."[6] Konrad provides a compelling critique of anthropological characterizations of anonymity, which, she argues, have tended to discount the imaginative possibilities of "not-knowing." If conventional anthropological treatments have portrayed anonymity as connotative of alienation, passivity, ahistoricity, and asociality, Konrad instead demonstrates that anonymity in the context of ova donation in Britain can produce "exciting connections between action and relatedness that cannot be reduced to the level of simple misrecognition or oblivious non-identity."[7] In this way, Konrad provides a powerful critique of biomedical and

[5] Monica Konrad, *Nameless Relations: Anonymity, Melanesia and Reproductive Gift Exchange between British Ova Donors and Recipients* (New York: Berghahn, 2005).

[6] Ibid., 117.

[7] Monica Konrad, "Ova Donation and Symbols of Substance: Some Variations on the Theme of Sex, Gender and the Partible Body," *Journal of the Royal Anthropological Institute* 4, no. 4 (1998): 659.

anthropological characterizations of anonymity that discount the imaginative possibilities of "not knowing." As we show in this chapter, Konrad's insistence on the imaginative possibilities of anonymity is strongly supported by the Indian experience of voluntary blood donation. Yet we also argue that just as blood donation practices demonstrate that we cannot reduce the complexities of anonymous formations to alienation and passivity, neither should we in reverse reductively restrict our analysis of anonymous formations to its utopic configurations. The alienability of anonymity is not easily suppressed. Anonymity, indeed, marks an ambivalent site of contraries, as well as troubled trafficking of desires, concepts, and cohabitation.

In particular, in this chapter we demonstrate that anonymity is a key mode through which practices of blood donation may be imagined to transgress and transcend social boundaries. Anonymity allows for discursive practices that promise all sorts of transgressions of division with an eye to larger integrations, even as such promises are hollowed out in the act of their making. Take for example the following case taken from a news report highlighting the capacity of blood donations to provoke integrative interpretations. After a series of bomb attacks in Mumbai in 2006, widely considered to have been carried out by militant Kashmiri separatists, Muslims in the city were reported to have rushed to donate blood for survivors of whatever hue: "Abdul Khan, waiting in line at the blood bank near one blast site at Jogeshwari station, said: 'We don't care whether it's a Hindu or a Muslim who gets our blood as long as we can save them.'" Blood donation was thus employed by donors and news reporters to provide a powerfully integrative conception of the nation at precisely the moment when the attackers were attempting to call into question such conceptions. Similarly, with the vexed question of caste, blood typing and donation have been engaged in attempts to "undivide" caste communities from one another. Caste is widely thought of as a quality inherent in the blood.[8] Blood donation across caste lines therefore holds the potential for transgressing this social divide. Anthropologist Jonathan Parry, in his work on industrial labor in Bhilai, central India, notes that when a worker at the local steel plant requires a transfusion, his workmates, of whatever caste, are quick to come forward to donate for him: "every worker knows that when it comes to life and death it is blood group not caste that counts."[9] In these examples, the social categories—religious or caste-based—of the persons subject to "integration" are known. And yet a key aim of ours is to demonstrate how the anonymity that characterizes voluntary blood donation, which disallows known identities, plays an important role in conceptions of integration. Such conditions, as we shall go on to show, create a kind of blank page that permits donors to engage in imaginative acts in regard to possible future beneficiaries.

[8] Christopher J. Fuller, *The Camphor Flame: Popular Hinduism and Society in India* (Princeton, NJ: Princeton University Press, 2004), 21.

[9] Jonathan Parry, "Two Cheers for Reservation: The Satnamis and the Steel Plant," in *Institutions and Inequalities: Essays in Honor of Andrei Beteille*, ed. Ramachandra Guha and Jonathan Parry (Delhi: Oxford University Press, 1999), 148.

[10] Projit Bihari Mukharji, "From Serosocial to Sanguinary Identities: Caste, Transnational Race Science and the Shifting Metonymies of Blood Group B, India c. 1918–1960," *Indian Economic and Social History Review* 51, no. 2 (2014): 143–76.

Caste and Nation

In this section we address how in an Indian context the anonymity of voluntary blood donation seems to promise caste reform and/or a more integrated nation. To begin with the vexed issue of caste: We have noted that reform of blood donation—from paid and replacement to voluntary and anonymous—may be made congruent with wider social reformist agendas, including to do with caste. Historian Projit Mukharji shows how caste and blood came to be scientifically linked.[10] He demonstrates how in the early twentieth century, multidisciplinary social scientists he calls "sero-anthropologists" sought to link blood to particular castes and regional groups. In doing so, they ran counter to what was the global scientific tendency to study blood for what it could reveal about race. Instead, Mukharji shows, Indian sero-anthropology postulated a "serosociality" in which blood groupings were associated with caste-based socialities of marriage rules and patterns. A later group of sero-anthropologists in the 1940s argued for region (and clustered caste groups) rather than pan-regional castes as co-relative with blood groups. However, according to Mukharji, this scientific interest in "serosocial identities" disappeared in the postindependence era. Mukharji thus traces a particularly interesting, albeit fleeting, hybrid discipline that produced an imagination of blood groups as constituted by and of caste and regional sociality. However, while the scientific "serosociality" that Mukharji describes waned in the mid-century, social practices that emphasize the relation between caste and blood persist. Anthropological accounts continue to document how a caste's "purity" is held to reside specifically in members' blood—with the policing of sexual liaisons that might result in "mixed blood offspring" to safeguard the purity of whole castes and disputes about one caste's status relative to another's continuing to take the form of arguments over whose blood is "purest."[11]

Ever since caste, race and blood began to be used interchangeably in policing social boundaries, anticaste activists have imagined intermixing as a potential antidote. As early as 1936, the foremost Dalit leader of the twentieth century B. R. Ambedkar used ethnological accounts of regional consanguinity to argue that the caste system had come into being after Indians were already commingled in blood, and therefore to confuse caste with race was scientifically incorrect.[12] At the same time, he understood the symbolic power of mixing blood—particularly through intercaste marriage—as a possible answer to caste discrimination: "Fusion of blood can alone create the feeling of being kith and kin, and unless this feeling of kinship, of being kindred, becomes paramount, the separatist feeling—the feeling of being aliens—created by caste will not vanish… Nothing else will serve as the solvent of caste."

Current attempts to promote a reformed voluntary and anonymous practice of blood donation thus appear to advance Ambedkar's idea that the mixing of blood can

[11] Christopher Fuller, *The Camphor Flame: Popular Hinduism and Society in India* (Princeton, NJ: Princeton University Press, 2004), 21; and Susan Bayly, *Caste, Society and Politics in India from the Eighteenth Century to the Modern Age* (New York: Cambridge University Press, 1999), 329.

[12] Bhimrao Ramji Ambedkar, *Annihilation of Caste* (London: Verso, 2014), 499.

serve as a "solvent" of caste boundaries. Take the typical Indian Red Cross slogan: "Your blood will be used to treat patients without any distinction of caste, creed, or status." Indeed, while an insistence that blood must flow "without any distinction" is a feature of voluntary blood donation ideology worldwide, the mutating significance of caste and communal boundaries in the region lends it a particular piquancy here. Much of the social reformist promise arising from the anonymity of voluntary blood donation has taken force precisely in the possibility of the transcendence of caste.

But crucially, *not so fast*. Utopic though such practices may initially appear, they contradict Ambedkar's desire for reform through the powerful transgression of intercaste marriage, which presents entirely a different order of "fusion." Many of the middle-class blood donors we met who demonstrate their progressive credentials by imagining their anonymously donated blood being transfused into the bodies of any others (specifically *beyond* their own castes), meanwhile do not interdine, and have little day-to-day contact with people belonging to communities other than their own. So, rather than a concrete and fraught presence, the stranger who receives anonymously donated blood is considered in absentia, via the abstracted medium of blood. The anonymous donation of blood by those who harbor misgivings about contact with "unclean" caste members allows a performance of anticaste sentiment, without troubling the ubiquity of caste segregation. What could be more anticaste than mixing one's blood with that of one from any conceivable caste community? And yet this is a mixing removed from the donor. Blood donation enables nonpolluting contact with others. The *anonymity* of blood donation, then, is consistently employed as a rhetorical means of transcending caste.

As several scholars of caste have noted, the postindependence emphasis on legal and governmental "caste-blindness" has encouraged and deepened the persistence of inequality.[13] We suggest that insofar as the Indian anonymous blood donation and transfusion field consists of practices that appear to transgress purity and pollution protocols, they form a species of material rhetoric concerning caste-blindness, or the becoming-obsolete of caste. The utopic promise of *using blood to go beyond blood* (where caste is figured as being locatable in the blood) is thus a central motif of anonymity here, with its very transcendental promise pressed into the support of self-serving claims to progressiveness that are not necessarily representative at all of other domains of donors' everyday lives. For all the transcategorial and utopic potential of anonymous blood donation, it is all too quickly liable to collapse back into regressive narratives of caste-based purity. If in one moment the practice's anonymity can appears to facilitate utopic and previously unthinkable "progressive transgressions," we might wish to retain a certain skepticism concerning the interests being served by such claims; and if bodies such as the Red Cross emphasize the progressive transgressions anonymity seems to afford, the purchase of such an ideology can appear shaky and uneven outside the doctrinally pure world of biomedicine and blood donor motivation. One may come across, for instance, news headlines such as "Now Available: Upper Class Blood," and "Caste Based Request for Blood Donation Causes Outrage on Twitter." In a news article about high-caste refusal of treatment by Dalit medics, principally in Tamil Nadu, we meet "N. Prabhu, who operates the Uyirthuli blood donation group… [and who] maintains a register of blood donors for […] emergencies. 'When we get requests for a rare blood group donor, often [the] patient's relatives will ask us to determine the caste of the donor before bringing him or her to the doctor. These cases are often emergency cases, and although we deny such requests to determine the caste, there have been a couple of cases where the donor has been sent away by the patient's family,' he says."

[13] Satish Deshpande and Mary E. John, "The Politics of Not Counting Caste," *Economic and Political Weekly* 45, no. 25 (2010): 39–42; and Surinder S. Jodhka and Ghanshyam Shah, "Comparative Contexts of Discrimination: Caste and Untouchability in South Asia," *Economic and Political Weekly* 45, no. 48 (2010): 99–106.

Of course, it is not only caste that the anonymity of voluntary blood donation can appear to allow donors to transcend but communal religious distinctions, too. A Kolkata blood donor recruitment poster draws out precisely this point: "Haru [a Hindu] donated blood and saved the life of Harun [a Muslim]. Rohim [a Muslim] has donated to Ram [a Hindu]. A little gift sometimes becomes much bigger [*asamanya*—rare, incomparable]." We can thus begin to glimpse how the anonymity of voluntary blood donation is a central factor that contributes to the perception of it as an act promoting "national integration" and "communal harmony," as well as transcendence of caste. After independence in 1947 the promotion of communal harmony and national integration became central concerns of the state, for "given its cultural diversity and religious plurality many were skeptical about the ability of the nascent state … to live beyond a couple of decades as a democratic nation. On more than one occasion, India has reached the brink of both disintegration and authoritarianism."[14] In considering now how the anonymity of blood donation has been key to its enrolment by the state and other actors as a means of promoting national integration, we draw on ideas from Michael Taussig who has argued that where there is facelessness, the face can stand for anyone.[15] Following from this, faceless transfusion recipients can, from the standpoint of donors, stand for any number of possible beneficiaries. Anonymity thus provides a key mode of imaginative engagement that amounts to an "active not knowing" on the part of donors and is in line with Donald Smith's famous definition of the Indian state policy of secularism as ideally involving "active non-preference" toward the different communities over which it governs.[16] Anonymous donors cannot specify the community to which the recipients of their donations will belong. They know their anonymous gift may literally be given to anyone; hence, donors' donations result from their enactment of active non-preference.

[14] K. N. Panikkar, "Introduction: Defining the Nation as Hindu," in *The Concerned Indian's Guide to Communalism*, ed. K. N. Panikkar (Delhi: Viking, 1999), vii.

[15] Michael T. Taussig, *Defacement: Public Secrecy and the Labor of the Negative* (Stanford, CA: Stanford University Press, 1999).

[16] Donald Eugene Smith, *India as a Secular State* (Princeton, NJ: Princeton University Press, 1963).

Consider also how the utopic and boundary-crossing imagery made possible by anonymity can become salient in respect of the unit of donated blood itself. Blood component separation is a technological procedure that separates donated blood into its constituent components so that several people may be treated from one donated unit. The development of this technology in the 1950s revealed that blood, instead of being a single, self-similar substance, is a "holding together" of red cells, platelets, and plasma—all useful in different ways for diverse types of treatment. Plasma can be further subdivided through a procedure called fractionation. Bayer and Feldman state that "As blood plasma is increasingly subject to transformation by pharmaceutical firms, it is difficult to sustain the symbolic attachments evoked by whole blood."[17] Our experience, however, suggests otherwise. When we asked donors what they thought about the separation of their donated blood, a recurring motif was the hope that their singularly donated unit would be transfused into three persons from three different communities. A woman we met at a camp in Delhi, well aware of and enthusiastic about the idea of component therapy, told us: "There is no discrimination, it is non-attachment. I am hopeful my blood will go to three different castes (*jatis*)." A Hindu devotee of the guru Sathya Sai Baba, whom we met at a donation camp organized by devotees, hoped his one donated unit would be split and transfused into a Christian, a Muslim, and a Sikh respectively, to show that all people and religions are one. He then pointed to Sai Baba's Sarvadharma symbol, assembled of emblems from the major world religions. The symbol, at that moment, seemed to merge with the unit of blood he had donated, both providing images of integration. Component therapy is evidently an act of technical decomposition rather than composition, but it reveals that the unit, prior to the separation procedure, is a gathered entity and thus, like the idealized nation, a holding together of the many in the one. In imagining their singularly offered donations as forming the transfusions of several persons belonging to different castes or

[17] Ronald Bayer and Eric A. Feldman, "Introduction: Understanding the Blood Feuds," in *Blood Feuds: AIDS, Blood, and the Politics of Medical Disaster*, ed. Eric A. Feldman and Ronald Bayer (Oxford: Oxford University Press, 1999), 8.

religions, donors see donation as an integrative action—all of India, as it were, in a unit of blood.

Competing Anonymities

So far, we have principally focused on utopic deployments of the anonymous structures of voluntary blood donation (even if those utopic deployments are not themselves straightforward). However, from the perspective of those invested in such progressive transgressions, a darker anonymity also haunts the Indic blood donation and transfusion field. We now elaborate this modality of anonymity to pinpoint a critical feature of the utopic anonymous form that it haunts: it's obvious, yet crucial, human-ness.

The Kolkata-based Association of Voluntary Blood Donors, West Bengal (AVBD) is a vanguard voluntary movement for the promotion of voluntary, anonymous blood donation in West Bengal. A significant part of the AVBD's pedagogical project is to characterize blood as what we might call "a substance of humanism." Take for example this excerpt from the inaugural address of the 2005 Parliament of Motivators conference, organized by the AVBD and held in Kolkata, which brought together amateur and professional blood donor recruiters from across India and the world: "Human blood possesses no caste, creed, religion or pedigree. No national or state boundaries can keep blood isolated in any domain. It is a symbol of unity and service of others."

It is not only for the AVBD but more widely still in the blood donor recruitment world (and beyond) that blood is figured as a substance of humanism, a kind of substance of humanistic connection. To paraphrase Marilyn Strathern, the nice thing about blood is that everyone has it: it is multicultural, with its uncontainable diverse symbolic associations, but also mononatural—everyone has it, as exemplified, for instance, in the way ABO blood groups crosscut caste distinctions otherwise said to be located in the blood: hence the ability of anonymously donated blood to act as a solvent of caste and other communal human distinctions.[18] Indeed, for the AVBD, that everyone has it is precisely the fortuitous thing about blood. It is this that makes the donation of blood an action that goes beyond itself—beyond even the invisible stitches holding society together as in Titmuss's famous account.[19] Anonymously donated blood opens up onto the universal—it is humanity at its highest pitch; and as the inaugural address makes clear, in the Indian context, it may well be figured as that which exceeds "caste, creed, religion [and] pedigree."

As will be clear, then, the AVBD harbors an ideology of blood donation that feeds it into a political aesthetic of integration; blood donation as a tool of progressive transgression and social reform. It is little wonder then that some of its members greet the prospect of artificial blood with extreme negativity. Scholars, too, have observed the ways in which the development of bloodless surgery and use of blood substitutes such as Hemopure and Biopure bring into question the model of anonymous, altruistic blood donation as advocated by the WHO.[20] For anthropologist Kath Weston, as well, "the quest for synthetic blood participates in a broader capitalization of nature that promises to domesticate kinship," where we understand "kinship" to stand for various symbolic and substantial ties not limited to the strictly familial.[21] Synthetic blood, then, promises a different kind of anonymity: one that moves beyond the human. Anonymously donated blood "deletes" human types but, critically, for the AVBD and allied progressive social reformers, it does not delete the human; on the contrary, it maximizes and universalizes the utopian humanistic potential of blood. Synthetic blood is no doubt anonymous (troublingly alienated in Weston's analysis), but at the same time, and necessarily, humanistically eviscerated. AVBD members understand that research work in this area is progressing, that currently employed

[18] Marilyn Strathern, "The Nice Thing about Culture Is That Everyone Has It," in *Shifting Contexts*, ed. Marilyn Strathern (London: Routledge, 1995), 165–88.

[19] Titmuss, *Gift Relationship*.

[20] Jean-Paul Lallemand-Stempak, "What Flows between Us: Blood Donation and Transfusion in the United States (Nineteenth to Twentieth Centuries)," in *Giving Blood: The Institutional Making of Altruism*, ed. Johanne Charbonneau and André Smith (London: Routledge, 2016), 33.

[21] Kath Weston, "Biosecuritization: The Quest for Synthetic Blood and the Taming of Kinship," in *Blood and Kinship: Matter for Metaphor from Ancient Rome to the Present*, ed. Christopher H. Johnson, Bernhard Jussen, David Warren Sabean, and Simon Teuscher (Oxford: Berghahn, 2013), 247.

blood substitutes have their place, and that development of universally transfusable lab-created nonhuman blood forms might well reduce human suffering. But this is also an organization for which, as we have seen, human blood is exalted as possessing "no caste, creed, religion or pedigree" and as being "a symbol of unity and service of others."

Here lies an important conflict between the AVBD as a recruitment organization and blood bank medics. While the two constituencies are close allies in the project of promoting blood science education and voluntary blood donation more generally, for doctors, unlike AVBD members, there exists an intense "professional longing" for the expedited development of viable artificial blood.[22] Such longing is informed not only by a possible solution to safety concerns, but also by the difficulties in combating the perceived general reluctance of Indian people to donate their blood voluntarily. Thus, if for the AVBD anonymous blood donation promises national and even international integration—beyond the more practical consequence of medical therapeutics—for medics the latter is both a more urgent, and more sufficient concern. We thus see two competing modes of promise—the promise of a hematological humanism of anonymous substantial flows versus a promise that is equally if not more anonymous, but which subtracts the human. Artificial blood thus contains the potential to disrupt the AVBD's commitment to blood donation as a consummately human practice with powers of social reform and progressive transgression.

At the above-mentioned conference in Kolkata there was a session on developments in synthetic biology (i.e. blood substitutes) in which doctors from blood substitute research teams gave updates on their research. An AVBD member in the audience bemoaned the effect that even the fantasy of viable artificial blood had begun to have on blood donor motivation: "College students say to us, "Artificial blood is now available, why should

[22] Lesley A. Sharp, *Strange Harvest: Organ Transplants, Denatured Bodies, and the Transformed Self* (Berkeley: University of California Press, 2006), 211.

I donate?" Another AVBD member stood up: "The cost of these substitutes will be so high that in our country they will not be feasible. Even if a substitute is found, blood doesn't cost anything from our bodies." Recalling Weston's argument about blood substitutes constituting yet another front in the capitalization of nature, the audience member's remarks are also suggestive of broader unease concerning how use of blood substitutes is likely to heighten even further our reliance on pharmaceutical companies.[23] Still another member of the audience rose to his feet: "There should be no artificial blood!" he shouted. Loud clapping followed. Such statements do not represent the official AVBD view, but they do tell us something about the hematological humanism of its members. The nonhuman anonymity of artificial blood, indeed, would be the end of the hematological humanism which rests on the utopic anonymity that obscures human typologies all the better to exalt the transcendent human.

[23] Lallemand-Stempak, "What Flows between Us," 33.

Conclusion

This chapter has presented examples of blood donations that hold a fantasy of transgressing community boundaries in the service of caste reform or national integration which demonstrate the power of anonymity in creating a space for prospective imaginings on the part of donors of their gifts' possible recipients. The anonymity of blood donation, as the condition of possibility of donors' prospective traversal of the nation's many distinct communities, forms the basis of a blood-based rhetoric of "national integration"—the enactment of threadlike imaginative extensions across diverse plurality as the folding of different constituencies into a "single" national field—and of moving beyond caste. If we have seen how the latter, especially, is problematic and unconvincing, both conceptions nevertheless remain rhetorically powerful and persuasive for many blood banking professionals and donors alike. If from the point of view of the donor the prospective transfusion recipient remains faceless, a space is opened up for imaginative engagement and fantasies of progressive transgression that accord well with varied projects of social reform. Indeed, the reform of blood donation closely allies with other reform projects besides. In this way donors come to enact a kind of "active non-preference" concerning the communities to which the recipients of their donations will belong, with the anonymity of such transactions both a figure and facilitator of transcendence.

In the final part of the chapter, however, we turned to a different form of anonymity, examining perceptions among promoters of voluntary blood donation of the imminent prospect of artificial blood. If theorists such as Konrad have sought to move beyond depictions of anonymity that equate it with alienation, passivity, ahistoricity, and asociality, here such connotations come back into the picture nonetheless, with this version of anonymity (blood minus the human) deeply at odds with (and threatening toward) the AVBD's hematological humanism, which draws its power and logic from another kind of anonymity: competing anonymities. From the point of view of medics, however, this is exactly the point: the hi-tech anonymity of artificial blood precisely promises to transcend the human (at least as a necessary source of blood for transfusion), with the aim of establishing a more stable and potentially safer supply. Such a return to the equation of anonymity with alienability and human passivity serves as a useful analytical reminder that even as we expand our analyses of anonymity beyond previous accounts and explore its creative, reformist potentials, it remains an ambivalent, graded site of contraries. If for the AVBD and others human blood flowing toward anonymous others provides a prefigurative politics of substantial flows beyond narrow distinctions and prejudice, such conceptions are fragile. Adequate accounts of anonymity must engage with and not occlude such fragility, ambivalences, and contradictions.

Bibliography

Ambedkar, Bhimrao Ramji. *Annihilation of Caste*. London: Verso, 2014.

Bayer, Ronald, and Eric A. Feldman. "Introduction: Understanding the Blood Feuds." In *Blood Feuds: AIDS, Blood, and the Politics of Medical Disaster*, edited by Eric A. Feldman and Ronald Bayer, 1–16. Oxford: Oxford University Press, 1999.

Bayly, Susan. *Caste, Society and Politics in India from the Eighteenth Century to the Modern Age*. New York: Cambridge University Press, 1999.

Bray, T. J., and K. Prabhakar. "Blood Policy and Transfusion Practice – India." *Tropical Medicine & International Health* 7, no. 6 (2002): 477–78.

Copeman, Jacob. "The Gift and Its Forms of Life in Contemporary India." *Modern Asian Studies* 45, no. 5 (2011): 1051–94.

Copeman, Jacob, and Dwaipayan Banerjee. *Hematologies: The Political Life of Blood in India*. Ithaca, NY: Cornell University Press, 2019.

Deshpande, Satish, and Mary E. John. "The Politics of Not Counting Caste." *Economic and Political Weekly* 45, no. 25 (2010): 39–42.

Fuller, Christopher J. *The Camphor Flame: Popular Hinduism and Society in India*. Princeton, NJ: Princeton University Press, 2004.

Graeber, David. "Anthropology and the Rise of the Professional-Managerial Class." *HAU* 4, no. 3 (2014): 73–88.

Jodhka, Surinder S., and Ghanshyam Shah. "Comparative Contexts of Discrimination: Caste and Untouchability in South Asia." *Economic and Political Weekly* 45, no. 48 (2010): 99–106.

Konrad, Monica. "Ova Donation and Symbols of Substance: Some Variations on the Theme of Sex, Gender and the Partible Body." *Journal of the Royal Anthropological Institute* 4, no. 4 (1998): 643–67.

Konrad, Monica. *Nameless Relations: Anonymity, Melanesia and Reproductive Gift Exchange between British Ova Donors and Recipients*. New York: Berghahn, 2005.

Lallemand-Stempak, Jean-Paul. "What Flows between Us: Blood Donation and Transfusion in the United States (Nineteenth to Twentieth Centuries)." In *Giving Blood: The Institutional Making of Altruism*, edited by Johanne Charbonneau and André Smith, 21–32. London: Routledge, 2016.

Mukharji, Projit Bihari. "From Serosocial to Sanguinary Identities: Caste, Transnational Race Science and the Shifting Metonymies of Blood

Group B, India c. 1918–1960." *Indian Economic and Social History Review* 51, no. 2 (2014): 143–76.

Panikkar, K. N. "Introduction: Defining the Nation as Hindu." In *The Concerned Indian's Guide to Communalism*, edited by K. N. Panikkar, vii–xxxv. Delhi: Viking, 1999.

Parry, Jonathan. "Two Cheers for Reservation: The Satnamis and the Steel Plant." In *Institutions and Inequalities: Essays in Honor of Andrei Beteille*, edited by Ramachandra Guha and Jonathan Parry, 128–69. Delhi: Oxford University Press, 1999.

Sharp, Lesley A. *Strange Harvest: Organ Transplants, Denatured Bodies, and the Transformed Self*. Berkeley: University of California Press, 2006.

Simpson, Bob. "Blood Rhetorics: Donor Campaigns and Their Publics in Contemporary Sri Lanka." *Ethnos* 76, no. 2 (2011): 254–75.

Smith, Donald Eugene. *India as a Secular State*. Princeton, NJ: Princeton University Press, 1963.

Strathern, Marilyn. "The Nice Thing about Culture Is That Everyone Has It." In *Shifting Contexts*, edited by Marilyn Strathern, 165–88. London: Routledge, 1995.

Taussig, Michael T. *Defacement: Public Secrecy and the Labor of the Negative*. Stanford, CA: Stanford University Press, 1999.

Titmuss, Richard Morris. *The Gift Relationship: From Human Blood to Social Policy*. London: Allen and Unwin, 1970.

Vanaik, Achin. *The Furies of Indian Communalism: Religion, Modernity, and Secularization*. London: Verso, 1997.

Weston, Kath. "Biosecuritization: The Quest for Synthetic Blood and the Taming of Kinship." In *Blood and Kinship: Matter for Metaphor from Ancient Rome to the Present*, edited by Christopher H. Johnson, Bernhard Jussen, David Warren Sabean, and Simon Teuscher, 244–65. Oxford: Berghahn, 2013.

Anonymity: The Politicisation of a Concept

Introduction

In May 2015 David Kaye, UN special rapporteur on the promotion and protection of the right to freedom of opinion and expression, submitted his first report to the Human Rights Council.[1] It focused on issues of encryption and anonymity, highlighting the important role these play regarding privacy and the right to free expression. The mere fact that such a report has been produced, and the debate it has engendered, indicates that anonymity has become a high-profile issue. Anonymity is, of course, nothing new in human history and has long been recognized as posing problems and providing solutions in several domains (investigative journalism and the handling of medical data are two such areas). But the intensity

[1] David Kaye, "Report on Encryption, Anonymity, and the Human Rights Framework" (Geneva: United Nations Human Rights Council, 2015).

of the current debate has shown just how hard it is to pinpoint anonymity—either as a normative concept or as an everyday practice. Only in the wake of the digital turn has the topic become politicized, in other words, transformed from a largely unmanaged determinant of social communication into a political issue. Until the late 1990s, there was a near-total absence of academic literature examining anonymity from a political point of view. Since the turn of the millennium and the heightened awareness of the digital condition we live in, this situation has changed radically. Discourse on the topic has become a scholarly and political battleground, and anonymity is widely understood as a cornerstone of the (normative) order governing our digital lives.

This chapter traces the changing conditions of anonymity in liberal Western societies. Political, technical, economic, and social developments have undermined the broad de facto anonymity of modern societies, and I ask whether the current politicization of anonymity is likely to have any impact on the steady disappearance of opportunities for anonymous communication. I argue that anonymity is an ambivalent but critical feature of the democratic public sphere. If we want to slow down or halt this trend, or actually reverse it, it will not be enough simply to politicize "deanonymizing" tendencies and whip up indignation.

My argument proceeds in three stages. I begin with several conceptual observations on anonymity. From these, a heuristic framework emerges with which the changes in anonymous communication, and in the role this form of communication plays in society, can be described. In very broad brushstrokes, I then describe and analyze the extent to which options for anonymity have been affected by the revolution in information and communication technologies (ICTs). I conclude by considering how anonymity is framed in public discourse and what effects this has. My aim in this last section is to provide a sketch of the main lines in the debates and show that none of the different layers of the anonymity discourse have generated any cogent ideas as to how the all-encompassing trend to deanonymization outlined in the second part of the chapter might be tackled. If we are to succeed in countering this trend, we will have to adopt a more political and institutional mode of thinking.

[2] Helen Nissenbaum, "The Meaning of Anonymity in an Information Age," *The Information Society* 15, no. 2 (1999): 141–44; Gary T. Marx, "What's in a Name? Some Reflections on the Sociology of Anonymity," *Information Society* 15, no. 2 (1999): 99–112; and Julie Ponesse, "The Ties That Blind: Conceptualizing Anonymity," *Journal of Social Philosophy* 45, no. 3 (2014): 304–22.

Anonymity: Conceptual Observations

The word "anonymity" literally means a condition of namelessness. But given that a name is only one—actually quite unreliable—identifier of a person, focusing on its absence does not exhaust the meaning of the concept of anonymity. A better way to understand the concept is to set it in a broader context of social communication. Viewed thus, anonymity describes a situation of intersubjective action in which it is not possible either to conclusively attribute a particular action or communication to an individual or subject or to render an individual or subject accessible and therefore accountable.[2] Greater precision can be introduced into this broad definition if we take into account four closely interrelated facts.

First, anonymity always relates to the question "Who?" It thus points to the combination of action/communication and actor. The "what"—in other words the object or content of the action/communication—can be known, provided it does not reveal the identity.

Second, anonymity is situational. It is not a characteristic of a person; it is the product of an intersubjective constellation and of the possibility/impossibility of identifying an actor in that constellation beyond the immediate context. This being the case, it is also an impermanent condition, always tied to specific delimitable actions, which themselves are visible as actions and produce effects. Anonymity is therefore distinct from invisibility.

Third, although anonymity can be produced intentionally (through disguise, for example, or the use of a pseudonym), it can also arise from a situation (as when one finds oneself in a crowd). Anonymity is generated by indistinguishability and therefore only succeeds where there are multiple possible authors of an action. This being so, anonymity always depends, at least indirectly, on others' either ignoring or accepting it and exercising restraint—by not insisting on identification, for example, or by not attempting to single out those performing an action. No individual can be sure that their action will in fact play out anonymously—especially since the possibility of identification persists after, or indeed arises from, the action. Anonymity therefore can never be established for good. Strengthening it would mean taking measures that render identification more difficult—by, for example, removing information from a situation.

The upshot of this, fourth, is that anonymity is best understood and analyzed in terms of its opposite—identification. Hence, anyone wishing to ascertain whether and to what degree anonymity exists in a particular situation must establish to what extent and by whom identification is possible.

With these observations in mind, we can set about constructing a heuristic framework that will help us trace the social and technological developments concerning the state of anonymity in liberal societies. To do this, we must first draw two distinctions.

The first differentiates horizontal from vertical anonymity. "Horizontal anonymity" refers to anonymity among peers and one's immediate surroundings. Such anonymity is obtained where one is not, or cannot be, identified by those observing a particular act or conversation. This is the situation, for example, in a café or bar, where we tend not to know the people around us and have no way of finding out who they are short of asking them to identify themselves. "Vertical anonymity," by contrast, refers to anonymity vis-à-vis well-resourced institutions. Most notable among these are states, which have a broad range of means available to identify people in situ and retrospectively. Such actors do not have to be present in the situation in order to make an identification.

This chronological aspect points to the second distinction, which relates to the fact that anonymity is not contained within the presence. On the contrary, it almost necessarily extends to the future. Being unidentified in a particular situation is different from being (or at least feeling) protected against later identification. We would not, for example, describe communication as anonymous if we were aware that it was possible, or even likely, that we would later be identified. Our second distinction is therefore between identification (which puts an end to anonymity within a situation) and identifiability (which implies that anonymity cannot be maintained beyond that situation). Whereas identification mostly has to be done overtly (a person presenting ID to board a plane is aware that they are not maintaining their anonymity), identifiability can be achieved without the knowledge or consent of those whose anonymity is being breached. Being aware of the possibility of later identification often prevents us from acting as if we were anonymous. It is possible to secure anonymity actively by introducing (effective, nonreversible) anonymizing procedures that restrict identifiability.

These two distinctions in themselves provide us with enough of a conceptual apparatus to trace the development of anonymity over the last three decades, in which we have experienced the advent of the public internet and the rise of mobile computing, triggering a deep meditization of our now digital lives. Before we do this, however, we need to make a short detour through normative territory.[3] Anonymity is, after all, most often discussed in relation to whether we have cause to fear its spread or demise. If, as previously proposed, anonymity is highly dependent on intersubjective constellations and

[3] For a more thorough discussion, compare Thorsten Thiel, "Anonymität und Demokratie," *Forschungsjournal Soziale Bewegungen* 30, no. 2 (2017): 152–61.

situational specifics, mounting a hardline defense of it (for example, according it the status of a human right) or, alternatively, banning it altogether would seem to be equally unpromising approaches. Normative evaluations of anonymity generally take the form of discussions about the presumed effects of anonymous communication. Although the language in these debates is normatively charged and seemingly general, these setups are better thought of as clashes between differing empirical expectations. The optimistic camp holds that facilitating anonymous or at least pseudonymous communication will engender authenticity since power relations can then be ignored, and the individual will be able to speak freely and openly.[4] The pessimists, by contrast, believe that giving up the possibility of holding someone to account will foster irresponsible and antisocial behavior.[5] These two sets of expectations are then tied into broader normative debates, such as those on privacy (where anonymity can be seen either as crucial to the creation of an inviolable personal sphere or as likely to foster negative behavior such as hate speech) and those on democracy (where anonymity may figure either as a necessary bulwark against the state or as a mechanism that can both facilitate collective action and undermine public discourse). The fact that both sides have a wealth of anecdotal evidence to draw on suggests that rather than treating anonymity as being of value in and of itself, we should look at it in specific contexts.[6] Indeed, to regard anonymity as being of inherent worth would seem, quite manifestly, to be a category error.

This being the case, rather than taking the abstract route and discussing potential effects of anonymous communication, I follow the heuristic framework established above and trace developments in the possibilities for such communication in society. By establishing what has changed, we get a different view of what these developments entail, and how we might respond.

[4] For example, Tony Doyle and Judy Veranas, "Public Anonymity and the Connected World," *Ethics and Information Technology* 16, no. 3 (2014): 207–18; Alfred Moore, "Anonymity, Pseudonymity, and Deliberation: Why Not Everything Should Be Connected," *Journal of Political Philosophy* 26, no. 2 (2018): 169–92; and Dongwon Lim, Hangjung Zo, and Dukhee Lee, "The Value of Anonymity on the Internet," in *Service-Oriented Perspectives in Design Science Research: 6th International Conference, DESRIST 2011, Milwaukee, WI, USA, May 5–6, 2011, Proceedings*, ed. Hemant Jain, Atish P. Sinha, and Padmal Vitharana (Berlin and Heidelberg: Springer-Verlag, 2011), 452–64.

[5] Ingrid Brodnig, *Der unsichtbare Mensch* (Vienna: Czernin, 2013).

[6] James Gardner, "Anonymity and Democratic Citizenship," *William & Mary Bill of Rights Journal* 19, no. 4 (2011): 927.

A Brief Overview of the Development of Anonymous Communication in the Digital Constellation

Guided by the conceptual framework laid down in the first section, we can now analyze the fortunes of anonymity in the digital constellation. To do this, we first need to ascertain the nature of anonymity—or more precisely, of the options for anonymous communication—prior to these events. Before we can focus on the specific scope and structure of anonymity in Western liberal societies in most of the second half of the twentieth century, we have to turn our attention to the abstract matter of historical representation.

Founding sociological text like those of Weber, Durkheim, and Simmel have often depicted modernity as an age of anonymity. In these accounts, the accelerated pace of life and the spread of impersonal modes of production and communication brought about by the Industrial Revolution has been precipitating the demise of community life. Bureaucracy, pluralism, and urban living are characterized as anonymous and contrasted with trust-based communication in small-scale communities. Overall, anonymity is described as ambivalent and often demanding for the individual but at the same time seen as inevitable, a necessary byproduct of the ongoing growth and differentiation of societies. Anonymity is conceptualized as a condition of modern life, less as something individual and situational that deserves protection.

Against this sociological background, what is the situation of anonymous communication in societies for most of the twentieth century? Two facts stand out from the above account: first, anonymity is a feature of society that points to broad development rather than intentional design; and second, anonymity is focused on the horizontal dimension, on societal experiences and peer-to-peer relations. Staying anonymous in a public setting is easily achieved, given that peers are not obliged to identify themselves, and it is not difficult to withhold information. Attempting to establish someone's identity is not only costly; in most situations, it also violates social and legal norms. Regarding vertical anonymity, there are specific areas—such as travel and taxation—in which identification has long been mandatory and is strictly enforced. Outside of these contexts, even the (liberal) state most often opts for modes of governance that are not based on establishing individual identities: besides being costly, it is a task that is feasible only for a limited number of individuals and that has to be performed more or less openly. Corporate actors play a minor role and are only able or inclined to enforce identification in very special circumstances.

A visual summary of the observations made so far is given in Table 1 This points to the centrality of de facto anonymity in societies before the last decade of the twentieth century. Private, public, and political spaces are mostly constituted in ways conducive to the spread of anonymity —provided this preservation does not entail the breaking of certain written and unwritten rules, and attempts to reach out to a wider public often brings with it a requirement for identification. At the same time, only a handful of actors are capable of breaching anonymity and curtailing the privacy it can afford to individuals moving in public spaces. Any actors (states, for example) who do seek to "unmask" an individual are often constrained by laws and social norms or deterred by the high cost and visibility of identification procedures. Even though anonymity, and the possibility of anonymous communication, is deeply inscribed in Western liberal societies of the twentieth century, the notion itself is viewed as negative and dangerous. As a result, social and legal norms aim chiefly to delimit anonymous spaces and tend to frame anonymity as a problem that must be tolerated for pragmatic reasons.

Anonymous communication before 1995

	Identification	Identifiability
Horizontal communication	- Regulated by social norms	- Weak
	- Identifiable communication in the wider public context enforced by strong gatekeepers	- Basically restricted to the immediate environment
Vertical communication	- Highly context specific	- Low to medium
	- Enforcement mainly by the state	- Very costly and resource intensive
	- Explicit and visible	- Mostly limited to states

Tab. 1

How, then, has the rise of ICTs influenced the discourse in this area, and what effect has it had on opportunities for anonymous communication? As early as 1993, in one of the best-known cartoons of the nascent internet age, Peter Steiner pictured two dogs in front of a computer, one of whom was saying to the other, "On the Internet, nobody knows you're a dog." This image sums up what the internet and ICTs were thought to be doing to social communication—namely, accelerating depersonalization.

From a technical point of view, the cartoon very much captures the idea of end-to-end communication and the fact that digital communications always have to be translated into bits and bytes and then transferred via a decentralized network using numbers and protocols. Therefore, every instance of such communication is in some sense pseudonymous. This circumstance brings with it a host of possibilities for covering one's tracks. As a result of these factors, early perceptions of digital communication assumed a wide gap between "the real world" and "cyberspace." In the latter, different norms seem to apply; social conventions and obligations appear less binding and less susceptible to legal enforcement. Today's debates about trolling and hate speech are still often understood in these terms and unsurprisingly often linked to the anonymous nature of the web.

The view that the digital constellation has facilitated and normalized anonymous communication with a broad public is widespread and has been reinforced by changes in the shape of collective action. This trend is perhaps most strikingly exemplified in the Anonymous protest movement and its emblem of a Guy Fawkes mask.[7] Even so, I argue that the assumption that digitalization fosters anonymity is misguided and does not take sufficient account of the further shifts that have occurred in technical infrastructure and political and social context.

Three Deanonymizing Trends of Critical Significance

The first deanonymizing trend is *technological*. The current ubiquity, locational capability, and 24/7 operation of technological devices seriously expand the potential for identification. Mobile computing precludes the levels of anonymous communication that were possible with stationary setups. Similarly, the increased potential for storing and analyzing data has hamstrung anonymization strategies to the point where attempts to resolve the tensions between big data and privacy through measures based on anonymity and consent are breaking down completely.[8]

The second trend is *economic* and involves a massive shift in the incentives for deanonymization. In a digitalized economy, identity drives profits—a situation aptly summed up in descriptions of data as the new gold or oil.[9] Alongside a growth in data mining, there has been a rise in the kinds of information monopolies that thrive on economies of scale and hence are hard to forgo.[10] In addition, new modes of digital communication—apps, streaming, SaaS (software as a service), and so on— reinforce the "identification and registration" logic and erode the notion of digital data as impersonal and

[7] Hans Asenbaum, "Cyborg Activism: Exploring the Reconfigurations of Democratic Subjectivity in Anonymous," *New Media & Society* 20, no. 4 (2018): 1543–63.

[8] Solon Barocas and Helen Nissenbaum, "Big Data's End Run around Anonymity and Consent," in *Privacy, Big Data, and the Public Good: Frameworks for Engagement*, ed. Helen Nissenbaum, Julia Lane, Stefan Bender, and Victoria Stodden (Cambridge: Cambridge University Press, 2014), 44–75; and Paul Ohm, "Broken Promises of Privacy: Responding to the Surprising Failure of Anonymization," *UCLA Law Review* 57 (2010): 1701–77.

[9] Constanze Kurz and Frank Rieger, *Die Datenfresser: Wie Internetfirmen und Staat sich unsere persönlichen Daten einverleiben und wie wir die Kontrolle darüber zurückerlangen*, 2nd ed. (Frankfurt: S. Fischer Verlag, 2011).

[10] Jodi Dean, "Communicative Capitalism: Circulation and the Foreclosure of Politics," *Cultural Politics* 1, no. 1 (2005): 51–74; and Sebastian Sevignani, "The Commodification of Privacy on the Internet," *Science and Public Policy* 40, no. 6 (2013): 733–39.

endlessly reproducible. All these developments shift electronic communication out of individual control and make it dependent on intermediaries who make vast profits from analyzing behavior and personalizing their offers accordingly.

The third deanonymizing trend results from changes in *social practice*, notably the rise of social networking, with its in-built spur to self-portrayal and its (often forced) reduction to a single fixed identity across the Net.[11] Mirroring these developments are various political attempts to make the web more "secure"—by, for example, requiring verification of identity in all sorts of digital settings. (A significant example here is the introduction by many countries of mandatory ID verification in internet cafes—one of several trends linking real and online identities.[12])

Together with other developments currently taking place, these trends are resulting in anonymous communication becoming much harder to achieve. Using my heuristic framework, we can determine where the relevant changes have occurred. In the horizontal dimension, the changes to anonymity have been less far reaching and, in terms of the present account, of less relevance than those in the vertical dimension. Although the possibilities for anonymous interaction appear, at first glance, to have multiplied (thanks to chat rooms, Twitter, and so on), and although the importance of gatekeepers in facilitating access to the broader public sphere has diminished, people's presence in social networks, and the data trails they leave behind, have in fact brought an increase in identifiability. Identification remains context dependent, and we see a simultaneous proliferation of contexts where all participants to a conversation are identified (as on Facebook) and contexts that permit peer-to-peer anonymity. It is the discourse surrounding horizontal anonymity that has largely shaped our public conception of the internet as a place where anonymity is still possible but may also pose a problem.

[11] Marc Andrejevic, "Facebook als neue Produktionsweise," in *Generation Facebook: Über das Leben im Social Net* (Bielefeld: Transcript-Verl, 2011); and Geert Lovink, "Facebook, Anonymität und die Krise des multiplen Selbst," in *Das halbwegs Soziale*, ed. Geert Lovink (Bielefeld: Transcript-Verl, 2011).

[12] See Kenneth Farrall, "Online Collectivism, Individualism and Anonymity in East Asia," *Surveillance and Society* 9, no. 4 (2012): 424–40.

Of much greater significance are the changes relating to vertical anonymity. Here the shifts have been not only more substantial but also distinctly one sided. The requirement for identification has become much more widespread and is now often mandatory for those seeking access to digital communication platforms. The result has been a proliferation in the number of private actors who are able—and motivated—to enforce identification. States too have extended their reach—not least by developing means of gaining access to, and combining, private data collections. Because the so-called digital public sphere is almost entirely privately owned and because the platform companies that grant access to it have enormous leverage when it comes to collecting all kinds of personal data, identifiability has burgeoned. Table 2 sums up these changes and allows comparison with conditions prior to the 1990s.

13 A. Michael Froomkin, "From Anonymity to Identification," *Journal of Self-Regulation and Regulation* 1 (2015): 121–38.

Anonymous communication in the digital constellation

	Identification	Identifiability
Horizontal communication	– Steady or decreasing – Weakening of social pressures	– Medium
Vertical communication	– Many contexts require identification or set it as a default – More actors are able to enforce identification	– Medium to high – Low costs – Easy to hide

Tab. 2

To sum up: over recent decades, the modalities of anonymous communication have undergone major change. Although this complex process has been driven by many different factors and trends, the shift away from de facto anonymity toward a "goldfish bowl" society has been unmistakable.[13] One particularly salient feature has been the growth in the identificatory powers wielded by well-resourced actors (whether states or private players). Given the added incentive that the falling costs of data storage and processing have created for generating personalized data, there seems little likelihood of this trend being reversed—particularly at a time when the distinction between the online and offline world is increasingly blurred. Digitalization is all pervading, even if we do have some power to shape it, and anonymity can no longer be achieved by switching off our computers or other devices.

The Politicization of Anonymity

Having outlined the general trends affecting anonymity, I now focus on how these developments have been taken up in the public discourse of Western liberal societies over the last twenty years. The concepts and convictions surrounding privacy have undergone enormous change, as the present volume demonstrates. Consequently, if we are to understand governance in this area, we need to analyze the various shifts and struggles in public discourse. Efforts at governance and regulation cannot be understood solely by looking at (external) challenges, such as changes in technological capacity. They need to be analyzed against the backdrop of changing expectations and demands. Therefore, the rest of this chapter gauges how successful attempts to politicize anonymity have been and whether there is any likelihood of current trends (particularly the diminution of vertical anonymity) being halted or reversed.

Before I embark on this task, a few remarks on terminology. As I use it here, "politicization" does not have the restricted meaning of getting an issue onto the agendas of political decision makers. Nor is it used in the sense of the extreme polarization of an issue. (Both of these are very common understandings of the concept.) Instead, I use the term in the "republican" sense of a topic of public discourse that gives rise to various alternative positions and is amenable to, and stands in need of, political resolution. Interpreted thus, politicization is not limited to professional politics but equally relates to the type, quality, and variety of arguments in the public sphere. From a normative point of view, politicization is here conceptualized as inherently positive, since reflexivity is encouraged (rather than discouraged), social conflicts are articulated, and inclusion is made possible. Empirically, too, this interpretation of politicization may have its advantages, given that acceptance becomes likelier and solutions can be verified by argumentation before they are implemented. That said, politicization does not mean that policies necessarily change, only that they become the object of contestation.

In what follows, I pick out four areas—technical, economic, legal, and sociopolitical—in which the issue of anonymity has become politicized, if in very different ways. I sketch what arguments and positions have taken shape and whether success in politicization has had any impact on the metatrend of diminishing anonymous communication. Interest in issues of anonymous communication has grown in all four areas, but the growth in each case has taken very different turns. My purpose here is not to carry out a comprehensive discourse analysis and map the entire argumentative field. What I am aiming for, rather, is an anecdotal overview that may serve as a starting point for a more thorough empirical investigation.

The Technical Domain

The technical domain is the one in which anonymity has been politicized for the longest time. Anonymity has been a concern from the early days of the internet, and sensitivity to changes in the normative fabric and the institutional and technical infrastructure of the Net is widespread among members of the active civil society of hackers, privacy advocates, and the like. The technical basis of the internet—protocols, routing logic, and so on, as well as advancing techniques of encryption—still leaves considerable room for anonymization, although the commodification of the Web and the framing of digital communication as a critical infrastructure (cyber security) has tightened control.[14] Still, every attempt to enforce personalized, verified identification necessitates the creation and acceptance of additional layers of communication. Cookies are one example of this—and also illustrate the characteristic "cat and mouse" game in which identification mechanisms are created and then repeatedly circumvented and refined. To secure acceptance of these kinds of identification mechanisms, the organizations concerned have mostly avoided directly raising the issue of anonymity, instead focusing on the benefits of identification (ease of use, elimination of the need to log in, etc.). Nowadays, many services are available only to registered users, and the processes used for verification are much more advanced. Mobile technology and the app economy have been game changers in this respect: logins here are often permanent, and much more metadata—notably regarding location—is collected by default. This reshaping of online communications has been met with vocal opposition. It has also triggered the development of alternatives that subvert or supplement the offers described above. Probably the most significant endeavor in this regard is TOR (The Onion Router), an anonymization network that one of the NSA slides leaked by Edward Snowden described as "the king of high-secure, low-latency Internet anonymity."

[14] Laura DeNardis, "Hidden Levers of Internet Control," *Information, Communication & Society* 15, no. 5 (2012); and Yochai Benkler, "Degrees of Freedom, Dimensions of Power," *Daedalus* 145, no. 1 (2016): 18–32.

Within public discourse, technical solutions that offer anonymity are mostly framed as a form of justified civilian self-defense. Anonymity itself is depicted as a weapon with which to resist state-based and commercial data collection to preserve the capacity to organize collective action and hold monopolies of force in check. It is thus represented as inherently democratic in both a participatory and a civil liberties sense. This framing has been met with attempts to criminalize traffic using anonymous networks or the equation of anonymizing mechanisms with fraud. As Helen Nissenbaum pointed out in regard to the hacker community, the contested ontology of cyberspace brings with it massive shifts in the normative evaluation of communication practices, even when these practices themselves change little.[15]

To sum up: in the technical domain, delegitimization discourses are on the rise, but significant factions in the tech community, especially in countries like Germany, have mostly remained on the side of anonymous communication. Several technical innovations for preserving anonymity have proliferated, although application rates in the wider public stay low. Because these tools are mostly geared to individual self-defense, often reduce ease of use, and entail regular checks and updates, their operation is restricted to a rather small group of technically literate users. Nevertheless, these tools and mechanisms are crucial, and internet-focused civil society has in Europe and the United States mostly succeeded in developing a political voice that commands a degree of attention.[16] All in all, though, the impact of these endeavors is tempered by developments in other sectors.

The Economic Domain

In the economic domain, anonymity is a latecomer and still "under construction." On the face of it, this is surprising, given the importance of anonymity in classical liberal theory. Here, markets are assumed to operate anonymously, and identification is regarded as unnecessary (or indeed likely to disrupt proper functioning), since goods can be exchanged by means of a mediation technique (money) that makes it irrelevant who is doing the buying and selling. In addition, modern economies are still viewed as being centered on markets, and they acquire much of their legitimacy by linking market exchange to the idea of freedom. The success of that

[15] Helen Nissenbaum, "Hackers and the Contested Ontology of Cyberspace," *New Media and Society* 6, no. 2 (2004): 195–217.

[16] Thorsten Thiel, "Turnkey Tyranny? Struggles for a New Digital Order," in *Resistance and Change in World Politics*, ed. Svenja Gertheiss, Stefanie Herr, Klaus Dieter Wolf, and Carmen Wunderlich (Basingstoke: Palgrave Macmillan, 2017), 215–42.

linkage depends, in its turn, on nondiscriminatory, anonymous markets.

Digitalization has clearly not resulted in the abandonment of the idea of markets. Instead it has reinforced a number of trends in capitalist economics that were already at work in postindustrialist societies generally; for example, the increased personalization of products, the localization of offers, and the shift from manufacturing to services. In this context, anonymity emerges as an obstacle to be overcome. The approach in the economic domain, therefore, has often been not to discredit anonymity but to highlight the virtues of identity and identification. Services have become increasingly personalized, social networking being the prime example.

The gradual disappearance of options for anonymous communication brought about by the changing behavior of commercial players has concerned privacy advocates and more recently also lawmakers. Although these diverse actors have vigorously condemned the kind of all-encompassing data collection pursued by business, they have mostly done so without referring to anonymity. Discussion here has generally taken place under the rubrics of data protection, responsible data use, and data minimization. Privacy, not anonymity, is the rallying cry. So, while there is, and always has been, a powerful anticonsumerist critique of the commercial internet, the argument is about collective goods and control of information and not about options for anonymous communication.

The Legal Domain

Because the issue of anonymity crops up in connection with many of the fundamental rights of liberal democracy, it presents a complex and persistent legal problem. Constitutionally, attempts have been made both to establish an abstract right to anonymity and to ban it.[17]

17 A. Michael Froomkin, "Legal Issues in Anonymity and Pseudonymity," *Information Society* 15, no. 2 (1999): 113–27;
Ian Kerr, Carole Lucock, and Valerie Steeves, eds., *Lessons from the Identity Trail: Anonymity, Privacy and Identity in a Networked Society* (Oxford and New York: Oxford University Press, 2009).

Discourse in the legal sphere tends to be more nuanced than in the other domains discussed here. In relation to digital issues, debates about recognizing anonymity as a right, or banning it, tend to develop out of specific legal concerns. The critique of copyright enforcement, for example, led to a discussion about legal responsibility in the context of peer-to-peer networks and cloud storage, and this in turn triggered a debate about anonymity and the necessity of identification for these kind of services. State-based attempts to expanding law enforcement pushed for data retention, framing anonymity as an obstacle to the application of the law (or to the prevention of its violation). These moves have at least in Germany been countered with a fierce defense of data protection and the right to "informational self-determination."

In legal discourses, those who support (qualified) rights to anonymity appear to be winning the argument. In regard to copyright infringement and data retention at least, a significant proportion of the relevant publics in democratic societies have become skeptical about proposals for an outright ban on anonymous communications. Still discursive framing does not translate directly into political power, and the current awareness might be temporal and specific to certain contexts and cases.

The Sociopolitical Domain

Within the wider sociopolitical domain, we find that many of the arguments from the other three areas also make an appearance here. The issue of anonymity has begun to excite interest and has been taken up by mass media. The way anonymity is framed in the public discourse continues to be more negative than positive, emphasizing the risks that anonymous communication brings with it and the antisocial behavior it is expected to engender. Attention is focused on the horizontal dimension and on the harm that can be done to private individuals in situations of direct interaction.

While the main triggers to the public debate about anonymity are still bad digital practices (such as cyberbullying and hate speech), the exposure of surveillance activities by states and corporations, such as the Snowden revelations or the Cambridge Analytica scandal, have given rise to counter-discourses. Although civil society activists often claim that not enough attention is paid to arguments about anonymity, issues relating to anonymity, privacy, and surveillance have undoubtedly gained considerable traction in the public sphere and have graduated from niche concern to major political battleground.

Concluding Remarks

The scope and diversity of discourse in these four different areas demonstrates the speed with which the debate on anonymity has evolved in the last decade. Arguments on both sides—for and against anonymity—have become much more sophisticated, and anonymity is now an object of political contestation rather than a minor determinant of modern life. Although politicization is clearly under way, one can foresee that the current attempts might not be enough to counter the powerful trend toward deanonymization. Politicization itself can only be a necessary step not a sufficient one—especially since the forces driving us toward identification are to an extent isolated from public debates and shifting sensitivities. Therefore, those who want to ensure that anonymous communication has a secured place in digitized societies will have to more radically rethink the way our digital societies are governed. The focus should be less on techniques of anonymization and more on a legal and an institutional setup that is robust enough to keep capitalist dynamics and governmental overreach in check. Ensuring that the horizontal and vertical dimension of anonymity are kept apart is as important as acknowledging the socioeconomic drivers of the development toward deanonymization. How and by whom the digital public sphere should be regulated is an open question and a major task of civil society and democratic politics.

Bibliography

Andrejevic, Marc. "Facebook als neue Produktionsweise." In *Generation Facebook: Über das Leben im Social Net*, edited by Oliver Leistert and Theo Röhle, 31–49. Bielefeld: Transcript-Verl, 2011.

Asenbaum, Hans. "Cyborg Activism: Exploring the Reconfigurations of Democratic Subjectivity in Anonymous." *New Media and Society* 20, no. 4 (2018): 1543–63. https://doi.org/10.1177/1461444817699994.

Barocas, Solon, and Helen Nissenbaum. "Big Data's End Run around Anonymity and Consent." In *Privacy, Big Data, and the Public Good: Frameworks for Engagement*, edited by Helen Nissenbaum, Julia Lane, Stefan Bender, and Victoria Stodden, 44–75. Cambridge: Cambridge University Press, 2014. https://doi.org/10.1017/CBO9781107590205.004.

Benkler, Yochai. "Degrees of Freedom, Dimensions of Power." *Daedalus* 145, no. 1 (2016): 18–32. https://doi.org/10.1162/DAED_a_00362.

Brodnig, Ingrid. *Der unsichtbare Mensch*. Vienna: Czernin, 2013.

Dean, Jodi. "Communicative Capitalism: Circulation and the Foreclosure of Politics." *Cultural Politics* 1, no. 1 (2005): 51–74. https://doi.org/10.2752/174321905778054845.

DeNardis, Laura. "Hidden Levers of Internet Control." *Information, Communication and Society* 15, no. 5 (2012): 720–38. https://doi.org/10.1080/1369118X.2012.659199.

Doyle, Tony, and Judy Veranas. "Public Anonymity and the Connected World." *Ethics and Information Technology* 16, no. 3 (2014): 207–18. https://doi.org/10.1007/s10676-014-9346-5.

Farrall, Kenneth. "Online Collectivism, Individualism and Anonymity in East Asia." *Surveillance and Society* 9, no. 4 (2012): 424–40. https://doi.org/10.24908/ss.v9i4.4344.

Froomkin, A. Michael. "From Anonymity to Identification." *Journal of Self-Regulation and Regulation* 1 (2015): 121–38. https://doi.org/10.11588/josar.2015.0.23480.

Froomkin, A. Michael. "Legal Issues in Anonymity and Pseudonymity." *Information Society* 15, no. 2 (1999): 113–27. https://doi.org/10.1080/019722499128574.

Gardner, James. "Anonymity and Democratic Citizenship." *William and Mary Bill of Rights Journal* 19, no. 4 (2011): 927.

Kaye, David. "Report on Encryption, Anonymity, and the Human Rights Framework." Geneva: United Nations Human Rights Council, 2015. https://www.ohchr.org/EN/Issues/FreedomOpinion/Pages/CallForSubmission.aspx.

Kerr, Ian, Carole Lucock, and Valerie Steeves, eds. *Lessons from the Identity Trail: Anonymity, Privacy and Identity in a Networked Society*. Oxford: Oxford University Press, 2009.

Kurz, Constanze, and Frank Rieger. *Die Datenfresser: Wie Internetfirmen und Staat sich unsere persönlichen Daten einverleiben und wie wir die Kontrolle darüber zurückerlangen*. 2nd ed. Frankfurt: S. Fischer Verlag, 2011.

Lim, Dongwon, Hangjung Zo, and Dukhee Lee. "The Value of Anonymity on the Internet." In *Service-Oriented Perspectives in Design Science Research: 6th International Conference, DESRIST 2011, Milwaukee, WI, USA, May 5–6, 2011, Proceedings*, edited by Hemant Jain, Atish P. Sinha, and Padmal Vitharana, 452–64. Berlin, Heidelberg: Springer-Verlag, 2011. https://doi.org/10.1007/978-3-642-20633-7.

Lovink, Geert. "Facebook, Anonymität und die Krise des multiplen Selbst." In *Das halbwegs Soziale. Eine Kritik der Vernetzungskultur*, edited by Geert Lovink, 53–68. Bielefeld: Transcript-Verl, 2012.

Marx, Gary T. "What's in a Name? Some Reflections on the Sociology of Anonymity." *Information Society* 15, no. 2 (1999): 99–112. https://doi.org/10.1080/019722499128565.

Moore, Alfred. "Anonymity, Pseudonymity, and Deliberation: Why Not Everything Should Be Connected." *Journal of Political Philosophy* 26, no. 2 (2018): 169–92. https://doi.org/10.1111/jopp.12149.

Nissenbaum, Helen. "Hackers and the Contested Ontology of Cyberspace." *New Media and Society* 6, no. 2 (2004): 195–217. https://doi.org/10.1177/1461444804041445.

Nissenbaum, Helen. "The Meaning of Anonymity in an Information Age." *Information Society* 15, no. 2 (1999): 141–44. https://doi.org/10.1080/019722499128592.

Ohm, Paul. "Broken Promises of Privacy: Responding to the Surprising Failure of Anonymization." *UCLA Law Review* 57 (2010): 1701–77. https://papers.ssrn.com/abstract=1450006.

Ponesse, Julie. "The Ties That Blind: Conceptualizing Anonymity." *Journal of Social Philosophy* 45, no. 3 (2014): 304–22. https://doi.org/10.1111/josp.12066.

Sevignani, Sebastian. "The Commodification of Privacy on the Internet." *Science and Public Policy* 40, no. 6 (2013): 733–39. https://doi.org/10.1093/scipol/sct082.

Thiel, Thorsten. "Anonymität und Demokratie." *Forschungsjournal Soziale Bewegungen* 30, no. 2 (2017): 152–61. https://doi.org/10.1515/fjsb-2017-0036.

Thiel, Thorsten. "Turnkey Tyranny? Struggles for a New Digital Order." In *Resistance and Change in World Politics*, edited by Svenja Gertheiss, Stefanie Herr, Klaus Dieter Wolf, and Carmen Wunderlich, 215–42. Basingstoke: Palgrave Macmillan, 2017. https://doi.org/10.1007/978-3-319-50445-2_7.

USAE

U

UNITED

S
STATES

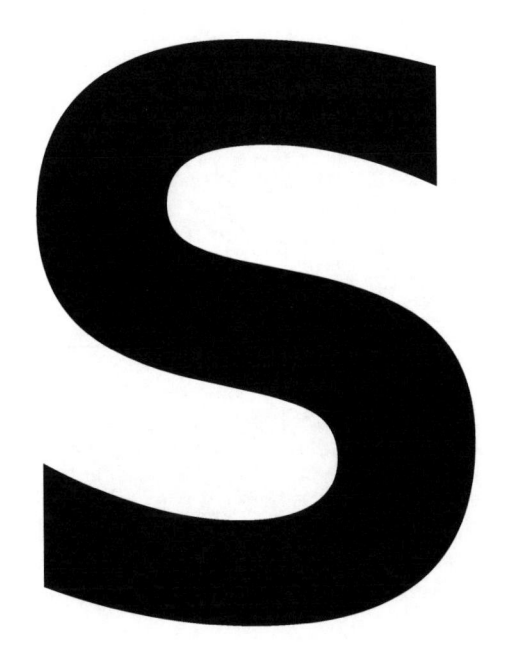

A

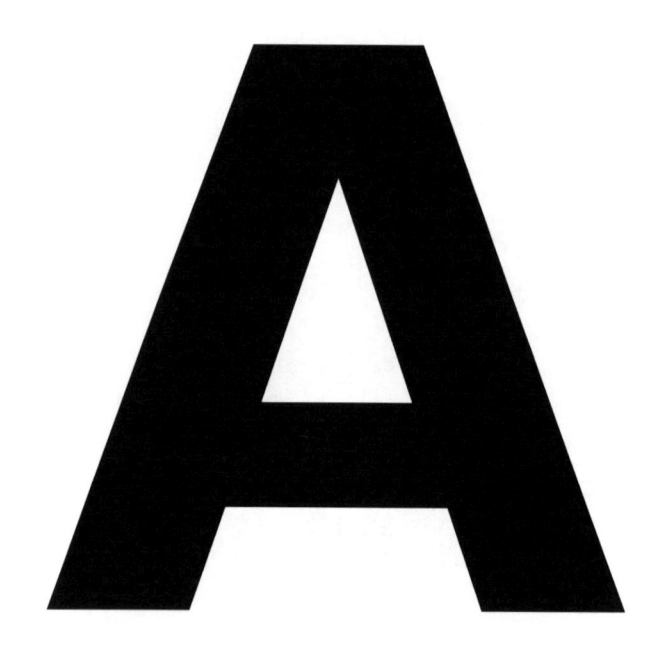

AMERICA

E

EMPIRE

Largest anonymous corporation

Big Data's End Run around Anonymity and Consent

Introduction

Big data promises to deliver analytic insights that will add to the stock of scientific and social scientific knowledge, significantly improve public and private decision making, and greatly enhance individual self-knowledge and understanding. It has already led to entirely new classes of goods and services, many of which have been embraced enthusiastically by institutions and individuals alike. And yet, where these data commit to record details about human behavior, they have been perceived as a threat to fundamental values, including everything from autonomy to fairness, justice, due process, property, solidarity, and, perhaps most of all, privacy.[1]

This ambivalent situation rehearses many of the long-standing tensions that have characterized each successive wave of technological innovation over the past half-century, as well as their inevitable disruption of constraints on information flows through which privacy had been assured. Anonymity and informed consent remain the most popular tools for relieving these tensions — tensions we accept, from the outset, as genuine and, in many cases, acute. Taking as a given that big data implicates important ethical and political values, we direct our focus instead on attempts to avoid or mitigate the conflicts that may arise.[2]

Anonymity and informed consent emerged as panaceas because they presented ways to "have it all"; they would open the data floodgates while ensuring that no one was unexpectedly swept up or away by the deluge. Now, as then, conscientious industry practitioners, policy-makers, advocates, and researchers across the disciplines look to anonymity and informed consent as counters to the worrisome aspects of emerging applications of big data. We can see why anonymity and consent are attractive: anonymization seems to take data outside the scope of privacy, as data no longer map onto identifiable subjects, while allowing information subjects to give or withhold consent maps onto the dominant conception of privacy as control over information about oneself. In practice, however, anonymity and consent have proved elusive, as time and again critics have revealed fundamental problems in implementing both.[3]

Those committed to anonymity and consent, however, do not deny the practical challenges; their solution is to try harder, to be more creative, to use more sophisticated mathematical and statistical techniques, and to become astute to the cognitive and motivational contours of users.

[1] For a wide-ranging survey of these issues, see David Bollier, *The Promise and Peril of Big Data* (Washington, DC: The Aspen Institute, 2010); and Janna Anderson and Lee Rainie, *The Future of Big Data* (Washington, DC: Pew Research Center, 2012).

[2] Solon Barocas "Data Mining: An Annotated Bibliography" (prepared for Cyber-Surveillance in Everyday Life: An International Workshop, University of Toronto, Ontario, Canada, May 12–15, 2011).

[3] See, for example, Latanya Sweeney, "K-Anonymity: A Model for Protecting Privacy," *International Journal of Uncertainty, Fuzziness, and Knowledge-Based Systems* 10, no. 5 (2002): 557–70; Arvind Narayanan and Vitaly Shmatikov, "Robust De-Anonymization of Large Sparse Datasets," in *Proceedings — IEEE Symposium on Security and Privacy* (Piscataway, NJ: IEEE, 2008), 111–25; Paul Ohm, "Broken Promises of Privacy: Responding to the Surprising Failure of Anonymization," *UCLA Law Review* 57, no. 6 (2010): 1701–77; Solon Barocas and Helen Nissenbaum, "On Notice: The Trouble with Notice and Consent" (presented at Engaging Data: First International Forum on the Application and Management of Personal Electronic Information, Cambridge, MA, October 12–13, 2009); Lorrie Faith Cranor, "Can Users Control Online Behavioral Advertising Effectively?" *IEEE Security and Privacy Magazine* 10, no. 2 (2012): 93–96; Lorrie Faith Cranor, "Necessary But Not Sufficient: Standardized Mechanisms for Privacy Notice and Choice," *Journal on Telecommunications and High Technology*

Although we accept that improvements can result and have resulted from these efforts (e.g., more digestible privacy policies, more robust guarantees of anonymity, more usable choice architectures, and more supple policy), the transition to big data has turned the definitional and practical fault lines that have worried policymakers, pundits, practitioners, and scholars into impassable chasms.

Even when individuals are not "identifiable," they may still be "reachable," may still be comprehensibly represented in records that detail their attributes and activities, and may be subject to consequential inferences and predictions made on that basis. In the case of consent, too, commonly perceived operational challenges have distracted from the ultimate inefficacy of consent as a matter of individual choice and the absurdity of believing that notice and consent can fully specify the terms of interaction between data collector and data subject.

Both, we argue, lead to the inescapable conclusion that procedural approaches cannot replace policies based on substantive moral and political principles serving specific contextual goals and values.

Definitions and Background Theory: Big Data and Privacy

Taking into consideration wide-ranging uses of "big data" in public discussions, specialized applications, government initiatives, research agendas, and diverse scientific, critical, and popular publications, we find that the term better reflects a paradigm than a particular technology, method, or practice.[4] There are, of course, characteristic techniques and tools associated with it, but, more than the sum of these parts, big data, the paradigm, is a way of thinking about knowledge through data and a framework for supporting decision making, rationalizing action, and guiding practice.[5]

Law 10, no. 2 (2012): 273–445;
Alessandro Acquisti and Jens Grossklags, "Privacy and Rationality in Individual Decision Making," *IEEE Security and Privacy Magazine* 3, no. 1 (2005): 26–33;
and Daniel J. Solove, "Privacy Self-Management and the Consent Dilemma," *Harvard Law Review* 126, no. 7 (2013): 1880, 1883–86.

4 For specialized applications, see James Manyika, Michael Chui, Brad Brown, Jacques Bughin, Richard Dobbs, Charles Roxburgh, and Angela Hung Byers, *Big Data: The Next Frontier for Innovation, Competition, and Productivity* (Washington, DC: McKinsey Global Institute, 2011).
For government initiatives, see *Tech America Foundation, Demystifying Big Data: A Practical Guide to Transforming the Business of Government* (Washington, DC: Tech America Foundation, 2012).
For research agendas, see the National Science Foundation news release "NSF Advances National Efforts Enabling Data-Driven Discovery," November 12, 2013.
For diverse publications, see, for example, the journals Big Data, on the Mary Ann Liebert, Publishers, website, www.liebertpub.com/big; and Big Data and Society, on the Sage journals website, www.journals.sagepub.com/home/bds.

5 See Tony Hey, Stewart Tansley, and Kristin Tolle, eds., *The Fourth Paradigm: Data-Intensive Scientific Discovery* (Redmond, WA: Microsoft Research, 2009); Mireille Hildebrandt, "Defining Profiling: A New Type of Knowledge?" in *Profiling the European Citizen: Cross-Disciplinary Perspectives*, ed. Mireille Hildebrandt and

There is some disagreement over how important privacy is among the various ethical and political issues raised by big data.[6] Downplaying privacy, the argument is that real problems include how we use the data, whether it is fair to treat people as part of a group, whether data are representative, whether we diminish the range of choices we make about our lives and fates, whether data about us and the data that we generate belong to us, thereby invoking justice, fairness, autonomy, and property rights. Revealing these wide-ranging ethical dimensions of big data is important, but an impoverished working conception of privacy can result in the failure to appreciate the crucial ways in which these other values and privacy interact.

To understand the concept's wider berth, we take privacy to be the requirement that information about people (personal information) flows appropriately, where appropriateness means in accordance with informational norms. According to the theory of contextual integrity, informational norms prescribe information flows according to key actors, types of information, and constraints under which flow occurs (transmission principles). Key actors include recipients, information subjects, and senders, where the last two are often one and the same. Social contexts form the backdrop for this approach to privacy, accounting for the range over which the parameters of actors, information types, and transmission principles vary. Put more concretely, informational norms for a healthcare context would govern flow between and about people in their context-specific capacities, such as physicians, patients, nurses, insurance companies, pharmacists, and so forth. Types of information would range over relevant fields, including, say, symptoms, diagnoses, prescriptions, as well as biographical information.

And notable among transmission principles, confidentiality is likely to be a prominent constraint on the terms under which information types flow from, say, patients to

Serge Gutwirth (Dordrecht: Springer, 2008), 17–45; danah boyd and Kate Crawford, "Critical Questions for Big Data," *Information, Communication, and Society* 15, no. 5 (2012): 662–79; Christopher Steiner, *Automate This: How Algorithms Came to Rule Our World* (New York: Portfolio/Penguin, 2012); and Viktor Mayer-Schönberger and Kenneth Cukier, *Big Data: A Revolution That Will Transform How We Live, Work, and Think* (New York: Houghton Mifflin Harcourt, 2013).

6 Oscar H. Gandy, "Consumer Protection in Cyberspace," *TripleC: Communication, Capitalism and Critique* 9, no. 2 (2011): 175–89; Cynthia Dwork and Deirdre K. Mulligan, "It's Not Privacy, and It's Not Fair," *Stanford Law Review Online* 66 (2013): 35–40; Omer Tene and Jules Polonetsky, "Judged by the Tin Man: Individual Rights in the Age of Big Data," *Journal on Telecommunications and High Technology Law*, August 15, 2013; Jonas Lerman, "Big Data and Its Exclusions," *Stanford Law Review Online* 66 (2013): 55–63; and Kate Crawford and Jason Schultz, "Big Data and Due Process: Toward a Framework to Redress Predictive Privacy Harms," *Boston College Law Review* 55, no. 1 (2014): 93–128.

physicians. In drawing comparisons between contextual integrity and other theories of privacy, one key difference is that control over information about oneself is merely one in an indefinitely large class of transmission principles, not presumed unless the other parameters—(context-specific) actors and information types—warrant it.[7]

Contextual informational norms, like other social norms generally, are not fixed and static but may shift, fade, evolve, and even reverse at varying rates, slowly or suddenly, sometimes as a result of deliberate cultural, legal, and societal alterations, and other times in response to contingencies beyond human or societal control. Science and technology is a significant agent of change; in particular, computing and information technologies have been radically disruptive, enabling information practices that frequently diverge from entrenched informational norms.

Big data involves practices that have radically disrupted entrenched information flows. From modes of acquiring to aggregation, analysis, and application, these disruptions affect actors, information types, and transmission principles. Accordingly, privacy, understood as contextual integrity, is fundamentally part of the big data story, for it immediately alerts us to how any practice conflicts with the expectations we may have based on entrenched information-flow norms. But that is merely the beginning.

Evaluating disruptive practices means judging whether they move us closer or farther from ideal informational flows, that is, whether they are more or less effective in promoting interests, general moral and political values, and context-specific ends, purposes, and values. Parsing cases in which big data gives rise to discrimination in terms of contextual integrity forces us to be much more specific about the source of that unfairness because it compels us to account for the disruption that made such discrimination possible.[8] And it likewise allows us

[7] Helen Nissenbaum, *Privacy in Context: Technology, Policy, and the Integrity of Social Life* (Stanford, CA: Stanford University Press, 2010).

[8] Solon Barocas, "How Data Mining Discriminates," in "Panic Inducing: Data Mining, Fairness, and Privacy" (Ph.D. diss., New York University, 2014).

to ask if anonymity and informed consent limit or mitigate the potential consequences of such disruptions—that is, whether they actually protect the values at stake when novel applications of big data (threaten to) violate contextual integrity.

Anonymity

Anonymity obliterates the link between data and a specific person not so much to protect privacy but, in a sense, to bypass it entirely. Anonymity is an attractive solution to challenges big data poses to privacy when identities associated with information in a dataset are not necessary for the analysis to proceed.

According to the literature, the promise of anonymity is impossible to fulfill if individual records happen to contain information—information that falls outside the scope of the commonly defined set of personally identifiable information—that nevertheless uniquely distinguishes a person enough to associate those records to a specific individual. The literature has also demonstrated many ways in which anonymity cannot be guaranteed because of the threat of so-called reidentification attacks.[9] These attacks depend on various methods: overlaying an anonymized dataset with a separate dataset that includes identifying information, looking for areas of overlap (commonly described as a linkage attack), or performing a sequence of queries on an anonymized dataset that allows the attacker to deduce that a specific person must be in the dataset because only one person has all the queried attributes (differencing attack).[10] Responding to these challenges, computer scientists have developed several approaches to limit, if not eliminate, the chances of deducing identity, such as k-anonymity and differential privacy, which work in certain settings by abstracting or perturbing data to a level or degree set by data controllers.[11]

[9] Khaled El Emam, Elizabeth Jonker, Luk Arbuckle, and Bradley Malin, "A Systematic Review of Re-Identification Attacks on Health Data," *PLOS ONE* 6, no. 12 (2011): e28071.

[10] See Narayanan and Shmatikov, "Robust De-Anonymization"; and Cynthia Dwork, "A Firm Foundation for Private Data Analysis," *Communications of the ACM* 54, no. 1 (2011): 86.

[11] Sweeney, "K-Anonymity"; and Cynthia Dwork, "Differential Privacy," in *Proceedings of the 33rd International Conference on Automata, Languages and Programming*, part 2 (Berlin: Springer, 2006), 1–12.

To see why anonymity does not solve ethical problems relating to privacy in a big data age, we should ask why we believe it does. And to do that, we need to ask not only whether in this age we are able to preserve the present-day equivalent of a traditional understanding of anonymity as namelessness, but also whether this equivalent preserves what is at stake in protecting anonymity. In short, we need to ask whether it is worthwhile to protect whatever is being protected when, today, we turn to anonymity to avoid the ethical concerns raised by the big data paradigm.

12 Helen Nissenbaum, "The Meaning of Anonymity in an Information Age," *Information Society* 15, no. 2 (1999): 141–44.

Anonymous Identifiers

First and perhaps foremost, many of anonymity's proponents have different meanings in mind. In earlier work, we argued that the value of anonymity inheres not in namelessness, and not even in the extension of the previous value of namelessness to all uniquely identifying information, but instead to something we called "reachability," the possibility of knocking on your door, hauling you out of bed, calling your phone number, threatening you with sanction, or holding you accountable.[12]

For example, when commercial actors claim that they rely on "anonymous identifiers," they rarely mean that they have no way to distinguish a specific person— or his browser, computer, network equipment, or phone —from others. Nor do they mean that they have no way to recognize him as the same person with whom they have interacted previously. They simply mean that they rely on unique persistent identifiers that differ from those in common and everyday use (i.e., a name and other so-called personally identifiable information, or PII).

The reasons for adopting this oxymoronic perspective on anonymity becomes clear when we explore why names in particular tend to generate such anxiety. As a persistent and common identifier, names have long seemed uniquely worrisome because they hold the potential to act as an obvious basis for seeking out additional information referring to the same person by allowing institutions to match records keyed to the same name.

Indeed, this is the very business of commercial data brokers: "Acxiom and other database marketing companies sell services that let retailers simply type in a customer's name and zip code and append all the additional profile information that retailers might want."[13] But this is highly misleading because, as scholars have long argued, a given name and address is just one of many possible ways to recognize and associate data with a specific person.[14] Indeed, any unique identifier or sufficiently unique pattern can serve as the basis for recognizing the same person in and across multiple databases.[15]

The history of the social security number in the United States is highly instructive here: as a unique number assigned to each citizen, it is a convenient identifier that other institutions can adopt for their own administrative purposes. Indeed, large institutions are often attracted to the social security number because it is necessarily more unique than given names, the more common of which (e.g., John Smith) could easily recur multiple times in the same database. That people had existing reasons to commit this number to memory also explains why other institutions would seize on it. In so doing, however, these institutions turned the social security number, issued by the government for administering its own welfare programs, into a common unique identifier that applies across multiple silos of information. A social security number is now perceived as sensitive, not because of any quality inherent to the number itself, but because it serves as one of the few common unique identifiers that enable the straightforward matching of the disparate and detailed records held by many important institutions.

[13] Natasha Singer, "Acxiom, the Quiet Giant of Consumer Database Marketing," *New York Times*, June 16, 2012.

[14] Gary Marx, "What's in a Name? Some Reflections on the Sociology of Anonymity," *The Information Society* 15, no. 2 (May 1999): 99–112.

[15] Arvind Narayanan and Vitaly Shmatikov, "Myths and Fallacies of 'Personally Identifiable Information,'" *Communications of the ACM* 53, no. 6 (2010): 24–26.

Comprehensiveness and Inference

A further worry is that the comprehensiveness of the records maintained by especially large institutions—records that contain no identifying information—may become so rich that they subvert the very meaning of anonymity.[16] Joseph Turow, for instance, has asked, "If a company knows 100 data points about me in the digital environment, and that affects how that company treats me in the digital world, what's the difference if they know my name or not?"[17] The answer from industry is that it seems to matter very little indeed: "The beauty of what we do is we don't know who you are.... We don't want to know anybody's name. We don't want to know anything recognizable about them. All we want to do is … have these attributes associated with them."[18] This better accounts for the common refrain that companies have no particular interest in who someone is because their ability to tailor their offerings and services to individuals is in no way limited by the absence of such information. And it helps to explain the otherwise bizarre statement by Facebook's chief privacy officer that they "serve ads to you based on your identity, … but that doesn't mean you're identifiable."[19] On this account, your legal or real-world identity is of no significance. What matters are the properties and behaviors that your identity comprises—the kinds of details that can be associated with a pseudonym assigned to you without revealing your actual identity. Where these details are sufficiently extensive, as with platforms that deal in big data, and where all these details can be brought to bear in deciding how to treat people, the protections offered by "anonymity" or "pseudonymity" may amount to very little. They may enable holders of large datasets to act on individuals, under the cover of anonymity, in precisely the ways anonymity has long promised to defend against. And to the extent that this results in differential treatment, limiting available choices and interfering with identity construction, it threatens individual autonomy and social justice. For these reasons, Serge Gutwirth and

[16] Emily Steel and Julia Angwin, "On the Web's Cutting Edge, Anonymity in Name Only," *Wall Street Journal*, August 4, 2010.

[17] "'Drinking from a Fire Hose': Has Consumer Data Mining Gone Too Far?," *Knowledge@Wharton*, November 22, 2011.

[18] Cindy Waxer, "Big Data Blues: The Dangers of Data Mining," *Computerworld*, November 4, 2013.

[19] Jennifer Valentino-Devries and Jeremy Singer-Vine, "They Know What You're Shopping For," *Wall Street Journal*, December 7, 2012.

Paul Hert have warned that if it is "possible to control and steer individuals without the need to identify them, the time has probably come to explore the possibility of a shift from personal data protection to data protection tout court."[20] In other words, we can no longer turn to anonymity (or, more accurately, pseudonymity) to pull datasets outside the remit of privacy regulations and debate.

But even this fails to appreciate the novel ways in which big data may subvert the promise of such protections: inference. As Brian Dalessandro has explained, "a lot can be predicted about a person's actions without knowing anything personal about them."[21] This is a subtle but crucial point: insights drawn from big data can furnish additional facts about an individual (in excess of those that reside in the database) without any knowledge of their specific identity or any identifying information. Data mining breaks the basic intuition that identity is the greatest source of potential harm because it substitutes inference for using identifying information as a bridge to get at additional facts. Rather than matching records keyed to the same name (or other PII) in different datasets, data mining derives insights that simply allow firms to guess at these qualities instead.

These indirect means may allow data collectors to draw inferences about precisely those qualities that have long seemed unknowable in the absence of identifying information. Rather than attempt to deanonymize medical records, for instance, an attacker (or commercial actor) might instead infer a rule that relates a string of more easily observable or accessible indicators to a specific medical condition, rendering large populations vulnerable to such inferences even in the absence of PII. Ironically, this is often the very thing about big data that generates the most excitement: the capacity to detect subtle correlations and draw actionable inferences. But this very same feature renders the traditional protections afforded by anonymity (again, more accurately, pseudonymity) much less effective.

[20] Serge Gutwirth and Paul Hert, "Regulating Profiling in a Democratic Constitutional State," in *Profiling the European Citizen: Cross-Disciplinary Perspectives*, ed. Mireille Hildebrandt and Serge Gutwirth (Dordrecht: Springer, 2008), 289.

[21] Brian Dalessandro, "The Science of Privacy," *Ad: Tech* (blog), July 30, 2013.

Informed Consent

The Transparency Paradox

Informed consent is believed to be an effective means of respecting individuals as autonomous decision makers with rights of self-determination, including rights to make choices, take or avoid risks, express preferences, and, perhaps most importantly, resist exploitation. Thus, where anonymity is unachievable or simply does not make sense, informed consent often is the mechanism sought out by conscientious collectors and users of personal information.

Understood as a crucial mechanism for ensuring privacy, informed consent is a natural corollary of the idea that privacy means control over information about oneself. For some, these are the roots of privacy that must be respected in all environments and against all threats. Its central place in the regulation of privacy, however, was solidified with the articulation and spread of the Fair Information Practice Principles (FIPPs) in the domains of privacy law and countless data protection and privacy regulation schemes around the world. These principles, in broad brushstrokes, demand that data subjects be given notice, that is to say, be informed of who is collecting, what is being collected, how information is being used and shared, and whether information collection is voluntary or required.

The internet challenged the "level playing field" embodied in FIPPs.[22] It opened unprecedented modalities for collecting, disseminating, and using personal information, serving and inspiring a diverse array of interests. Mobile devices, location-based services, the internet of things, and ubiquitous sensors have expanded the scope even more. This need has long been answered by online privacy policies offered to individuals as unilateral terms-of-service contracts (often dubbed "transparency and choice" or "notice and consent"). In so doing, privacy

[22] OECD, "The Evolving Privacy Landscape: 30 Years after the OECD Privacy Guidelines," OECD Digital Economy Papers, no. 176, April 6, 2011.

questions have been turned into practical matters of implementation.

Over the course of roughly a decade and a half, privacy policies have remained the linchpin of privacy protection online, despite overwhelming evidence that most of us neither read nor understand them. Sensitive to this reality, regulatory agencies, such as the Federal Trade Commission, have demanded improvements focusing attention on (1) ways in which privacy policies are expressed and communicated so that they furnish more effective notice, and (2) mechanisms that more meaningfully model consent, reviving the never-ending stalemate over opt-in versus opt-out.[23] While the idea that informed consent may no longer meet the challenges posed by big data has been floated by scholars, practitioners, advocates, and even some regulators, such thinking has not entered the mainstream. As before, the challenge continues to be perceived as purely operational, as a more urgent need for new and inventive approaches to informing and consenting that truly map onto the states of understanding and assenting that give moral legitimacy to the practices in question.

Online tracking has been one such highly contentious debate—one in which corporate actors have glommed onto the idea of plain language, simple-to-understand privacy policies and plain-to-see boxes where people can indicate their assent or consent. But situations involving complex data flows and diverse institutional structures representing disparate interests are likely to confront a challenge we have called "the transparency paradox," meaning that simplicity and clarity unavoidably result in losses of fidelity.[24] Typical of the big data age is the business of targeted advertising, with its complex ecology of backend ad networks and their many and diverse adjuncts. Simplified, plain-language notices cannot provide information that people need to make such decisions. The detail that would allow for this would overwhelm even savvy users because the practices themselves are

[23] Yannis Bakos, Florencia Marotta-Wurgler, and David R. Trossen, "Does Anyone Read the Fine Print? Testing a Law and Economics Approach to Standard Form Contracts," *SSRN Electronic Journal*, August 4, 2009; Aleecia M. McDonald and Lorrie Faith Cranor, "The Cost of Reading Privacy Policies," *I/S: A Journal of Law and Policy for the Information Society* 4, no. 3 (2008): 540–65; Aleecia M. McDonald, R. W. Reeder, P. G. Kelley, and Lorrie Faith Cranor, "A Com-parative Study of Online Privacy Policies and Formats," *Lecture Notes in Computer Science* 5672 (2009): 37–55; Helen Nissenbaum, "A Contextual Approach to Privacy Online," *Daedalus* 140, no. 4 (2011): 32–48; and Omer Tene and Jules Polonetsky, "To Track or 'Do Not Track': Advancing Transparency and Individual Control in Online Behavioral Advertising," *Minnesota Journal of Law, Science and Technology* 13, no. 1 (2013): 281–357.

[24] Nissenbaum, "Contextual Approach."

volatile and indeterminate as new parties come on board and as new practices, squeezing out more value from other sources of information (e.g., social graphs), are constantly augmenting existing flows.

Empirical evidence is incontrovertible: the very few people who read privacy policies do not understand them.[25] But the paradox identified above suggests that even when people understand the text of plain-language notices, they still will not—indeed cannot—be informed in ways relevant to their decisions whether to consent.

[25] Solove, "Privacy Self-Management."

Indeterminate, Unending, Unpredictable

What we have said thus far emerges from a discussion of notice and choice applied to online behavioral advertising, but with clear parallels for the big data paradigm generally. Consider typical points of contact for data gathering: signing up for a smart utility meter; joining an online social network; joining a frequent flier program; buying goods and services; enrolling in a MOOC (massive open online course); enrolling in a health self-tracking program; traveling; participating in a medical trial; signing up for a supermarket loyalty card; clicking on an online ad; commenting on a book, a movie, or a product; or applying for insurance, a job, a rental apartment, or a credit card. Because these mundane activities may yield raw material for subsequent analysis, they offer a potential juncture for obtaining consent, raising the natural question of how to describe information practices in ways relevant to privacy so that individuals meaningfully grant or withhold consent. The machinations of big data make this difficult because data move from place to place and recipient to recipient in unpredictable ways.

While questions of information type and use might, at first, seem straightforward, they are extremely difficult when considered in detail: it may be reasonably easy for a utility company to explain to customers that, with smart meters, it can monitor usage at a fine grain, can derive aggregate patterns within and across customers, and can use these as a basis for important decisions about allocation of resources and for targeted advisement about individual customers' energy usage. It may clearly explain who will be receiving what information and to what end.

With notice such as this, consent is meaningful. Big data analytics typically do not stop here, however; an enterprising company may attempt to figure out how many people are associated with a given account, what appliances they own, and what their routines are (work, bedtime, and vacation). It may fold other information associated with the account into the analysis and other information beyond the account—personal or environmental, such as weather. The company may extract further value from the information by collaborating with third parties to introduce additional data fields.

If the more encompassing approach is taken, how does the data controller explain that it is impossible to know in advance what further information might be discoverable? These factors diminish the value of informed consent because they seem to require notice that does not delimit future uses of data and the possible consequences of such uses. As many have now argued, consent under such conditions is not meaningful.[26]

The Tyranny of the Minority

Big data troubles the long-standing focus on individual choice in a slightly more roundabout way because the willingness of a few individuals to disclose certain information implicates everyone else who happens to share the more easily observable traits that correlate with the revealed trait. This is the tyranny of the minority: the volunteered information of the few can unlock the same information about the many.

[26] Herman T. Tavani, "KDD, Data Mining, and the Challenge for Normative Privacy." *Ethics and Information Technology* 1, no. 4 (1999): 265–73; Mireille Hildebrandt, "Who Is Profiling Who? Invisible Visibility," in *Reinventing Data Protection?*, ed. Serge Gutwirth, Yves Poullet, Paul de Hert, Cécile de Terwangne, and Sjaak Nouwt (Dordrecht: Springer, 2009), 239–52; Mireille Hildebrandt, "Profiling and AmI," in *The Future of Identity in the Information Society*, ed. Kai Rannenberg, Denis Royer, and André Deuker (Berlin: Springer, 2009), 273–310; Serge Gutwirth and Mireille Hildebrandt, "Some Caveats on Profiling," in *Data Protection in a Profiled World*, ed. Serge Gutwirth, Yves Poullet, and Paul de Hert (Dordrecht: Springer, 2010), 31–41; Fred H. Cate and Viktor Mayer-Schönberger, "Notice and Consent in a World of Big Data," *International Data Privacy Law* 3, no. 2 (2013): 67–73; Omer Tene and Jules Polonetsky, "Big Data for All: Privacy and User Control in the Age of Analytics," *Northwestern Journal of Technology and Intellectual Property* 11, no. 5 (April 2013): 239–272; and Ira Rubinstein, "Big Data: The End of Privacy or a New Beginning?" *International Data Privacy Law* 3, no. 2 (2013): 74–87.

This differs markedly from the suggestion that individuals are ill equipped to make choices serving their actual interests; rather, even if we accept that individuals can make informed, rational decisions concerning their own privacy, these decisions nonetheless affect what institutions (to whom these individuals have disclosed information) can now know (i.e., infer) about others.

In registering some kind of connection to another person through the formal process of "friending" on a social networking site, for example, we signal that this is a person with whom we share certain interests, affinities, and history. In associating with this person, we open ourselves up to inferences that peg us as people who share certain qualities with this other person, hence danah boyd's point that "it's no longer about what you do that will go down on your permanent record. Everything that everyone else does that concerns you, implicates you, or might influence you will go down on your permanent record."[27] Computer scientists have turned this into a formal problem, asking whether techniques drawn from social network analysis and data mining can be used to infer undisclosed attributes of a user based on the disclosed attributes of the user's friends on social networking sites.[28]

When we move away from discussions of online social networking, however, we find that no such explicit associations are necessary to engage in this same kind of guesswork. More significantly, similar inferences can be made about an entire population even if only a small fraction of people who share no ties are willing to disclose. This describes the dynamics of the Target pregnancy prediction score.[29] Target did not infer the likelihood of a woman giving birth by looking at her group of friends; rather, the company looked over the records from its baby shower registry to find women who had actively disclosed that they had given birth and then went about trying to figure out if these women's shopping habits, leading up to the baby shower, seemed to differ

[27] danah boyd, "Networked Privacy" (presented at the Personal Democracy Forum 2011, New York University, June 6–7, 2011).

[28] Alan Mislove, Bimal Viswanath, Krishna P. Gummadi, and Peter Druschel, "You Are Who You Know: Inferring User Profiles in Online Social Networks," *Proceedings of the Third ACM International Conference on Web Search and Data Mining* (New York: ACM Press, 2010), 251–60; Carter Jernigan and Behram F. T. Mistree, "Gaydar: Facebook Friendships Expose Sexual Orientation," *First Monday* 14, no. 10 (2009); and Emöke-Ágnes Horvát, Michael Hanselmann, Fred A. Hamprecht, and Katharina A. Zweig, "One Plus One Makes Three (for Social Networks)," *PLOS ONE* 7, no. 4 (2012): e347402012.

[29] Charles Duhigg, "How Companies Learn Your Secrets," *New York Times Magazine*, February 16, 2012.

from other customers' habits such that Target could then recognize the telltale signs in the future shopping habits of other women.[30] Which is to say that Target was able to infer a rule about the relationship between purchases and pregnancy from what must have been a tiny proportion of all its customers who actually decided to tell the company that they recently had a baby. Not only is this the tyranny of the minority, it is a choice forced on the majority by a minority with whom they have no meaningful or recognized relations.

Computer science researchers are tackling this question head on: What proportion of people need to disclose that they possess a certain attribute for an adversary to then be able to identify all the other members in the population who also have this attribute? The findings from Mislove et al.'s study are rather startling: "Multiple attributes can be inferred globally when as few as 20% of the users reveal their attribute information."[31] Of course, reaching this minimum threshold is really just a matter of arriving at a sufficiently representative sample whose analysis generates findings that are generalizable to an entire population.

So long as a data collector can overcome sampling bias with a relatively small proportion of the consenting population,[32] this minority will determine the range of what can be inferred for the majority, and it will discourage firms from investing their resources in procedures that help garner the willing consent of more than the bare minimum number of people. In other words, once a critical threshold has been reached, data collectors can rely on more easily observable information to situate all individuals according to these patterns, rendering irrelevant whether those individuals have consented to allowing access to the critical information in question. Withholding consent will make no difference to how they are treated!

[30] Rachel Nolan, "Behind the Cover Story: How Much Does Target Know?" *New York Times*, February 21, 2012.

[31] Mislove et al., "You Are Who You Know," 255.

[32] Christina Aperjis and Bernardo A. Huberman, "A Market for Unbiased Private Data: Paying Individuals According to Their Privacy Attitudes," *First Monday* 17, no. 5 (2012).

Conclusion

Those swept up in the great excitement that has placed big data at the forefront of research investment and the national scientific policy agenda may take courage. For them, these findings, particularly those concerning consent, prove once and for all that privacy is an unsustainable constraint if we are to benefit, truly, from big data. Privacy and big data are simply incompatible, and the time has come to reconfigure choices that we made decades ago to enforce certain constraints. The arguments presented here give further reason to dislodge privacy from its pedestal and allow the glorious potential of big data to be fulfilled.[33] We think these people are wrong in part because they adhere to a mistaken conception of privacy, often as control or as secrecy. Because they see privacy at odds with any distribution and use of data instead of focusing only on the inappropriate, they set up a false conflict from the start. They also may wrongly be conflating the operationalization of informed consent with informed consent itself.

Others say that we should remain concerned about ethical issues raised by big data, that, while privacy may be a lost cause, the real problems arise with use.[34] Those deserving urgent attention include being discriminated against, limited in one's life choices, trapped inside stereotypes, unable to delineate personal boundaries, and wrongly judged, embarrassed, or harassed.[35] Pursuing privacy as a way to address these issues is not only retrograde but a fool's errand, a conclusion reinforced by the arguments in our chapter. Better to route around privacy and pursue directly its ends. To fathom the ways in which big data may threaten interests and values, we must distinguish among the origins and nature of threats to individual and social integrity, between, say, unfair discrimination originating from inappropriate information flows and discrimination originating from other causes. For one thing, different sources may indicate different solutions.

[33] Jane Yakowitz, "Tragedy of the Data Commons," *Harvard Journal of Law and Technology* 25, no. 1 (2012): 1–67.

[34] Tal Z. Zarsky, "Desperately Seeking Solutions: Using Implementation-Based Solutions for the Troubles of Information Privacy in the Age of Data Mining and the Internet Society," *Maine Law Review* 56, no. 1 (2004): 14–59; Cate and Schöneberger, "Notice and Consent"; Omer Tene and Jules Polonetsky, "Big Data for All: Privacy and User Control in the Age of Analytics," *Northwestern Journal of Technology and Intellectual Property* 11, no. 5 (2013): 239–72; and Rubinstein, "Big Data."

[35] Oscar H. Gandy, *Coming to Terms with Chance: Engaging Rational Discrimination and Cumulative Disadvantage* (Burlington, VT: Ashgate, 2009); Dwork and Mulligan, "It's Not Privacy"; Tene and Polotensky, "Judged by the Tin Man"; Omer Tene and Jules Polotensky, "A Theory of Creepy: Technology, Privacy and Shifting Social Norms," *Journal on Telecommunications and High Technology Law*, September 16, 2013; Gutwirth and Hildebrandt, "Some Caveats on Profiling"; Tal Z. Zarsky, "'Mine Your Own Business!': Making the Case for the Implications of the Data Mining of Personal Information in the Forum of Public Opinion," *Yale Journal of Law and Technology* 5 (2004): 1–57.

We are not yet ready to give up on privacy, nor completely on anonymity and consent.

Let us begin with informed consent and imagine it foregrounded against a social landscape. In academic and regulatory circles, attention has focused on the foreground, suggesting ways to shape, tweak, and augment informed consent so that it covers everything important about the relationship between a data controller and a data subject. FIPP and its innumerable descendants are a case in point. These efforts ensure that, in principle, nothing goes unremarked, unrevealed, unnoticed; in practice, informed consent has groaned under the weight of this burden, with results—such as the transparency paradox—that have been noted here and elsewhere. In *Rethinking Informed Consent in Bioethics*, philosophers Neil Manson and Onora O'Neill address a concern, analogous to the one confronted by privacy researchers and regulators, over how to communicate with human subjects to ensure that consent is meaningful.[36] When individuals—human subjects—enter into a study or treatment regime, they engage not as tabula rasa in a vacuum, expecting that the protocol of informed consent will specify fully what will happen and respective rights, obligations, and responsibilities. It does not and cannot constitute the complete relationship between the medical researcher or practitioner and the subject. Instead, the protocol is set against a rich background of social and professional roles, ethical standards, and legal and other obligations, which shape a subject's reasonable expectations. Notice generally covers only notable departures from these expectations, and consent is a limited and selective waiver of rights that subjects normally would expect to have respected.[37]

When they are waived by giving consent, they are not discarded or marginalized: they are merely waived in limited ways, for a limited time, for a limited purpose. In consenting to take part in a clinical trial, I do not consent to swallow other novel medicines, let alone medicines that are irrelevant to my condition. Informed consent

[36] Neil Manson and Onora O'Neill, *Rethinking Informed Consent in Bioethics* (New York: Cambridge University Press, 2012).

[37] Ibid., 73.

matters because it offers a standard and controllable way of setting aside obligations and prohibitions for limited and specific purposes.

38 Ibid., 75.

39 Ibid., 73.

According to Manson and O'Neill, consent is not required for acceptable, expected behaviors, but only for those that depart from it. The burden on notice, therefore, is to describe clearly the violations of norms, standards, and expectations for which a waiver is being asked and not to describe everything that will be done and not done in the course of treatment or research, which both the researcher and the subjects can safely presume.

Manson and O'Neill decline to produce a general or universal list of legal and ethical claims that applies to all treatment and research scenarios because, while all would surely include a common set of obvious prohibitions on, say, killing, stealing, injury, torture, fraud, deception, manipulation, and so forth, each would further include prohibitions and prescriptions relevant to the particular treatment or study in which subjects are engaged.

It is not sufficient for researchers to provide assurances that subjects are given a choice to waive or not to waive; they must be able to justify "actions that otherwise violate important norms, standards or expectations."[38]

According to O'Neill and Manson, "Any justification of informed consent has therefore to start from a recognition of the underlying legal and ethical claims and legitimate expectations that are selectively waived by consent transactions, and the reasons individuals may have for waiving them in particular cases."[39] In other words, selective waivers may not be requested for just anything but are acceptable under two conditions, either concerning actions for which individuals are presumed to have reasons to waive rights and obligations, or concerning actions that promise significant benefits to others and to society at large.

Scientists requesting a limited waiver must ensure that subjects are well informed of departures from expected behaviors, and they should ensure that the waiver they are requesting is consistent with the reasons their subjects have for waiving these rights. But informed consent is constrained in one further, crucial way—namely, by the requirements of beneficence, nonmaleficence, and justice. These constrain what a subject can be asked to consent to.

When we understand informed consent as a limited waiver of rights and obligations, certain aspects of existing practices applied to privacy come to light. To begin, since FIPPs have served as a guide to law and policy, the focus has been on specifying the characteristics of notice and consent and very little on rights and obligations. Drawing on Manson and O'Neill, why this has not worked is quite clear; it is impossible, even absurd, to believe that notice and consent can fully specify the terms of interaction between data collector and data subject.

For too long, we have focused on the foreground, working at it from every angle. In good faith, we have crammed into the notice and consent protocol all our moral and political anxieties, believing that this is the way to achieve the level playing field, to promote the autonomy of data subjects, to energize a competitive marketplace for good data practices, and more. It is time to contextualize consent by bringing the landscape into focus. It is time for the background of rights, obligations, and legitimate expectations to be explored and enriched so that notice and consent can do the work for which it is best suited.

Until now, the greatest obligation of data gatherers was either to anonymize data and pull it outside various privacy requirements or to inform and obtain consent. After charting the increasing difficulty of fulfilling these obligations in the face of big data, we presented the ultimate challenge: not of practical difficulty but of irrelevance. Where, for example, anonymizing data, adopting pseudonyms, or granting or withholding consent makes no difference to outcomes for an individual, we had better be sure that the outcomes in question can be defended as morally and politically legitimate. When anonymity and consent do make a difference, we learn from the domain of scientific integrity that simply because someone is anonymous or pseudonymous, or has consented, does not by itself legitimate the action in question.

We have argued that background and context-driven rights and obligations have been neglected in favor of anonymity and consent to the detriment of individuals and social integrity. Although our chapter will be deeply vexing to those who have placed anonymization and consent at the foundation of privacy protection, we welcome the shift in focus to the purposes to which data practices are being put and how these comport with individual interests as well as ethical, political, and context-driven values.

Acknowledgments

The authors gratefully acknowledge research support from Intel Science and Technology Center for Social Computing, DHHS Strategic Healthcare Information Technology Advanced Research Projects on Security (SHARPS), NSF Cyber-Trust Collaborative Research (CNS-0831124), and Lady Davis Trust, The Hebrew University of Jerusalem.

Bibliography

Acquisti, Alessandro, and Jens Grossklags. "Privacy and Rationality in Individual Decision Making." *IEEE Security and Privacy Magazine* 3, no. 1 (2005): 26–33.

Anderson, Janna, and Lee Rainie. *The Future of Big Data*. Washington, DC: Pew Research Center, 2012.

Aperjis, Christina, and Bernardo A. Huberman. "A Market for Unbiased Private Data: Paying Individuals According to Their Privacy Attitudes." *First Monday* 17, no. 5 (2012). https://firstmonday.org/ojs/index.php/fm/article/view/4013.

Bakos, Yannis, Florencia Marotta-Wurgler, and David R. Trossen. "Does Anyone Read the Fine Print? Testing a Law and Economics Approach to Standard Form Contracts." *SSRN Electronic Journal*, August 4, 2009. https://papers.ssrn.com/sol3/papers.cfm?abstract_id=1443256.

Barocas, Solon. "Data Mining: An Annotated Bibliography." Prepared for Cyber-Surveillance in Everyday Life: An International Workshop. University of Toronto, Ontario, Canada, May 12–15, 2011. http://www.digitallymediatedsurveillance.ca/wpcontent/uploads/2011/04/Barocas_Data_Mining_Annotated_Bibliography.pdf.

Barocas, Solon. "How Data Mining Discriminates." In "Data Mining: Episteme, Ethos, and Ethics." Ph.D. diss., New York University, 2014.

Barocas, Solon, and Helen Nissenbaum. "On Notice: The Trouble with Notice and Consent." Presented at Engaging Data: First International Forum on the Application and Management of Personal Electronic Information, Cambridge, MA, October 12–13, 2009.

Bollier, David. *The Promise and Peril of Big Data.* Washington, DC: The Aspen Institute, 2010.

boyd, danah. "Networked Privacy." Presented at the Personal Democracy Forum 2011, New York University, June 6–7, 2011.

boyd, danah, and Kate Crawford. "Critical Questions for Big Data." *Information, Communication, and Society* 15, no. 5 (2012): 662–79.

Cate, Fred H., and Viktor Mayer-Schönberger. "Notice and Consent in a World of Big Data." *International Data Privacy Law* 3, no. 2 (2013): 67–73.

Cranor, Lorrie Faith. "Can Users Control Online Behavioral Advertising Effectively?" *IEEE Security and Privacy Magazine* 10, no. 2 (2012): 93–96.

Cranor, Lorrie Faith. "Necessary but Not Sufficient: Standardized Mechanisms for Privacy Notice and Choice." *Journal on Telecommunications and High Technology Law* 10, no. 2 (2012): 273–445.

Crawford, Kate, and Jason Schultz. "Big Data and Due Process: Toward a Framework to Redress Predictive Privacy Harms." *Boston College Law Review* 55, no. 1 (2014): 93–128.

Dalessandro, Brian. "The Science of Privacy." *Ad: Tech* (blog), July 30, 2013. http://blog.ad-tech.com/the-science-of-privacy/.

"'Drinking from a Fire Hose': Has Consumer Data Mining Gone Too Far?" Knowledge@Wharton, November 22, 2011. http://knowledge.wharton. upenn.edu/article/drinking-from-a-fire-hose-has-consumer-data-mining-gone-too-far/.

Duhigg, Charles. "How Companies Learn Your Secrets." *New York Times Magazine*, February 16, 2012.

Dwork, Cynthia. "Differential Privacy." In *Proceedings of the 33rd International Conference on Automata, Languages and Programming*, part 2, 1–12. Berlin: Springer, 2006.

Dwork, Cynthia. "A Firm Foundation for Private Data Analysis." *Communications of the ACM* 54, no. 1 (2011): 86.

Dwork, Cynthia, and Deirdre K. Mulligan. "It's Not Privacy, and It's Not Fair." *Stanford Law Review Online* 66 (2013): 35–40.

El Emam, Khaled, Elizabeth Jonker, Luk Arbuckle, and Bradley Malin. "A Systematic Review of Re-Identification Attacks on Health Data." *PLOS ONE* 6, no. 12 (2011): e28071.

Gandy, Oscar H. *Coming to Terms with Chance: Engaging Rational Discrimination and Cumulative Disadvantage*. Burlington, VT: Ashgate, 2009.

Gandy, Oscar H., Jr. "Consumer Protection in Cyberspace." *TripleC: Communication, Capitalism and Critique* 9, no. 2 (2011): 175–89.

Gutwirth, Serge, and Paul Hert. "Regulating Profiling in a Democratic Constitutional State." In *Profiling the European Citizen: Cross-Disciplinary Perspectives*, edited by Mireille Hildebrandt and Serge Gutwirth, 289. Dordrecht: Springer, 2008.

Gutwirth, Serge, and Mireille Hildebrandt. "Some Caveats on Profiling." In *Data Protection in a Profiled World*, edited by Serge Gutwirth, Yves Poullet, and Paul de Hert, 31–41. Dordrecht: Springer, 2010.

Hey, Tony, Stewart Tansley, and Kristin Tolle, eds. *The Fourth Paradigm: Data-Intensive Scientific Discovery*. Redmond, WA: Microsoft Research, 2009.

Hildebrandt, Mireille. "Defining Profiling: A New Type of Knowledge?" In *Profiling the European Citizen: Cross-Disciplinary Perspectives*, edited by Mireille Hildebrandt and Serge Gutwirth, 17–45. Dordrecht: Springer, 2008.

Hildebrandt, Mireille. "Profiling and AmI." In *The Future of Identity in the Information Society*, edited by Kai Rannenberg, Denis Royer, and André Deuker, 273–310. Berlin: Springer, 2009.

Hildebrandt, Mireille. "Who Is Profiling Who? Invisible Visibility." In *Reinventing Data Protection?*, edited by Serge Gutwirth, Yves Poullet,

Paul de Hert, Cécile de Terwangne, and Sjaak Nouwt, 239–52. Dordrecht: Springer, 2009.

Horvát, Emöke-Ágnes, Michael Hanselmann, Fred A. Hamprecht, and Katharina A. Zweig. "One Plus One Makes Three (for Social Networks)." *PLOS ONE* 7, no. 4 (2012): e34740.

Jernigan, Carter, and Behram F. T. Mistree. "Gaydar: Facebook Friendships Expose Sexual Orientation." *First Monday* 14, no. 10 (2009). https://firstmonday.org/article/view/2611/2302.

Lerman, Jonas. "Big Data and Its Exclusions." *Stanford Law Review Online* 66 (2013): 55–63.

Manson, Neil C., and Onora O'Neill. *Rethinking Informed Consent in Bioethics*. New York: Cambridge University Press, 2012.

Manyika, James, Michael Chui, Brad Brown, Jacques Bughin, Richard Dobbs, Charles Roxburgh, and Angela Hung Byers. *Big Data: The Next Frontier for Innovation, Competition, and Productivity*. Washington, DC: McKinsey Global Institute, 2011.

Marx, Gary. "What's in a Name? Some Reflections on the Sociology of Anonymity." *The Information Society* 15, no. 2 (May 1999): 99–112.

Mayer-Schönberger, Viktor, and Kenneth Cukier. *Big Data: A Revolution That Will Transform How We Live, Work, and Think*. New York: Houghton Mifflin Harcourt, 2013.

McDonald, Aleecia M., and Lorrie Faith Cranor. "The Cost of Reading Privacy Policies." *I/S: A Journal of Law and Policy for the Information Society* 4, no. 3 (2008): 540–65.

McDonald, Aleecia M., R. W. Reeder, P. G. Kelley, and Lorrie Faith Cranor. "A Comparative Study of Online Privacy Policies and Formats." *Lecture Notes in Computer Science*, no. 5672 (2009): 37–55.

Mislove, Alan, Bimal Viswanath, Krishna P. Gummadi, and Peter Druschel. "You Are Who You Know: Inferring User Profiles in Online Social Networks." *Proceedings of the Third ACM International Conference on Web Search and Data Mining*, 251–60. New York: ACM Press, 2010.

Narayanan, Arvind, and Vitaly Shmatikov. "Myths and Fallacies of 'Personally Identifiable Information.'" *Communications of the ACM* 53, no. 6 (2010): 24–26.

Narayanan, Arvind, and Vitaly Shmatikov. "Robust De-Anonymization of Large Sparse Datasets." In *Proceedings—IEEE Symposium on Security and Privacy*, 111–25. Piscataway, NJ: IEEE, 2008.

Nissenbaum, Helen. "A Contextual Approach to Privacy Online." *Daedalus* 140, no. 4 (2011): 32–48.

Nissenbaum, Helen. "The Meaning of Anonymity in an Information Age." *Information Society* 15, no. 2 (1999): 141–44.

Nissenbaum, Helen. *Privacy in Context: Technology, Policy, and the Integrity of Social Life*. Stanford, CA: Stanford University Press, 2010.

Nolan, Rachel. "Behind the Cover Story: How Much Does Target Know?" *New York Times*, February 21, 2012. http://6thfloor.blogs.nytimes.com/2012/02/21/behind-the-cover-story-how-much-does-target-know/.

OECD. "The Evolving Privacy Landscape: 30 Years after the OECD Privacy Guidelines." OECD Digital Economy Papers, no. 176, April 6, 2011.

Ohm, Paul. "Broken Promises of Privacy: Responding to the Surprising Failure of Anonymization." *UCLA Law Review* 57, no. 6 (2010): 1701–77.

Rubinstein, Ira. "Big Data: The End of Privacy or a New Beginning?" *International Data Privacy Law* 3, no. 2 (2013): 74–87.

Singer, Natasha. "Acxiom, the Quiet Giant of Consumer Database Marketing." *New York Times*, June 16, 2012.

Solove, Daniel J. "Privacy Self-Management and the Consent Dilemma." *Harvard Law Review* 126, no. 7 (2013): 1880, 1883–86.

Steel, Emily, and Julia Angwin. "On the Web's Cutting Edge, Anonymity in Name Only." *Wall Street Journal*, August 4, 2010.

Steiner, Christopher. *Automate This: How Algorithms Came to Rule Our World*. New York: Portfolio/Penguin, 2012.

Sweeney, Latanya. "K-Anonymity: A Model for Protecting Privacy." *International Journal of Uncertainty, Fuzziness, and Knowledge-Based Systems* 10, no. 5 (2002): 557–70.

Tavani, Herman T. "KDD, Data Mining, and the Challenge for Normative Privacy." *Ethics and Information Technology* 1, no. 4 (1999): 265–73.

Tech America Foundation. *Demystifying Big Data: A Practical Guide to Transforming the Business of Government*. Washington, DC: Tech America Foundation, 2012.

Tene, Omer, and Jules Polonetsky. "Big Data for All: Privacy and User Control in the Age of Analytics." *Northwestern Journal of Technology and Intellectual Property* 11, no. 5 (2013): 239–72.

Tene, Omer, and Jules Polonetsky. "Judged by the Tin Man: Individual Rights in the Age of Big Data." *Journal on Telecommunications and High Technology Law*, August 15, 2013.

Tene, Omer, and Jules Polonetsky. "A Theory of Creepy: Technology, Privacy and Shifting Social Norms." *Journal on Telecommunications and High Technology Law*, September 16, 2013.

Tene, Omer, and Jules Polonetsky. "To Track or 'Do Not Track': Advancing Transparency and Individual Control in Online Behavioral Advertising." *Minnesota Journal of Law, Science and Technology* 13, no. 1 (2013): 281–357.

Valentino-Devries, Jennifer, and Jeremy Singer-Vine. "They Know What You're Shopping For." *Wall Street Journal*, December 7, 2012.

Waxer, Cindy. "Big Data Blues: The Dangers of Data Mining." *Computerworld*, November 4, 2013. https://www.computerworld.com/article/2485493/enterprise-applications-big-data-blues-the-dangers-of-data-mining.html.

Yakowitz, Jane. "Tragedy of the Data Commons." *Harvard Journal of Law and Technology* 25, no. 1 (2012): 1–67.

Zarsky, Tal Z. "Desperately Seeking Solutions: Using Implementation-Based Solutions for the Troubles of Information Privacy in the Age of Data Mining and the Internet Society." *Maine Law Review* 56, no. 1 (2004): 14–59.

Zarsky, Tal Z. "'Mine Your Own Business!': Making the Case for the Implications of the Data Mining of Personal Information in the Forum of Public Opinion." *Yale Journal of Law and Technology* 5 (2004): 1–57.

A List of Famous Artists

Who Used to Be Invigilators

Famous Artists Who Used to Be Invigilators[1]
Listed by Date of Birth

[1] Invigilator is the British term for Art Gallery Security Guard

Karl Knaths—Art Institute of Chicago
Beauford Delaney—Whitney, New York
Louise Bourgeois (docent)—Louvre, Paris
LeLand Bell—Museum of Non-Objective Painting
  (later the Guggenheim), New York
Charles Brady—Metropolitan Museum of Art, New York
Francois-Xavier Lalanne—Louvre, Paris
Regina Bogat (docent)—Whitney, New York
Nicholas Krushenick—Whitney, Met, MoMA,
  all New York
Robert Ryman—MoMA, New York
Willem De Looper—Phillips Collection, Washington, DC
Dan Flavin—MoMA, American Museum of Natural
  History, both New York
Hans Haacke—Documenta 2, Kassel
Gene Beery—MoMA, New York
Robert Mangold—MoMA, New York
Brice Marden—Jewish Museum, New York
Mel Bochner—Jewish Museum, New York
Haim Steinbach—Dia, New York
Allan McCollum—Whitney, New York
Eric Fischl—Chicago Museum of Contemporary Art
Kevin Atherton—Whitechapel Gallery, London
David Ward—Serpentine Gallery, London
John Miller—Dia, New York
Fred Wilson—Neuberger Museum, New York
Chris Martin—unkown
Alison Turnbull—Serpentine Gallery, London
Donald Baechler—Dia, New York
Cerith Wyn Evans—Tate, London
Charles LeDray—Seattle Art Museum
Mamma Andersson—Moderna Museet, Östasiatiska
  Museet, Nationalmuseum, Stockholm
Rachel Whiteread—Serpentine Gallery, London
Andrea Fraser—Dia, New York
Dominique Gonzalez-Foerster—unkown, Grenoble
Dean Marsh—Wallace Collection, London

Ceal Floyer—ICA, London
David Shrigley—CCA, Glasgow
Marianne Heier—National Museum of Art, Architecture and Design, Oslo
Wade Guyton—Dia, New York
Anna Barriball—Serpentine Gallery, London
Jessica Dickinson—Metropolitan Museum of Art, New York
Laura Aldridge—Serpentine Gallery, London
Rashaad Newsome—Contemporary Arts Center, New Orleans
Nate Lowman—Dia, New York
Ryan Mosley—National Gallery, London
Daniel Turner—New Museum, New York
Dan Shaw-Town—unkown, London
They Are Here—Whitechapel Gallery, London
Nils Guadagnin—Mackintosh Museum, Glasgow

Famous Artists Who Were Gallery Assistants

Vincent van Gogh (clerk) — Goupil and Cie, Paris
Jackson Pollock (framer, visitor counter) — Museum of Non-Objective Painting (later the Guggenheim), New York
Nigel Henderson (assistant picture restorer) — National Gallery, Washington, DC
Henry Mundy (gallery assistant) — AIA Gallery, London
Larry Rivers (delivery man) — "an art supply shop"
Alex Katz (carver) — "a frame shop"
Sol LeWitt (night desk) — MoMA, New York
Claes Oldenburg (library assistant) — Cooper Union, New York
John Button (front desk) — MoMA, New York
Gillian Ayres (gallery assistant) — AIA Gallery, London
Richard Anuszkiewicz (model restorer) — Metropolitan Museum of Art, New York
Ruth Wolf-Rehfeldt (department for exhibitions) — Academy of Arts East Berlin
Joan Jonas (assistant to Richard Bellamy) — Green Gallery, New York
Richard Tuttle (assistant to Betty Parsons) — Betty Parsons Gallery, New York
Stephen Willats (gallery assistant) — Drian Galleries, London
Ib Benoh (assistant to Betty Parsons) — Betty Parsons Gallery, New York
Harvey Tulcensky (art handler) — MoMA, New York
Louise Lawler (administrative assistant) — Metro Pictures, New York
Cindy Sherman (bookkeeper) — Hallwalls, Buffalo, New York; (receptionist) — Artists Space, New York
Jeff Koons (ticket seller, membership desk) — MoMA, New York
Christopher D'Arcangelo (technician and cleaner) — John Webber Gallery, New York
Mark Flood (museum assistant) — Menil Collection, Houston, Texas

Keith Haring (gallery assistant) — Tony Shafrazi Gallery, New York
Jack Pierson (gallery assistant) — Pat Hearn Gallery, New Yrok
Adam Fuss (waiter at previews) — MoMA, New York
Cary Leibowitz, "Candy Ass" (print specialist) — Christie's, New York
Damien Hurst (technician) — Anthony d'Offay Gallery, London
Andrea Zittel (gallery assistant) — Pat Hearn Gallery, New York
Alec Soth (darkroom technician) — Minneapolis Institute of Art
Oscar Murillo (installer) — "small local galleries in East London"
Khadija Saye (intern) — PEER, London

A Provisional List of Artists Who Had Jobs That Are Similar, in Some Aspects, to Invigilation

Henri Rousseau was a toll collector
Henry Darger was a hospital janitor
Abraham Rattner was a porter
Dorothea Tanning was an extra in films
Jackson Pollock was a school janitor
Agnes Martin was a janitor
Philip Guston was an extra in films
Ellsworth Kelly was a janitor
Edward Paolozzi was a fire watcher (per the Ashmolean Museum)
Edward Kienholz was an attendant in a mental institution
Malcolm Morley was a prisoner in Wormwood Scrubs for three years
Mihail Chemiakin was a night watchman
Ai Weiwei was a babysitter
Stewart Home was a life model
Conrad Shawcross was an extra in films

A Partial List of Exhibitions of Works by Invigilators

Turpentine (2003), Studio Voltaire, by current and former Serpentine Gallery invigilators

Private: Staff Only (2006), private areas at the ICA, by all staff members at the ICA

Guard Art II: Guards Gone Wild (2007), SSCA Gallery, by museum guards from the Minneapolis Institute of Arts, the Walker Art Center, and the Frederick R. Weisman Art Museum

SW!PE MAGAZINE: Guards Matter (2010), 25CPW, by Met museum guards

Guardists (2011), Towson Arts Collective, by security personnel at the Baltimore Museum of Art

The Invigilators (2012), Glasgow School of Art, by Mackintosh Museum invigilators

Inside Job (2018), Tate Modern, by all staff members at Tate

A Partial List of Invigilators Who Are/Were Other Things

Authors
Sara Baume
Thomas Brusig
Frank O'Hara
Imogen Hermes Gowar
Nicolas Fargues
Thomas Beller
John Freeman
Peter Rock
Paul T. Gilbert
Jen Miller

Filmmakers/Directors
Ken Russell
Kurt Kren

Musicians
Pavement (band)
Hindi Zahra

Comedians
Alistair McGowan
Kevin Allison

Actors
Rob Corddry

Graphic Novelists
Karl Stevens

Poets
Janette Ayachi
Graham Foust

Journalists
Russ Pitts

Textile Designers
Maija Isola

Poster Designers
Lee Corklin

Reality Television Stars
Garland Brown

Boxers
Dick Tiger

Art Critics
Jerry Saltz
Michael Archer

Anonymity as an Everyday Phenomenon and as a Topic of Research

> All relationships of people to each other rest, as a matter of course, upon the precondition that they know something about each other.
>
> Georg Simmel
> *The Sociology of Georg Simmel*

Anonymity as a Term and a Practice

Anonymity is foremost not a sociological or philosophical concept but an everyday term with very different meanings for the people involved. The different studies on the topic, some of which also aim to develop the term from a theoretical perspective, illustrate that anonymity points to practices of very different qualities in everyday life based on the areas treated in them, ranging from activism and authorship to self-help groups and sperm donation. In contrast to some other everyday terms, which have been taken up and developed scientifically, anonymity has largely remained without reference in social and cultural theory to date. The relevant handbooks also illustrate that anonymity as a sociological concept might need to be developed and supplemented from a theoretical perspective. To begin with, however, I would like to share a perspective on how anonymity has so far been a topic in the social sciences, especially in the social theory of modernity.

Those who are often quoted as social science pioneers of anonymity, particularly sociologists Georg Simmel and Zygmunt Bauman, do not define the term.[1] Simmel, who is seen as a founder of sociology, does not use the term in his studies; rather, he argues from a phenomenological point of view. Bauman, a widely read and well-received sociologist who, with more than ninety years of life, has observed societal developments over a span of time longer than hardly anyone else can claim, does use the term, at least sporadically, but in a more general manner, such as when he takes a look at estrangement from the social and humane, never in the sense of sociological work on the theory of the concept.[2] In total, anonymity is not given a significant role in either the development of early sociological theory on modernity or its aftermath, yet it has not gone without notice, even if only implicitly so.[3]

In Simmel's works, different figures of thought become apparent that were later taken up as important dimensions

1 Georg Simmel, "Money in Modern Culture," *Theory, Culture and Society* 8, no. 3 (1991), first published 1900 as "Philosophie des Geldes"; Georg Simmel, "The Metropolis and Mental Life," in *The Blackwell City Reader*, ed. Gary Bridge und Sophie Watson, Blackwell Readers in Geography (Malden, MA: Blackwell Publishing, 2002), 11–19, first published 1903 as "Die Großstädte und das Geistesleben";
Zygmunt Bauman, "Modernity and Ambivalence," *Theory, Culture and Society* 7, no. 2 (1990): 143–69;
Zygmunt Bauman, "Making and Unmaking of Strangers," *Thesis Eleven* 43, no. 1 (1995): 1–16;
and Zygmunt Bauman, "Identity in the Globalising World," *Social Anthropology* 9, no. 2 (2001): 121–29.
The sociologists who are named in this chapter have worked at very different times, so their lines of argumentation partly build on each other but also partly differentiate and modify each other. In the interest of readability, this contribution forgoes a detailed presentation of the individual respective reception and presents only selective references. To aid in orientation, readers may wish to refer to the dates of publication of the references used, as well as to the overview at the end of this chapter of sociological theorists quoted here, with their individual biographical details.

2 Zygmunt Bauman, "Is This the End of Anonymity?" *The Guardian*, June 28, 2011.

3 The term modernity has rightly been criticized in many regards (e.g., Shmuel N. Eisenstadt, "The Civilizational Dimension of Modernity: Modernity as a Distinct Civilization," *International Sociology* 16, no. 3 [2001]:

of anonymity. These make the individualization and subjectification of humanity a topic by means of and based on several interlinked developments in the constitutional phase of modernity—the spread of the money economy; the dissolution of the traditional, rather more rurally characterized economic systems and living conditions; the growth and thus increasing heterogeneity of cities; the budding of mass production, mass consumption, and mass society; and others that Simmel witnessed and made the starting point of his scholarly observations. The observation of these developments is characterized by a central moment of tension, the motive of the freedom connected to it for humanity as a positive state, free from estatist constraints on the one hand, and on the other, from the necessity of making oneself at home in this new freedom in order not to become lost in the mass of the urban population, not to lose face in it. At stake is the Janus-faced character of the developing mass society's freedoms and the psychological demands placed on the identity work of individuals here. At its center, modernity is about being able to locate oneself, to gain a place and a face among the many in order not to lose oneself. The loneliness and estrangement of modern humans from their contemporaries in an urban environment become apparent as key themes in Simmel's thinking, even if he does not use the terms. This can be demonstrated in Georg Simmel's elaborations on the increasing spread of money—a central part of his sociological studies from today's point of view. Money as a symbolically generated medium formalizes and standardizes relationships of exchange. It can thus be used as an abstract medium for all interests of exchange to fulfill our own needs, such as the need for goods, without having to enter into a personal relationship with the fulfiller of those needs, such as the owner of the goods. The exchange of goods can thus be organized solely based on the goods and the market, without distinguishing particular people or the character of the trader. The symbolically generated exchange of money for goods independent of personal relationships is an important precondition for the

320–40); however, no other term so far has evolved from this criticism to grasp, as modernity does, the developments of the Enlightenment, rationalization through technology and science, the development of a national state supported by the military, and secularization. I use the term here to refer to these phenomena, albeit in recognition of the problems connected with it, such as its Eurocentric point of view as well as the temporal disparities of these developments in different parts of the world.

development of mass consumption, the beginnings of which Simmel witnessed. In a way, both buyer and seller thus remain—not necessarily, but usually—anonymous in the innumerous situations of purchase that are common today, from the department store to online trading. They do not enter into a relationship with each other that transcends the trade and only know of each other in an abstract way, without any individuality.

If anonymity was discussed in Simmel's time, it referred to the identifiability of authors and creators—for instance, in the context of the (missing) freedom of the press— or in tenders and contests engaged in using pseudonyms.[4] With the sociological thematization of modernity also came an extension of what is understood as anonymity, including impersonal forms of relationships that disregard individual identities, depersonalizing or ignoring them, as well as forms of relationships and life in a mass society, which can be described as anonymous. These meanings, however, did not yet appear in Simmel's work but were simply a consequence of his description of the phenomenon in which a central sociological problem becomes apparent: How do people organize their relationships without knowing one another? How does socialization occur in these circumstances? And how do they orient themselves in the social structure in times of rapid political, technological, and economic change, when traditional ties of estate and familial life forms are dissolving? Simmel stated that people need to know about one another to enter into relationships, which in sociology becomes the question, How do people (in modernity) know about one another, and how does this influence their actions with and toward each other? Considerations of relationships and individual handling of them already take quite a bit of space in Simmel. A paradigmatic example is his considerations of the "stranger," which has remained his central figure of societal-theoretical reflection in theoretical work in sociology.[5]

[4] See also, for example, K. Kern, "Die Anonymität bei Konkurrenzen," *Wochenblatt* (Architektenverein, Berlin) 1, no. 24 (1867): 229–30.

[5] Georg Simmel, *Soziologie: Untersuchungen über die Formen der Vergesellschaftung*, Suhrkamp Taschenbuch Wissenschaft 811, 8th ed. (1908; Frankfurt: Suhrkamp, 2016).

Different Forms of Knowing about Each Other

Social theory of the interwar era is interested in understanding this changed relationship in the transition from "traditional" to "modern" ways of living, and in grasping it terminologically. The new relationship between traders and buyers, or consumers, which originated with money as a means of exchange and which, in everyday language, would probably be described as anonymous, has become the norm. Moreover, this type of relationship has emerged as the norm of coexistence in urban environments, in which people encounter and interact with each other on a large scale every day without knowing one another. How can coexistence take place in such a situation? What is necessary for people not to lose their orientation in such situations and remain able to act? How does socialization take place, and what demands does this place on people in terms of coping psychologically? These are the questions that sociology asks as a consequence of societal changes, which Simmel describes in such an impressive manner that his considerations continue to be adopted to this day. Against the backdrop of the premise that people's relationships rest on knowing about each other, new forms of knowing about each other have to develop in modern living conditions, a fact that becomes apparent in cities. Urban dwellers must act constitutively in their socialization, that is, in a structure-incorporating way that stabilizes the social structure and forms institutions. The relationship between buyer and seller in a consumer society, or the encounters between strangers, which is termed as anonymous in everyday language, is described more generally and less judgmentally in sociology with the concept of the *symbolically generalized other*. To perceive the other in a symbolically generalized manner means to see him or her as an ideal type, as a social figure—as a stranger, buyer, trader, factory worker, citizen, vagabond—and to act accordingly. The other is classified according to what one knows (stereotypically) about this societal figure. The recourse to stereotypical images aids in reducing social complexity in a mass society, which differentiates into ever more diverse forms of living. In the works of the sociologists who deal with the symbolically generalized other, anonymity has not become a category of social thinking but is seen as an everyday phenomenon quickly dissolved in the framework of personal, individually shaped encounters and as something that can be overcome.[6] The symbolically generalized other is the conceptual starting point for considerations in sociology in general on how social order is known and translated into action in a mass society, which tends to be confusing. Departing from this, in further sociological thinking, highly different answers on how socialization takes place have been deduced, such as social constructivism and systems theory.[7] In the face of the magnitude of current societies as well as the mobility of today's world, the state of being a symbolically generalized other has to be seen as normality. Life as a stranger has become the original mode of being, as Zygmunt Bauman states in his considerations on today's societies, which he terms postmodern.[8] In this sense, and in an everyday language turn on Bauman's insights, anonymity can thus be assumed to be a normal situation that is inherent to today's way of life in cities and that furthermore has become an everyday reality in many other places as well. The stranger in this is a social figure, that is, a figure who is characteristic for this time. From exile, Austrian-born American sociologist Alfred Schütz describes life as a stranger as being a difference in knowing and a lack of intimacy with the fundamental assumptions that guide everyday life in another country.[9] In this context, his use of the term anonymity is instructive. It takes place in the context of the unknown and refers to both observed behavior as well as typecasting of behaviors for successful communication.[10] "Anonymous" is used here as a differentiation from the individual; it refers to the exemplary and typical in behavior that explicitly *does not belong to identity but to the intersubjective in-between sphere of conventions and social relations* between individuals. In this, conventions are learned to facilitate

[6] Alfred Schütz, *The Phenomenology of the Social World* (1932; Evanston, IL: Northwestern University Press, 1967); Alfred Schuetz, "The Stranger: An Essay in Social Psychology," *American Journal of Sociology* 49, no. 6 (1944): 499–507; Talcott Parsons, Edward Albert Shils, and Neil J. Smelser, *Toward a General Theory of Action: Theoretical Foundations for the Social Sciences* (Piscataway, NJ: Transaction, 1965); and Niklas Luhmann, *Vertrauen: Ein Mechanismus der Reduktion sozialer Komplexität* (Stuttgart: Verlag, 1968).

[7] Peter L. Berger and Thomas Luckmann, *The Social Construction of Reality: A Treatise in the Sociology of Knowledge* (Garden City, NY: Anchor Books, 1967); Talcott Parsons, *Structure and Process in Modern Societies* (New York: Free Press, 1960); and Niklas Luhmann, *Soziale Systeme* (Frankfurt: Suhrkamp, 1984).

[8] Zygmunt Bauman, *Intimations of Postmodernity* (London: Routledge, 1992); and Zygmunt Bauman, *Postmodernity and Its Discontents* (Cambridge: Polity Press, 1997).

[9] Schuetz, "Stranger."

[10] Ibid., 503, 505.

mutual security in terms of behavior and to ritualize socially typical behaviors. "For the strangers the observed actors within the approached group are not—as for their co-actors—of a certain presupposed anonymity, namely, mere performers of typical functions, but individuals."[11] Anonymity is understood as a dimension of behaviors and relationships between social figures and thus faces the individual with his or her specific personhood (neither individuality nor identity).

Even if anonymity is not explicitly reflected as a category of modern social theory, it is nevertheless implicit in sociological thinking. Anonymity is a relational state between social figures, that is, between the symbolically generalized others, while knowledge about their individual positions in the social order defines the frame of reference for behaviors and interactions in this encounter. Without having further information about each other's lives, individuals who are unknown to each other can thus nevertheless enter into more or less appropriate personal contact with each other. Anonymity is given when the personal, in the sense of a particular social role within society, is put into the foreground and individual identity is blinded out of the encounter, as well as when one speaks and acts based on typecasting and stereotypes. A specific knowledge about the relationship with the other is at base here. In sociological social theory, the term anonymity is thus extended and elaborated as a figure of deindividualized social relationships between strangers. This elaboration, however, remains implicit and is not further theorized. It complements and stands next to the understanding of anonymity as a lack of identifiability that occurs in everyday urban life, accidentally or on purpose (for instance, through the use of pseudonyms or other strategies of hiding).

[11] Ibid., 506.

Freedom and the Price of Being a Social Figure

Encountering the other as a social figure and thus de-individualized, reduced to social standing and anonymity, carries degrees of freedom that facilitate the exuberant life in cities that Simmel describes. Because direct personal relationships play less of a role there, a space has developed in which new behaviors and concepts of identity can be explored. Society thus becomes more diverse, and social orders continue to fan out, which in turn lets social complexity continue to grow. This occurs at the price of reduction to the exemplary and deindividualized encounters, linked with the danger of being perceived only as a part of the masses and dissolving in it. A contemporary of Georg Simmel, the journalist, intellectual, and film theorist Siegfried Kracauer, born in 1889, about thirty years after Simmel, takes a similar perspective. Kracauer is also interested in the changes emerging with modernization and is fascinated by the loss of individuality. He speaks of the "ornament of the masses," which formed in the entertainment industry with the origin of large stage shows and cinema performances in the time between the wars and thus points to the estrangement of the individual as a small cog in the gears that went along with these developments.[12] Even though Kracauer does not elaborate his considerations on anonymity further in his oeuvre, he stands exemplary for other intellectuals and scientists and their observations of the emergence of anonymity between the world wars. They have addressed in different ways the idea of anonymity, which has inscribed itself as a topos in the thinking of critical social theory and philosophy in multiple ways. Even without becoming a key concept in sociology, anonymity remains a central element in the writings of scholars in sociology and philosophy during the postwar years, such as Hannah Arendt, Zygmunt Bauman, and many others who cope with societal changes in mass societies related to industrial production, Fordist work regimes, and capitalist economic systems as typical

[12] Siegfried Kracauer, *The Mass Ornament: Weimar Essays* (1927; Cambridge, MA: Harvard University Press, 1995).

features of modernism.[13] The negative consequences of mass societies with the anonymous imperatives of the systems, the market, and the state are critically and intensely reflected in these scholars' works. The main representatives of the Frankfurt school—notably Theodor Adorno, Max Horkheimer, and later Jürgen Habermas—have outlined in detail these problematic aspects as a general fundamental characteristic of modern rationality.[14] This indirect problematization of anonymity as an estranging effect of systems in modern societies, markets, and states, and these societies' loss of a collective cohabitation orientation, continues in the tension between freedom and estrangement as it is linked to the term anonymity in everyday language. As a consequence of the insight generated through sociological studies, sociology certainly contributes to designing such social figures and to making them describable in a social statistical manner.[15]

The (New) Relevance of Anonymity

For anonymity as discussed in modernity social theory, the digital turn has brought new qualities that have probably caused the current heightened attention to the topic. In this discussion, two dimensions of anonymity have become apparent, which are not synonymous and can be distinguished from each other. One dimension, which I describe as mode 1, aligns anonymity conceptually to nonidentifiability of an individual, a topic that emerges under the impression of new modes of surveillance and traceability resulting from the digital data economy; nonidentifiability seems to be the only shelter against tracking and surveillance. In the other dimension, mode 2, the understanding of anonymity emphasizes deindividualized action toward a typified fellow being in the sense of social figures, which is an outcome of the social theory of modernity, as outlined above.

[13] Hannah Arendt, *The Origins of Totalitarianism* (New York: Houghton Mifflin Harcourt, 1973); and Zygmunt Bauman, *Modernity and the Holocaust* (Ithaca, NY: Cornell University Press, 1989).

[14] Max Horkheimer and Theodor W. Adorno, "The Culture Industry: Enlightenment as Mass Deception," 1947, in *Media and Cultural Studies: Keyworks*, ed. Meenakshi Gigi Durham and Douglas Kellner (Malden, MA: Blackwell, 2006), 41–72; Theodor W. Adorno and Max Horkheimer, "Kulturindustrie: Aufklärung als Massenbetrug," in *Dialektik der Aufklärung: Philosophische Fragmente* (Amsterdam: Querido, 1947), 108–50; Jürgen Habermas, *The Theory of Communicative Action*, vol. 2 (Boston, MA: Beacon Press, 1984); and Jürgen Habermas, *Moral Consciousness and Communicative Action* (Cambridge, MA: MIT Press, 1990).

[15] Stephan Moebius and Markus Schroer, eds., *Diven, Hacker, Spekulanten: Sozialfiguren der Gegenwart* (Berlin: Suhrkamp, 2010); and Jürgen Schupp, "25 Jahre Sozio-oekonomisches Panel – Ein Infrastrukturprojekt der empirischen Sozial- und Wirtschaftsforschung in Deutschland / Twenty-Five Years of the German Socio-Economic Panel—An Infrastructure Project for Empirical Social and Economic Research in Germany," *Zeitschrift für Soziologie* 38, no. 5 (2009): 350–57.

Mode 1

With the internet and other digital media, the identifiability and visibility of individuals has grown enormously; increasingly, these technologies facilitate transparency in individuals' ways of life. Each individual who is active on the internet carries the threat of a loss of anonymity, even if pseudonyms are used. This makes it necessary to rethink anonymity in times of digital communication.[16] The idea of a virtual community in the global village (McLuhan), which used to be thought of as a positive vision of a large interconnected translocal community that develops via the internet, has reappeared in new clothing, now associated with the less comfortable qualities of communal life: the manifold possibilities of social control in immediate proximity.[17] Through use of the internet, these possibilities are not limited to fellow beings in the immediate vicinity but are also open to many institutions hungry for information: the state, the economy, and the sciences have a great interest in the data available on the internet.[18] Against this background of new possibilities for identifiability and the threat of loss, the productivity of anonymity comes into the focus of cultural and social sciences, and the necessity of defining these possibilities and threats more closely is formulated.[19]

Mode 2

Because of available computer technologies with automatic evaluation options, new possibilities for typecasting have evolved, moving the second mode of anonymity to the center of attention with and through social theory considerations on the symbolically generalized other. Typecasting and deindividualized action because of this typecasting are principles of orientation in situations of high social complexity, not just in face-to-face relationships but also in internet communication. Typecasting can be generated even more efficiently based on parameters

[16] Helen Nissenbaum, "The Meaning of Anonymity in an Information Age," *Information Society* 15, no. 2 (1999): 141–44.

[17] Howard Rheingold, *The Virtual Community: Finding Connection in a Computerized World* (Boston, MA: Addison-Wesley, 1993).

[18] José van Dijck, "Datafication, Dataism and Dataveillance: Big Data between Scientific Paradigm and Ideology," *Surveillance and Society* 12, no. 2 (2014): 197–208.

[19] Götz Bachmann, Michi Knecht, and Andreas Wittel, "The Social Productivity of Anonymity," *ephemera* 17, no. 2 (2017).

evident in the data of internet users. Mode 2 of anonymity in encounters and in the actions of generalized others should initially be thought of as independent of the first mode of anonymity—the lack of identifiability, or potentially an identifiability generated only at a later stage. Although the interlacing of both modes of anonymity creates special efficiency, even without the identifiability of individuals, mode 2 alone—the typified treatment of internet users—enables the pursuit of manifold economic uses, such as in pricing policies, the steering of supply and demand, and the generation of consumer profiles. Equally, the biopolitical concerns of state supervision and regulation of population behavior are favored by information on the internet. Of interest here is the ornament of the masses, in regard to both economic use and governance approaches of the state.[20] The ornament of the masses rests on reducing, typecasting, and treating individuals independently of their individual circumstances of life in particular areas (e. g., shopping behavior, information behavior, etc.) according to these types. Amazingly, this dimension of anonymity (mode 2) presents but a marginal topic in current literature. Typecasting in particular, which can be undertaken based on internet data, is part of a significant moment of the political economy of the internet, even more so when linked with mode 1, loss of identifiability.[21]

For both understandings of anonymity, scenarios increasingly occur in everyday action that are experienced from an individual point of view as a (technocratic) limitation of degrees of freedom in social action and that entail corresponding perspectives in academic research.[22] Anonymity thus also becomes an object of theoretical considerations. These aim, for instance, at what constitutes "identifiers" and what it means to become identifiable.[23] Furthermore, anonymity in reference to interpersonal relationships and identity is discussed but not linked with social theoretical considerations. While social theorists have centered their understanding of modernity's sociological problem on how the growing societal complexity

[20] Kracauer, *Mass Ornament*.

[21] José van Dijck, *The Culture of Connectivity: A Critical History of Social Media* (Oxford: Oxford University Press, 2013).

[22] Nevertheless, expectations of anonymity may vary depending on the social standpoint. The child conceived through sperm donation and the father who remains unknown because of legal regulations will have quite different assessments on this.

[23] Gary T. Marx, "What's in a Name? Some Reflections on the Sociology of Anonymity," *Information Society* 15, no. 2 (1999): 99–112.

of mass society can be overcome individually and collectively by means of social forms of engagement, today's central problem is more about moral and ethical questions of anonymity. In this, the positive and negative forms of anonymity for a social entity are a topic not least from a philosophical point of view, insofar as it is about systematically determining different purpose-oriented qualities of anonymity.[24] At its base, in the overwhelming majority of studies, anonymity is about protecting current degrees of individual freedom from supervision by various information-hungry actors.[25]

Today, the term anonymity, as well as the changes that have without doubt constituted themselves in this figure of relationship in the course of modernity in the way in which individuals coexist, have moved more strongly into the focus of studies and theoretical considerations in sociological thinking—albeit without arriving at a precise definition of the term by means of conceptual inclusion in social theory considerations. The low degree of discriminatory power from a plenitude of aspects of the term "privacy" will most likely play a role in this; this term has been elaborated on comprehensively in the context of theories on the political public, which has been discussed for decades, particularly in the tradition of critical theory by different authors, and which has time and again been supplemented and made more precise as a theoretical concept. "Privacy" and "public" have thus proved to be a central duality in the organization of coexistence in today's societies as long as these are democratically organized and allow for civil society to have a sphere beyond state raison and economic instrumentalization. Anonymity, on the other hand, has remained a term of everyday life that presents an important and differently experienced quality in coexistence. The social practice in dealing with anonymity varies enormously across time, with manifold effects for different areas of life. A theoretical definition of the term anonymity has not been undertaken yet in the context of social theory of modernity. There is much to

[24] Nissenbaum, "Meaning of Anonymity"; Kathleen Wallace, "Anonymity," *Ethics and Information Technology* 1, no. 1 (1999): 31; Julie Ponesse, "Navigating the Unknown: Towards a Positive Conception of Anonymity," *Southern Journal of Philosophy* 51, no. 3 (2013): 344; and Julie Ponesse, "The Ties That Blind: Conceptualizing Anonymity," *Journal of Social Philosophy* 45, no. 3 (2014): 304–22.

[25] Paula Helm, "Transparenz und Anonymität: Potentiale, Grenzen, Irrtümer," *Forschungsjournal Soziale Bewegungen* 30, no. 2 (2017): 142–51; Catherine Frois, *The Anonymous Society: Identity, Transformation and Anonymity in 12 Steps* (Cambridge: Cambridge Scholars, 2009); Steve Matthews, "Anonymity and the Social Self," *American Philosophical Quarterly* 47, no. 4 (2010): 351–63; K. D. Haggerty and R. V. Ericson, "The Surveillant Assemblage," *British Journal of Sociology* 51 (2000): 605–22; and Finn Brunton and Helen Fay Nissenbaum, *Obfuscation: A User's Guide for Privacy and Protest* (Cambridge, MA: MIT Press, 2016).

be said for undertaking this endeavor against the background of social theory considerations of modernity.[26]

[26] Gertraud Koch and Anna Henke, "Disentangling Anonymity and Privacy: Theoretical Reflections in the Light of the Conceptual History of Both Terms" (discussion paper, December 11, 2017, University of Hamburg).

Social Theorists Mentioned in This Chapter

Simmel, Georg (March 1, 1858–September 26, 1918), German sociologist
Kracauer, Siegfried (February 8, 1889–November 26, 1966), German writer and sociologist
Horkheimer, Max (February 14, 1895–July 7, 1973) German philosopher
Schütz, Alfred (April 13, 1899–May 20, 1959), Austrian-born American sociologist and philosopher
Parsons, Talcott (December 13, 1902–May 8, 1979), American sociologist
Adorno, Theodor (September 11, 1903–August 6, 1969), German philosopher and music critic
Arendt, Hannah (October 14, 1906–December 4, 1975), German-born American political scientist
Bauman, Zygmunt (November 19, 1925–January 9, 2017), Polish-born sociologist
Luckmann, Thomas (October 14, 1927–May 10, 2016), German American sociologist
Luhmann, Niklas (December 8, 1927–November 6, 1998), German sociologist, educator, and legal and administrative scientist
Berger, Peter L. (March 17, 1929–June 27, 2017), Austrian American sociologist and philosopher
Habermas, Jürgen (born June 18, 1929), German philosopher and sociologist.

Notes

This chapter was translated by Stefanie Everke Buchanan.

Epigraph: Georg Simmel, *The Sociology of Georg Simmel*, trans., ed., and with an introduction by Kurt H. Wolff (New York: The Free Press, 1967), 307.

Bibliography

Adorno, Theodor W., and Max Horkheimer. "Kulturindustrie: Aufklärung als Massenbetrug." In *Dialektik der Aufklärung: Philosophische Fragmente*, 108–50. Amsterdam: Querido, 1947.

Arendt, Hannah. *The Origins of Totalitarianism*. New York: Houghton Mifflin Harcourt, 1973.

Bachmann, Götz, Michi Knecht, and Andreas Wittel. "The Social Productivity of Anonymity." *ephemera* 17, no. 2 (2017). http://www.ephemerajournal.org/contribution/social-productivity-anonymity.

Bauman, Zygmunt. *Modernity and the Holocaust*. Ithaca, NY: Cornell University Press, 1989.

Bauman, Zygmunt. "Modernity and Ambivalence." *Theory, Culture and Society* 7, no. 2 (1990): 143–69.

Bauman, Zygmunt. *Intimations of Postmodernity*. London: Routledge, 1992.

Bauman, Zygmunt. "Making and Unmaking of Strangers." *Thesis Eleven* 43, no. 1 (1995): 1–16.

Bauman, Zygmunt. *Postmodernity and Its Discontents*. Cambridge: Polity Press, 1997.

Bauman, Zygmunt. "Identity in the Globalising World." *Social Anthropology* 9, no. 2 (2001): 121–29.

Bauman, Zygmunt. "Is This the End of Anonymity?" *The Guardian*, June 28, 2011. https://www.theguardian.com/commentisfree/2011/jun/28/end-anonymity-technology-internet.

Berger, Peter L., and Thomas Luckmann. *The Social Construction of Reality: A Treatise in the Sociology of Knowledge*. Garden City, NY: Anchor Books, 1967.

Brunton, Finn, and Helen Fay Nissenbaum. *Obfuscation: A User's Guide for Privacy and Protest*. Cambridge, MA: MIT Press, 2016.

Eisenstadt, Shmuel N. "The Civilizational Dimension of Modernity: Modernity as a Distinct Civilization." *International Sociology* 16, no. 3 (2001): 320–40.

Frois, Catherine. *The Anonymous Society: Identity, Transformation and Anonymity in 12 Steps*. Cambridge: Cambridge Scholars, 2009.

Habermas, Jürgen. *The Theory of Communicative Action*. Vol. 2. Boston, MA: Beacon Press, 1984.

Habermas, Jürgen. *Moral Consciousness and Communicative Action*. Cambridge, MA: MIT Press, 1990.

Haggerty, K. D., and R. V. Ericson. "The Surveillant Assemblage." *British Journal of Sociology* 51 (2000): 605–22.

Helm, Paula. "Transparenz und Anonymität: Potentiale, Grenzen, Irrtümer." *Forschungsjournal Soziale Bewegungen* 30, no. 2 (2017): 142–51. https://doi.org/10.1515/fjsb-2017-0035.

Horkheimer, Max, and Theodor W. Adorno. "The Culture Industry: Enlightenment as Mass Deception." 1947. In *Media and Cultural Studies: Keyworks*, edited by Meenakshi Gigi Durham and Douglas Kellner, 41–72. Malden, MA: Blackwell, 2006.

Stier, H. "Die Anonymität bei Konkurrenzen." *Wochenblatt* (Architektenverein, Berlin) 1, no. 24 (1867): 229–30. https://books.google.de/books?id=mHc_AAAAcAAJ.

Koch, Gertraud, and Anna Henke. "Disentangling Anonymity and Privacy: Theoretical Reflections in the Light of the Conceptual History of Both Terms." Discussion paper, December 11, 2017. University of Hamburg. http://reconfiguring-anonymity.net/blog/wp-content/uploads/2018/01/Koch-Henke_2017_Disentangling-anonymity-and-privacy_DISCUSSION-PAPER.pdf.

Kracauer, Siegfried. *The Mass Ornament: Weimar Essays*. 1927. Cambridge, MA: Harvard University Press, 1995.

Luhmann, Niklas. *Vertrauen: Ein Mechanismus der reduktion sozialer Komplexität*. Stuttgart: Verlag, 1968.

Luhmann, Niklas. *Soziale systeme*. Frankfurt: Suhrkamp, 1984.

Marx, Gary T. "What's in a Name? Some Reflections on the Sociology of Anonymity." *Information Society* 15, no. 2 (1999): 99–112.

Matthews, Steve. "Anonymity and the Social Self." *American Philosophical Quarterly* 47, no. 4 (2010): 351–63.

Moebius, Stephan, and Markus Schroer, eds. *Diven, Hacker, Spekulanten: Sozialfiguren der Gegenwart*. Berlin: Suhrkamp, 2010.

Nissenbaum, Helen. "The Meaning of Anonymity in an Information Age." *Information Society* 15, no. 2 (1999): 141–44.

Parsons, Talcott. *Structure and Process in Modern Societies*. New York: Free Press, 1960.

Parsons, Talcott, Edward Albert Shils, and Neil J. Smelser. *Toward a General Theory of Action: Theoretical Foundations for the Social Sciences*. Piscataway, NJ: Transaction, 1965.

Ponesse, Julie. "Navigating the Unknown: Towards a Positive Conception of Anonymity." *Southern Journal of Philosophy* 51, no. 3 (2013): 344.

Ponesse, Julie. "The Ties That Blind: Conceptualizing Anonymity." *Journal of Social Philosophy* 45, no. 3 (2014): 304–22.

Rheingold, Howard. *The Virtual Community: Finding Connection in a Computerized World*. Reading, MA: Addison-Wesley, 1993.

Schuetz, Alfred. "The Stranger: An Essay in Social Psychology." *American Journal of Sociology* 49, no. 6 (1944): 499–507. https://doi.org/10.1086/219472.

Schupp, Jürgen. "25 Jahre Sozio-oekonomisches Panel – Ein Infrastrukturprojekt der empirischen Sozial-und Wirtschaftsforschung in Deutschland / Twenty-Five Years of the German Socio-Economic Panel—An Infrastructure Project for Empirical Social and Economic Research in Germany." *Zeitschrift für Soziologie* 38, no. 5 (2009): 350–57.

Schütz, Alfred. *The Phenomenology of the Social World*. 1932. Evanston, IL: Northwestern University Press, 1967.

Simmel, Georg. "Money in Modern Culture." *Theory, Culture and Society* 8, no. 3 (1991): 17–31. https://doi.org/10.1177/026327691008003002. First published 1900 as "Philosophie des Geldes."

Simmel, Georg. "The Metropolis and Mental Life." In *The Blackwell City Reader*, edited by Gary Bridge und Sophie Watson, 11–19. Blackwell Readers in Geography. Malden, MA: Blackwell Publishing, 2002. First published 1903 as "Die Großstädte und das Geistesleben."

Simmel, Georg. *Soziologie: Untersuchungen über die Formen der Vergesellschaftung*. Suhrkamp Taschenbuch Wissenschaft 811. 8th ed. 1908. Frankfurt: Suhrkamp, 2016.

van Dijck, José. *The Culture of Connectivity: A Critical History of Social Media*. Oxford: Oxford University Press, 2013.

van Dijck, José. "Datafication, Dataism and Dataveillance: Big Data between Scientific Paradigm and Ideology." *Surveillance and Society* 12, no. 2 (2014): 197–208.

Wallace, Kathleen. "Anonymity." *Ethics and Information Technology* 1, no. 1 (1999): 31.

Anonymity on Demand
The great Offshore

Since 2016, we have undertaken a large-scale investigation on the offshore banking industry, the industry that manages the opaque financial flows of money laundering, tax evasion, and tax optimization. The investigation was primarily led through field research, starting with the major central nodes of the identified networks—The City of London, Delaware, and Zurich—followed by their respective satellites—Jersey, Guernsey, the Cayman Islands, the Bahamas, Liechtenstein, Malta, Luxembourg, and the Netherlands. We empirically forged a specific set of methods to face the impossibility of catching such a deterritorialized phenomenon in any given territory: data-driven walks, psychogeographic GPS, paranoid semiotic investigations, and the creation of a series of algorithms that cumulate and aggregate sophisticated singular tax evasion schemes.[1] The investigation also mixed together research in national and private archives; walks through the city centers and financial neighborhoods; collections of coincidences, signs, relations, and correlations; meetings with researchers, artists, and activists; data analysis; and other methods. This field research was conducted according to the extradisciplinary methodology, following Brian Holmes's proposition of artistic intrusions into ultraspecialized fields of interests to generate a public discussion outside the reserved area of experts.[2] The investigation was guided through an extended documentary corpus, combining financial reports, patents, press articles, anticolonial pamphlets, short stories, touristic guides, novels, and other written works.

While the *dérives* (drifts) in the research and in the cities were fueled by the offshore leaks data, the conclusions we have reached at the end of our investigation were slightly different from those newspapers and media in general have reached with the same data[3]:

1. The offshore banking system, far from being a marginal phenomenon, is central within the global banking system and no longer deserves to be differentiated

[1] "Psychogeography" was defined in 1955 by Guy-Ernest Debord, as "the study of the precise laws and specific effects of the geographical environment, consciously organized or not, on the emotions and behavior of individuals." Guy-Ernest Debord, "Introduction to a Critique of Urban Geography" (1955), in *Situationist International Anthology*, ed. and trans. by Ken Knabb, rev. ed., (Minneapolis, MN: Bureau of Public Secrets, 2006), 8–11.

[2] Brian Holmes proposes the extradisciplinary investigation method, in opposition to the multidisciplinary, where ultraspecialized topics are approached by artists into long-term investigation, to generate a discussion outside the field of expertise. Brian Holmes, *Extradisciplinary Investigations: Towards a New Critique of Institutions*, www.eipcp.net, 2007.

[3] Offshore Tour Operator is a prototype of a psychogeographic GPS, based on the geolocalized addresses taken from the Panama papers, Paradise papers, offshore leaks, and Bahamas leaks databases. See "Offshore Tour Operator," www.cutt.ly/offshore-tour-operator

from the onshore system. In other words, offshore is the new onshore, or, quoting Reijer Hendrikse and Rodrigo Fernandez, "Offshore is the new norm."[4] And this is corroborated by the following facts:

- The geographies of the onshore and offshore overlap quite perfectly if we take the common offshore agents (Panama, Caymans, Bahamas, BVI, etc.) as the dependencies of the onshore established financial centers. Then the UK, United States, Switzerland, and Luxembourg reveal themselves as the main offshore centers.
- The offshore and onshore major architects are the same: big accounting companies (KPMG, Deloitte, EY, PWC), institutional banks (UBS, HSBC, Barclays, Deutsche Bank, BNP, Société Générale, etc.).
- The beneficiaries of the offshore circuits are the same actors involved in the stock markets' big capitalizations—Amazon, Apple, Google, Starbucks, and so forth—through the intricate mechanisms of tax optimization and the exploitation of legislation loopholes.
- All those actors, agents, and beneficiaries are participating in the construction of normalized jurisdictions, through lobbying and job changes from public to private sectors, in which deregulation— i.e., market compatibility—is becoming the norm.

2. Our inability to address the offshore as the onshore is maintained and reinforced by the generalization of "proxy politics," a term coined by the Research Center for Proxy Politics.[5] All the above-mentioned actors, private or public, have managed to set up a series of intermediaries (or proxies), to create subsidiaries, as financial and political doppelgängers, to obfuscate their traces and their influence, liquefy their identities, and become as fluid and as liquid as capital can be in the twenty-first century.

[4] Reijer Hendrikse and Rodrigo Fernandez, "Offshore Finance: How Capital Rules the World," *Longreads* (blog), Transnational Institute, 2019.

[5] Referring here to the research of Vera Tollmann and Boaz Levin, from the RCPP, Research Center on Proxy Politics, and their beautiful text on the City of London: "The City and Its Double," RCPP, June 10, 2016.

3. This perspective bias is maintained by this proxy architecture but also by semantic misformation. A specific and restricted vocabulary has been designed to attenuate, mislead, or blur our understanding of the actual capitalist system and neutralize its critiques. One example among the many: in the newspeak of fiscal lawyers and companies, taxes are not evaded nor avoided but *optimized*. By restricting the vocabulary aimed to describe the system properly, we lose the ability to judge it in the right terms. The debate is then unable to focus on the offshore systemic integration within the onshore and becomes restricted to a mere moral issue: that's the reason public discussion of the Paradise papers has stagnated on the problem of "not moral but legal." To elaborate on this, we refer to the works of Alain Deneault, and his concept of "laundering by language." The transformation of semantics not only reduces our abilities to criticize, but also opens the door to the legitimation and legalization of illegal activities.[6]

4. The offshore banking system reveals itself a simple illusionist trick, whose function is to capture maximum financial assets to assimilate and digest within the onshore system, outside the control of nation-states. In the process, the money feeds a whole series of intermediaries, in a very limited circuit of specialized services—yachting, private jets, freeports to store artworks, specialized tax lawyers, wealth managers, and so forth. The admission prices to those services, and their nature, shed a crude light on the social class that has access to them and benefits from such a system.

5. To achieve the trick, the core ingredients required are anonymity and secrecy policies. Through simple contracts, identities are deported and persons are transformed into private companies and legal, judicial, and economic entities, sometimes on the fly, where the links between one organization and its assets are diluted.

[6] Alain Deneault, *Legalizing Theft: A Short Guide to Tax Havens*, trans. Catherine Browne (Halifax, NS: Fernwood, 2018).

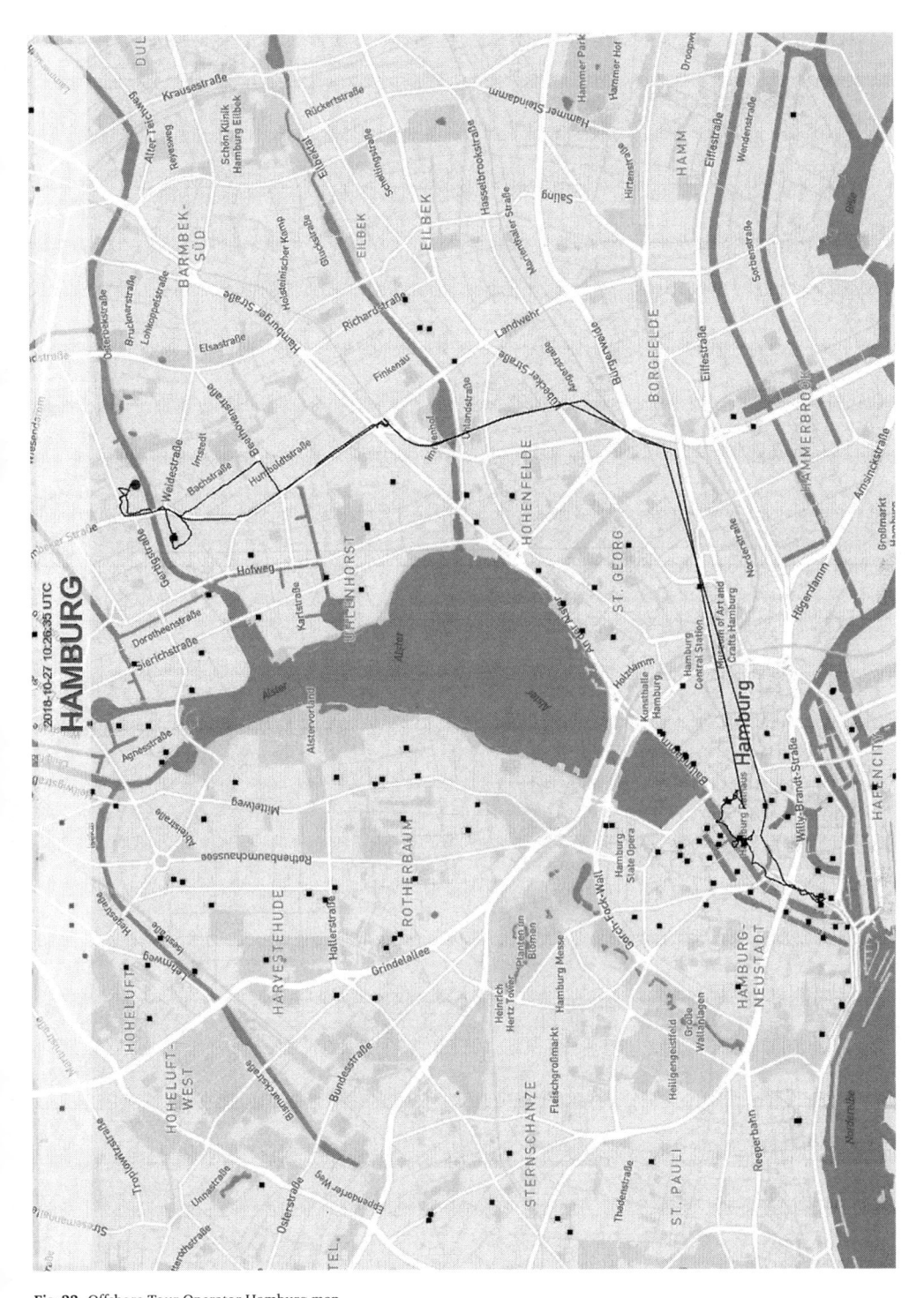

Fig. 23 Offshore Tour Operator Hamburg map.

B — RECONFIGURATION
Anonymity on Demand

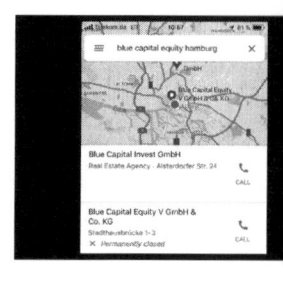

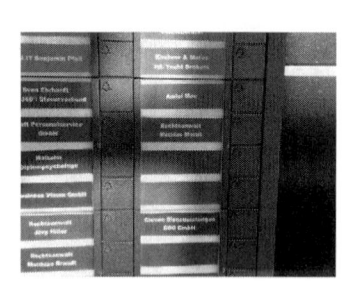

Fig. 24–43 Photographs collected during the Offshore Tour in Hamburg, workshop organized in the context of the exhibition A = ANONYM, Kampnagel, 2018.

6. Anonymity is provided as a privileged service to any client of a wealth management service or private banking and audit services. These services are provided by all the major banks of the onshore world (UBS, Crédit Suisse, HSBC, BNP, Commerzbank, etc.) and by the accounting firms (KPMG, Deloitte, EY, PwC) subcontracted by their subsidiaries (Offshore Magic Circle, Mossack Fonseca, Appleby, etc.). Clients are transformed into shell corporation swarms in the British Virgin Islands, or in the Bermudas, to disappear from the lists exchanged by countries within bilateral tax agreements. Despite the announced end of banking secrecy in Switzerland, those bilateral agreements target only individuals, not legal entities.

7. Protected by the legal structure of the trust, one can operate a network of shell companies that will continue to dissolve identity and ownership, transferring parts of one's assets within companies that are bounded together only by this trust. The assets will be accessible through another endpoint structure, usually a foundation in Liechtenstein. While all claim offshore financial packages are complex, they are in fact always based on a very simple and repetitive scheme, leading economist Gabriel Zucman, in his book *The Hidden Wealth of Nations*, to assert that there is no complex offshore scheme. "If we believe most of the commentators, the financial arrangements among tax havens rival one another in their complexity. In the face of such virtuosity, citizens are helpless, nation-states are powerless, even the experts are overpowered. So the general conclusion is that any approach to change is impossible. In reality, the arrangements made by bankers and accountants are often quite simple. Some have been functioning unchanged for close to a century."[7]

Like all illusionist tricks, to operate properly, attention has to be derived. We need to focus on the right point of attention to reveal the trickery. As part of our research,

[7] In *The Hidden Wealth of Nations*, Gabriel Zucman has calculated that the amount of money in the tax havens is about 7.3 billion US dollars. Gabriel Zucman, *The Hidden Wealth of Nations: The Scourge of Tax Havens*, trans. Teresa Lavender (Chicago: University of Chicago Press, 2019).

we tried to complete a speculative model of a tax optimizer algorithm, with a primary focus on anonymity.[8] This virtual model tries to elaborate on Zucman's assertion. To achieve this model, we have collected all possible resources on tax avoidance into an encyclopedia.

[8] "Algoffshore: The Anonymization Swarm," no. 3.

The continuation of this article presents a few entries of this Great Offshore Encyclopedia, with a selection of entries connected to anonymity. These entries, presented in alphabetical order, document a series of schemes, techniques, events, and case studies of "anonymity as a mean" in offshore banking, aiming to draw a panorama of a banking industry all directed toward tax avoidance, an industry that provides anonymity on demand.

Encyclopedia Entries

A

Anonymous Companies

"This is a more insidious form of secrecy, in which authorities and bankers do not bother to ask for names.... For shady clients, this is a far better proposition: what their bankers do not know, they can never be forced to reveal. And their method is disarmingly simple. Instead of opening bank accounts in their own names, fraudsters and money launderers form anonymous companies, with which they can then open bank accounts and move assets."

SOURCE: Nicholas Shaxson, *Treasure Islands: Uncovering the Damage of Offshore Banking and Tax Havens* (New York: Palgrave Macmillan, 2011) 30.

Anonymous Corporations

"One of the first reports to put the issue of anonymous corporations at center stage was commissioned by the United Nations in 1998 on the tenth anniversary of the first international convention against money laundering, in this case connected with the illegal drug trade (the Vienna Convention). Financial Havens, Banking Secrecy and Money Laundering explains that 'Despite a myriad of complications, there is a simple structure that underlies almost all international money-laundering

SOURCE: Jason Sharman, "Behind the Corporate Veil: A Participant Study of Financial Anonymity and Crime" (presented at ECPR Joint Sessions, Lisbon, Portugal, April 14–19, 2009).

activities.... The launderer often calls on one of the many jurisdictions that offer an instant corporation manufacturing business. ....Once the corporation is set up in the offshore jurisdiction, a bank deposit is made in the haven country in the name of that offshore company.' The report estimated that at time of writing there were over a million anonymous corporations in existence."

B

Bankgeheimnis, Switzerland, 1934

The Swiss Banking Code specifically prohibits violations of banking secrecy and outlines the consequences under criminal law of such a violation. Article 47 of the Bank and Savings Bank Federal Act of June 8, 1934, as amended in 1971, provides the language that prohibits bankers and other professionals from revealing secret information:

1. Every person working at a bank has a duty to keep secrets;
2. Third parties who lead others to infringe the secrecy duty are also to be punished, even if the offense never takes place;
3. Infringement due to pure negligence, as well as intentional infringement, is to be punished;
4. The infringement of bank secrecy may be prosecuted by the court on its own initiative;
5. The penalties are a prison term not to exceed six months or a fine not to exceed Sfr. 50,000; either penalty may be cumulated;
6. Breach of professional secrecy remains punishable even after termination of a public or private employment relationship or the practice of a profession;
7. Bank secrecy is not absolute; in specific legal circumstances, Swiss authorities are to be granted the right of access to private banking records. Several qualifications to banking secrecy have been provided for under Swiss domestic law. Exceptions may arise in civil proceedings.

SOURCE: Michele Moser, "Switzerland: New Exceptions to Bank Secrecy Laws Aimed at Money Laundering and Organized Crime," *Case Western Reserve Journal of International Law* 27, no. 2 (1995): 321–57.

Bermuda Black Hole

"Bermuda black hole is the term given to the final destination of corporate tax avoidance schemes which end up in an offshore tax haven/offshore financial center. The term 'black hole' is mostly used in relation to a corporation because once the money enters Bermuda, it does not emerge again (or it could be subject to corporation tax). Instead, the money is 'lent out' to the corporate parent (or its subsidiaries) to avoid repatriation (and taxing). This has led to US corporations amassing over $1trn in locations like Bermuda by 2017."

SOURCE: Wikipedia, s.v. "Bermuda Black Hole," last modified June 28, 2018.

C

Cooking the Book, or Creative Accounting

"Creative accounting consists of accounting practices that follow required laws and regulations, but deviate from what those standards intend to accomplish. Creative accounting capitalizes on loopholes in the accounting standards to falsely portray a better image of the company. Although creative accounting practices are legal, the loopholes they exploit are often reformed to prevent such behaviors."

SOURCE: Investopedia, s.v., "Cook the Books," last updated April 11, 2019.

Corruption

"In December 2006 the UK government canceled a corruption probe into an 86 billion dollar arms deal between BAE Systems and Saudi Arabia.... The scheme is described by Leigh and Evans as follows ("BAE's Secret Money Machine," *Guardian*, July 9, 2007). BAE allegedly paid bribes to officials from Saudi Arabia and elsewhere in return for arms contracts using agents, the latter being separated from both BAE and bribe recipients by shell companies. The first intermediary company was Novelmight, until 1999 incorporated in the UK before then being reincorporated in the British Virgin Islands. A second company, Red Diamond, was set up to channel payments via accounts in New York (Chase

SOURCE: Sharman, "Behind the Corporate Veil."

Manhattan), London (Lloyds TSB) and Switzerland (the ever-obliging UBS) to agents, and to officials from the governments purchasing BAE's wares. These payments were excluded from mention in the public contracts but included in parallel covert contracts for the same deals. Once more, maintaining the corporate veil was key: British police had just obtained crucial documentation elaborating on beneficial ownership of corporate bank accounts when the government canceled the investigation, citing 'a lack of evidence' as well as national security concerns."

Cross-Border Workshop

"Exhibit No. 92.1, which purports to be information that comes from UBS, ... was used at UBS workshops, training for some of their client advisors. It was given to us by Mr. Birkenfeld. I think he delivered that, and I will be asking the UBS folks about this. But if you look at Case 4—which the Chairman mentioned in his opening statement—and it gives a case study, and it says, 'After passing the immigration desk during your trip to the USA/Canada, you are intercepted by the authorities. By checking your Palm, they find all your client meetings. Fortunately, you stored only very short remarks of the different meetings and no names.' Then it goes on to say, 'You are staying at a hotel. You are being observed.' And what they are reflecting is being observed by authorities, and that you are then intercepted by an FBI agent, and he is looking for information about one of your clients, explains to you your client is involved in illegal activities. Then they ask, 'What are the signs indicating something is going on?' In other words, this purports to be directions to folks coming in to do business here— and we are going to find out that they are not registered securities folks, that many of them that came, that on their entry documents saying they were here for personal reasons, not for business reasons[,] were in fact here solely for the business of inducing and abetting tax evasion."

SOURCE: US Senate, *Hearings Before the Permanent Subcommittee on Investigations of the Committee on Homeland Security and Governmental Affairs*, 110th Cong., 2nd sess. (July 17 and 25, 2008).

D

Double Irish with a Dutch Sandwich

"The double Irish with a Dutch sandwich is a tax avoidance technique employed by certain large corporations, involving the use of a combination of Irish and Dutch subsidiary companies to shift profits to low or no tax jurisdictions. The scheme involves sending profits first through one Irish company, then to a Dutch company, and finally to a second Irish company headquartered in a tax haven. This technique has made it possible for certain corporations to reduce their overall corporate tax rates dramatically."

SOURCE: Investopedia, s.v. "Double Irish with a Dutch Sandwich," last updated April 20, 2019, www.investopedia.com/terms/d/double-irish-with-a-dutch-sandwich.asp.

Doe, John

"Historians can easily recount how issues involving taxation and imbalances of power have led to revolutions in ages past. Then, military might was necessary to subjugate peoples, whereas now, curtailing information access is just as effective or more so, since the act is often invisible. Yet we live in a time of inexpensive, limitless digital storage and fast internet connections that transcend national boundaries. It doesn't take much to connect the dots: from start to finish, inception to global media distribution, the next revolution will be digitized."

SOURCE: "John Doe's Manifesto," Panama Papers, *Süddeutsche Zeitung*, n.d.

Domino Effect

"This is the 'domino effect' of company law: if this type of regulation seeks to maximize anonymity in financial transactions, enabling the creation of shell or shelf companies whose owners remain largely unknown... such anonymity will be transferred to other sectors of the law. Thus the names of ultimate beneficial owners or the beneficiaries of financial transactions will remain obscure, which thwarts criminal investigation and prosecution.... [I]f company law maximizes anonymity, then the ineffectiveness of criminal law and police and judicial cooperation is inevitable. The same

SOURCE: Sharman, "Behind the Corporate Veil."

effect arises in banking law, where bank secrecy becomes a marginal issue owing to the anonymity enjoyed by the companies operating the bank accounts under surveillance."

H

H29, Luxembourg, 1929

"The 1929 holding (H29) was a vehicle for holding capital and enjoyed a favorable tax regime, in return for which its range of activities was confined to taking participations in other companies, managing bond loans, and managing patents and licenses under certain conditions. The holding was not allowed to engage in any commercial activities, failing which it would forfeit its tax regime. In 2006 the European Commission found the new H29 tax regime to be non-compliant with European legislation on State aid, leading to the government decision to phase out the scheme by 2010. H29s were excluded from double taxation treaties and were not allowed to benefit from the tax regime common to parent companies and their subsidiaries resident in the European Union. This characteristic therefore restricted the use of H29s as vehicles in international acquisition structures. These structures were in fact mainly used by private individuals as wealth management products."

SOURCE: OECD, *OECD Economic Surveys: Luxembourg 2008* (Paris: OECD Publishing, 2008).

K

K2

"There are different types of tax avoidance schemes, such as K2—the Jersey-based tax scheme. This is where an individual resigns from his/her job in the UK and becomes an employee of an offshore company such as K2. The individual receives a minimal salary from that company. K2 seconds (or hires out) the employee to his/her original employer, and the original employer pays a fee to K2. The offshore company, via

SOURCE: Financial Times Lexicon, s.v., "K2," last updated April 2019.

an employee benefits trust it sets up, lends this money to the individual. So the individual takes part of their income in the form of a loan and pays a lower amount of tax on the minimal income and not the loan."

L

LLP

"An LLP for accountancy firms is an example of having your cake and eating it: An LLP partner not only gets the benefits of being in a partnership—less disclosure, lower taxes, and weaker regulation—but it gets the limited liability protection too. And if a partner commits wrongdoing or is negligent, other partners who are not involved aren't accountable."

SOURCE: Shaxson, *Treasure Islands*, 175–76.

Loan-Back

"Lansky began with Swiss offshore banking in 1932, perfecting the loan-back technique. This involved first moving money out of the United States—in suitcases stuffed with cash, diamonds, airline tickets, cashier's checks, untraceable bearer shares, or whatever. Next, he would put the money in secret Swiss accounts, perhaps via a Liechtenstein anstalt (an anonymous company with a single secret shareholder). The Swiss bank would loan the money back to a mobster in the United States, who could then deduct the loan interest repayments from his taxable business income there."

SOURCE: Ibid.

P

Panama

"The biggest tax haven in the US zone of influence is Panama. It began registering foreign ships from 1919 to help Standard Oil escape US taxes and regulations, and offshore finance followed: Wall Street interests helped Panama introduce lax company incorporation laws in 1927, which let anyone open tax-free, anonymous,

SOURCE: Shaxson, *Treasure Islands*.

unregulated Panama corporations with few questions asked."

Proxy Politics

"These proxy politics have fueled the global economy, where the Delaware Freeport, nation states, anonymous trusts, shell companies and Mossack Fonseca among others are treated as equal entities, with these acts of depoliticizing and cover-up resulting in 'netscapes that are partly unlinked from geography and national jurisdiction.'"

SOURCE: Vera Tollmann and Boaz Levin, "The City and Its Double," *RCPP*, June 10, 2016.

S

Sealand

"You won't find it on any map of the world nor see it mentioned in any geography book. And yet it certainly exists. In the middle of the North Sea, surrounded by nothing but waves and wind, is the smallest self-proclaimed state in the world. The Principality of Sealand, as its inhabitants call it, is a small artificial island made of steel and anchored by two concrete pillars. To the east is a seemingly endless horizon. To the west is mainland Britain, some thirteen kilometers away. When the weather is right, the Roughs Tower platform rests about twenty meters above the surging sea. The surface area, however, is smaller than a football pitch. Sealanders have their own passports and currency—even their own constitution. But they can't travel with those passports or use the currency to buy anything outside Sealand. And no other state in the world recognizes the constitution. To some, the principality offers an alternative way of life, one with a dash of Robinson Crusoe. To others it is just a place where a handful of people, trying to exempt themselves from obligations imposed by the state, have taken advantage to create a tax haven and host computer servers."

SOURCE: Katrin Langhans, "Micronation, Offshore: Panama Papers Wash Up In Sealand," *Worldcrunch*, April 30, 2016.

Sharman, Jason

Jason Sharman is Professor and Queen Elizabeth II Fellow at the Centre for Governance and Public Policy and Griffith Asia Institute, Griffith University. In 2009 he conducted a study to open shell companies with a budget of 20,000 dollars. The *Economist* picked up on this study regarding the United States: "For foreigners, America is a particularly attractive place to stash cash, because it does not tax the interest income they earn. Thus with both anonymity and no taxation, America offers them all the elements of a tax haven." And about Britain: "In 45 minutes on the internet he formed a company without providing identification, was issued with bearer shares (which have been almost universally outlawed because they confer completely anonymous ownership) as well as nominee directors and a secretary. All was achieved at a cost of £515.95 ($753)." Sharman's conclusion? "The United States, Great Britain and other OECD states have chosen not to comply with the international standards which they have been largely responsible for putting in place."

SEE also Jason Sharman, "Shopping for Anonymous Shell Companies: An Audit Study of Anonymity and Crime in the International Financial System," *Journal of Economic Perspectives* 24, no. 4 (2010): 127–40.

Shell Bank

"They worked with what were euphemistically called 'managed banks' or shell banks, an offshore specialty. These have no real presence where they are incorporated, so they can escape supervision by responsible regulators. A shell bank will typically be operated through an agent in the tax haven jurisdiction, perhaps a famous global bank, which provides a reassuringly solid name and address to back the shell but will otherwise carry no responsibility or even real knowledge of what the shell is actually up to. So a shell bank might be incorporated in the Bahamas, for example, but its owners and managers could be anywhere. Shell banks handle business that many banks will not touch. US senator Carl Levin notes that they are generally not examined by regulators, and virtually no one but the shell bank owner really knows where the bank is, how it operates, or who its customers are."

SOURCE: Shaxson, *Treasure Islands*.

Shell Companies

"The use of anonymous shell corporations makes it increasingly hard to identify the beneficial owners of the wealth held offshore. In the macroeconomic data we use, a growing amount of wealth is assigned to the British Virgin Islands, Panama, and similar tax havens where most of the world's shell corporations are domiciled. The use of shell companies increased after 2005, when in the context of a law known as the Saving Tax Directive, the European Union introduced a tax on interest income earned by EU residents in Switzerland and other tax havens. Because the tax did not apply to accounts nominally owned by shell companies, European depositors massively shifted their assets to shell companies."

SOURCE: Annette Alstadsæter, Niels Johannesen, Gabriel Zucman, "Who Owns the Wealth in Tax Havens? Macro Evidence and Implications for Global Inequality" (National Bureau of Economic Research working paper series, no. 23805, 2017).

Special Purpose Vehicle

"Ramón Fonseca and Jürgen Mossack would have us believe that their firm's shell companies, sometimes called 'special purpose vehicles,' are just like cars. But used car salesmen don't write laws. And the only 'special purpose' of the vehicles they produced was too often fraud, on a grand scale."

SOURCE: "John Doe's Manifesto"

U

UBS

"It is germane to look briefly at two applied examples of the utility of anonymous shell corporations. The first relates to large-scale tax evasion carried out by US citizens assisted by UBS, using intermediary shell companies. This involved 19,000 undeclared accounts holding about $20 billion, earning UBS $200 million a year in fees. Although the UBS scheme did involve some genuinely innovative stratagems (e.g., smuggling diamonds inside tubes of toothpaste, "Ex-UBS Banker Pleads Guilty to Tax Evasion," *New York Times*, June 20, 2008), much more conventional was establishing offshore vehicles for US citizens and transferring their accounts to the new shell entities. UBS and their US clients then

SOURCE: Sharman, "Behind the Corporate Veil."

collaborated in the fiction that the accounts were held by non-US persons, and thus that assets and income passing through was not liable for US tax."

W

Wyoming

"A Wyoming website boasts that 'Wyoming Corporations and LLCs have a tax haven within the United States with no income taxation, anonymous ownership and bearer shares.... Shelf Corporations and LLCs: Anonymous entity where YOUR NAME IS ON NOTHING! These companies already exist and are complete with Articles, Federal Tax ID numbers and registered agents.... You may have these complete companies by TOMORROW MORNING!"

SOURCE: Shaxson, *Treasure Islands*.

Bibliography

Debord, Guy-Ernest. "Introduction to a Critique of Urban Geography" (1955). In *Situationist International Anthology*, edited and translated by Ken Knabb, 8–11. Rev. ed. Minneapolis, MN: Bureau of Public Secrets, 2006.

Deneault, Alain. *Legalizing Theft: A Short Guide to Tax Havens*. Translated by Catherine Browne. Halifax, NS: Fernwood, 2018.

Hendrikse, Reijer, and Rodrigo Fernandez. "Offshore Finance: How Capital Rules the World." *Longreads* (blog), Transnational Institute, 2019. http://longreads.tni.org/state-of-power-2019/offshore-finance/.

Tollmann, Vera, and Boaz Levin. "The City and Its Double." *RCPP*, June 10, 2016. http://rcpp.lensbased.net/the-city-and-its-double-2/.

Zucman, Gabriel. *The Hidden Wealth of Nations: The Scourge of Tax Havens*. Translated by Teresa Lavender. Chicago: University of Chicago Press, 2019.

C
ASSAULT

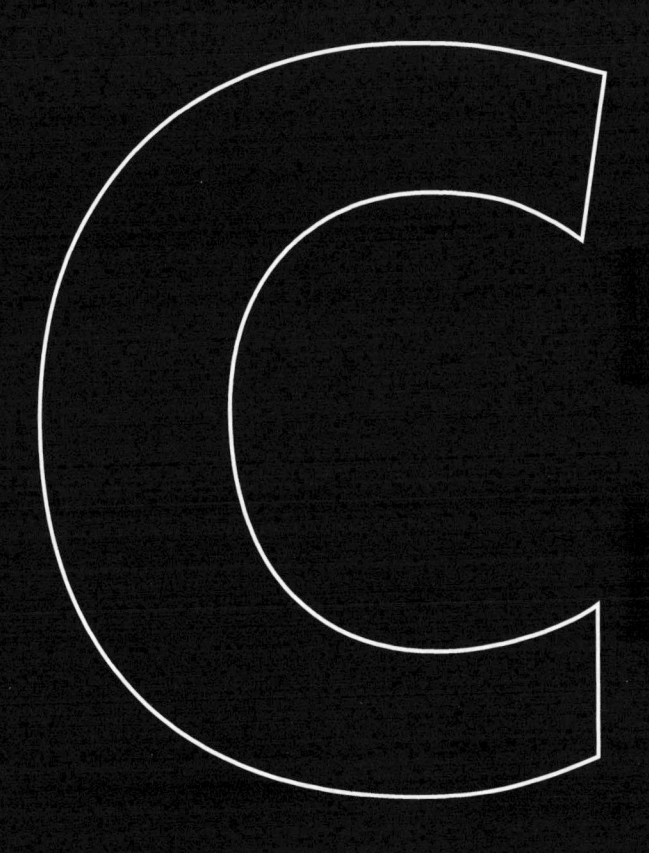

DNA Works! Merging Genetics and the Digital Realm

Introduction

Elizabeth Chapman, a donor-conceived person from the UK, was an inexhaustible source of knowledge for everything that had to do with genealogy and genetic testing, and she clearly enjoyed sharing this knowledge with me.[1] When I visited her at her and her husband's home in 2018 for the second time, she told me a story that, given the degree of vigor and enthusiasm in her voice, I initially believed to be about a close friend of hers. It turned out, however, to be about a distant relative who had been born in the eighteenth century, and to whom she was related through her maternal family. She had come across his story for the first time while researching her family tree, with the help of genealogy websites that contain digitized historical records. Although his baptism document was available on several of them, it contained only the name of his mother, suggesting that her ancestor

[1] The names of all donor-conceived persons mentioned have been pseudonymized.

had been an illegitimate child. She had therefore been unable to trace his paternal line. With the help of Ancestry, however, Chapman was eventually successful in finding out who the father was: the commercial service enables users to do genealogical research with the help of genetic analysis of a saliva sample that customers submit, as well as with a collection of digitized records that can be accessed online. Notably, the possibility of doing a DNA test distinguished Ancestry from the genealogy websites she had used in the past. Chapman had bought a test kit and added her DNA profile to Ancestry's database. She had chosen to do so because she wanted to find out who her anonymous sperm donor was; to clarify the origins of her long-deceased ancestor had not been her actual motivation. I explain in this chapter how exactly the donor conceived make use of these tests, which were originally designed for a different purpose. Ancestry eventually published the scanned pages of the church register in which her ancestor's baptism had been registered, and Chapman discovered that the vicar who had registered it had in fact written in the margin of a book the name of the man he suspected was the father. This was information that she had not had before. Ancestry's analysis of her saliva sample then linked her to a person in Australia, who had also added his DNA to the database, and who was (albeit distantly) genetically related to her. Through combining the results of the DNA test, the digitized records available on Ancestry, and her own detective skills, she found out that this person was also related to the man the vicar had thought was her ancestor's father. By finding the intersection between her and her Australian relative's family trees, she had eventually been able to confirm the vicar's suspicion. Chapman was clearly delighted with the results of her investigation and smilingly declared: "DNA works!" Indeed, DNA, or rather testing via Ancestry, seemed to have worked for and with her in multiple ways: It had helped her pursue her interest in genealogy, which resulted in her telling her distant and deceased relative's story with joy and elation. Through combining the results of the DNA test, which linked her to other members of the online database who shared portions of her DNA and thus were genetic relatives, with the digitized records that are available to Ancestry's customers, she had also been able to identify her previously anonymous donor, although official regulations in the UK do not grant her the right to information. Her experience is a prime example of how commercial genetic testing merges participation in a digital world with genetic material.[2] DNA testing had worked for her, but she had also worked with the results of her Ancestry test and put all her investigative skills to work to identify her donor.

Chapman's story shows that in the case of anonymous gamete donation, commercial genetic testing changes dramatically what can be known by whom and at what point. It affects what kind of knowledge the donor-conceived can potentially access about their donor, who was supposed to stay anonymous from the time of conception. It changes the status of the donor's anonymity from something that was supposed to be permanent to something that can possibly and sometimes actually be dissolved. The regulation and organization of donor conception, as well as the management of information storage and release, have changed considerably since Chapman was conceived with anonymous sperm in the 1950s. Instead of going into details regarding the development of the legal regulation of gamete donation in the UK and Germany, the two countries where I have conducted ethnographic research, this chapter focuses on genetic testing and anonymity. I first explain why and how Ancestry and similar databases are used by the donor-conceived in their attempts to find donors, genetic half-siblings, and other relatives. I then give two examples of women who have undergone genetic testing and argue that this technology does not lead to the "end of anonymity"—which was never "complete" to begin with.

[2] Minna Ruckenstein "Keeping Data Alive: Talking DTC Genetic Testing," *Information, Communication and Society* 20, no. 7 (2017): 1026.

Enforcing the "Right to Know" via Genetic Testing

Whereas donors were supposed to remain anonymous permanently, donor anonymity became temporally limited in the UK in 2005, and a few years later in Germany.[3] This means that donor offspring conceived today will be able to access identifying information about the donor when they reach a certain age (also referred as "identity release" (IR) donors). The donor-conceived persons I met in the UK and in Germany, however, had all been conceived when anonymity was either mandated by law or made a common practice through the destruction of records after an obligatory storage period. The regulations that controlled the storage and release of identifying and nonidentifying information (not only to the offspring, but also, to some extent, to parents and donors) were not retroactive in either country, which meant that the people I interviewed did not directly profit from them. Nonetheless, most people I met insisted on having a moral and ethical right to know, which they interpreted as outweighing any legal regulations. Like Chapman, they very much adhered to one view: as you *need to know* about your genetic origins, you should be given the *right to know*. Anonymity was described to me as being harmful to one's "identity formation," as it resulted in people not knowing where they "come from." Many of my interlocutors insisted on the state having a duty to protect its citizens from such harm by issuing appropriate laws.[4] Retroactive legislation similar to that issued in Victoria, Australia, in 2017 was not on the legal horizon in the UK or in Germany at the time of my ethnographic research in 2016 and 2017, so donor-conceived persons oftentimes reverted to more subversive practices to find information about their donor and/or genetic half-siblings.[5]

Notably, commercial genetic testing has significantly contributed to making temporally unlimited but always inherently partial anonymity potentially fragile. Chapman

3 When exactly (permanent) anonymity began to be limited or prohibited in Germany has been highly controversial among various actors in the field; donor-conceived activists often argue that anonymity has never been legal, which is contested by medical professionals. Since 2007, the Tissue Law has required donor data to be stored for thirty (instead of ten) years, which at least theoretically made it possible for donor-conceived adults to retrieve the data. It was not clear at that time, however, how the information should be kept and released. A central donor register, which allows donor-conceived persons aged sixteen or older to access information, has only existed since 2018.

4 See Kimberly Leighton, "Geneticizing the Desire to Know: Analogies to Adoption in Arguments against Anonymous Gamete Donation," in *Family-making: Contemporary Ethical Challenges*, ed. Françoise Baylis and Carolyn McLeod (Oxford: Oxford University Press, 2014), 239–64, for an analysis and critique of the right-to-know argument.

5 Sonia Allan, "Donor Identification: Victorian Legislation Gives Rights to All Donor-Conceived People," *Family Matters* 98 (2016): 43–55.

described it to me as "the holy grail" of the donor-conceived because of the revolutionary chances and changes it had brought about for those using genetic testing technologies to enforce their "right to know" and to identify genetic relatives. Such testing has significantly shifted the boundaries not only between what can be known and what remains hidden, but also between what can be classified as identifying and nonidentifying information in the realm of donor conception. Tests sold by mostly American companies such as Ancestry and FamilyTreeDNA are a way to circumvent official regulations regarding the anonymity of donors. They can enable the donor-conceived to identify donors who are not even registered themselves, or half-siblings who do not know yet that they have been conceived with donated gametes. These databases have a fast-growing worldwide membership and are increasing rapidly in terms of scope and accuracy, while being sold at more and more affordable prices. FamilyTreeDNA's popular Family Finder test is usually sold for 79 US dollars but is frequently on sale and was available for 59 US dollars during the company's "summer sale" in August 2019; in contrast, Family Finder was first sold for 300 US dollars when it was launched in 2010.[6]

In the context of these online databases, genes are presented "as digital big data to be browsed, uploaded and shared."[7] After buying a test kit online, sending in a saliva sample for analysis to the company's laboratory, and receiving a notification email about the results, customers can log in to their accounts and view their own data online. The database will also show them how they are related to other registered persons and suggest possible relationships—although the exact nature of the relationship, as I will explain in more detail, cannot be determined by DNA analysis alone. Most people I interviewed initially found only very distant relatives, or "matches," as they are oftentimes referred to, with whom they shared only an ancestor several generations ago. They can also connect with other users, discuss

[6] Hallam Stevens, "Genetimes and Lifetimes: DNA, New Media and History," *Memory Studies* 8, no. 4 (2015): 394.

[7] Stuart Hogarth and Paula Saukko, "A Market in the Making: The Past, Present and Future of Direct-to-Consumer Genomics," *New Genetics and Society* 36, no. 3 (2017): 202.

their findings, exchange messages and family trees. Additionally, "raw genetic data" can usually be exported and uploaded to other databases. Using these tests to identify donors or donor-conceived half-siblings is clearly not the aim of those providing the services, nor of the main user community. Instead, such databases are mostly joined by people interested in genetic ancestry research or personalized health reports. Nonetheless, they allow the donor-conceived to identify half-siblings and even donors, who might get inadvertently identified and "exposed" by unknowing relatives who join to do ancestry research and "match" with the donor-conceived. Whereas anonymizing the donor cut relations between the donor and recipient parents and offspring, commercial genetic testing can be a means to make new, unprecedented relations.[8] Contact between these different persons was not originally foreseen; the families of donors and of their donor-conceived offspring were to be protected from external intrusion, and any contact (and anticipated problems) was to be prevented by anonymity.

Genetic testing, particularly when employed in forensics, has in the past been ascribed an "allegedly unlimited evidential power."[9] It is oftentimes seen as an infallible "truth machine" that can eliminate any kind of uncertainty, for example, when traces found at a crime scene have to be attributed to one particular individual.[10] Scholars from the social sciences and Science and Technology Studies (STS) in particular, however, have long offered a much more critical perspective on the kind of results genetic testing can yield. Their perspective destabilizes the almost unquestionable certainty attributed to DNA testing.[11] It has been pointed out that "even disregarding the risk of contamination and human error, absolute certainty is unattainable," since "a high probability that the trace has indeed been left by the suspect is not the same thing as absolute certainty."[12] The impossibility of having results that operate without possibilities is linked to the kind of testing technology commonly employed in forensics: It is not the entire genome that is examined but only a set of

[8] Maren Klotz, "Wayward Relations: Novel Searches of the Donor-Conceived for Genetic Kinship," *Medical Anthropology* 35, no. 1 (2016): 45–57.

[9] Antonio Amorim, "Opening the DNA Black Box: Demythologizing Forensic Genetics," *New Genetics and Society* 31, no. 3 (2012): 259.

[10] Michael Lynch, Simon A. Cole, Ruth McNally, and Kathleen Jordan, *Truth Machine: The Contentious History of DNA Fingerprinting* (Chicago: University of Chicago Press, 2008).

[11] Torsten Heinemann, Thomas Lemke, and Barbara Prainsack, "Risky Profiles: Societal Dimensions of Forensic Uses of DNA Profiling Technologies," *New Genetics and Society* 31, no. 3 (2012): 249–58.

[12] Corinna Kruse, "Producing Absolute Truth: *CSI* Science as Wishful Thinking," *American Anthropologist* 112, no. 1 (2010): 86.

specific so-called short tandem repeat (STR) loci. Since testing looks at very specific points, or "markers," in the genome, "there is a fair chance that two individuals might 'look alike' for one of the markers."[13]

The Donor Conceived Register (DCR), a voluntary register that has its own DNA database for those who donated or were conceived in the UK before the establishment of the central register (which is not DNA-based), is an example of how the testing technology employed in forensics is repurposed for and by the donor-conceived. Unlike a commercial site, a voluntary register is specifically designed for the purpose of identifying matches between donors and their offspring and between genetic half-siblings conceived with gametes from the same anonymous donor. Researchers and social work professionals involved in the DCT have repeatedly pointed out that the kind of testing employed by the voluntary register always operates with levels of probability and is always uncertain.[14] At the time of my ethnographic research in the UK, the DCR was trying to overcome these difficulties by adding more genetic markers, which were supposed to eliminate any sources of uncertainty. These "technical fixes," however, cannot alter the fact that genetic test results are inherently uncertain.

It is important to highlight that tests such as FamilyTreeDNA's popular Family Finder are in fact based on a different type of testing (although, for example, FamilyTreeDNA does offer additional, more expensive STR-based tests, which are commonly used for ancestry research). Instead of examining STRs, they look at single-nucleotide polymorphisms (SNPs), which are more suited to determine degrees of relatedness.[15] Forensic laboratories have in fact also started to incorporate the analysis of SNPs, combined with established methods.[16] While siblings and other close relatives will share enough DNA for the relationship to be detected by a genetic genealogy test such as Family Finder, SNP tests are likely to miss a large proportion of more distant relatives.

[13] Amâde M'charek, "Technologies of Population: Forensic DNA Testing Practices and the Making of Differences and Similarities," *Configurations* 8, no. 1 (2000): 131.

[14] See, for example, Olga van den Akker, Marilyn Crawshaw, Eric Blyth, and Lucy Frith, "Expectations and Experiences of Gamete Donors and Donor-Conceived Adults Searching for Genetic Relatives Using DNA Linking through a Voluntary Register," *Human Reproduction* 30, no. 1 (2015): 118f; and Marilyn Crawshaw, Lucy Frith, Olga van den Akker, and Eric Blyth, "Voluntary DNA-Based Information Exchange and Contact Services Following Donor Conception: An Analysis of Service Users' Needs," *New Genetics and Society* 35, no. 4 (2016): 388. See also Jenni Millbank, "Identity Disclosure and Information Sharing in Donor Conception Regimes: The Unfulfilled Potential of Voluntary Registers," *International Journal of Law, Policy and the Family* 28, no. 3 (2014): 223–56, for a general analysis of voluntary registers.

[15] Maren Klotz, *(K)information: Gamete Donation and Kinship Knowledge in Germany and Britain* (Frankfurt: Campus, 2014), 273.

[16] John M. Butler, "The Future of Forensic DNA Analysis," *Philosophical Transactions of the Royal Society* B 370 (2015): 20140252.

Regardless of how accurate a test is, many relatives will remain "inaccessible" simply because one does not share any DNA with them, which is in turn related to the "randomness of genomic patterns of inheritance."[17] A distant genetic relative who might constitute a link to one's donor might thus be registered but remain undetectable. More importantly, tests can not determine the exact nature of a relationship—they can only determine what testing sites refer to as a "relationship range." Since one might share the same amount of DNA with different types of relatives, the amount of shared DNA alone is not enough to determine the genealogical nature of a relationship. For example, tests cannot distinguish between an aunt and a niece; therefore, a test taker will usually need additional information to determine the nature of a relationship.[18] The search for genetic relatives with the help of DNA testing can be much more complicated than one might assume, and as my fieldwork and the examples I give in this text show, it may require a lot more effort than merely purchasing a test kit.

Nevertheless, commercial genetic testing certainly has an almost revolutionary potential: as my first vignette shows, a donor does not need to be tested and registered to be identified. It may be sufficient if close but also more distant relatives of the donor are registered. In contrast, voluntary registers such as the DCR can match only people who have already joined. Unsurprisingly, an article by Joyce C. Harper, Debbie Kennett, and Dan Reisel has been titled "The End of Donor Anonymity: How Genetic Testing Is Likely to Drive Anonymous Gamete Donation out of Business." It focuses exclusively on SNP-based testing.[19] To proclaim "the end of anonymity" does indeed seem plausible and tempting given these new technological possibilities. Yet, my ethnographic record belies such a broad statement and highlights that unmaking anonymity in gamete donation is a much more complex matter. Genetic tests do not bring about the hoped-for results for everyone, and even if some matches are made, they do not completely dissolve the

[17] Sarah Abel, "What DNA Can't Tell Us: Problems with Using Genetic Tests to Determine the Nationality of Migrants," *Anthropology Today* 34, no. 6 (2018): 4.

[18] Ibid.

[19] Joyce C. Harper, Debbie Kennett, and Dan Reisel, "The End of Donor Anonymity: How Genetic Testing Is Likely to Drive Anonymous Gamete Donation out of Business," *Human Reproduction* 31, no. 6 (2016): 1137.

element of the unknown. To demonstrate these points, I briefly present two vignettes from my ethnographic material before discussing them in relation to the question of what happens to anonymity in genetic testing—if we assume it does not merely end. They both demonstrate the complexity that characterizes present-day anonymity regimes in gamete donation and allow implicit presumptions to be examined in detail.

[20] See the Human Fertilisation and Embryology Act 1990, last updated October 1, 2019, www.legislation.gov.uk/ukpga/1990/37/contents.

Vignette 1: Anonymity and the Brick Wall

Sarah Holmes had been conceived with anonymous sperm in the UK in the 1980s, before the founding of the Human Fertilisation and Embryology Authority (HFEA) in 1991 and the establishment of a central register, which is still managed by the HFEA.[20] When she was thirteen, she learned about the circumstances of her conception during an argument with her mother, who had already planned on telling her in a more controlled situation. After initially not talking about it anymore with her parents and only rarely discussing it with friends, Holmes started to address it when she entered university and had more space for "reevaluating [her] identity." After having a look on the internet, which had just gotten more widely available—a memory that made her laugh in our talk, given the current omnipresence of the online world ("And I think the internet then just came, just came out [laughs]. That's crazy, isn't it?!")—she came across the Donor Conception Network (DCN). The DCN is a nongovernmental organization that aims to support donor-conception families and promotes openness, which she soon decided to join. She also registered with UK Donor Link, the DCR's predecessor and submitted a saliva sample for their internal register. The DNA test did not yield any results, and despite her low expectations, Holmes was taken aback by this: "And I didn't have any matches. And I didn't expect any matches, but when I actually got the confirmation through, it was, I was surprised that I was quite upset by it." According to information given to her mother at the time of her conception, her donor had been a medical student in the town where she had been conceived. Yet, neither contacting the university nor getting in touch with her mother's fertility doctor had brought her any closer toward knocking down the "brick wall" of anonymity, which meant that she "couldn't go anywhere for that information." Holmes explained to me that the donor and the circumstances of her conception were not always at the forefront of her mind; instead, it was something that got foregrounded when she was faced with major events in her life.

> SH: Being donor-conceived, it's like a tap that drips. So it doesn't affect you every moment of every day. But it's there in the background, and at certain points in your life, the tap becomes more forceful and it turns on, and you, you sort of then go, "Okay, I'm gonna do this, I'm gonna figure it out once and for all."

When she was pregnant with her second child, Holmes decided to register with a commercial genetic database. Whereas her registration with the voluntary register had still not produced any results, she learned that she had a "close match," with whom she shared a relatively large amount of DNA, on the commercial site. Her match, with whom she was still in contact at the time of my research and occasionally exchanged emails, turned out to be her donor's cousin (and therefore her first cousin once removed), who was living abroad. Although he decided to respect the donor's wish to not have his identity disclosed, he provided Holmes with a family tree (that he had "shortened" by two generations to keep the donor's identity hidden), medical history, as well as pictures of her genetic grandparents. Although she still did not know her donor's identity, she mentioned that she had regained her inner equilibrium as a result of these unexpected developments, which had in turn made her a lot more open to talking about the circumstances of her conception.

SH: I'm much more open about it now, yeah. And I think that finding out about the donor and having real information from his cousin, it was huge, I felt like; I don't know how to describe it. But it was just so much a weight that was lifted off my shoulders. I felt so relaxed and comfortable and at peace—I think that's the right words. I felt at peace, knowing who I was, and that wall that had been there for twenty years had suddenly been knocked down. And it had been knocked down enough that I didn't need to search for anything else. I had the information that I needed. And I still don't think of him as my dad. I still don't know who he is. There's still a definite boundary around him being anonymous, but I have that information about the family. I have that information about the genetic stuff, the medical history. I have some photographs. And it's, it's really comforting to have that information.

When I emailed her the following year to send New Year's greetings and to give her an update on how my work was progressing, I also inquired whether the tap had been dripping again since we had met up. Holmes replied that, indeed, her interest in the donor had once again been triggered by a major life decision that she and her husband had been required to make that year. Without reflecting about this link at the time, she started to continue her search and used the names mentioned in the (shortened) family tree given to her by her donor's cousin to search the medical directory for doctors that could potentially have been donors. She eventually found a physician who had studied in the town where she had been conceived, just as her mother had been told at the time of her conception. Since Holmes knew from his cousin that he did not want to be contacted, she looked him up on Facebook instead, where she managed to find a photograph of him, which she saved and attached to her reply when I got in touch with her. She also informed her cousin about her discovery, the accuracy of which he did not deny. He even told her more about her already deceased genetic grandparents, whose identity she had also figured out. Since the donor had in the past declined to be in contact, Holmes had made no further attempts to contact him and did not say in the email if she would want to do so in the future.

Vignette 2: As Good as a Paternity Test

For other donor-conceived persons I interviewed, searching for their donor had not been crowned with success. I had originally chosen Nadine Fuchs's story for this chapter as she was one of my interlocutors who had not yet been lucky despite putting a lot of effort in her search. Even though she eventually found her donor after I had already finished the first draft of this text, I have chosen to still include her story, as Fuchs, too, had some "unfinished relations."[21] This phenomenon was in a way predicted by Monica Konrad in her ethnography on anonymous egg donation in the UK. Konrad argued that those searching for their donor-conceived genetic half-siblings would "build … networks around the non-traceable," but she added that "there will always be the curiosity and determination to know more, the disappointments of 'dead ends' and thwarted non-reunion."[22] Commercial DNA databases such as Ancestry were not yet available when Konrad did her research. Nevertheless, the "non-reunions" that Konrad predicted are particularly present again because of new technological possibilities, even if DNA tests allegedly lead to the "end" of anonymity.

A couple of years ago, Fuchs had found out that she and her brother had been conceived with anonymous sperm in the late 1970s, in a German university town. When Fuchs was in her midthirties, her parents had started seeing a psychologist because of her mother's mental health. He had advised them to tell Fuchs and her brother about the circumstances of their conception. Whereas several of my research contacts did not properly start their actual search until several years after the initial "revelation talk," Fuchs mentioned that she had decided to look for him straight away:

[21] Monica Konrad, *Nameless Relations: Anonymity, Melanesia and Reproductive Gift Exchange between British Ova Donors and Recipients* (Oxford: Berghahn, 2005), 119.

[22] Ibid., 216.

NF: Because at the beginning it was just so bad, that whenever I was standing in front of a mirror, my own face somehow didn't fit anymore. I was looking at myself in the mirror, and I somehow thought "A foreign being is standing there." That really was very, very odd. And I somehow had the desire to find that person, so that this gap would be closed. So that someone would be there.

23 See Samenspenderregistergesetz, July 17, 2017, *SaRegG* BGBl I, S. 2513.

As she had always had the feeling of not fitting in to the family because her interests and talents differed considerably from those of her parents, the fact that she was not genetically related to her father came not as a surprise or shock to her but as a relief: her feelings had always pointed her in the right direction, which renewed her trust in her intuition. Whereas her parents insisted on her and her brother keeping the details of their conception a secret, as they feared the father's reputation would be damaged if others knew the truth about their conception, Fuchs did not want to stick to such secretive behavior. Although she was still obliging to her parents' request and had, for example, not revealed her real name in a newspaper article on donor conception for which she had been interviewed, she emphasized that she felt an incredible need to talk about her experience, because not being completely open about it with her family, friends, and the public felt like a form of self-denial to her. Fuchs was a member of the German advocacy group Spenderkinder, which she had found online and joined its internal mailing list, which is open to only donor-conceived persons. She was also registered with several commercial genetic testing companies. At the time of my fieldwork, she had found neither any half-siblings nor her donor. The fact that a central sperm donor register was established in Germany in 2018 did not change her situation, as the legislation was not retroactive.[23] Nevertheless, the results of her and her brother's registration with FamilyTreeDNA had been insightful, as they had revealed that she and her younger brother were in fact full siblings, since they shared more DNA than half-siblings would. They thus knew that they had been conceived with sperm from the same donor. This had surprised her, as her parents had been told that another donor had been used for her brother, who was six years younger. The result would not have been surprising or revealing if it had already been customary at this time to use cryopreserved instead of "fresh" sperm. If cryopreserved sperm had been used, Fuchs could not even have assumed that the donor had ever been in the city where she and her brother were conceived; with cryopreservation, it had become possible to separate the act of donation and conception both spatially and geographically, as sperm could now be stored and posted. Yet, the cryopreservation of sperm had not yet become a common practice when Fuchs was conceived in the 1970s. Therefore, the information about their "full" genetic relatedness was an important starting point for her subsequent search: their donor had most likely been in contact with her mother's physician between at least the years of her conception and that of her younger brother. As her parents had been told that her donor had been a medical student at the time of her conception, Fuchs started to look online for doctors who had studied in the town where she and her brother had been conceived during the respective years. During her search, she came across the picture of a physician who bore a remarkable resemblance to her brother. Yet, he denied ever having been a sperm donor when Fuchs subsequently contacted him. Despite his answer, she continued to follow up this lead to figure out whether he had told her the truth: after some research in physical archives (instead of digital ones, as are the records provided by Ancestry), where she went through old newspaper magazines, she found a notice about his registration of birth. With the help of her daughter, who managed to find his grandparents' grave and thereby their names and dates of birth and death, she was able to start building his family tree through searching in on- and offline archives. The goal of her search was to find an intersection between the doctor's family tree and information she had obtained via her registration on several genetic databases and through her own 'detective work.' By meticulously examining several trees that had been put online by several of her matches, Fuchs had managed to identify the person who constituted the "most recent common ancestor" of her and her distant American cousins, who had all registered to do ancestry research. These persons had been shown to her as genetic relatives in her "match lists." The relationships were so distant, however, that the exact type of connection could not be determined by the tests alone; her American matches were therefore listed as cousins of a certain degree (the list will, for example, show them as a "3rd cousin–4th cousin").

As she had been able to test her maternal aunt in order to "filter out" her maternal matches from her own test results, she knew that this person who had been born in the eighteenth century was linking her and her distant cousins to her unknown paternal family. Therefore, she was convinced that if she managed to build the family tree of her "most common recent ancestor" and prove that her physician was related to him as well, it would be "as good as a paternity test." Although she had already invested a considerable amount of time and effort into tracing the clinician's family tree, Fuchs was determined not to focus her search solely on him.

> NF: I somehow try not to be guided by my emotions, but I rather try to really think out of the box, and I take everything into consideration. I consider that the professor [her mother's gynecologist] himself may have done it, that our parents are lying, that it actually was the neighbor.

The family tree that she had managed to compile for the doctor had in the meantime become quite comprehensive. Fuchs laughingly remarked that should she eventually figure out that he was indeed not her genetic father, she would probably just anonymously send it his way.

At the time of my ethnographic research, Fuchs had not yet been successful at finding her donor. Her dedication

to her search and her creativeness continued to impress me throughout my research, and I mentioned in the first draft of this chapter that I would not be surprised if her investigative skills led her to success by the time this text gets published. Back then, her experiences still confirmed a point made by Chapman, who had praised genetic testing as a revolutionary technology, but who also pointed out that "not everybody's gonna be lucky."
But it turned out that I had been right: Fuchs eventually registered with another testing site. A genetic cousins that she found on that database was close enough for her to eventually track down her donor when she combined that information with the data she had already gathered. Fuchs then contacted her donor, who agreed to meet up with her. It was not the doctor, nor the professor, nor the neighbor. Instead, it had been a man whose wife had been treated during pregnancy by the professor, who was a gynecologist and who had persuaded him to become a donor to help infertile couples.

She had not yet made contact with the (non-donor-conceived) children of her donor, who were also her genetic half-siblings; her donor seemed uninterested in further contact with her or in facilitating contact between her and his children. Fuchs wanted contact, but she did not want to contact them against his will. In addition, she had not found any donor-conceived half-siblings yet and could not even be sure that they existed.

Working with DNA

The two case studies I have chosen depict two different experiences shaped by two different sets of circumstances, but they do have several important elements in common that must be identified if one is to develop a deeper understanding of the kind of "DNA work" that donor-conceived persons are doing. First of all, both Holmes and Fuchs were conceived at a time when neither UK nor Germany had legislated a centralized or decentralized system of storing and releasing donor information; additionally, anonymity had not yet become temporally limited. Second, for this reason, both women had to revert to other ways of obtaining information that circumvent the regulations and practices established by law and the medical profession. Third, both case studies demonstrate that genetic testing neither dictates practices nor replaces other knowledge infrastructures. Donor-conceived persons who buy a test kit are neither passive users of what is technically possible nor passive consumers of the results of a certain test. In Holmes's case, her search was interrupted by several years-long breaks in which "the tap [was] turned off." She did not immediately seek to identify her donor based on the information given to her by her match but was moved to do so only by other events in her life. This time she had to actively access other online infrastructures and combine information from different sources. Anthropologist Janet Carsten has observed a similar phenomenon in her research on adoption reunions: the adoptees she met had oftentimes put their search for their birth parents aside for several years and were triggered to restart it by significant life events.[24] Carsten argues that "the fact that new moves are often linked to the present family circumstances of adoptees, particularly the birth of children, suggests a rather complex intertwining of past, present, and future chronologies of kinship."[25] She concludes that adoptees can actively "limit or accommodate [the] effects" of kinship knowledge.[26] My second case study, too, is more than just a testimony of what is made possible by technological developments. Instead, it should be read as bearing witness to human creativity and inventiveness. Fuchs is a prime example of a donor-conceived person who would continuously interlace on- and offline search strategies and come up with new ideas of how to best combine results from different sources. Her resourcefulness suggests that instead of a certain technology dictating and shaping search practices, it might be more helpful to think of complex "practices of infrastructuring," which interweave databases, genetic tests, archives, and other

[24] Janet Carsten, "Constitutive Knowledge: Tracing Trajectories of Information in New Contexts of Relatedness," Anthropological Quarterly 80, no. 2 (2007): 403–26.

[25] Ibid., 419.

[26] Ibid., 422.

sources of knowledge. Both case studies demonstrate how knowledge can circulate in new ways and establish new forms of collaboration, as both Holmes and Fuchs formed new relations with (distant) genetic relatives. These relations enabled them to access new kinds of information that would have remained inaccessible if they had not been able to interact with other registrants.

Unfinished Relations and Loose Ends

Both women eventually managed to identify their donor, although neither of the two men had themselves registered with a genetic testing company. At first glance, their stories do indeed seem to support those who claim that anonymity has come to an end: after all, they were conceived at a time when anonymity was not yet temporally limited—and yet, they still managed to identify their donor. Holmes was left with questions that were unanswerable, as her donor did not wish to be put in contact with her. She did not mention any further open questions that she wanted him to answer, although she would have liked to meet up with him in person: "You're only in this life once. You might as well go for things. If it doesn't work out, then I don't have to see him again." Yet, her comments regarding her tap opening at turning points and pivotal moments in her life and causing a renewed curiosity made me wonder whether figuring out the donor's name would really lead to the permanent closing of the tap. Would the apparent closure of finding out her donor's name and a photograph online really permanently destroy the "brick wall"? Or was there rather a potential for more uncertainty that might resurface when more important events occurred in her life? Besides, anonymity might be "dead" in the sense that the donor's name was no longer hidden in records or behind a donor number; however, Holmes still did not know whether she had any half-siblings. Half-siblings who know or do not know that they are donor-conceived might join the database anytime, and her kinship network will continue to be potentially incomplete and expandable, despite, or because of, genetic testing. Fuchs was still following up several leads when I got in touch with her a couple of months after our encounter, but she had identified and met up with her donor by the time I started revising this text. He had so far not put her in contact with his children, however, and out of respect for his privacy, she had not contacted them on her own initiative. Like Holmes, she had not found any donor-conceived half-siblings either, so there were other potential connections that she might make in the future. If the goal of registering with a commercial testing site is to find genetic relatives, then "DNA work" is likely an ongoing project. People might register in the hope to "complete" themselves and (re)establish perceived continuity in their lives and in their kinship network, but my research suggests that genetic testing creates conditions under which this is not possible.[27]

I do not disagree with Harper and colleagues, who claim that anonymity cannot be guaranteed anymore as a result of developments in genetic testing.[28] A broad statement like the one made in their title ("The End of Donor Anonymity"), however, does not accurately reflect the "nature" of anonymity in gamete donation, which was also never complete or total before the introduction of genetic testing: Holmes's and Fuchs's donors were, for example, not anonymous to the medical professionals who treated their mothers. The same can be said about the situation of IR donors, who are mostly referred to as "nonanonymous" donors. IR donors remain anonymous in the beginning but agree to their identifying information being released (usually only to the child). Likewise, any recipient parents might indeed not know who "their" donor is when they receive treatment, but information will already have been recorded and stored by official and clinical authorities. Even if they are supposed to remain anonymous—for example, until the child reaches majority—they are only ever anonymous in relation to certain persons or parties but nonanonymous to others.

[27] This is reminiscent of an observation made by Sarah Franklin in her analysis of early IVF practices and experiences. Women might decide to try IVF because they feel that they have to at least try and "hope for the certainty of knowing they did everything possible to succeed." Franklin argues, however, that "this is precisely the certainty that IVF takes away." Sarah Franklin, *Embodied Progress: A Cultural Account of Assisted Conception* (New York: Routledge, 1997), 173.

[28] Harper, Kennett, and Reisel, "The End of Donor Anonymity," 1138.

Given the nature of anonymity in gamete donation, it might be more apt to say that genetic testing has the potential for introducing new possible players in the field of anonymity instead of ending it. Distant genetic cousins who can help identify or track down one's donor are an example for such transformative figures. Since sites can predict only a relationship range, the "DNA work" that these new players can accomplish is not an automatic one. People commonly need to engage in exchange with other users (who are their genetic relatives) and conduct more inquiries to see how a match fits into their genetic family tree and might link them to their donor. Given the growing popularity of commercial DNA testing—statistics indicate that it started to become a lot more popular in 2017, and several of my interlocutors seemed to believe, in the words of Chapman, that it had "blossomed" that year, especially in the second half, when I had already mostly finished my fieldwork—"finding" relatives might become more and more common; but as the case studies presented in this text show, the process of *searching* and "working with DNA" had not yet come to an end for my interlocutors.[29]

In conclusion, it can be stated that in the "DNA work" of donor-conceived persons, a far-reaching transformation of anonymity, which in itself is always partial and relational, is emerging. These changes are not prescribed or dominated by new technical possibilities but take place at the intersection of various technologies, regulations, and social practices. Through these intersections, new actors enter the arena in which anonymity is done and undone, establishing new modes of being anonymous through new collaborations. Information from different sources, which were previously neither linked nor relevant for a question like "Who is my donor" can now be linked and become relevant through this connection. The possibility of a clear demarcation between information that can identify a person and information that is supposedly nonidentifying and can maintain anonymity is becoming more and more questionable.

[29] Razib Khan and David Mittelman, "Consumer Genomics Will Change Your Life, Whether You Get Tested or Not," *Genome Biology* 19 (2018): 120.

Bibliography

Abel, Sarah. "What DNA Can't Tell Us: Problems with Using Genetic Tests to Determine the Nationality of Migrants." *Anthropology Today* 34, no. 6 (2018): 3–6.

Allan, Sonia. "Donor Identification: Victorian Legislation Gives Rights to All Donor-Conceived People." *Family Matters* 98 (2016): 43–55.

Amorim, Antonio. "Opening the DNA Black Box: Demythologizing Forensic Genetics." *New Genetics and Society* 31, no. 3 (2012): 259–70.

Butler, John M. "The Future of Forensic DNA Analysis." *Philosophical Transactions of the Royal Society B* 370 (2015): 20140252.

Carsten, Janet. "Constitutive Knowledge: Tracing Trajectories of Information in New Contexts of Relatedness." *Anthropological Quarterly* 80, no. 2 (2007): 403–26.

Crawshaw, Marilyn, Lucy Frith, Olga van den Akker, and Eric Blyth. "Voluntary DNA-Based Information Exchange and Contact Services Following Donor Conception: An Analysis of Service Users' Needs." *New Genetics and Society* 35, no. 4 (2016): 372–92.

Franklin, Sarah. *Embodied Progress: A Cultural Account of Assisted Conception.* New York: Routledge, 1997.

Harper, Joyce C., Debbie Kennett, and Dan Reisel. "The End of Donor Anonymity: How Genetic Testing Is Likely to Drive Anonymous Gamete Donation out of Business." *Human Reproduction* 31, no. 6 (2016): 1135–40.

Heinemann, Torsten, Thomas Lemke, and Barbara Prainsack. "Risky Profiles: Societal Dimensions of Forensic Uses of DNA Profiling Technologies." *New Genetics and Society* 31, no. 3 (2012): 249–58.

Hogarth, Stuart, and Paula Saukko. "A Market in the Making: The Past, Present and Future of Direct-to-Consumer Genomics." *New Genetics and Society* 36, no. 3 (2017): 197–208.

Khan, Razib, and David Mittelman. "Consumer Genomics Will Change Your Life, Whether You Get Tested or Not." *Genome Biology* 19 (2018): 120.

Klotz, Maren. *(K)information: Gamete Donation and Kinship Knowledge in Germany and Britain.* Frankfurt: Campus, 2014.

Klotz, Maren. "Wayward Relations: Novel Searches of the Donor-Conceived for Genetic Kinship." *Medical Anthropology* 35, no. 1 (2016): 45–57.

Konrad, Monica. *Nameless Relations: Anonymity, Melanesia and Reproductive Gift Exchange between British Ova Donors and Recipients.* Oxford: Berghahn, 2005.

Kruse, Corinna. "Producing Absolute Truth: *CSI* Science as Wishful Thinking." *American Anthropologist* 112, no. 1 (2010): 79–91.

Leighton, Kimberly. "Geneticizing the Desire to Know: Analogies to Adoption in Arguments against Anonymous Gamete Donation." In *Family-making: Contemporary Ethical Challenges*, edited by Françoise Baylis and Carolyn McLeod, 239–64. Oxford: Oxford University Press, 2014.

Lynch, Michael, Simon A. Cole, Ruth McNally, and Kathleen Jordan. *Truth Machine: The Contentious History of DNA Fingerprinting.* Chicago: University of Chicago Press, 2008.

M'charek, Amâde. "Technologies of Population: Forensic DNA Testing Practices and the Making of Differences and Similarities." *Configurations* 8, no. 1 (2000): 121–58.

Millbank, Jenni. "Identity Disclosure and Information Sharing in Donor Conception Regimes: The Unfulfilled Potential of Voluntary Registers." *International Journal of Law, Policy and the Family* 28, no. 3 (2014): 223–56.

Ruckenstein, Minna. "Keeping Data Alive: Talking DTC Genetic Testing." *Information, Communication and Society* 20, no. 7 (2017): 1024–39.

Stevens, Hallam. "Genetimes and Lifetimes: DNA, New Media and History." *Memory Studies* 8, no. 4 (2015): 390–406.

van den Akker, Olga, Marilyn Crawshaw, Eric Blyth, and Lucy Frith. "Expectations and Experiences of Gamete Donors and Donor-Conceived Adults Searching for Genetic Relatives Using DNA Linking through a Voluntary Register." *Human Reproduction* 30, no. 1 (2015): 111–21.

Sanitary Police and the Politics of Anonymity

Observations on a Game about Endocrine Disruptors

The anonymity we wish to address in this chapter relates to a category of substances that have been gradually and often controversially identified as endocrine disruptors. An endocrine-disrupting substance is a natural or synthetic substance that interferes with the hormonal system of living organisms. Scientific studies have confirmed, denied, or underplayed the impact these substances can have on organisms, resulting in their illness, deformation, alteration, or death.

The endocrine-disruptor game is an investigation into the means through which these endocrine disruptors emerge from anonymity and become associated with effects on the organisms or environments they transform. The game is designed to be activated in a given territory by the key players of this territory. It is about endocrine disruptors but could equally be about any entity that does not have an established social existence, and that affects organisms or environments. The point of the game is to highlight the process through which social agents are established. The endocrine disruptor game uses various categorization and identification systems and formats, which also means multiple ways of establishing identities. The idea is to take an agent out of anonymity, to establish its sanitary existence as well as its associated social network.

Working on establishing existence and assigning names, which may appear rather abstract, should not make us forget what is at stake here: organisms are affected, become sick or die because substances circulate freely and anonymously without leading to their social identification or legal prohibition.

Sanitary Police and the Politics of Endocrine Disruptors

In the context of this game, the word "anonymous" qualifies that which is not endowed with a clearly defined sanitary identity, and whose identity is restricted to a specific field. In the latter case, "anonymous" qualifies that which is outside that field, imperceptible or unperceived, unlocatable or even undetermined, masked or secret. Anonymity therefore qualifies what precedes or escapes the ontological process through which an entity is established within a field.

Conversely, giving something a name within a certain frame of reference, or categorizing something within a new frame of reference it did not have before, means taking it out of its anonymity, in other words, establishing it. This act of establishing is a political enterprise.
It is also, in the case of endocrine disruptors, an operation carried out by sanitary police. Ontology as a naming activity is a political activity that provides the necessary conditions for any sanitary police operation. It establishes substances (as potential endocrine disruptors) then enacts them (as recognized endocrine disruptors). Conversely, it can also dismiss them. Dismissal can, for example, constitute an anonymization operation, in the way that glyphosate, following a scientific study sponsored by an industrial group, will be removed from the "endocrine disruptor" category.

Though designation is a political enterprise, anonymization, the act of removing something's designation, of taking away the possibility of being identified, or even the act of removing the substance's ability to be designated, or taking away the properties that qualify its presence in the eyes of the world, is also a political enterprise. It is the act of protecting something from the sanitary police's authority: the nameless substance that is not hidden or secret is outside the sanitary police's field of action. It cannot be acted on, from a regulatory standpoint, since it is not listed as a substance that should not exist or that needs to be regulated.

This game about endocrine disruptors is our attempt to address this activity of taking a substance in and out of certain categories, allowing it to circulate freely within bodies. The game deals with the liminal area where substances (molecules in this case), though named and recognized, have not yet been identified in terms of the effects they have, or are just beginning to be identified. Since they are named only in an abstract way, their effects remain concretely anonymous. They still have not been registered in a sanitary police's jurisdiction. An arena can then take shape as a conflict unfolds, intending to subject the anonymous entity (a molecule) to a naming power (expertise, victim, social group) that will enact its name by associating it with an effect.

Bringing the Real Out of Anonymity: Placing a Name within a Categorical Mesh

What is anonymous is first what is indeterminate; what is indeterminate has no qualities, no value. The object, as it is unidentified, can generate a feeling of horror, anxiety, or wonder: it is a black box whose contents are unknown. It can refer back to indeterminate, unlocalized, unobservable authority. We know that a chemical or semiotic authority is present, but it is blurred, hidden, or imperceptible. Or, it cannot give rise to the unequivocal attribution of qualities without getting mixed up with neighboring authorities that could also possess the same ones.

Assigning a noun or name is not enough to extract the real from the indeterminate and coax it out of anonymity. The name or noun must also enter into a network of qualities, categories, and oppositions, which will lead to the ontological as well as epistemological, social, and even economic existence of the named thing. The identity of the thing named by the common noun or proper name is thus nested, inserted into a tangle of other identities and named things, making anonymity just one among many cases within a foliage of names and attributions.

The endocrine disruptions provoked by chemical authorities are effects attributed to substances enabling the classification of said substances as public health issues. Medical then sanitary classification identifies the substance, endows it with qualities. It forces the substance out of inexistence, out of anonymity, and gives the named matter, endowed with qualities, an additional quality that identifies it within the medical or sanitary field.

Beforehand, the substance is outside the field of reference. It exists within a botanical (soy, hops, etc.) or industrial (phthalate, bisphenol A) nomenclature; in other words, it is endowed with a name that distinguishes it from others. It is not anonymous within botanical or industrial nomenclature since it has been recognized, identified: it is bisphenol A from petrochemistry or a contraceptive pill from the pharmaceutical industry. But this identification is relative to a field. It is not universal. The substance, though named within biochemistry or industrial chemistry, remains anonymous from the standpoint of public health: it has not been identified as a disruptive agent. It is not part of the list of toxic or disruptive substances. And because it is not listed, classified, identified as disruptive, the substance—for example, bisphenol A—can be present in baby bottles, phthalates can appear in plastic bottles, and contraceptive pill residue can circulate in tap water.

In France, the level of nitrate or the presence of heavy metals is mapped. By doing so, it is possible to correlate these substances with effects on the endocrine system. But contraceptive pill residues are not listed as substances that need to be detected and reported in quality analysis reports. They can circulate freely in water and affect bodies. The substance, though known, remains anonymous, unidentified in the water. It has a name only in certain areas of social reality. It is anonymous in others.

Taking the substance out of anonymity by creating a record of it, by putting it on a list of toxic or disruptive substances, is the product of an epidemiological, medical, and biological investigation. But often, it is also the result of a social effort, when the substance is controversial, or when it is supported by lobbies and local interests.

Once the newly recognized quality is attributed to the substance, once its toxic or disruptive effects have been measured and recognized as posing a threat to public health, then the anonymous circulation of the substance can potentially stop. The exit from anonymity is the official establishment at once of a chemical social actor and its possible eradication.

Subjecting the endocrine disruptor to sanitary police by taking it out of anonymity is one of the products of social, sanitary, political struggles. The recent debate over Gaucho (a neurotoxin blamed for the mass destruction of bees) demonstrated this. How is it possible to prohibit Gaucho before there's any proof—identification certified by a competent authority—of the danger posed by the substance?

The action can take place without scientific proof recognized by the institution, as we saw with genetically modified organisms, when the GMO reapers destroyed the organisms without waiting for scientific evidence. The anonymous action of the "voluntary reapers" removed the confidential or invisible work from private and public labs, disseminating modified organisms in the environment without the initiation of an open and public debate. The direct action of the reapers—the destruction of the GMO plants—resulted in taking away anonymity by attributing nominal responsibility, that is, political and even legal, to a stakeholder involved in research, to publicly reveal its activity and the disturbances that activity is likely to produce: in short, to generate controversy.

The controversy is created around the production and *political* administration of the proof and conviction beyond a reasonable doubt. The proof removes Gaucho from its neutrality, from the indifference that allows it to circulate anonymously throughout society. The conviction reveals this anonymity to the greater public through direct action and creates something visible by giving it a personality.

Emerging from Anonymity: A Game about Attribution Systems

The categorization of something within a specific section, the allocation of a quality or attribute, subjects that thing to the order and governmentality of names, removing that thing from the anonymity of what is vague, undetermined, and thus without names, properties, or attributes. Being a human, earthling, Asian is not enough to be anonymous, or being a dog instead of being Rex. Being a blade of grass is not even sufficient, as it is not one of those plants that cannot be said to have a tip, a definite beginning or end, because, unlike animals, they do not have an envelope, an edge, that gives them a body that allows us to say "it is that" or "it is him." The human, the dog, and the blade of grass are each endowed with a set of properties that tie them to an identity like this envelope known as a dog, this bag of skin that ties the dog to a body that makes it a "dog." And even if it is "a" dog rather than "the" or "that" dog, it is still not anonymous, despite appearing to be *anonymous as an individual within the general context* of its category. The same applies to an endocrine-disrupting substance, which is endowed with a general name, such as atrazine, that assigns to it an identity without pushing the investigation any further, enabling the recognition of the specific signature of this atrazine, attributable to Syngenta, who produces it.

Name attribution operations

	Spatial system (geographic)	Existential system	Perceptive system	Property or attribute system	Agency	Expressive system	Political system
Cultural attribution system	Attributing a location	Becoming oneself, being oneself	Attributing an observability	Attributing determinations, qualities	Attributing a personality, being granted a role (e.g., neighbor)	Original, subjective	Custom
Official attribution system	Land register	Birth certificate	Anthropometrics	Legally or scientifically identified attributes	Having an identified, recognized power, responsibility (expert, witness, etc.)	Legal, statistical identity	Summons in court, establishment of a norm
Anonymity system	A-local, nonlocalized	Becoming impersonal, becoming imperceptible	Imperceptible, nonobservable	Indeterminate, without qualities	Impersonal	Banal, common, mundane	Direct action

Tab. 3

Here we point out six possible name attribution operations, including four used in the game. The lack of one of these attribution modes, their confinement to a given field, opens the possibility of a form of anonymity akin to the example of the plasticizing agent phthalate existing in the field of chemistry and not in that of public health.

Playing the game leads to the emergence of agents to which responsibilities are assigned. Having a location, being granted at least one type of agency, and bearing a responsibility are three major elements in the establishment of identity in this context. That which has no location and remains undetermined is out of scope. The agent is formed at the convergence of a geographic location, an evidence-producing event, and a group of social actors and experts who influence whether a responsibility will be recognized.

THE FROG WITH THREE LEGS

ABSTRACT
Since five years the inhabitants of a territory have been experiencing unusual, and not yet determined health problems.

Could these problems be caused by an unknown hazard, such as the presence of one or several toxins? If so, what kind of poison could it be, and what or who has spread it in the environment?

Five players investigate to identify the real source of the disorder.

FORMATION OF THE PLAYING BOARD
- 6 producer cards
- 6 agent cards
- 6 lobbyist cards
- expert cards
- 1 event card

RULES
- the first player places one event card on the playing board.

- he or she then places one producer, one agent and one lobbyist card in the envelope without showing them.

- next, the player mixes the remaining cards and distributes them. Each player also receives a survey sheet that lists all the game elements, allowing them to check which cards they do and do not have.

- talking turns, each player then picks one "expert card" and reads it aloud.

- if any player thinks that they know who the producer, agent or lobbyist might be, they can share their hypothesis. Players can share their hypothesis at every turn. An hypothesis could, for example, look like this

  "I think Bayer, the contraceptive consumers and the coalition of anonymous monsters" are the responsible trio."

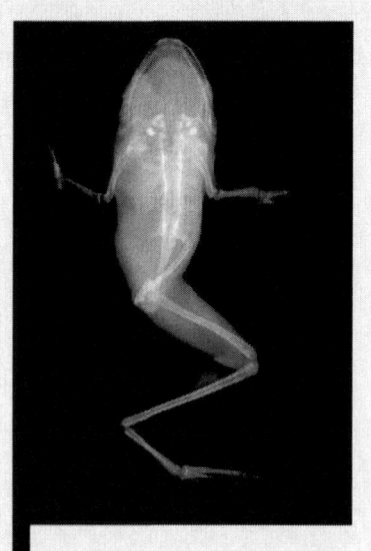

- if one of the other players has one of the cards named in that trio, he or she must show it discreetly to the player who shared the hypothesis. In this way, players can eliminate producer, agent or lobbyist cards and get closer to solving the enigma.

- when a player thinks he or she has found the answer to the enigma, he or she makes an accusation and then check it in the enigma case. Note that each player can only make one accusation per game.

- if the player is wrong, he or she is out of the game. Players who are out of the game cannot share any further hypothesis or accusations but must still show their cards if they are part of another players hypothesis. The remaining players continue the game until the enigma is solved, or all players are out of the game.

Fig. 44 Rules of the game "The frog with three legs"

Geographic Identification

The first identification of a person or event within the game is geographic. The establishment of the geographic space is determined through the attribution of unique positions, which establishes objects (a river, a farm, a factory, etc.). This attribution provides an environment for mobile objects, such as people for whom part of their identity refers to their dwelling. Living somewhere therefore already means carrying a name, and this general name (city, region, area) comes associated with secondary names and qualities. These qualities, some of which are stable, almost immutable (latitude, climate type, sunlight) are associated with other, more mobile and temporary ones.

Geographic anonymity is not merely a result of lacking a name, as could still be seen in nineteenth-century maps, which included blank areas to indicate places that had not yet been subject to a topographical survey. Contemporary cartographic anonymity, except voluntary anonymization, say, for security purposes (military zones that have been deliberately masked or blurred in Google Maps), is manifested as an absence of precision and as weak informational density, as found in rural areas, which are not regularly surveyed by Google vehicles and whose satellite images are sometimes up to ten years old. In these areas of low attention, elements of the landscape are also subject to very little documentation.

Yet maps remain inefficient at showing blurred objects at a micro or nano level, which only become visible or representable when they exist on a large scale, like a source of pesticides in a river that immediately points to the farmer who caused it.

This attribution is the condition for the potential assignment of responsibility, the condition for the production of evidence. It is based on the relational ontology of geography, built in relation to the inclusion of a part into

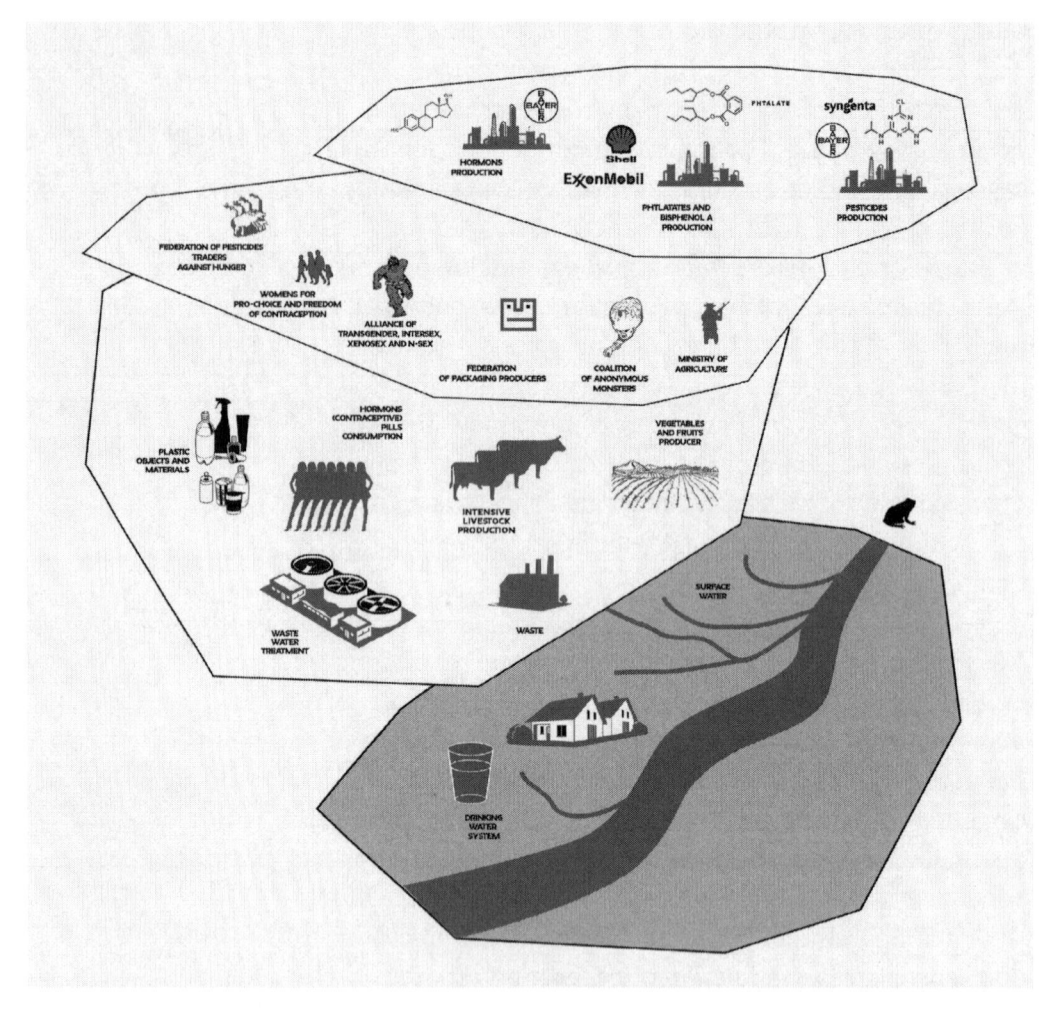

Fig. 45 Game board of "The frog with three legs"

a whole, which uses the concepts of identity and dependence. These relations are at once antisymmetric (if A is included in B, B is not included in A) and transitive (if A is included in B and B is C, then A is included in C). Knowing the properties of A allows us to deduce the properties of B. This suggests the existence of ultimate (simple) elements, and a logic of thing formation based on combining simple elements (interlocking, arranging, aggregating, joining, etc.). The real is thus divided into two classes: that of simple elements, and that of combined or complex elements. And the relation between one and the other is the system that determines the methods used to combine basic elements into statements.

In this case, geographic identification is also, simultaneously, a cartographic identification: a position is given on a map, which shows where objects are located with respect to one another according to geometric or topographical relations. Geometric relations include measured space, since distance is defined by a pair of points. Euclidean space is a topographic space at once measurable and mappable where changes in terrain are translated into angles and distances between points that remain constant regardless of the transformations. Every spot has an identity because it has one and only one location. The source of the pesticides is located at these precise coordinates, and because it is located in this specific spot, it can be attributed to a cause, which is then tied to an agent.

Player Identification

The players themselves, their identity or biography, are of capital importance in determining the methods of attribution that will be deployed in the game. They are the ones who will bring into play the clues and assets, who will decide to act to "invent" an identity, remove a being from anonymity, or qualify its previously unknown toxic force of action. In the game, every player is granted a biography, which remains secret and which cannot be revealed other than through an action activating clues and assets, forcing the players to unmask themselves.

Establishment through Clues

A molecule disseminated in a lake through the discharge of drinking water will thus be considered the cause of the endocrine disruption that provoked the frog's sex change. The clue is the frog's sex change. The clue generates an event.

PLACE
HORMONS PRODUCTION (Bayer)

The plant specializes in the manufacture of contraceptive pills and steroids. The plant uses a pipe coming from the river and rejects filtered water. The Bayer plant has 500 jobs. Controversy has arisen regarding workers affected by the hormones produced in the factory.

MOLECULES
Oestrogens
Androgenes

PLACE
PESTICIDES PRODUCTION (Monsanto / Bayer)

Monsanto sells more than 825,000 tonnes a year of Roundup, which represents 40% of its turnover. The company presented studies concluding that glyphosate was "probably not carcinogenic".

MOLECULES
Pesticides

PLACE
PLASTIZER PRODUCTION (Shell)

Royal Dutch Shell produces Bisphenol A, a plastizer.

MOLECULES
Bisphenol A

PLACE
PLASTIZER PRODUCTION (ExxonMobil)

Exxon Mobil produces Phtalates, a plastizer.

MOLECULES
Phtalates

PLACE
PESTICIDES PRODUCTION (syngenta)

Atrazine, the active ingredient in a pesticide produced by Syngenta, has been the subject of intense controversy over the past 15 years. This powerful herbicide has been banned by the European Union since 2003 and by Switzerland since 2012. But it continues to be used in a large number of countries.

PLACE
HORMONS PRODUCTION (Pfizer)

Pfizer CentreOne specializes in steroid and hormone production.

MOLECULES
Progesterone,
Testosterone,
Éthinylestradiol,
somatropin (Growth hormone)

POLITICS
MINISTRY OF AGRICULTURE

According to the Minister of Agriculture, farmers need pestoids even if they know the danger: "If I banned them, what would farmers tell me? People will tell me: you are destroying agricultural production» Stéphane W., Minister for Agriculture, about pesticides.

POLITICS
COALITION OF ANONYMOUS MONSTERS

This coalition includes individuals considered monstrous because of their deformity or abnormality. They fight against discrimination against monsters.

POLITICS
ALLIANCE OF TRANSGENDER, INTERSEX, XENOSEX AND N-SEX

The Alliance criticizes eco-normativity that asserts the abnormality of the sex change of frogs. It militates for the abrogation of all normativities relative to sex, gender and sexualities.

POLITICS
WOMENS FOR PRO-CHOICE AND FREEDOM OF CONTRACEPTION

This association, which inherited feminist struggles, campaigns for the distribution of female or male oral contraceptives, and for their repayment.

POLITICS
FEDERATION OF PESTICIDES TRADERS AGAINST HUNGER

The Federation of Pesticides Traders Against Hunger defends the increase in agricultural production to fight hunger in the world. For this it promotes the use of pesticides.

POLITICS
FEDERATION OF PACKAGING FOR HYGIENE

Packaging producers advocate for the use of plastic, which helps maintain food hygiene.

AGENTS
WASTE WATER TREATMENT PLANT

Waste water treatment has not been designed for the elimination of endocrine disruptors, xenoestrogens and anti-androgens, pesticides.

MOLECULES
Pesticides
Oestrogens
Androgenes
Phtalates
Bisphenol A

AGENTS
FRUITS AND VEGETABLE PRODUCER

This vegetable and fruit producer is applying pesticides that affect both the nearby residential area and the environment. Nobody knows around that these pesticides are carcinogenics. Culture effluents, especially when it rains, arrive in the river. The farmer is a pesticide user for 20 years, with Parkinson's disease.

MOLECULES
Pesticides

AGENTS
CONTRACEPTIVE PILLS CONSUMPTION

Birth control pills have a combination of estrogen and progesterone.

MOLECULES
Oestrogens
Oestradiol

AGENTS
WASTE

Uncontrolled waste incinerators (solid waste and hospital waste) produce dioxins. Dioxins are highly toxic and can cause reproductive and developmental problems, damage the immune system, interfere with hormones and also cause cancer. More than 90% of human exposure to dioxins is through the food supply, mainly meat and dairy products, fish and shellfish.

MOLECULES
Dioxins

Fig. 46 Some cards of the game "The frog with three legs"

The event is the first public manifestation of the clue: an anomaly is detected, and a cause is sought out. The events express the signature of a molecule that acts on a body in a given space and time: the anonymous and unclear pesticide emerges from its dissolution into the real. It affects a body and creates a trauma, a sanitary problem.

The work to produce evidence establishes the identity of the acting entity, to take it out of anonymity. The continuity of the real is broken down into discrete components, enabling at once the production of evidence, the attribution of responsibility, and the socialization of the entity, which until then had no social existence.

The analysis of water or organic fragments allows for the detection of the entity's presence, to assign it a name—that is, to remove it from indifferentiation, from anonymity. The clue points toward a still-unidentified agent that has caused the sex change. It gives meaning to the event, which without it would remain incomprehensible. It is used in the process of producing evidence, the basic material to confirm or disprove guilt and responsibility, that is, to remove an actor from anonymity, from indifferentiation. The accumulation of clues gradually shapes an identity, building a social actor who will be endowed with the power to act.

Establishment by Experts

Experts are the authorities who bring into play their knowledge and power to establish and recognize, or to deny or rescind, a clue. These experts will have a decisive impact on the establishment of an agent. The players rely on experts to deduce a responsibility. Controversy arbitration takes place in an arena. Information is compiled to form a coalition that establishes the agent.

Establishing Agents in the Arena

While the clues and the experts are both deanonymizing or reanonymizing agents, the authorities that categorize, produce, and establish the real institute substances inside the arena, where series of clues and experts are pitted against one another: Is it acceptable to assign clues to a responsibility? What is the configuration of the network of stakeholders contributing to the establishment of the substance? The arena arises through actions that do not activate the same powers. Some of them activate identification and categorization methods by relying on scientific investigations, expert authority, and the order of laws and norms. Others can also attack anonymity systems directly without bothering with the burden of proof. Of course, such an attack presupposes the recognition of an existence and the attribution of a name, thus an exit from anonymity. This is what we were referring to before when discussing the direct action of the often anonymous GMO reapers.

It is important here to distinguish between the tactical and the strategic moment of naming. In the direct action of the GMO reapers, the coming out of anonymity was tactical: it aimed to reveal what was invisible, to call attention to it. This is the logic behind the people's court pointing fingers at the executioners. The other tactic is a summons to appear in court, which uses police and control measures to divert the purpose of the inspection. These tactical naming actions contribute to the regeneration of a henceforth toxic and definitively transformed world.

Notes

This chapter was translated by Toby Cayouette.

INVESTIGATION CARD   −   +

public power
- Colation of anonymous monsters ☐☐☐☐☐☐☐☐
- Ministry of agriculture ☐☐☐☐☐☐☐☐
- Alliance of transgender, xeno-sex,... ☐☐☐☐☐☐☐☐
- Women for pro-choice ☐☐☐☐☐☐☐☐
- Federation of pesticides traders ☐☐☐☐☐☐☐☐
- Federation of packaging producers ☐☐☐☐☐☐☐☐

agent
- Women consumption of contraceptive pills ☐☐☐☐☐☐☐☐
- Waste water treatment ☐☐☐☐☐☐☐☐
- Waste ☐☐☐☐☐☐☐☐
- Vegetables and fruits producers ☐☐☐☐☐☐☐☐
- Livestock producers ☐☐☐☐☐☐☐☐
- Plastics packaging ☐☐☐☐☐☐☐☐

producer
- Pesticides producer Monsanto/Bayer ☐☐☐☐☐☐☐☐
- Pesticides producer Syngenta ☐☐☐☐☐☐☐☐
- Phtalate or Bisphenol A producer Shell ☐☐☐☐☐☐☐☐
- Phtalate or Bisphenol A producer Exxon ☐☐☐☐☐☐☐☐
- Hormons producer Bayer ☐☐☐☐☐☐☐☐
- Hormons producer Pfizer ☐☐☐☐☐☐☐☐

- Number of true affirmations ☐☐☐☐☐☐☐☐

INVESTIGATION CARD   −   +

public power
- Colation of anonymous monsters ☐☐☐☐☐☐☐☐
- Ministry of agriculture ☐☐☐☐☐☐☐☐
- Alliance of transgender, xeno-sex,... ☐☐☐☐☐☐☐☐
- Women for pro-choice ☐☐☐☐☐☐☐☐
- Federation of pesticides traders ☐☐☐☐☐☐☐☐
- Federation of packaging producers ☐☐☐☐☐☐☐☐

agent
- Women consumption of contraceptive pills ☐☐☐☐☐☐☐☐
- waste water treatment ☐☐☐☐☐☐☐☐
- Waste ☐☐☐☐☐☐☐☐
- Vegetables and fruits producers ☐☐☐☐☐☐☐☐
- Livestock producers ☐☐☐☐☐☐☐☐
- Plastics packaging ☐☐☐☐☐☐☐☐

producer
- Pesticides producer Monsanto/Bayer ☐☐☐☐☐☐☐☐
- Pesticides producer Syngenta ☐☐☐☐☐☐☐☐
- Phtalate or Bisphenol A producer Shell ☐☐☐☐☐☐☐☐
- Phtalate or Bisphenol A producer Exxon ☐☐☐☐☐☐☐☐
- Hormons producer Bayer ☐☐☐☐☐☐☐☐
- Hormons producer Pfizer ☐☐☐☐☐☐☐☐

- Number of true affirmations ☐☐☐☐☐☐☐☐

Fig. 47 Investigation factsheet for the game "The frog with three legs"

Where Do the Data Live?

Anonymity and Neighborhood Networks

In 2016 Amazon's Prime service excluded predominantly African American neighborhoods in six major US cities from its twenty-four-hour free delivery service. According to a Bloomberg analysis that compared the same-day delivery areas with US Census Bureau data, this holds, for example, in the Bronx in New York and in Chicago's South Side.[1] The most striking gap was in Boston, where three ZIP codes encompassing Roxbury, a neighborhood where most residents are people of color, are excluded from the service, while the areas that surround it on all sides are eligible. Amazon might not have deliberately

[1] David Ingold and Spencer Soper, "Amazon Doesn't Consider the Race of Its Customers: Should It?" *Bloomberg*, April 21, 2016.

supported a cartography evolved from a long history of redlining efforts when it calculated the locations where the service would get the highest expected yield. The discriminatory bias was implemented into their anonymized dataset based on neighborhoods. Yet, what can we learn about current issues of anonymity from this example of segregating and discriminating against certain neighborhoods?

Neighborhood data, like a postal code, is seen as valuable for product development and marketing purposes because it does not just inform about locality; it is connected to lots of information, for example, average income, without using personally identifiable information (PII).[2] Marketing information systems combine databases of consumer information with geographic information systems to understand and predict what people do and want, and what they buy based not on private declared information but on the behavior of their neighbors.[3] Crucially, the terms "neighbor" and "neighborhood" function here in a twofold dimension. On one hand, the neighborhood means a physical urban space, with people living next to each other in a defined district, like the Bronx or Roxbury. On the other hand, the term is used in network science to designate a cluster of data with the same characteristics. If a user searches on Amazon for Gabriella Coleman's book *Hacker, Hoaxer, Whistleblower, Spy: The Many Faces of Anonymous*, the results shown are sorted not just by the user's search history, but also by the online behavior of others who searched for the same—interestingly called neighbors. Recommendations for other products, for example, that one might also be interested in the book *Ghost in the Wires: My Adventures as the World's Most Wanted Hacker*, are based on which links data neighbors clicked on, what they looked for next, or what they also bought. One specific network science method is called k-nearest neighbor, which is used for supervised machine-learning algorithms to automatize the classification of neighbors based on data points, which ones are close to each other

[2] So-called linkage attacks (see Arvind Narayanan and Vitaly Shmatikov, "Robust De-Anonymization of Large Sparse Datasets," *Proceedings of the 2008 IEEE Symposium on Security and Privacy* [Los Alamitos, CA: IEEE, 2008], 111–25) have proved many times the high potentials to reidentify individuals by matching anonymized datasets with publicly available information. The EU General Data Protection Regulations are an example of new regulations trying to rethink how personal data is defined under the conditions of networked information. Effective since May 2018, Article 4(1) says, "'Personal data' means any information relating to an identified or identifiable natural person ('data subject'); an identifiable person is one who can be identified, directly or indirectly, in particular by reference to an identification number or to one or more factors specific to his physical, physiological, mental, economic, cultural or social identity." How to control potential ways for indirect reidentification with the use of networked data remains unclear.

[3] Jon Goss, "'We Know Who You Are and We Know Where You Live': The Instrumental Rationality of Geodemographic Systems," *Economic Geography* 71, no. 2 (1995): 171–98.

and therefore potentially similar. The curation of so-called personalized digital services, like the selection of certain online newsfeeds, by a search engine, or in recommendation systems are functioning with the same logic of neighborhood clustering. As Wendy Chun describes, "If Big Data predictive analytics work, it is not because everyone is treated like a special snowflake but because network analyses segregate users into 'neighborhoods' based on their intense likes and dislikes."[4]

On the first glimpse, urban neighborhoods and data neighborhoods and their segregation mechanisms might seem to be two different phenomena sharing the same name because people or data are located close to each other, but there is much more to the story, as their history is deeply entangled. This, the entanglement of the history of urban neighborhoods and today's networking algorithms shaping social interactions online, has subsequent effects on anonymity.

In "Homophily: The Urban History of an Algorithm," Laura Kurgan et al. demonstrate how the impact of homophily, namely, to think of and construct neighborhoods as homogeneous formations or, in other words, as clusters based on similarities, has become a grounding axiom in network science.[5] Drawing on an influential and highly contestable biracial housing study in Pittsburgh from 1947 by Paul F. Lazarsfeld and Robert K. Merton, their work reveals that the study "is not simply something from the past. It speaks directly to our present, our segregated cities and our polarized platforms, where the effects of research in a housing project now reverberate at much greater scale in networks and networked cities."[6] The online and offline segregation caused by exclusion from an Amazon Prime service is one incident that exemplifies the interconnectedness. But what role does anonymity play in this example and what issues are caused?

[4] Wendy H.K. Chun, "Queerying Homophily," in *Pattern Discrimination*, ed. Clemens Apprich, Wendy H.K. Chun, Florian Cramer, and Hito Steyerl (Minneapolis: University of Minnesota Press, 2018), 61.

[5] Laura Kurgan, Dare Brawley, Brian House, Jia Zhang, and Wendy Hui Kyong Chun, "Homophily: The Urban History of an Algorithm," *e-flux*, October 4, 2019.

[6] Laura Kurgan et al.'s work was produced for the 2019 Chicago Architecture Biennial. It is part of a collaborative research project on the historical roots of homophily of neighborhoods undertaken by the Center for Spatial Research at Columbia University and the Digital Democracies Group at Simon Fraser University.

Anonymization in times of big data analysis takes (data) neighborhoods outside the applicability of privacy, as it no longer maps onto identifiable individuals, although, as Solon Barocas and Helen Nissenbaum argue, certain people remain reachable with, for example, advertisements, while others are not addressed and are (unwillingly) excluded for certain services, like twenty-four-hour delivery of purchases they might not be able to buy in their area.[7] For various reasons rooted in urban inequalities, "white areas get organic grocers and designer boutiques. Black ones get minimarts and dollar stores," as the Bloomberg authors comment on the Amazon case in the United States.[8] The Amazon example shows that the use of (data) neighborhoods for allegedly anonymized big data analysis causes problems that go beyond privacy issues: in cities where most paying members of a Prime online service are concentrated in predominantly white parts of town caused by the long tradition of redlining in the United States, a solely data-driven calculation that focuses on *where the data live* (that is, concentrating on data subjects in data neighborhoods), instead of considering the history of segregation implemented within the data, can reinforce long-entrenched inequality in access to retail services.

Currently discussed under the term "echo chambers," online networks reproduce gender and racial biases, as well as reinforcing social and economic inequalities embedded within society.[9] As online communities have become more homogeneous, they have also shifted from the nineties cyberutopian vision of fluid, anonymous *online beings* to an imperative of an *authentic,* consistent social media *profile.*[10] Social media networks became a place for *real* data, *real* names, *real* places, and *real* neighbors. Neighborhood platforms like Nextdoor or Amazon's Neighbors by Ring see the relevance of their product in focusing on connecting *real* people living next to each other rather than people in a global online network. But what happens when neighborhood districts and data neighborhoods get linked in a social media

[7] Solon Barocas and Helen Nissenbaum, "Big Data's End Run around Anonymity and Consent," in this volume.

[8] Ingold and Soper, "Amazon Doesn't Consider the Race of Its Customers."

[9] Chun, "Queerying Homophily"; Cathy O'Neil, *Weapons of Math Destruction: How Big Data Increases Inequality and Threatens Democracy* (London: Penguin, 2016); Safiye U. Noble, *Algorithms of Oppression: How Search Engines Reinforce Racism* (New York: New York University Press, 2018); and Virginia Eubanks, *Automating Inequality: How High-Tech Tools Profile, Police, and Punish the Poor* (London: St. Martin's Press, 2018).

[10] Andreas Bernard, *The Triumph of Profiling: The Self in Digital Culture* (Oxford: Polity, 2019).

neighborhood network? Networks of hybrid offline and online information based on small-scale areas and groups of people connected to machine-readable user profiles owned by private tech companies create various political and ethical problems, like the potential for surveillance, privacy and security concerns, and issues of discrimination.

Two important implications of anonymity arise in the context of network science and the neighborhoods it produces. One has to do with a representation of *identity* based on groups of actors with the same characteristics, and the other with techniques and regulations of *(non) identification*. Both concepts influence and shape each other; their history and their interdependence with social and technical conditions have to be understood. By tracing the history of neighborhood developments like the *neighborhood unit* that evolved from the industrial city, the *block* regime in Nazi Germany, the countercultural idea of *alternative ways of communal living*, the vision of a virtual *global village*, and social media neighborhood networks linked to *nearest-neighbor analytics*, this chapter traces how historically developed relations of anonymity and neighborhoods affect subjectivity, fairness, and relations of equality and difference today.

The Metropolitan City and the Neighborhood Unit

In "The Metropolis and Mental Life," Georg Simmel describes how the development of big and more anonymous cities in the industrialization of the nineteenth century changed the concept and coordination of life and altered the subject toward a "metropolitan individuality."[11] Following Simmel, this new individuality evolved because the social and spatial organization of the city encouraged multiplicity and opened up a bigger and more anonymous living space. This social development proceeds simultaneously in two divergent but nonetheless corresponding directions. On the one hand, the anonymity of the

[11] Georg Simmel, "The Metropolis and Mental Life." In *Georg Simmel on Individuality and Social Forms*, edited by D. N. Levine (Chicago: Chicago University Press, 1903), 325.

many-membered urban organism in contrast to the small, closed, and conformed circles of narrow familial groups and village communities offers more space for freedom and peculiarities in the inner and external creation of individuality. On the other hand, the spacious, crowded, diverse city is linked to difficulties of control, fears of missing security, depersonalized modes of exchange, and experiences of alienation. This position gained further traction from the strong influence of the Chicago school of sociology during the twenties and thirties. Amid the urban dynamism of Chicago's explosive growth, Robert E. Park, William I. Thomas, Ernest W. Burgess, and Park's student Louis Wirth were early representatives of this new school of urban sociology focused on questions around the city from the perspective of human behavior and social structures. One of their critical standpoints was that the city and its heterogeneous urban environment is characteristic of an absence of intimate community and instead dominated by anonymous, superficial, and transitory relations among segmented people.[12] In a similar regard, Simmel emphasizes that the new market system of the metropolitan city operates for purchasers who never appear within the actual field of vision of the producers or marketers themselves. What he calls "the structure of highest impersonality"[13] involves a loss of trust and lack of control through failures of identification in cases of fraud or deception. The opaque system also makes an understanding of the customers' needs more difficult.

The more anonymous market conventions raised new challenges for how to manage business and people, accompanied by efforts to measure, coordinate, predict, and identify. In this regard, the money economy produced a need for practices like weighing, calculating, and enumerating, as well as a reduction of qualitative values to quantitative terms. Evolving logistical media for coordinating humans and their practices in time and space, like the tower, the calendar, and the clock, as explored by John Durham Peters, are related to the

[12] Louis Wirth, "Urbanism as a Way of Life," *American Journal of Sociology* 44 (1938): 3–24.

[13] Simmel, "The Metropolis and Mental Life," 329.

increasing desire for calculability, precision, and certainty in definitions of equalities and inequalities and unambiguousness in agreements.[14] The impact of "the machine" during the age of industrialization was not just seen in the context of technological innovation but also referred to the social world of the metropolitan city that had become increasingly organized around information and information technics. William F. Ogburn, a professor in the University of Chicago's Department of Sociology and the director of a countrywide investigation of social development and trends in the metropolis, writes in *You and Machines*:

> The city has done things to us. More crimes are committed in the city than in the country. Not so many people get married. Families have fewer children. More women are employed outside the home. Suicides are more frequent in cities. City people are more nervous and more of them go insane. There is more wealth in the city, more conveniences. We don't know many of our neighbors in the cities. There is not so much gossip. There is more music, more books, more education. All these differences between city and country life, the machine has caused.[15]

The industrial city and its space for anonymity were connected to the "machine" as a technical and social development, which caused visions of potential personal growth, creativity, and empowerment because one is liberated from rural traditions and intellectualism, but also more crime, asociality, loneliness, more health issues, and the withering of social communities have been associated with the city.[16] But it is not just that the city brought forth the need for new logistical media and sociotechnical practices to reinsure a form of trust in people and business deals; these practices also pervaded the design of the city itself.[17]

As a reaction to the intensified population shift from the homogeneous agrarian community to the vast heterogeneous industrial metropolis, and the problems of

[14]. John Durham Peters, "Calendar, Clock, Tower," in *Deus in Machina: Religion, Technology, and the Things in Between*, ed. Jeremy Stolow (New York: Fordham University Press, 2013), 25–42.

[15] William F. Ogburn, *You and Machines* (Chicago: University of Chicago Press, 1934), 33.

[16] Clarence Perry, *Housing for the Machine Age* (New York: Russell Sage Foundation, 1939).

[17] Armin Beverungen and Florian Sprenger, eds., "Introduction: Computing the City," *Fibreculture Journal* 212, no. 29 (2017).

controlling time, space, and people, the concept of the neighborhood gained importance. With the engagement of urban sociology like the Chicago school, social mathematics, and city planning, the neighborhood was reinvented in the early twentieth century as the smallest local unit in the social, economic, and political organization of a city.[18] The neighborhood was interpreted as a key unit between the individual and the metropolis. To offer a design framework for city planners to disseminate the city into smaller spatial subsets, as well as to provide a concept of the neighborhood as a social community, the urban planner and sociologist Clarence Perry developed a design model in 1929. The formula, which became influential as the "neighborhood unit," has been enormously important in the evolution of the modern city form to this day. In its geometric distribution and the relation to perimeter street patterns, Perry's model, like several other variations, standardized the components of a neighborhood by population size connected to certain institutions. Standardized increments are mainly designed for convenience for the people living in the neighborhood, but with a strong vision of a traditional small family with a perimeter that restricts the maximum distance that inhabitants have to cover to reach a shopping center, a church, and an elementary school: "Not more than one-quarter to one-half mile radius from the school; total area is a function of density."[19] To some degree, the unit seeks to standardize the factor of sociality as a group of neighbors and their interactions. This vision of social engineering through a spatial cluster supporting a social network has high impact on concepts of *neighborhood identity* and conditions for *identification*, and it raises the question of how one should live (connected to space and people). The effects of certain assumptions regarding categories like class, race, and gender roles are implemented into the design of the neighborhood unit. The sharpest criticism in a controversial debate against the neighborhood unit has focused on the degree to which diverse urban society can or should resemble the neighborly community Perry imagined.

[18] Christina Vagt, "Neighborhood Design: Buckminster Fuller's Planning Tools and the City," in *Neighborhood Technologies: Media and Mathematics of Dynamic Networks*, ed. Tobias Harks and Sebastian Vehlken (Zurich: Diaphanes, 2015), 81–95.

[19] Clarence Perry, *Regional Survey of New York and Its Environs, Neighborhood and Community Planning*, vol. 3 (1929; London: Routledge, 1998); on Perry's neighborhood unit, see also Thomas Reiner, *The Place of the Ideal Community in Urban Planning* (Philadelphia: University of Pennsylvania Press, 1963), 60.

Opponents have pointed to the parochial and excessively homogeneous ethnic, racial, or religious formation of neighborhoods, questioning besides economic factors like rent and taxes the assumption that the segment should be, for example, limited to one-school-oriented areas or a Christian church. Shortly after World War II, the neighborhood unit came under attack from Reginald Isaacs, who studied sociology and planning at the University of Chicago. Isaacs discusses in his prominent paper "The Neighborhood Theory: An Analysis of Its Adequacy" that the overwhelming endorsement of the imagined neighborhood unit, as "a panacea for all urban ills," can be misused as an instrument for the segregation of racial, ethnic, religious, and economic groups by city planners willing to use the gated-community aspects of the neighborhood design for this purpose.[20] Its most extreme consequences show up in the totalitarian control apparatus of Nazi Germany, its "micromanagement" of the Blockwart system that controlled the neighborhoods, the ghettoization, and, for example, the technical impact of IBM's punch card system in organizing the mortal analytics and logistics of the fascist regime.

[20] Reginald Isaacs, "The Neighborhood Theory: An Analysis of Its Adequacy," *Journal of the American Institute of Planners* 14, no. 2 (1948): 15–23.

[21] Edwin Black, *IBM and the Holocaust: The Strategic Alliance between Nazi Germany and America's Most Powerful Corporation* (New York: Crown, 2001). There can't be one single-sided answer to the question of how the genocide of 5.5 to 6.3 million people could happen—and of course, it shouldn't imply a technical determinism, which could open doors for the worst misinterpretation to absolve people's responsibility or accountability for human rights violations and genocide. This is not what this chapter is offering. It is a reminder of the history of an automated system for identification misused for the purposes of fascist identity politics.

The Block

One simple and horrifying question regarding anonymity, identification, and the Holocaust is how the Nazi regime could know who of Germany's sixty million citizens were not conforming with their ideological categories, such as "Jewish," "Sinti and Roma," "homosexual," "communist," or "disabled." How did they know their names and where they lived? To find answers to how the Nazis ascertained, identified, and counted them, Edwin Black documented the involvement of statistics and the company IBM in the organization of the Holocaust.[21] Before explaining the role of the neighborhood as a key control segment between the state and the individual, I need to explain how the Nazi regime used computation to quickly acquire information about German society.

Even though surveys in Germany had asked questions about, for example, religious affiliation before the first census in the Third Reich, the European population shifts and dislocations caused by the Great War had brought, among others, Jewish people from Poland to Germany. The fascist regime wanted to know how many, their names, where they lived, and what jobs they held. IBM's business in Germany, called Dehomag, handled almost the entire project to count and classify every citizen in 1933 as well as later in a second census, after the expansion of the Reich in 1939. Herman Hollerith, the German inventor of the Hollerith punching card system, founded the company in 1896 as a census-tabulating company. In the early twentieth century, Thomas J. Watson Sr. combined several small companies to form the International Business Machines Corporation (IBM), building a broad lineup of commercial products like scales, clocks, and typewriters.[22] With the punching card machine, IBM became one of the pioneers in computation.

But how did a concept of massively organized identification quietly emerge to become a means of social control, a weapon of war, and a roadmap for group destruction? And how is the power apparatus connected to the neighborhood cluster? On June 16, 1933, one-half million census takers went from door to door through every neighborhood. Information gathered was represented on a card with different combinations of holes and columns. For a bigger spectrum of possible combinations, the standard forty-five-column card moved to a sixty-column format. Sixty columns, each with ten horizontal positions, created six hundred punch holes per card, which were used to identify everyone by county, community, gender, age, religion, mother tongue, number of children, and current occupation. Column 22, "Religion," was to be punched at hole 1 for Protestant, hole 2 for Catholic, or hole 3 for Jewish. The combinations of numbers did not *just* identify people as, for example, "Jew"—the numbers also affected the classification of what "counts" as a "Jewish identity." The information was used to define a

[22] Louis Gerstner Jr., *Who Says Elephants Can't Dance? Inside IBM's Historic Turnaround* (New York: Harper Collins, 2002).

new binary for pseudoscience and official race hatred. Correlated with data of ancestors, terms like "first-degree Jew," "racial Jew," "Mischling," "half Jew," or "quarter Jew" appeared and were combined with generation-to-generation histories, such as remarriages and divorces.[23] People, their history, and their social relationships became transformed in the logic of the totalitarian regime to combinations of numbers, deciding about categories like "Jew" or "Aryan," about those worth being allowed to live and those to be sentenced to death. The system of *highest impersonality* became the system of *highest inhumanity*.

People who were able to escape the identification process or fall through the network of the binary logic had a chance to disappear in the technical system. Anonymity could protect peoples' lives, but the information network was based on decreasing granularity. All cards identifying "non-Aryan" were processed separately, and the information was aligned with land registers, community lists, and church authorities: "What emerged was a profession-by-profession, city-by-city, and indeed a block-by-block revelation of the Jewish presence."[24] Friedrich Zahn, publisher of Germany's general statistical archive (*Allgemeines Statistisches Archiv*), summed up the process when he wrote, "in using statistics, the government now had the road map to switch from knowledge to deeds."[25]

Lists of "non-Aryan" registries were maintained at police stations and local Nazi departments.[26] The largest concentration of Jewish people was found in the Berlin district Wilmersdorf: approximately twenty-six thousand "Observant Jews" accounted for 13.54 percent of the neighborhood. The areas themselves were defined in the tradition of Charlemagne by a system based on the Gau. The thirty-three and later forty-three Gau districts were systematized by postal code numbers in 1941 to be compatible with the logic of automation. The Reichspost was just one of many important German clients of IBM. Transportation schedules, food plans, properties, and zones were processed in the new tabular systems. The

[23] In August 1934 the Dehomag publication *Hollerith Nachrichten* published the article "An Improved Analysis of Statistical Interdependencies via Hollerith Punch Cards Process," using examples of how the new statistics are used for improvements in the field of medicine and the science of genetics and race.

[24] Black, *IBM and the Holocaust*, 58.

[25] Friedrich Zahn, "Die Statistik im nationalsozialistischen Großdeutschland," *ASA* 29, no. 40 (1939): 370.

[26] Black, *IBM and the Holocaust*, 92.

standardized numbers of one to two digests per Gau became the basis for the German post code system.

Even the National Socialist German Workers' Party (NSDAP) was organized into Gau segments. A Gau defined the local affiliation and area of authorization of the NSDAP members.[27] The strict hierarchy was structured in decreasing segments under Führer Adolf Hitler, his deputy Rudolf Hess, and 18 high-rank Reichsleiter into 40 Gauleiter, 813 Kreisleiter, 26,138 Ortsgruppenleiter, 97,161 Zellenleiter, and 5,111,689 Blockleiter (also known as the Blockwart during the second period of the census, in 1939). The Blockwart was responsible for controlling the smallest segments of around 170 people and 40 to 60 households. They were the informers and abettors of daily National Socialist (NS) terror and constitutive elements of the NS persecution machine focusing on their neighborhood. They were responsible for the enforcement of Nazi politics on the micro scale, functioning as an intermediate between the NSDAP leadership and their neighbors—or, as Black puts it, "Population statistics had crossed the fiery border from a science of anonymous masses to the investigation of individuals."[28]

There is a long tradition of research around power distribution of the Reich in which, surprisingly, the Blockwart is still underrepresented although their role in the enforcement of disciplinary mechanisms is immensely important.[29] During all of World War II, more than two million of them acted not only as ideological propagandists for numerous NS organizations, but also as effective instruments of widespread information gathering in the neighborhoods. A neighborhood block was the systematic set size, which is controllable, and the Blockwart organized the inner front. They registered non-Aryan households and their properties and denunciated "Judenfreunde," who were later persecuted by other institutions. They were in charge of food supplies for the civilian population, maintaining public order, and diffusing regulation into even the smallest details of

[27] The implication of Gau came to mean much more than a cluster based on and defining neighborhoods; the symbol is used even today in right-wing extremist groups. German law has forbidden the fascist symbol since 2002.

[28] Black, *IBM and the Holocaust*, 57. The powerful positions of the Gauleiter and the Blockwart within the control apparatus are understandable in the context of the roles of intendant and syndic governing the districts of the city when the plague appeared at the end of the seventeenth century, as described by Michel Foucault in *Discipline and Punish* (1975; New York: Vintage Books, 1995), 196: "Every day, the intendant visits the quarter in his charge, inquires whether the syndics have carried out their tasks, whether the inhabitants have anything to complain of; they 'observe their actions.' Every day, too, the syndic goes into the street for which he is responsible; stops before each house: gets all the inhabitants to appear at the windows (those who live overlooking the courtyard will be allocated a window looking onto the street at which no one but they may show themselves); he calls each of them by name; informs himself as to the state of each and every one of them—'in which respect the inhabitants will be compelled to speak the truth under pain of death'; if someone does not appear at the window, the syndic must ask why: 'In this way he will find out easily enough whether dead or sick are being concealed.'... This surveillance is based on a system of permanent registration: reports from the syndics to the intendants, from the intendants to the magistrates or mayor." Foucault describes

everyday life, for example, harassing house rules that prohibited pets in Jewish homes. As the watchdogs of the block, they were known as the Treppenterrier (staircase terrier), sniffing and snooping at doors to make sure nobody was roasting meat on the cost-saving Soup Sundays. Everything was constantly documented in a formalized register, the Haushaltskartei (housekeeping file), in which any statement critical of the regime or signs of depreciated behavior would be archived and delivered to the NSDAP. The Blockwart registered the information within his block and managed the transfer from the neighborhood to the Nazi state. He was on the ground level of ramifications of power structured in a hierarchical organization with in-depth surveillance and control.

During wartime, the city and its neighborhoods were "exempt" from "Jewish business" and "non-Aryan" people. The fatal pogroms as well as the establishment of "Jewish housing" within Germany and the more than five hundred ghettos in the expanding Nazi Reich were part of the racial segmentation of people in different districts. In Warsaw, for instance, the city was divided into Jewish, Polish, and German quarters. The ghettoization was a provisional measure to control and manage the mortal logistics of killing as many as possible as quickly as possible. In many places, ghettos lasted a short time. Some existed for only a few days; others lasted for months or years. Many people died in the ghettos; others were deported to death camps. The organization of the ghettos and the death camps was based on the automated systematization of people. Their names were taken from them, and they became standardized and numbered. The anonymization practices in the camps were part of the brutal formalization and dehumanization necessary to systematically kill a group of people categorized and identified as Jews, gay, disabled, or non-Aryan. Culture of memory engagement and research are working on filling the gaps with personal stories to deanonymize the numbers of people who lost their lives in the genocide.

how the complete hierarchy ensured that the granular functioning of the control regime worked with the registration of each individual with a "true" name, a "true" place, and a "true" body.

29 Detlef Schmiechen-Ackermann, "Der Blockwart: Die unteren Parteifunktionäre im nationalsozialistischen Terror- und Überwachungsapparat," *VfZ* 48, no. 4 (2000): 575–602.

Anonymity and anonymization practices in a multifaceted context can be "both under threat, and threatening".[30]

The Global Village

The traumatic history of World War II had a big impact on both the idea of depersonalization through computing and the repoliticization of small communities, like the communes in the counterculture movement of the sixties and seventies. As inspiring precursor for an international protest wave in the sixties, activists from University of California, Berkeley, formed what became famous as the free speech movement. In 1964, Cal students marched against the Vietnam War, centralized bureaucracy, the rationalization of human life, and the idea of being treated as a piece of data. "At Cal you are little more than an IBM card," claimed their nonofficial spokesperson Mario Savio, and other students wore computing cards with punched patterns of holes saying, "I am a UC student. Please do not fold, bend, spindle or mutilate me."[31]

Similar to the concerns expressed against the industrial city envisioned as the "machine," the computer in the sixties was imagined as a systematizing technology causing alienation and depersonalization, now combined with the fear of surveillance through automated identification. This is the starting point of Fred Turner's book *From Counterculture to Cyberculture*, in which he describes how the imaginary of the depersonalized computer system completely changed within the next thirty years: the machines that had served as the identifying and defining devices in the wake of World War II and Cold War technocracy emerged in the nineties as the symbols of a countercultural ideology, with visions of alternative identity politics addressing an empowered individualism and collaborative community.

Although mostly people remain fascinated with the Summer of Love and its sex, drugs, and rock 'n' roll attitude,

[30] Götz Bachmann, Michi Knecht, and Andreas Wittel, eds., "The Social Productivity of Anonymity," *ephemera* 17, no. 2 (2017): 242.

[31] Quoted in Fred Turner, *From Counterculture to Cyberculture: Stewart Brand, the Whole Earth Network, and the Rise of Digital Utopianism* (Chicago: University of Chicago Press, 2006), 12, 2.

Fred Turner emphasizes the importance of the evolvement from a group he calls the "new communalist" and their alternative visions of *living*—in the sense of "being" and "being together." In 1967 many of the hippies who had made Haight-Ashbury *the* neighborhood of the movement left San Francisco to begin the largest wave of communalization in American history. Moved by ideas of finding decentralized ways to de- and reorganize life and living, Americans established between several thousand and several tens of thousands of communes between 1965 and 1972 nationwide, where around 750,000 people lived.[32] The movement envisioned something that could become a new nation, a generation of "small communities linked to one another by a network of shared beliefs."[33] Californian hippies saw the key to social change not in traditional politics, which was in their eyes the reason for most of the grievances they tried to subvert, but through the *mind*.[34] With the help of psychedelic drugs like LSD, a disembodied form of identity could be explored, freed from secular limitations. Ideas of disconnecting from embodied markers engendered a shift toward a positive valuation of a form of *unlinkability*, producing a liberating space for the individual as well as for building community beyond traditional regulations. Technics like the use of drugs but also technology were seen as tools for making this transformation possible.

Turner argues that although members of the counterculture rejected the military-industrial complex as a whole, as well as the political process that brought it into being, they were at the same time highly inspired by the cybernetic discourse.[35] Through the writings of Norbert Wiener, Buckminster Fuller, and Marshall McLuhan, the hippies encountered a cybernetic version of the world, which could be imagined as an information network system. Even without knowing about the internet in 1962, Marshall McLuhan pronounced that people were becoming linked by communication media in a "global village," and architect, designer, and traveling speechmaker Buckminster Fuller declared a new awareness of

[32] The social movements in the sixties were highly fragmented, but countercultural slogans like "Make love not war" were an inspiration for an international flower power wave and served as an input into new ideas of identity and visions of alternative, egalitarian communities in postwar Germany, too. In divided Germany the countercultural movement triggered the idea that the traditional structure of the nuclear family life and the philistine neighborhood is a nucleus for fascism, fueling the development of alternative communities and communes in the city and the German countryside.

[33] Turner, *From Counterculture to Cyberculture*, 33.

[34] In 1996 the entrepreneur and founder of the NGO Electronic Frontier Foundation John Perry Barlow transposed this way of thinking in his famous "Declaration of the Independence of Cyberspace": "Governments of the Industrial World, you weary giants of flesh and steel, I come from Cyberspace, the new home of Mind. On behalf of the future, I ask you of the past to leave us alone. You are not welcome among us. You have no sovereignty where we gather." John Perry Barlow, "A Declaration of the Independence of Cyberspace," Electronic Frontier Foundation, February 8, 1996.

[35] Turner, *From Counterculture to Cyberculture*, 4.

a global neighborhood as "the result of a new and vivid awareness of all other humans around our space vehicle Earth, a vivid awareness of neighbors, never before experienced by humanity."[36]

The neighborhood community became connected to the vision of a whole earth network and system theory as an alternative way of life. The cybernetic rhetoric of information systems, combined with the countercultural ideas of communities and the influence of the emerging technological hub of Silicon Valley, helped to redefine the invention of the microcomputer as a *personal* machine, computer communication as *virtual communities*, and the internet as a *global village*. Similar to the enthusiastic hopes connected to the openness of the big anonymous city was the vision of a *world wide web* celebrated as a potential for exploration of individuality and for building alternative communities by overcoming entrenched social frontiers. Influenced by the ideas of poststructuralists, the academic answers came from Howard Rheingold's *Virtual Community* or Sherry Turkle's *Life on the Screen: Identity in the Age of the Internet*, who proposed that online, the subject has to be understood in its fluidity with the help of categories like heterogeneity and fragmentation.[37] The internet, similar to the countercultural idea of psychedelic drugs, could disconnect the human from the information linked to the body and connect minds of freed *online beings* without the restrictions of locality.

The global reach and new social conditions also raised the fear that a world wide web and its virtual networks would destroy local neighborhood communities.[38] These deterministic visions are matched by the earlier fears of the Chicago school of sociology that a heterogeneous urban environment would be characteristic of an "absence of intimate personal acquaintanceship" and would result in "the segmentation of human relations" into those that were "largely anonymous, superficial, and transitory."[39] From today's standpoint, the internet imagined as cyberspace did not provide fewer possibilities for identification

[36] Vagt, "Neighborhood Design," 88; Marshall McLuhan, *The Gutenberg Galaxy* (1962; Hamburg: Gingko Press Verlag, 2011); and Buckminster. Fuller, "World Game," *Ekistics* 28 (1969): 286–92.

[37] Howard Rheingold, *The Virtual Community: Finding Connection in a Computerized World* (Reading, MA: Addison-Wesley, 1993); Sherry Turkle, *Life on the Screen: Identity in the Age of the Internet* (New York: Simon and Schuster, 1995).

[38] Keith Hampton and Barry Wellman, "Neighboring in Netville: How the Internet Supports Community and Social Capital in a Wired Suburb," *City and Community* 2, no. 4 (2003): 277–311.

[39] Wirth, "Urbanism as a Way of Life," 1.

via its media-technological conditions, nor did it make locality less important.[40] What seems different today is an idea of the individual imagined as a fluid online being. In *The Triumph of Profiling: The Self in Digital Culture*, Andreas Bernard argues that during the time of Turkle and Rheingold's ideas, another concept was on the way to success: the *online profile*.[41] The profile, counter to the imaginary of the fluid online being, is a format based on standardization, calculation, and continuity. This imperative of an *authentic*, consistent profile of the online user relates back to economic rather than philosophical reasons in times of "platform capitalism."[42]

Neighborhood Networks

The commercialization of the internet and, in this context, the ascendency of promoting real data caused a shift in online policies to real name standards on many social media platforms as well as a constant localization.[43] The trend of social media neighborhood networks is based on both. Neighborhood platforms like Nextdoor or Neighbors by Ring shape communities of people by linking them in a small clustered social network. Aligned with the fear of the Chicago school that the city causes anonymous, superficial, and transitory relations among segmented people, digital neighborhood services draw on the assumption that people miss a sense of human (online) connections and community with people in the area they live in. Their forums are an easy way of information transfer about a very small segment of people and places. Neighbors keep one another informed about events, sales, or recommendations in the area, forming a sense of neighborhood community. Connection via an online neighborhood network just like the neighborhood unit in the industrial city can be experienced as something positive against alienation, as a feeling of home, or as a higher level of trust and security. Just as in the critique of the neighborhood unit, however, the question is not whether a neighborly community, where people

[40] Hampton and Wellman, "Neighboring in Netville."

[41] Bernard, *Triumph of Profiling*.

[42] Nick Srnicek, *Platform Capitalism* (London: Polity, 2016).

[43] Bernard, *Triumph of Profiling*.

feel comfortable and safe, is something desirable, but instead who gets included and who excluded based on the assumptions inherent to the design and the conditions supported by it.

Nirav Tolia, the CEO of the world's largest neighborhood platform, Nextdoor, proclaims that we are trending toward "localized discussion facilitated through the internet, and made easier through the mutual trust gained in accountability."[44] To secure the relation to both locality and accountability, a user account has to be linked to a real name and a real residency in a neighborhood. The information has to be verified either by a neighbor who is a current user or by submitting evidence of residency to the company. That people working but not living in the district, just like people living in the district without any residency, are not included in the social media service illustrates that the proclaimed *authenticity* presented on social media (which is commonly used as a counter-argument against online anonymity), which in this case is the real, authentic neighborhood, is replaced by *authentication*.[45] A tech company from San Francisco developed a map of residential areas combined with authenticated and machine-readable profiles—which brings potentials for surveillance from a nexus of other neighbors, private tech companies, and the state.

Nextdoor launched their "forward to police" button in 2016, and Amazon's Neighbors by Ring partners with local law enforcement across the United States to share crime and safety updates. Neighborhood online forums are commonly used to talk about crimes and suspicious behavior or people in the neighborhood. Now users can report these observations directly online to the local police. Ring is additionally connectable to a whole toolbox of home security systems, like a video doorbell, smart lights, and cameras. The footage is easily shareable with neighbors, with the police, and with Amazon. Amazon seems aware of upcoming privacy and security issues and encourages users on their website "to carefully consider

[44] Quoted in Mike Isaac, "Nextdoor, the Private Social Network, Hooks Up with the City of San Jose," *All Things D* (blog), August 7, 2012. Meanwhile, Nextdoor has appointed Sarah Friar as the new CEO.

[45] Liz Losh, based on her collaborative work with Nishant Shah, argues in her lecture "Fake News for Real People" that through processes of automation, authenticity gets replaced by authentication, authority by authorization, and veracity through verification, which has high impact on, for example, the spread of misinformation, and can support processes of polarization. See Losh, "Fake News for Real People," 13th Tack Faculty Lecture, William and Mary, March 22, 2018.

the behavior that made them suspicious of others and whether such suspicion is reasonable, and not post pictures or videos of people taken where they had a reasonable expectation of privacy without their knowledge or consent (for example, users should not post photos or videos of their neighbor's backyard)."[46] Nonetheless, a system to register and deliver observations from the neighborhood to the state continues to evolve.

Regarding the ongoing public discourse on racial profiling on Nextdoor, privacy issues are not the only problem neighborhood networks can potentially proliferate. The debate started with a local newspaper article in the *East Bay Express*, which reported about serious consequences families of color have to face in the context of the racial online posting in Oaklands' Nextdoor group, because the neighborhood platform was increasingly used to report "suspicious activity" of people of color.[47] After the article was published, a public debate started about the discriminating and defaming tendencies of a "crime & safety" forum, where people were posting about activity that wouldn't have been suspicious if the subject hadn't been black—and wearing a hoodie—while most of the people who were accused were also excluded from partaking in the dialogues. Even though targets mostly stay anonymous, it doesn't protect them against the violation. As an answer, Nextdoor redesigned the interface of the reporting system, which complicates the process for the user and generally caused postings to decrease by around 25 percent, exemplifying that how technology is designed can be effective and political.[48] Additionally they created a Racial Profiling Resource Center, which than eliminated anonymity from online posts. Now reports must include specific charactestics of the suspect, not just race or sex.[49] Following the 2020 Black Lives Matter protests Nextdoor reacted to allegations that the platform facilitates racial profiling and surveillance 'by design,' by removing its controversial 'forward-to-the-police' button. Keen to demonstrate support for social justice, the company also has to take responsibility for their biased content moderating

46 Neighbors by Ring, app download page, Ring, last updated October 10, 2019, www.shop.ring.com/pages/neighbors.

47 People of color described stories of white residents running away from them, screaming at them to leave a shared garden space, and calling police on young children in their own home. In some areas, the profiling is further exacerbated by the growing presence of private patrol officers, whom residents have hired to guard the streets. Sam Levin 2015. "Racial Profiling Via Nextdoor.com" *East Bay Express,* October 7, 2015.

48 The online tech magazine *Wired* titled a 2016 story about this "Nextdoor Breaks a Sacred Design Rule." The example illustrates how questions of anonymity are deeply entangled with the design of the neighborhood platform itself. Margaret Rhodes, "Nextdoor Breaks a Sacred Design Rule," *Wired*, August 31, 2016. Another *Wired* article, from 2017, discusses the difficulties that evolve by trying to find a technical fix for racist use of the neighborhood website. Jessi Hempel, "For Nextdoor, Eliminating Racism Is No Quick Fix," *Wired*, February 16, 2017.

49 See "Preventing Racial Profiling on Nextdoor," Nextdoor website, accessed November 28.

system, that censored activist posts.[50] Whether a more detailed observation system and registration is an adequate solution to the problem is questionable. Eliminating racism is not an easy technical fix, but using anonymity as a scapegoat for harmful effects or usage seems to play into the hands of gatekeepers of social media sites, with business models based on authenticated datasets.

With the shift of cyberspace to the internet as a huge online market, the *being online* became a *user* of digital products—and the *user data* a valuable product itself. Data mining opens up a huge potential and even bigger hopes for new knowledge production about individuals and their everyday life, but similar to the challenges occurring with the market system in the metropolitan city, the online system operates for purchasers who don't appear in the actual field of vision of the producers or marketers themselves. As in the industrial city, the digital marketplace brought new challenges in how to manage business and people, accompanied by new practices to measure and predict. As Brunton and Nissenbaum pointed out, "Counteracting the visions of doom, 'Big Brother,' exposure, oppression, surveillance, and losses of privacy and freedom are the celebratory visions of enlightenment, knowledge, transparency, understanding, efficiency, and security through data analysis."[51] Network scientist like Albert-László Barabási see in big data analytics a new, direct, and *pure* way to understand human beings, much better than they could ever understand themselves, because people themselves are not *trustworthy*, as Seth Stephens-Davidowitz argues in *Everybody Lies: Big Data, New Data, and What the Internet Can Tell Us about Who We Really Are*.[52] The logic behind this form of social mathematics is built in a way on the same idea of the punch cards; it creates "user" as systematically readable for the machine. What is readable is the trace of events caused by certain behaviors and relations. As Nishant Shah shows, this produces an imagination of "the individual as atomic, deconstructing the individual not as an actor, but as produced through

[50] Some of the neighbors, who moderate the crime & safety forum flagged and blocked BLM supporters during the protests. Nextdoor promised to offer training against unconscious bias for their moderators. How unconscious the bias in the BLM censorship has been and how willing and able unpaid moderators are to tackle this bias remains questionable.

[51] Finn Brunton and Helen Nissenbaum, *Obfuscation* (Cambridge, MA: MIT Press, 2015), 3.

[52] Albert-László Barabási, *Bursts: The Hidden Pattern behind Everything We Do* (London: Dutton, 2010); and Seth Stephens-Davidowitz, *Everybody Lies: Big Data, New Data, and What the Internet Can Tell Us about Who We Really Are* (New York: Dey Street Books, 2018).

a series of actions, understood as a networked entity that can be mined for data and information, ranging from genetic blue-prints to socio-cultural profiles."[53] The data economy makes a user synonymous with his or her usage, more specifically with the usage of like users, the data neighbors. As explained earlier, the clustering of data neighborhoods functions with correlations based on shared characteristics, what Hito Steyerl describes as, "If white men mostly have strawberries and cream with white men, this means that whoever a white man has strawberries with is most likely a white man. This is what Facebook packages into the idea that you are like what you like, and that you will like the things that people who are like you like."[54]

Obviously this form of standardization behind what is ironically called "personalized" services also means accepting the computational reductionism and decontextualization inherent in systematizing and quantifying people, their behaviors, and their identities.[55] Data neighboring is implemented into recommendation systems or shows in the automated placement of advertisements in newsfeeds of certain groups, based, for example, on targeted ZIP codes, a marketing service Nextdoor is offering. This means, as in the introductory example of Amazon's twenty-four-hour Prime delivery, that some ZIP codes get other advertisements or services from Nextdoor's business partners, ranging from real estate agents, home renovation and insurance companies to home mortgage experts, rental property experts, and so forth.[57] As illustrated with the Amazon Prime example, using neighborhood-based data like postal codes for decision-making processes, such as who gets access to what kind of offer or service, is problematic because it is connected to a long history of urban segregation. In *The Color of Law: A Forgotten History of How Our Government Segregated America*, Richard Rothstein unpacks how systematic and forceful public policies explicitly segregated every metropolitan area in the United States until the last quarter of the

[53] Nishant Shah, "Identity and Identification: The Individual in the Time of Networked Governance," *Socio-Legal Review* 11, no. 2 (2015): 24.

[54] Wendy H. K. Chun, "Queerying Homophily"; Hito Steyerl, "A Sea of Data: Pattern Recognition and Corporate Animism (Forked Version)," in *Pattern Discrimination*, ed. Clemens Apprich, Wendy H. K. Chun, Florian Cramer, and Hito Steyerl (Minneapolis: University of Minnesota Press, 2018), 13.

[55] Noëmi Manders-Huits, "Practical versus Moral Identities in Identity Management," *Ethics and Information Technology* 12, no. 1 (2010): 43–55.

[56] "About Advertising on Nextdoor," Nextdoor Help Center, accessed November 28, 2019.

twentieth century, and the effects are still showing in all kinds of urban inequalities.[57] Additional important effects of racial zoning besides private prejudice and white flight are, for example, income differences; accessibility to education (as US schools are tied to the district one lives in), healthcare, or supermarkets; real estate steering; and denial of financial services such as insurance or banking. If Nextdoor and its business partner implement neighborhood data, such as the statistical income of a certain district, to decide which areas will (or will not) get offers for certain properties, insurances, mortgages, and so on, without considering the historical complex power structure inherent to their data, they can potentially reinforce a discriminatory system. As Sorelle Friedler, a computer science professor at Haverford College who specializes in data bias, warns, "As soon as you try to represent something as complex as a neighborhood with a spreadsheet based on a few variables, you've made some generalizations and assumptions that may not be true, and they may not affect all people equally.... There is so much systemic bias with respect to race. If you aren't purposefully trying to identify it and correct it, this bias is likely to creep into your outcomes."[58] Following Chun's work on *Updating to Remain the Same: Habitual New Media*, we need to understand how seemingly personalized services correspond with former racial and class categories and historically developed power systems—which doubles up if seemingly anonymized neighborhood data and data neighborhoods get correlated in a hybrid online/offline neighborhood network.[59]

[57] Richard Rothstein, *The Color of Law: A Forgotten History of How Our Government Segregated America* (London: Liveright, 2017).

[58] Sorelle Friedler quoted by Ingold and Soper, "Amazon Doesn't Consider the Race of Its Customers."

[59] Wendy H. K. Chun, *Updating to Remain the Same: Habitual New Media* (Cambridge, MA: MIT Press, 2016).

Anonymity and the History of Neighborhoods

We live in an era of networks, which causes fragile conditions for anonymity. By looking into the entangled history of neighborhood networks and corresponding platforms and algorithms, which are shaping personalized digital services, we gain understanding of the mechanisms behind its fragility. To do so, we need to address two main questions: first, how is anonymity understood in the context of network science and personalized digital services, tied to a genealogy of neighborhoods? And second, how does this understanding of anonymity play out today in issues of information governance?

Tracing notions of neighborhoods historically developed by city planning, urban sociology, and social mathematics, diverse valuations of anonymity appear. It is not always clear whether anonymity itself is at issue or some other values driven by fears of crime, deception, alienation, asociality, or hopes of empowerment and the right to peculiarities and personal freedom already appealed to in the debate caused by the industrial city. The various valuations of anonymity combine divergent, sometimes paradoxical, but connected strands of a multilinear history of neighborhoods. The history entangles extremes like the surveillance apparatus of the fascist Blockwart regime in Nazi Germany with a nineties techno-enthusiasm for alternative communities of virtual connected online beings inspired by the countercultural era. What this illustrates is that anonymity can have rather different meanings. What this also means is that how anonymity is currently applied on social media, such as neighborhood platforms, or more broadly in the logic of big data analytics could be changed. Connected to understandings of anonymity are emerging imaginaries of an individual, personhood, and personalization as well as techniques of identification. The market logic of the data economy creates a new imaginary of the individual understood as a series of quantifiable information of behavior and relationships, living segregated in homogenous neighborhoods of anonymous data subjects. It seems like a grotesque irony that neighborhoods get used for big data analytics because the data implied count as *anonymous* and therefore applicable to *privacy standards*, even though, as history has shown, neighborhoods can and have worked as a systematic set size for surveillance, as in the Nazi control apparatus. What neighborhoods and data neighborhoods have in common is that they create a space that interlaces anonymity and surveillance. Furthermore, if neighborhoods and data neighborhoods are interlinked without caution, new and complex effects evolve, whose consequences are difficult to foresee. Drawing on the history of neighborhoods and the sociotechnical conditions it developed for or against anonymity, I put forward two main characteristics that create the fragility of anonymity, which is lying at the heart of current information governance problems.

First, the neighborhood designed and regulated *as a small set* of information, locations, and people makes anonymity more difficult to produce and maintain. This aggravates on neighborhood platforms, which demand real, authentic, validated profiles linked to networked information of hybrid online/offline worlds. In contrast to the fear that the global reach of the internet would destroy local communities, people next to each other get linked in a "glocal village." In the name of alleged security and hope of a better understanding of the human being, the information network of the neighborhood machine becomes a technique of governmental control as well as a business model in times of surveillance capitalism.[60] Without the need for any census takers walking from door to door, social media neighborhood platforms develop small-scaled location maps combined with machine-readable profiles. As in the history of the block regime and IBM's involvement in the Holocaust, this technology could be misused as an instrument for exploitation and surveillance on an everyday level, stemming from a nexus of the government, private companies, and people living next door to each other. As neighborhoods are developed as a key unit between governmental power and the individual and therefore play an important political role, it is important to raise awareness that anonymity has to be protected against a digital version of the Haushaltskartei, where everyone is profiled and their doings constantly documented with the aid of neighbors.

[60] David Lyon, *Surveillance Society: Monitoring Everyday Life* (Buckingham: Open University Press, 2002); and Shoshana Zuboff, *The Age of Surveillance Capitalism: The Fight for a Human Future at the New Frontier of Power* (New York: Public Affairs, 2019).

Second, the concept of neighborhoods as homogeneous formations became central for current anonymization techniques used in big data statistics, which causes various problems. Data neighbors are used to develop so-called personalization of digital services, especially because they do not fall under privacy regulations, as they do not lead to identifiable individuals, even though users remain *addressable* as standardized clusters. In that sense, the practice of anonymization doesn't result in anonymity, at least not in a resilient way. The high potential to reidentify individuals by matching anonymized datasets with publicly available information poses both political and technical challenges. It raises the question of what should be regulated as PII, and how anonymity should be understood and regulated under these complex conditions.

[61] Barocas and Nissenbaum, "Big Data's End Run."

[62] Kurgan et al., "Homophily."

Drawing on the example of the punch cards used for the census in the Nazi regime, I want to furthermore make clear that certain forms of profiling are harmful without exposing single individuals. In this context, the problem goes beyond the need for new privacy regulations. Various ethical and political questions regarding how we use social mathematics arise, such as how (data) neighborhoods get defined, whether (data) neighborhoods are representative for what they are supposed to represent, and whether it is fair to treat people differently in regard to their (data) neighbors.[61] What the example of Amazon Prime reinforcing discriminatory redlining practices shows is that "the ties between network science, urban planning, and social engineering are deeply historical, conceptual, and bi-directional. Network science is haunted by the consequences of urban planning, and vice versa," as the team of Laura Kurgan et al. points out.[62]

The difficulty for single users is to understand the reason they've been excluded from certain services or that they have been excluded in the first place. It is even more difficult to prove that they are part of a whole neighborhood (and this means urban as well as data neighborhoods) that has been systematically discriminated against by exclusions based on categories like race, class, and gender, as private companies keep the systems behind these decision-making processes a corporate secret. As long as their digital services stand up to the endurance test of being able to understand their users with the help of data analysis based on data neighborhoods in which individuals are "not identifiable," tech companies conform with privacy policies. In this context the question is not so much who can still be anonymous but what gets anonymized and what kind of power relations can become untraceable in current dynamics of neighborhood networks. In the way that anonymity is regulated and implemented in data neighborhoods, it doesn't offer an effective weapon against either the new potentials for surveillance (namely because privacy and security issues emerge with the high potential to reidentify individuals by matching supposedly anonymous data neighborhoods with publicly available information), or the clustering of discriminatory classifications (because the data used for personalization is allegedly anonymized data). Connected to a vision to transform subjects into "something that can be easily fed into the machines that convert data into meaningful information or actionable insight," anonymity gets exploited for the purposes of the data economy.[63] A reconfiguration between (non)identification and identity in networks of data neighborhoods occurs, which makes anonymity fragile. To work against the fragility of anonymity and to make the inherent power relations visible, interdisciplinary approaches stemming from network science, data analytics, media and feminist theory, cultural studies, urban planning, infrastructure and algorithm studies, science and technology studies, and political economy are needed.

[63] Anna Laura Hoffmann, "Making Data Valuable: Political, Economic, and Conceptual Bases of Big Data," *Philosophy and Technology* 31 (2018): 210.

Bibliography

Bachmann, Götz, Michi Knecht and Andreas Wittel, eds. "The Social Productivity of Anonymity." *ephemera* 17, no. 2 (2017): 241–58.

Barabási, Albert-László. *Bursts: The Hidden Pattern behind Everything We Do*. London: Dutton, 2010.

Barlow, John Perry. "A Declaration of the Independence of Cyberspace." Electronic Frontier Foundation, February 8, 1996. https://www.eff.org/cyberspace-independence.

Bernard, Andreas. *The Triumph of Profiling: The Self in Digital Culture*. Oxford: Polity, 2019.

Beverungen, Armin, and Florian Sprenger, eds. "Introduction: Computing the City." *Fibreculture Journal* 212, no. 29 (2017). https://www.doi.org/10.15307/fcj.29.212.2017.

Black, Edwin. *IBM and the Holocaust: The Strategic Alliance between Nazi Germany and America's Most Powerful Corporation*. New York: Crown, 2001.

Brunton, Finn, and Helen Nissenbaum. *Obfuscation*. Cambridge, MA: MIT Press, 2015.

Chun, Wendy H. K. "Queerying Homophily." In *Pattern Discrimination*, edited by Clemens Apprich, Wendy H. K. Chun, Florian Cramer, and Hito Steyerl, 59–97. Minneapolis: University of Minnesota Press, 2018.

Chun, Wendy H. K. *Updating to Remain the Same: Habitual New Media*. Cambridge, MA: MIT Press, 2016.

Eubanks, Virginia. *Automating Inequality: How High-Tech Tools Profile, Police, and Punish the Poor*. London: St. Martin's Press, 2018.

Foucault, Michel. *Discipline and Punish*. 1975. New York: Vintage Books, 1995.

Fuller, Buckminster. "World Game." *Ekistics* 28 (1969): 286–92.

Gerstner, Louis. *Who Says Elephants Can't Dance? Inside IBM's Historic Turnaround*. New York: Harper Collins, 2002.

Goss, Jon "'We Know Who You Are and We Know Where You Live': The Instrumental Rationality of Geodemographic Systems." *Economic Geography* 71, no. 2 (1995): 171–98.

Hampton, Keith, and Barry Wellman. "Neighboring in Netville: How the Internet Supports Community and Social Capital in a Wired Suburb." *City and Community* 2, no. 4 (2003): 277–311.

Hempel, Jessi. "For Nextdoor, Eliminating Racism Is No Quick Fix," *Wired*, February 16, 2017, https://www.wired.com/2017/02/for-nextdoor-eliminating-racism-is-no-quick-fix/.

Hoffmann, Anna Laura. "Making Data Valuable: Political, Economic, and Conceptual Bases of Big Data." *Philosophy and Technology* 31 (2018): 209–12.

Ingold, David, and Spencer Soper. "Amazon Doesn't Consider the Race of Its Customers: Should It?" *Bloomberg*, April 21, 2016. https://www.bloomberg.com/graphics/2016-amazon-same-day/.

Isaacs, Reginald. "The Neighborhood Theory: An Analysis of Its Adequacy." *Journal of the American Institute of Planners* 14, no. 2 (1948): 15–23.

Kurgan, Laura, Dare Brawley, Brian House, Jia Zhang, and Wendy H. K. Chun. "Homophily: The Urban History of an Algorithm." *E-flux*, October 4, 2019. https://www.e-flux.com/architecture/are-friends-electric/289193/homophily-the-urban-history-of-an-algorithm/.

Lyon, David. *Surveillance Society: Monitoring Everyday Life*. Buckingham: Open University Press, 2002.

Manders-Huits, N. "Practical versus Moral Identities in Identity Management." *Ethics and Information Technology* 12, no. 1 (2010): 43–55.

McLuhan, Marshall. *The Gutenberg Galaxy*. 1962. Hamburg: Gingko Press Verlag, 2011.

Narayanan, Arvind, and Vitaly Shmatikov. "Robust De-Anonymization of Large Sparse Datasets." *Proceedings of the 2008 IEEE Symposium on Security and Privacy*, 111–25. Los Alamitos, CA: IEEE, 2008.

Noble, Safiye U. *Algorithms of Oppression: How Search Engines Reinforce Racism*. New York: New York University Press, 2018.

Ogburn, William F. *You and Machines*. Chicago: University of Chicago Press, 1934.

O'Neil, Cathy. *Weapons of Math Destruction: How Big Data Increases Inequality and Threatens Democracy*. London: Penguin, 2016.

Perry, Clarence. *Housing for the Machine Age*. New York: Russell Sage Foundation, 1939.

Perry, Clarence. *Regional Survey of New York and Its Environs, Neighborhood and Community Planning*. Vol. 3. 1929. London: Routledge, 1998.

Peters, John Durham. "Calendar, Clock, Tower." In *Deus in Machina: Religion, Technology, and the Things in Between*, edited by Jeremy Stolow, 25–42. New York: Fordham University Press, 2013.

Reiner, Thomas. *The Place of the Ideal Community in Urban Planning*. Philadelphia: University of Pennsylvania Press, 1963.

Rheingold, Howard. *The Virtual Community: Finding Connection in a Computerized World*. Reading, MA: Addison-Wesley, 1993.

Rhodes, Margaret. "Nextdoor Breaks a Sacred Design Rule." *Wired*, August 31, 2016. https://www.wired.com/2016/08/nextdoor-breaks-sacred-design-rule-end-racial-profiling/.

Rothstein, Richard. *The Color of Law: A Forgotten History of How Our Government Segregated America*. London: Liveright, 2017.

Schmiechen-Ackermann, Detlef. "Der Blockwart: Die unteren Parteifunktionäre im nationalsozialistischen Terror- und Überwachungsapparat." *VfZ* 48, no. 4 (2000): 575–602.

Shah, Nishant. "Identity and Identification: The Individual in the Time of Networked Governance." *Socio-Legal Review* 11, no. 2 (2015): 22–40.

Simmel, Georg. "The Metropolis and Mental Life." In *Georg Simmel on Individuality and Social Forms*, edited by D. N. Levine, 324–39. Chicago: Chicago University Press, 1903.

Srnicek, Nick. *Platform Capitalism*. London: Polity, 2016.

Stephens-Davidowitz, Seth. *Everybody Lies: Big Data, New Data, and What the Internet Can Tell Us about Who We Really Are*. New York: Dey Street Books, 2018.

Steyerl, Hito. "A Sea of Data: Pattern Recognition and Corporate Animism (Forked Version)." In *Pattern Discrimination*, edited by Clemens Apprich, Wendy H. K. Chun, Florian Cramer, and Hito Steyerl, 1–22. Minneapolis: University of Minnesota Press, 2018.

Turkle, Sherry. *Life on the Screen: Identity in the Age of the Internet*. New York: Simon and Schuster, 1995.

Turner, Fred. *From Counterculture to Cyberculture: Stewart Brand, the Whole Earth Network, and the Rise of Digital Utopianism*. Chicago: University of Chicago Press, 2006.

Vagt, Cristian. "Neighborhood Design: Buckminster Fuller's Planning Tools and the City." In *Neighborhood Technologies. Media and Mathematics of Dynamic Networks*, edited by T. Harks and S. Vehlken, 81–95. Zurich: Diaphanes, 2015.

Wirth, Louis. "Urbanism as a Way of Life." *American Journal of Sociology* 44 (1938): 3–24.

Zahn, Friedrich. "Die Statistik im nationalsozialistischen Großdeutschland." *ASA* 29, no. 40 (1939): 369–92.

Zuboff, Shoshana. *The Age of Surveillance Capitalism: The Fight for a Human Future at the New Frontier of Power*. New York: Public Affairs, 2019.

Fraught Platform Governmentality

Anonymity, Content Moderation, and Regulatory Strategies over Yik Yak

This chapter unpacks how user behavior is governed in anonymous social media platforms. The communities formed within social media platforms have become a locus of various forms of e-bile, vitriol, trolling, flaming, and harassment. Though such behavior does exist on platforms where user identities are publicly visible, the severity and frequency of vitriolic practices are intensified on platforms that are organized around user anonymity or pseudonymity. Exploring a social context where users couldn't be held accountable for the content they post, my ethnography investigated how an anonymous platform called Yik Yak regulated content across its feeds through complex interactions between institutional and vernacular social practices. Yik Yak was an anonymous, location-based social network that championed a central feed regulated by upvotes and downvotes. Users were able to post anonymous content, comment on posts, and engage in discussion about that content within a five-mile radius of other users. I conducted my ethnographic work on the Queen's University Yik Yak feed in Kingston, Ontario, Canada. When I first began doing research on anonymous social media communities, I was astounded by how seemingly chaotic and messy feeds of diverse anonymous user-generated content were patterned by sociocultural norms and practices unique to the Yik Yak platform. I became interested in the opaque social processes that led to the creation and enforcement of these norms. Like other anonymous social media before it, such as 4chan and Whisper, Yik Yak was shaped by moral ambivalence and a focus on leisure and entertainment, with frequent instances of trolling and bullying, as well as instances of caretaking and an escape from social stigmatization.[1] This moral ambivalence characterizing Yik Yak's platform made regulation of its feeds incredibly challenging as a substantial number of users engaged in undisciplined, vitriolic, and bigoted behavior.

Yik Yak began as a venture capitalist endeavor founded and engineered by Brooks Buffington, Tyler Droll, and Douglas Warstler, who hatched their business plan while attending Furman University in South Carolina in 2013. Once developed, the application spread virally across the North American mediascape, appealing largely to undergraduate students at university and college

[1] Abigail E. Curlew, "Undisciplined Performativity: A Sociological Approach to Anonymity," *Social Media + Society* 5, no. 1 (2019): 1–14.

campuses. Unlike 4chan, Yik Yak became a mainstream service that began to rival social media behemoths Twitter and Instagram on the campuses of colleges and universities. *TechCrunch* reported that within a year of being launched, Yik Yak had accumulated roughly seventy-five million dollars in capital investments.[2] It eventually earned a place among the top ten social media applications on the Apple App Store and Google Play Store in the United States.

As on most anonymous social media platforms, public controversies began to plague Yik Yak's reputation after news reports began exposing what seemed to be a proliferation of bullying, harassment, and toxic behavior within the platform's countless feeds. A series of scathing opinion pieces and editorials were published throughout the application's tenure, highlighting its inability to sufficiently moderate content and stem the flow of abuse. Journalists and critics published opinion pieces that called for Yik Yak's closure as well as banning the platform across college and university campuses.[3] This brewing controversy was bolstered by serious criminal acts linked to the platform, including a series of bomb threats, gun threats, and threats of racially motivated lynching.[4] CBC News highlighted one instance where a threat triggered a lockdown at the All Saints Catholic High School in Ottawa, Ontario, which resulted in growing concern from parents and educators over young students using this application.[5] Because of the severity of some of these occurrences, police agencies, working with Yik Yak, used location-based metadata attached to problematic posts to identify the users who had threatened to commit acts of violence.

Yik Yak's decline was almost as swift as its development. In October 2015, Yik Yak began to drop from the app store charts. In an article for *TechCrunch*, Sarah Perez wrote, "It's unheard of for a popular social app like Yik Yak to go from riding the top of the app store to dropping off like this without some sort of intervention."[6] Among the most

[2] Jonathan Shieber, "Yik Yak Closes To Closing On Roughly $75 Million," *Techcrunch*, November 14, 2014.

[3] Marty Swant, "Does Yik Yak Have an Anonymity Problem? App Drew Criticism at SXSW," *Adweek*, March 17, 2016; and Ryan Chapin Mach, "Why Your College Campus Should Ban Yik Yak," *Huffington Post*, October 3, 2014.

[4] Julia Glum, "In Growing Trend, Yik Yak Users Post Anonymous School Bomb Threats—and Get Caught," *IBT*, November 2014; CBC News, "Yik Yak App: Why Schools Are Concerned," *CBC News*, January 20, 2015; and Caitlin Dewey, "What is Yik Yak, the app that fielded racist threats at University of Missouri?" *Washington Post*, November 11, 2015.

[5] CBC News, "Yik Yak App."

[6] Sarah Perez, "Amid Bullying and Threats of Violence, Anonymous Social App Yik Yak Shuts off Access to US Middle and High School Students," *TechCrunch*, March 13.

significant consequences of this public controversy was the response from the Google Play Store, as it revoked its endorsement of the application and removed it from its top charts because of the alleged toxic environment the platform fostered. Users could still search and install the application, but it was no longer visible to new users.[7]

The mounting public pressure eventually motivated Yik Yak to ban the usage of its platform on high school campuses across North America. Using a third-party application called Maponics, Yik Yak gathered GPS data on the locations of high schools and private schools across North America to set up hundreds of thousands of geofences. If a student were to try to access the application within a geofence, they would receive a message reading, "It looks like you're trying to use Yik Yak on middle school or high school grounds. Yik Yak is intended for people college-aged and above. The app is disabled in this area."[8] As the platform was primarily organized around location-based data, the company was able to obfuscate its usage for users under the age of eighteen. The geofence was bolstered by an algorithm designed to detect potentially inflammatory language and remove it from Yik Yak's local feeds. Most notably, on August 16, 2016, Yik Yak removed the ability for users to post anonymously through a user handle update that gave all users a mandatory username and a bio. Though users were still pseudonymous, these updates shifted the affordances of the platform and radically rewrote the platform's identity. In an effort to stem the abusive content, Yik Yak strayed too far from the application's original purpose, and users abandoned the platform en masse. One user expressed frustration: "What the actual eff, is there any point to using this app anymore?" Another user mused, "Yik Yak's update is a classic example of Icarus flying too close to the sun." The platform operators stumbled into an identity crisis that eventually led to Yik Yak's servers shutting down and the company selling off its assets on April 28, 2017.

[7] Rob Price, "Google Has Dropped Yik Yak from Its App Store Charts," *Business Insider,* March 11, 2015.

[8] Perez, "Amid Bullying."

The regulatory strategies used to moderate content on anonymous social media are often fraught with difficulty due to the competing interests of pleasing investors, maintaining profits, having a compelling public relations image to remain competitive and visible on the mobile app stores, and providing a platform that is compelling to its user base. When a platform such as Yik Yak is unable to successfully navigate the friction between these competing interests, the social and institutional bonds that hold together its internal sense of community begin to collapse. In this chapter, I explore how behavior on Yik Yak was governed through a complex interplay of vernacular user practices and institutional operator practices. Using a Foucauldian framework, I refer to the fraught governing practices used to navigate this social friction as "platform governmentality." Through this modality of governance, Yik Yak as a corporation enlisted the aid of both human and technical actors to shape and discipline how users shared and consumed user-generated content over an anonymous social media platform.

Undisciplined Social Media

Social media platforms are digital bounded web applications that use the internet to facilitate social connections and the creation and sharing of user-generated content.[9] As Susan Scott and Wanda Orlikowski have argued, enactments of anonymous communication are always a relational effort.[10] A social media platform can be analytically understood as a set of relations among an application's physical and technical infrastructure, the platform operators, and a platform's users to maintain a wider public or community. The physical and technical infrastructure of a platform is a form of "digital affordances" that act to shape how social media platforms silently mediate the anonymous communicative acts of users.[11] A platform's affordances comprise both "protocols" and "interfaces" that underlie the technical constitution of a platform as a medium for communi-

9 Andreas M. Kaplan and Michael Haenlein, "Users of the World, Unite! The Challenges and Opportunities of Social Media," *Business Horizons* 53 (2010): 59–68.

10 Susan V. Scott and Wanda J. Orlikowski, "Entanglements in Practice: Performing Anonymity through Social Media," *MIS Quarterly* 38, no. 3 (2014): 873–93.

11 Angela M. Cirucci, "Redefining Privacy and Anonymity through Social Networking Affordances," *First Monday* 20, no. 7 (2015); and Emily van der Nagel, "From Usernames to Profiles: The Development of Pseudonymity in Internet Communication," *Internet Histories: Digital Technology, Culture and Society* 1 (2017): 312–31.

cation. Jose van Dijck defines protocols as the "formal descriptions of digital message formats complemented by rules for regulating those messages in or between computing systems."[12] Interfaces, on the other hand, are the visual components that make a platform accessible to both platform operators and users. These can be broken down into "internal" and "visible" interfaces. The visible interface is the branded visual aspect of a platform; it is what the user can access through images, text, and hyperlinks on a digital screen. The internal interface is only accessible to the platform operators and consists of administrative features for platform governance and maintenance. Through the internal interface, platform operators can mediate and shape, and thus regulate, how users are able to engage with both the platform and other users. For instance, the visual interface of Yik Yak is designed to afford users the ability to communicate anonymously with one another, and thus the platform operators set the boundaries of available behavior within a platform. These boundaries are mediated by protocols and interfaces designed to silently steer the social traffic on the platform to appear in predetermined ways. An example of this is how Yik Yak was designed to mobilize its user base to regulate their own content through an up- and down-vote system. Once a user's post receives a total of minus five votes, the post automatically becomes invisible on the public feed, thus enlisting users to discipline their own feeds.

Social media platforms fundamentally rely on users' performance and presentation of self and how they seek to communicate their performances of self to others using user-generated content mediated by a platform's social, cultural, and historical context. A useful frame of reference for approaching digital forms of identity is Erving Goffman's dramaturgical approach to social interactions.[13] According to Goffman, social actors use techniques of "impression management" to influence social situations and, furthermore, perform different renditions of self based on sociocultural contexts, or the "stage."[14] In this

[12] Jose van Dijck, "Facebook and the Engineering of Connectivity: A Multilayered Approach to Social Media Platforms," *Convergence: The International Journal of Research into New Media Technology* 19, no. 2 (2012): 144.

[13] Laura Robinson, "The Cyberself: The Self-ing Project Goes Online, Symbolic Interaction in the Digital Age," *New Media and Society* 9, no. 1 (2007): 93–110; Bernie Hogan, "The Presentation of Self in the Age of Social Media: Distinguishing Performances and Exhibitions Online," *Bulletin of Science, Technology, and Society*, 30, no. 6 (2010): 377–86; and Bernie Hogan, "Pseudonyms and the Rise of the Real-Name Web," in *A Companion to New Media Dynamics*, ed. J. Hartley, J. Burgess, and Bruns (Chichester: Blackwell, 2012), 290–308.

[14] Erving Goffman, *The Presentation of Self in Everyday Life* (New York: Anchor Books, 1959).

context, the "stage" is the visible interface of a social media platform and fundamentally shapes the terms of communication. As Lee Knuttila observes, "In social media terms: Facebook wants to know who you are, Twitter wants to know what you are, and Foursquare wants to know where you are. Social media relies on an articulation of a lived social self."[15] This social phenomenon is evident when users are engaged in curating content for platforms like Facebook or Twitter, which are organized around an articulation of (usually) legal identities.[16] The Yik Yak users I spoke to shared a general understanding of social media like Facebook and Instagram as indicative of inauthentic performances of identity, where users were made to filter their content in accordance with social norms and appropriate behavior. One user told me, "When you're anonymous, you don't really have a filter, and you post on the app what you truly think. It's more like an honest opinion than on Facebook." Another user observed, "Because I mean, social media as a whole is fake. Right? We all know people on Facebook and Instagram have this front of being perfect. You know they have a perfect family, a perfect life. But really, they are just falling apart. You know what I mean?" Such behavior can be understood through the scope of disciplinary power, where social actors begin to discipline their own behavior when they are aware of the presence and gaze of others.[17] Disciplinary power is especially acute when surveillance is being exerted at the lateral level, where a social actor's family and peers are watching and accessing their behavior.[18] Where real-name social media facilitate a concern of the strategic maintenance of a perceived self and reputation, anonymous social media allow users to dissociate from their legal identity and post more "honestly." As I explore later, this disciplinary power can be utilized by platform operators who enlist users to police their own behavior.

Anonymous social media is characterized by a phenomenon I've termed elsewhere as "undisciplined performativity."[19] When users participate in an anonymous

[15] Lee Knuttila, "User Unknown: 4chan, Anonymity and Contingency," *First Monday* 16, no. 10 (2011).

[16] Alice E. Marwick and danah boyd, "I Tweet Honestly, I Tweet Passionately: Twitter Users, Context Collapse, and the Imagined Audience," *New Media and Society* 13, no. 1 (2012): 114–33.

[17] Michel Foucault, *Discipline and Punish: The Birth of the Prison* (New York: Vintage Books, 1995).

[18] Mark Andrejevic, "The Work of Watching One Another: Lateral Surveillance, Risk, and Governance," *Surveillance and Society* 2, no. 4 (2005): 479–97; and Mark Andrejevic, "The Discipline of Watching: Detection, Risk, and Lateral Surveillance," *Critical Studies in Media Communication* 23, no. 5 (2006): 391–407.

[19] Curlew, "Undisciplined Performativity."

social media platform, they can post content without concern for the laborious work of curating an identity in relation to the expectations of others. In other words, a user is free from the disciplinary influence of lateral surveillance. One user told me, "It's like a community with no faces. It's all about who you are inside—it's like, who you are, what you think, what you believe in. It's not what you want people to think about you." As I have observed elsewhere, "The inability to link a performative digital act to an identifiable person allows for such an act to become dissociated from a user's overall identity and untethers that user from being held accountable for the content they post."[20] It is important to note that just because users become undisciplined through enactments of anonymity, their behavior is still shaped in accordance with socialized norms, and thus anonymous communication isn't just a performative free-for-all. Consequently, users may behave in unconventional or cruel ways, through acts of trolling or vitriolic behavior, but users also engage in forms of caretaking, entertainment and leisure, and flight from social stigmatization. Nonetheless, the existence of undisciplined performative acts poses challenging obstacles to regulating content on anonymous social media platforms like Yik Yak.

The platform operators played an important role in the constitution of Yik Yak's social media platform. By platform operators, I mean the social actors involved in founding, funding and managing a platform's technical, legal, and financial infrastructure. Yik Yak, as mentioned earlier, was a start-up business that emerged from the work of university graduates, Brooks Buffington, Tyler Droll, and Douglas Warstler. They developed the application and marketed it to wealthy venture capitalists, who invest a great deal of capital in emerging firms. Yik Yak's economic structure is akin to other businesses in venture capitalism. As Vincent Mosco describes of venture capitalists, "The visionary wins some venture capital funding, hires a public relations firm and goes after media attention."[21] In this case, the appeal

[20] Ibid., 5.

[21] Vincent Mosco, *The Digital Sublime: Myth, Power, and Cyberspace* (Cambridge, MA: MIT Press, 2005), 26.

to venture capitalists was immensely successful, and Yik Yak's founders secured up to 75 million dollars in investments.[22] With little return on investments and no monetization in sight, however, Yik Yak had become emblematic of the failure of anonymous social media. One investor, Bill Gurley, told *Business Insider*, "I think it's going to be really hard to monetize. I think there's potential that they are a false positive."[23] A few years later, Yik Yak had shut down after being in the center stage of several public controversies and unable to monetize its platform or user (meta)data. Throughout the platform's bid to continue operating through the public controversy that plagued their operations, the platform operators were tasked with the challenge of monetizing Yik Yak and thus were predominantly concerned with a public relations image in the face of controversy, experimenting with methods of governing behavior, and finding ways to make profits on the backs of anonymous users.

As I explore in the following sections, digital affordances are by no means static. Platform operators regularly introduce new features and updates that change how users engage with a social media platform.[24] Over the course of Yik Yak's existence, the platform operators made use of a steady flow of updates and new features that reshaped how behavior was governed. Some of these updates were useful and popular. For instance, the original application was designed to be fully anonymous so that no identifiers linked a poster to his or her content. Yik Yak introduced an update that temporarily assigned a user with an innocuous random icon, such as a boat or a tree, that would allow users to identify who was speaking in a single thread. Communication was still anonymous, but it allowed for smooth conversations within its feeds. After the thread disappeared, the user's assigned icon would as well. Other updates proved unpopular, or even catastrophic, when rolled out over the platform. As mentioned earlier, the August 16 update that removed anonymity as a key affordance in the platform set off a chain of events that led to the company folding and selling off its assets. So,

[22] Jonathan Shieber, "Yik Yak Is Close to Closing on Roughly 75 Million," *TechCrunch*, November 14, 2014.

[23] Alyson Shontell, "One of the World's Smartest Investors Thinks Anonymous Apps Like Whisper and Secret Are Fads that Won't Make Money," *Business Insider*, March 31, 2014.

[24] Van der Nagel, "From Usernames to Profiles."

not only are digital affordances characterized by flux, but as Emily van der Nagel has pointed out, they are only "ideal forms of engagement" designed by platform operators to encourage certain types of behavior.[25] If users do not approve of the new digital affordances that are introduced by platform updates, they can and sometimes will revolt. Yik Yak's attempts to stem the flow of vitriolic and trolling behavior largely failed. Arguably because the platform operators did not properly enlist the support of their user base before implementing major changes to the platform's overall identity, users ultimately abandoned the platform.

[25] Ibid., 326.

Fraught Platform Governmentality

All social media platforms are exposed to an array of regulatory practices that constitute a wider modality of platform governmentality. Such efforts aren't entirely relegated to the platform operators but are shared practices that include the roles of users and automated algorithms. Social media platforms are designed using software to construct a visual interface with the intentional purpose of directing digital affordances to the work of channeling and controlling the flow of user traffic. The power of digital affordances as a regulatory tool, however, are constantly hampered by the diverse range of interests, visions, and desires put forward by platform users. For instance, on the Queen's University Yik Yak feed, there was a constant tension between users who were entertained by vitriol, bigotry, and trolling and those who eschewed vitriolic behavior in favor of taking on the role of caretaking other anonymous users. These two different user groups had very different ideals for what Yik Yak's feeds should look like. The user base of a platform is rarely unified or in agreement on the ideal identity of the platform's multiple communities. The reality of an anonymous platform's divergent social constitution is incredibly consequential for platform operators, as the diverse range of user ideals and expectations, compounded with the ephemerality of anonymous content, mean that user behavior is largely unpredictable, which makes the project of platform governmentality a complex endeavor.

As mentioned earlier, platform governmentality refers to a modality of varied social practices from a wide range of social and technical actors that shape and discipline the sharing and consumption of user-generated content in social media platforms. Often it is easy to think of governing practices as being the exclusive task of institutional actors such as Yik Yak's platform operators. In the case of the Queen's University Yik Yak feed, however, this is far from true. For a social media platform to survive, the whole array of social and technical actors needs to be enlisted into its regulatory practices. This means that enlisting the support of users through intentional designs in a platform's digital affordances is essential to regulating behavior within a digital public. Governmentality can be understood as a divergent sets of practices centrally concerned with the "conduct of conduct" or, in other words, shaping how actors be have in any social context. As Stuart Elden points out, governmentality can be understood as a constant and emergent process that is subject to change and modification, as opposed to a static "state of being."[26] In relation to platform governmentality, this means that the strategies employed by all actors within a social media platform are constantly changing to account for fluctuations in a platform's social, cultural, political, and historical context. Within these constant fluctuations, friction is produced between vernacular and institutional social practices as they go about the labor of shaping the platform's identity. And as I explore in the final sections, this friction-laden process means that platform governmentality is a fraught process always on the verge of crisis and collapse.

[26] Stuart Elden, *Foucault's Last Decade* (Cambridge: Polity Press, 2016).

Vernacular Regulatory Strategies

The governing practices that Yik Yak's users engaged in to shape the overall identity of their local feeds constitute what I call "vernacular regulatory strategies." "Vernacular" refers to the production and practices of informal cultural knowledge that is produced on the level of everyday life interaction.[28] In other words, knowledge that is not produced by institutions or experts and is varied according to the affordances of a platform. Importantly, my use of vernacular doesn't merely refer to how users might undermine or subvert institutional intentions, but refers to how users are ofttimes encouraged by the structure of a platform to use their own cultural norms and mores to discipline themselves. As mentioned above, this process of enlisting vernacular regulatory strategies is fraught with difficulty: sometimes users are enlisted, but other times they are not; sometimes they undermine the institutional intentions, but other times they do not. The important point here is that a platform is unable to tame undisciplined behavior without enlisting the support of vernacular regulatory practices.

[28] Robert Glen Howard, "Electronic Hybridity: The Persistent Processes of the Vernacular Web," *Journal of American Folklore* 121, no. 480 (2008): 192–218.

To users of Yik Yak, its anonymous feeds were primarily a community where they could "be themselves," and thus, they took ownership of the feeds they participated in. One user observed:

> Yik Yak was a site where you could anonymously post opinions or jokes or just observations and people would determine as a collective whether or not that thing was valuable or valid. So like, if you get more than five down votes and no up votes, your comment is automatically removed. It's very democratic in that way. But in a very harsh way. It was cool just to see what would survive and what wouldn't because it was like a self-regulatory community. Even though it was all anonymous, people could be more free in what they were saying. There was regulation within it from every person participating.

Most users were quite active in participating in vernacular efforts to regulate the feeds. They did so in various ways: through the up-vote/down-vote system, through discussion and debate, and in extreme circumstances, through reporting users to the platform operators. Because of the location-based affordance, which allowed users to communicate with others within a five-mile radius, the ideological and cultural textures of Yik Yak's feeds were incredibly divergent from each other. Up voting and down voting were a primary source of regulatory activity for respondents. As one respondent reported, "Because I saw this happen quite a bit, where someone is like ripping on an ex-spouse or an ex-lover, and they are like, 'you're being an asshole,' and they get down voted. And it's kind of nice to see, like, that social feedback." The platform infrastructure often successfully enlisted the participation of users through the up-vote/down-vote affordance as a primary tool for regulating the feeds.

Enlisting users to the task of regulating one another's content in an anonymous context can backfire spectacularly. In many cases, users' practices will go against the grain of platform design in unexpected ways as users navigate the visual interface.[29] A substantial population of users were primarily interested in entertainment through trolling. For instance, some users engaged in practices of up voting unfolding drama to keep the content in the feed longer so that they could spectate the drama for entertainment. One user reported, "There wasn't much that I would down-vote. I was pretty neutral. I would either up-vote stuff because I thought it was funny or interesting or want other people to see it, or I would scroll past it. I never actively sought to get rid of a post unless bummed." Another respondent demonstrated a similar practice: "But actually, I will usually change my down-vote on those if a discussion develops. If other people start talking about it, then I want to see this discussion continue. And I will just not up vote it. But I won't continue to down-vote it." It was clear in my research that the regulatory strategies

[29] Jose van Dijck, *The Culture of Connectivity: A Critical History of Social Media* (New York: Oxford University Press, 2013).

employed by users were not unified toward any singular goal but were multiple and often divergent.

Other vernacular regulatory strategies include the use of debate, discussion, and argument to challenge undesirable content. One user felt that debating trolls or abusive users in the feed was among the reasons that he found the platform appealing. He explained, "I kind of feel a responsibility to balance out the trolling." All social media platforms are tasked with the challenge of regulating vitriolic behavior, and a major component of that is other users engaging in oppositional rhetoric to trolls and abusers within a feed. These balancing practices were enacted through either providing a counter-narrative to vitriolic or bigoted content or posting positive content to the feed. For many users, the use of the "report post" feature was considered a last resort used only in the most extreme circumstances. One respondent told me, "It's funny that I didn't even [report] when those rape posts were up. I still didn't report it. I just assumed that other people would. I rarely report anything online anyways." Respondents generally wanted to maintain control over the regulatory features in their local Yik Yak feeds and would typically resort to institutional remedies only if all other vernacular regulatory strategies failed. The user continued, "If there was someone saying that they are going to bomb the school, I would report that. But, beyond that ... I would down vote if it was particularly repulsive." Vernacular regulatory strategies are an inherent feature of platform governmentality and play a substantial role in regulating Yik Yak's feeds. Users exploit the digital affordances of the social media platform to shape an idealized identity for the overall platform, while platform operators attempt to steer that behavior toward a productive goal of having manageable communities. And though platform operators can use these practices as a way of keeping the platform's feeds clean of vitriolic content, users are largely unpredictable and can use the platform's affordances in ways not accounted for in the platform's design.

Institutional Regulatory Strategies

Yik Yak had various regulatory strategies for institutionally governing the platform, which were informed by their Code of Conduct and Terms of Service. These strategies were primarily enacted by algorithms designed to automatically flag problematic content, the ability to suspend or ban user accounts for breaching Yik Yak's policies, and the occasional major update that shifted the design of the platform's digital affordances. Yik Yak used the platform's technical infrastructure and visual interface to facilitate a digital public that allowed users to regulate their own feeds through voting or through reporting problematic users. For these institutional strategies to work effectively, the platform needed to enlist users to facilitate regulatory practices. Yik Yak's platform operators had an extensive array of resources and capital at their disposal to shape practices designed to facilitate particular behavior on the platform. When I refer to institutional regulatory strategies, I mean the methods that platform operators use, sometimes through the deployment of software, to regulate the posting of user-generated content to its feeds.

According to federal law in the United States during my fieldwork, social media platforms are not legally obligated to moderate and censor problematic user-generated content on their feeds.[30] This legislation is relevant for most major social media platforms, as their servers are typically hosted within US jurisdiction. Julia Angwin and Hannes Grassegger write, "A 1996 federal law gave most tech companies, including Facebook, legal immunity for the content users post on their services."[31] This law has a very practical implications, allowing the operators of a platform to let users post a wide array of content without having to "legally vet" each post before it is made public. This legislation provides the legal scaffolding for developing platforms that will inevitably be plagued with vitriolic and abusive content by shifting legal liability for illegal or criminal content from the company to the

[30] Julia Angwin and Hannes Grassegger, "Facebook's Secret Censorship Rules Protect White Men from Hate Speech but Not Black Children," *ProPublica,* June 28, 2017.

[31] Ibid.

user. Technically, a server doesn't legally need to clean up its newsfeeds, but it's within a platform's interest to moderate its feeds to attract users, investors, and revenue.

[32] Rob Kitchin and Martin Dodge, *Code/Space: Software and Everyday Life* (Cambridge, MA: MIT Press, 2011), 85.

One of the primary institutional regulatory strategies used by Yik Yak was the ability to suspend or ban users who broke the Code of Conduct. This process of using the "banhammer" was automated through algorithms that combed through content for inappropriate language or photos. This is what Rob Kitchin and Martin Dodge have called "automated management," which they describe as a mode of governmentality particular to the digital context: "Put simply, automated management is the regulation of people and objects through processes that are *automated* (technologically enacted), *automatic* (the technology performs regulation without prompting or direction), and *autonomous* (regulation, discipline, and outcomes are enacted without human oversight) in nature."[32]

The use of automation alone, however, was insufficient to govern the Yik Yak platform. Platform operators also facilitated legal intervention from policing or security agencies for content that was thought to pose a criminal threat. According to Yik Yak's Guidelines for Law Enforcement, the company urges users to report extreme content to emergency services directly. The document also explains that police must send a request with a warrant or notification of an emergency to Yik Yak to authorize the release of nonpublic information. Without a sizable department of content moderators to review and verify whether banned content or users were legitimately guilty of problematic practices, however, the algorithm was not alone reliable. The consequence of this is that platform operators were left with no choice but to attempt to enlist vernacular regulatory strategies to self-discipline their own feeds.

Conclusion

Despite the many strategies Yik Yak deployed to respond to mounting public controversies and a rapidly growing notoriety, the social network was unable to recover from the damages it incurred when it nullified the affordance of anonymity. The failure of the platform to sustain itself is an apt case study of the fraught process of successfully governing user practices within a platform. This case study represents an important lesson about facilitating a practical model of platform governmentality—if platform operators can't navigate the friction generated between the divergent social and technical actors within a platform's multiple communities by enlisting them to self-moderate their newsfeeds, the platform will eventually dissolve. The use of a Foucauldian framework for approaching platform governmentality allows us to conceptualize how the work of governance must include the consent and participation of members of a platform and is not the sole responsibility of institutional actors. For smaller social media platforms (i.e., those without the financial bulk of Facebook or Twitter), platform governmentality is always a fraught process teetering on failure. Yik Yak could not afford to staff a department of content moderators in the same way other larger platforms can. This was an especially challenging project considering that Yik Yak was never able to monetize its platform to produce any revenue.

Thus, the challenge becomes one of aligning diverse interests. It takes both the platform operators and its users to make any worthwhile attempt to shape behavior in a feed. Users are exposed to a varied, messy, and multidimensional array of vernacular and institutional regulatory strategies designed to govern the conduct of users engaged with the platform. It is important to note that though I separated the vernacular from the institutional, this was done for analytical purposes. Vernacular and institutional regulatory strategies are constantly entangled, as well as constantly incomplete and partial. Despite the wide array of governing strategies employed by social media platforms, there is still a significant presence of trolls, bullies, and bigots, who engage in problematic behavior that is toxic for both platform operators and users alike. Notably, at the same time, there is a significant presence of users with various intentions that span from entertainment, therapy, and flight from social stigmatization. In lieu of the popular stigmatization of anonymous social media that illustrates anonymity as the cause of toxic behavior, it is essential that we continue to scrutinize the complexities of platform governmentality.

Bibliography

Andrejevic, Mark. "The Discipline of Watching: Detection, Risk, and Lateral Surveillance." *Critical Studies in Media Communication* 23, no. 5 (2006): 391–407.

Andrejevic, Mark. "The Work of Watching One Another: Lateral Surveillance, Risk, and Governance." *Surveillance and Society* 2, no. 4 (2005): 479–97.

Angwin, Julia, and Hannes Grassegger. "Facebook's Secret Censorship Rules Protect White Men from Hate Speech but Not Black Children." *ProPublica,* June 28, 2017. https://www.propublica.org/article/facebook-hate-speech-censorship-internal-documents-algorithms.

CBC News. "Yik Yak App: Why Schools Are Concerned." *CBC News*, January 20, 2015. http://www.cbc.ca/news/technology/yik-yak-app-why-schools-are-concerned-1.2920155.

Cirucci, Angela M. "Redefining Privacy and Anonymity through Social Networking Affordances." *First Monday* 20, no. 7 (2015). https://firstmonday.org/ojs/index.php/fm/article/view/5465/4672.

Curlew, Abigail E. "Undisciplined Performativity: A Sociological Approach to Anonymity." *Social Media + Society* 5, no. 1 (2019): 1–14.

Dewey, Caitlin. "What is Yik Yak, the App That Fielded Racist Threats at University of Missouri?" *The Washington Post*, November 11, 2015. https://www.washingtonpost.com/news/the-intersect/wp/2015/11/11/what-is-yik-yak-the-app-that-fielded-racist-threats-at-university-of-missouri/.

Elden, Stuart. *Foucault's Last Decade*. Cambridge: Polity Press, 2016.

Foucault, Michel. *Discipline and Punish: The Birth of the Prison*. New York: Vintage Books, 1995.

Glum, Julia. "In Growing Trend, Yik Yak Users Post Anonymous School Bomb Threats—and Get Caught." *IBT*, November 2014. http://www.ibtimes.com/growing-trend-yik-yak-users-post-anonymous-school-bomb-threats-get-caught-1721543.

Goffman, Erving. *The Presentation of Self in Everyday Life*. New York: Anchor Books, 1959.

Hogan, Bernie. "The Presentation of Self in the Age of Social Media: Distinguishing Performances and Exhibitions Online." *Bulletin of Science, Technology, and Society*, 30, no. 6 (2010): 377–86.

Hogan, Bernie. "Pseudonyms and the Rise of the Real-Name Web." In *A Companion to New Media Dynamics*, edited by J. Hartley, J. Burgess, and A. Bruns, 290–308. Chichester: Blackwell, 2012.

Howard, Robert Glen. "Electronic Hybridity: The Persistent Processes of the Vernacular Web." *Journal of American Folklore* 121, no. 480 (2008): 192–218.

Kaplan, Andreas M., and Michael Haenlein. "Users of the World, Unite! The Challenges and Opportunities of Social Media." *Business Horizons* 53 (2010): 59–68.

Kitchin, Rob, and Martin Dodge. *Code/Space: Software and Everyday Life*. Cambridge, MA: MIT Press, 2011.

Knuttila, Lee. "User Unknown: 4chan, Anonymity and Contingency." *First Monday* 16, no. 10 (2011). http://firstmonday.org/article/view/3665/3055.

Mach, Ryan Chapin. "Why Your College Campus Should Ban Yik Yak." *Huffington Post*, October 3, 2014. https://web.archive.org/web/20180310181721/https://www.huffingtonpost.com/ryan-chapin-mach/why-your-college-campus-should-ban-yik-yak_b_5924352.html.

Marwick, Alice E., and danah boyd. "I Tweet Honestly, I Tweet Passionately: Twitter Users, Context Collapse, and the Imagined Audience." *New Media and Society* 13, no. 1 (2012): 114–33.

Mosco, Vincent. *The Digital Sublime: Myth, Power, and Cyberspace*. Cambridge, MA: MIT Press, 2005.

Newman, Lily Hay. "Open Secrets: The New Wave of Anonymous Social Networks Is Neither New nor Anonymous." *Slate*, March 21, 2014. http://www.slate.com/articles/technology/technology/2014/03/whisper_secret_yik_yak_new_anonymous_social_networks_are_neither_new_nor.html.

Perez, Sarah. "Amid Bullying and Threats of Violence, Anonymous Social App Yik Yak Shuts off Access to US Middle and High School Students." *TechCrunch*, March 13, 2014. https://techcrunch.com/2014/03/13/amid-vicious-bullying-threats-of-violence-anonymous-social-app-yik-yak-shuts-off-access-to-u-s-middle-high-school-students/.

Price, Rob. "Google Has Dropped Yik Yak from Its App Store Charts." *Business Insider*, March 11, 2015. http://uk.businessinsider.com/google-drops-yik-yak-android-play-store-app-charts-2015-3.

Robinson, Laura. "The Cyberself: The Self-ing Project Goes Online, Symbolic Interaction in the Digital Age." *New Media and Society* 9, no. 1 (2007): 93–110.

Scott, Susan V., and Wanda J. Orlikowski. "Entanglements in Practice: Performing Anonymity through Social Media." *MIS Quarterly* 38, no. 3 (2014): 873–93.

Shieber, Jonathan. "Yik Yak Is Close to Closing on Roughly 75 Million." *TechCrunch*, November 14, 2014. https://techcrunch.com/2014/11/14/yik-yak-is-close-to-closing-on-roughly-75-million/.

Shontell, Alyson. "One of the World's Smartest Investors Thinks Anonymous Apps Like Whisper and Secret Are Fads that Won't Make Money." *Business Insider*, March 31, 2014. http://www.businessinsider.com/bill-gurley-on-anonymous-apps-like-whisper-and-secret-2014-3.

Swant, Marty. "Does Yik Yak Have an Anonymity Problem? App Drew Criticism at SXSW." *Adweek*, March 17, 2016. http://www.adweek.com/news/technology/yik-yak-drew-bunch-criticism-sxsw-over-anonymity-its-platform-170186.

van der Nagel, Emily. "From Usernames to Profiles: The Development of Pseudonymity in Internet Communication." *Internet Histories: Digital Technology, Culture and Society* 1 (2017): 312–31.

van Dijck, Jose. *The Culture of Connectivity: A Critical History of Social Media*. New York: Oxford University Press, 2013.

van Dijck, Jose. "Facebook and the Engineering of Connectivity: A Multilayered Approach to Social Media Platforms." *Convergence: The International Journal of Research into New Media Technology* 19, no. 2 (2012): 141–55.

Anonymity
Obsolescence and Desire

Is This You in the Video?
2018

During the setup of my solo exhibition *Is This You in the Video?* at La Chaufferie Hear, a pole with a surveillance camera attached to it was found lying on a Strasbourg street. It was unclear whether this camera pole had been pushed over by someone or had just fallen down by itself. Surprisingly, the surveillance camera was still working, following the movements of passersby and recording them. The pole was partially blocking the sidewalk, forcing pedestrians to step around it or over it, and its inconvenient position was even affecting traffic. Eventually, the object was retrieved from the street and silently became part of the *Is This You in the Video?* exhibition. The camera was still working. Like the pigeons' best friend, CCTV cams squat in every high corner of the city, protecting us from the future. Will they fall off or be released from their stoical nonpresence?

Figure 48 *Is This You in the Video?* 2018. Installation and performance in public space; metal, wood, plaster, camera, cables, battery; 134 × 19.7 × 19.7 inches (340 × 50 × 50 cm).

Keepalive
2015

Seen from the outside, *Keepalive* looks like a normal rock. There is no sign that the stone, which lies inconspicuously on the edge of the idyllic village of Hartböhn in the Lüneburger Heide, contains hundreds of digital books. By lighting a small campfire underneath the stone, a thermoelectric generator and a Wifi router inside are activated, giving access to an electronic library with survival guides of all kinds. Visitors can add their own data and texts via smartphone or laptop. In a very archaic but also conspiratorial manner, information can only be exchanged locally. In contrast to globally networked servers, services, and clouds, this rock is not connected to the internet.

Figure 49 *Keepalive*, 2015. Outdoor sculpture; rock, steel, router, USB key, thermoelectric generator, fire, software, PDF database; 39.3 × 43.3 × 35.4 inches (100 × 110 × 90 cm). Exhibited at Landart Kunstverein Springhornhof Neuenkirchen, Lower Saxony, Germany; commissioned by the Center for Digital Cultures, Leuphana University, Lüneburg; curated by Andreas Broeckmann, Leuphana Arts Program; and realized as part of the Innovation Incubator Lüneburg, a large EU project funded by the European Fund for Regional Development and the German state of Lower Saxony.

If you take the advice from the survival-guide collection to heart, you're armed—at least that's their big promise—for lonely survival in the chaos of the world of computer programs, as well as in the wilderness. *Keepalive* poses the question of what "survival" really means, and sounds out our needs. The work opposes the forces of internet centralization of the Internet, raises questions about the democracy of knowledge management, and ignites a counter-movement to autonomy. (Jennifer Bork)

BYOD—Bring Your Own Disk (and Crush It)
2014
Destroying data is a widespread cultural phenomenon— from professional hard-drive punch systems to art projects and DIY thermite melting. Usually, data are stored on technically sensitive systems and can easily be lost. At the same time, files appear as indestructible once uploaded to the internet. Inspired by the Edward Snowden case, and referring to the bizarre act of the forced destruction of hard drives at the *Guardian* newspaper offices in 2013, *BYOD—Bring Your Own Disk (and Crush It)* asks the public to bring their old disks to the artist's exhibition. Visitors are invited to have them crushed with the IDEAL 0101 hard-drive punch, a commercially available

Figure 50 *BYOD—Bring Your Own Disk (and Crush It)*, 2014. Installation and performance; hard-drive punch shredder; size variable.

device. In the course of the exhibition, destroyed data carriers pile up. (Edward Snowden, former National Security Agency (NSA) contractor, is one of the best-known whistleblowers of our time. In 2013, aided by several news publishers, he revealed to the public the enormous scale of surveillance that British and American governments were carrying out in other countries, as well as over their own citizens.)

Forgot Your Password?
2013

In recent years, internet platforms have increasingly experienced security problems. Insufficiently protected databases have been hacked with the goal of retrieving large amounts of user data. The data—email addresses and passwords—are then traded on the darknet or through hidden forums. In summer 2012 the social network LinkedIn got hacked and lost its whole user database. A few months later, parts of the decrypted password list surfaced on the internet. The *Forgot Your*

Figure 51 *Forgot Your Password?* 2013. Book series, 8 hardcover volumes, each 8.3 × 10.6 inches (21 × 27 cm).

Password? series started with a set of eight books. These eight volumes contain 4.7 million LinkedIn clear-text user passwords printed in alphabetical order. Visitors are invited to look up their own password. The work is part of a series of works, mostly shown in public spaces in cities around the world, whereby the content changes according to the location.

KILLYOURPHONE.COM
2014

KILLYOURPHONE.COM is as an open workshop format, which premiered in a live participatory event at the Chaos Communication Congress in Hamburg in late December 2013. Participants were invited to craft a Faraday cage pouch for their cellular telephones using coated cloth or fleece specially developed for electromagnetic protection. The mobile phone can then no longer be located or listened to—unless a Trojan is installed on it. I developed the protective cover ten years earlier but updated it on the occasion of the NSA affair. Committed to a DIY

Figure 52 *KILLYOURPHONE. COM*, 2014. Open workshop format, with variable materials and sizes.

approach, the project additionally unfolds on a project website, which provides the audience with all necessary advice on how to run this workshop on their own. Protect your privacy! Discuss surveillance and learn how to sew!

How to Vacuum Form
2012

Figure 53 *How to Vacuum Form*, 2012. Performance, installation, DIY activity; Guy Fawkes mask, white Guy Fawkes mask copies, transparent Guy Fawkes mask, polysterol, plaster, hose, hose connectors, clamps, vacuum hand pump, toaster, wooden board, rods, stop watch, cutters, cutting mat, black pens, photo album, table, wooden pole; 118 × 197 × 137.8 inches (300 × 500 × 350 cm).

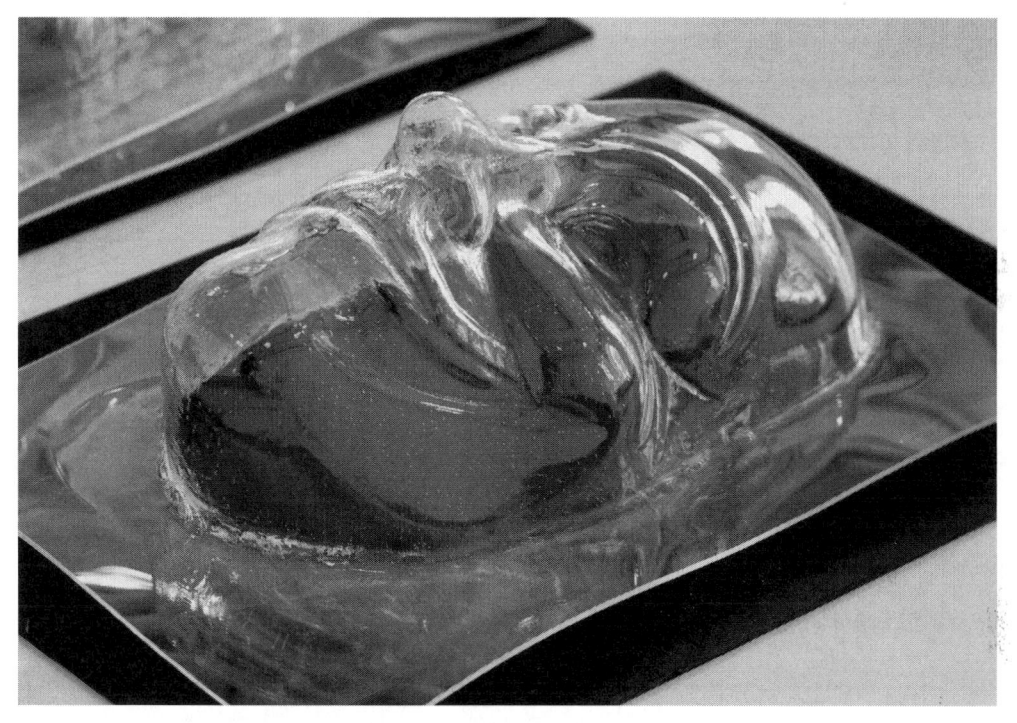

The human face plays a particularly prominent role in images of anonymity. Homing in on what Dutch critic Daniel de Zeeuw has referred to as "mask culture," this project points to the multiplicity of meanings associated with anonymity: the mask, originally a stylized portrait of the English Catholic revolutionary Guy Fawkes and later adopted by the Anonymous hacker collective, appears here in a transparent version. Like the questionable protection offered by this mask, anonymity is never absolute but relative to the context and the particular circumstances under which it is constructed and performed. In many cases, it is merely imagined, though no less empowering and affective. *How to Vacuum Form* comments on ideas of radical anonymity in online hacker communities as well as on transformations in the sphere of (design) production. Giving out a description on how to build a DIY vacuum former, the artist's mask is meant to be copied. *How to Vacuum Form* therefore also contributes to recent debates on copyright issues for digitally printed physical objects.

15 Seconds of Fame
2010

In 2007 Google began to photograph streets around the globe for its Street View service. In a spontaneous performance I ran behind a Google Street View car to get in as many pictures as possible in Berlin in 2009. The somewhat "hacked" images later appeared in Google's application. Using the enterprise's image cartography tool as a portrait camera, I inscribed myself in the photographic landscape of the city and was, from then on,

Figure 54 *15 Seconds of Fame*, 2010. Performance, video, and photo series.

visible for the uncounted Google Street View users who examine the Earth by means of the online service. Street View's ongoing picture taking led to widespread discussions about privacy and image rights in public space in Germany and in many other countries. Concealment requests by citizens resulted in partly blurred images on Germany's Street View. Faces or number plates that Google's visual recognition software detects in these photographic images are also blurred, and in this project, recognizable only to people who are familiar with my characteristic physique. On the company's servers, image files of faces, number plates and facades are of course properly visible, waiting for examination and further usage.

Figure 55 *Dead Drops*, 2010–ongoing. Public intervention; offline peer-to-peer file-sharing network.

Dead Drops
2010–Ongoing

Dead Drops is an anonymous, offline, peer-to-peer file-sharing network in public space. In an era of so-called clouds and new devices without access to local files, the project invites us to rethink the freedom and distribution of data. It started in 2010 as a participatory project at five different public spaces in New York. Each Dead Drop is a naked piece of passively powered Universal Serial Bus technology embedded into the city, the only true public space. USB flash drives are fixed into walls, buildings, and curbs. Each Dead Drop is installed empty except for a readme.txt file explaining the project and inviting visitors to drop or to access files. To date, more than 1,400 of these "dead letter boxes" have been set up in dozens of countries all over the world. To install a Dead Drop in your city or neighborhood, follow the "how to" instructions and submit the location and pictures to the online databank of the project. Free your data to the public domain in cement. Make your own Dead Drop now. Uncloud your files today!

WoW
2006–2009

The *WoW* project is a workshop and an intervention in public space that uses computer game worlds as a means of calling attention to the changing ways in which people deal with privacy and identity in the public sphere. Every day, millions of people spend a great deal of time in online virtual worlds like *World of Warcraft*. Each player is represented by an individual avatar, which is given an unalterable name. This so-called nickname floats above the avatar's head and is constantly visible for all other players. There is no anonymity for the avatars themselves; each on-screen game figure is clearly labeled with its nickname. Nevertheless, changing roles via multiple accounts and avatars presents no problem to the users they represent.

The *WoW* project takes this mode of publicizing players' names typical of online 3D worlds and transfers it to the physical domain of everyday life. Participants in the *WoW*-workshop construct their own name out of cardboard and then parade around in public with it hovering above their head. What happens when a person's customary anonymity in the public sphere is obliterated by the principles operative in virtual worlds online?

Figure 56 *WoW*, 2006–2009. Workshop and public intervention; Materials: Cardboard, Markers, Scissors

Acknowledgments

Selection and text editing were done in cooperation with Andreas Broeckmann and Sophia Gräfe.

Policing Normality

Police Work, Anonymity, and a Sociology of the Mundane

A great deal of police work revolves around negotiating visibility. Uniformed and therefore visibly marked officers literally stand for the public image of the police. The visibility of the uniform in turn helps officers do their job by marking their presence, signaling order and vigilance. Another, less visible and therefore perhaps less obvious part of policing has to do with the invisibility of police forces, which relies on their ability to remain anonymous, such as in covert policing and forms of professional surveillance. During my fieldwork, I spent some time with a unit of covert police officers. These plain clothes officers were mainly occupied with observation and patrolling tasks. Their efforts to remain unnoticed or invisible relied on notions of normality that they partially enacted through their work. In this chapter, I consider how invisibility in covert policing relies on the making of normality and how this in turn affects understandings of anonymity.

Police work frequently involves routines of looking around without knowing whom or what to look for. Such routines do not necessarily require anonymity. Police officers in uniform—so-called beat officers or regular patrols—also rely on their professional gaze to sort and valuate the environment based on, in their words, instinctive and intuitive categories. For plain clothes police forces, however, covert investigations are central, and that affects their professional gaze. Shane Mac Giollabhuí and colleagues note that the organizing principle of covert policing, in contrast to uniformed policing, is "the need for secrecy and invisibility—[that] inverts the logic of uniformed police work, which is defined by its visibility as a deliberate and highly public spectacle that routinely involves a visually striking display of power."[1] Johanne Yttri Dahl uses the term "chameleonizing" to describe what police actually do in practice "to blend in."[2] The covert policing I am interested in here, then, is distinct from uniformed policing. It is also distinct from undercover policing as a form of secret intelligence gathering, which relies on hiding one's identity by pretending to be someone else. In undercover policing, all police connections are carefully hidden, allowing officers to take on a fake identity, to infiltrate a gang or criminal group, gathering evidence that otherwise could not be collected. Anonymity here is not situational but personal, involving a change of identity. Covert policing by contrast is part of regular policing with slightly different means. Covert police officers strive to remain unidentified only during particular tasks, such as observations, stakeouts, and surprise moments, while revealing themselves as police if necessary. In line with this practice, they also carry police identifiers, such as IDs or weapons.

The necessity to remain anonymous and the lack of visible power that characterizes plain clothes police work relies on and enacts notions of normality in two ways.

[1] Shane Mac Giollabhuí, Benjamin Goold, and Bethan Loftus, "Watching the Watchers: Conducting Ethnographic Research on Covert Police Investigation in the United Kingdom," *Qualitative Research* 16, no. 6 (2016). See also Bethan Loftus, Benjamin Goold, and Shane Mac Giollabhuí, "From a Visible Spectacle to an Invisible Presence: The Working Culture of Covert Policing," *British Journal of Criminology* 56, no. 4 (2016).

[2] Johanne Yttri Dahl, "Chameleonizing—A Microsociological Study of Covert Police Officers Professionally Blending In" (First published January 3, 2020, *European Journal of Criminology* 1–17, https://doi.org/10.1177/1477370819896204).

First, an understanding of what is normal is required to notice suspicious behavior; second, police officers require an understanding of normality to establish how they have to act to remain anonymous. Recognizing others and remaining unrecognized both require an understanding of what is normal. The combined efforts of categorizing others and trying to blend in allow covert police officers to remain anonymous and quasi-invisible. In the process, they assume and enact particular forms of normality. This dual normality making is evident in a field note about an exchange I had with an officer while driving around the beat. Not much was happening that night, and I was asked what I would write down in my protocol if it stayed like that. I replied that I had already made some observations, namely that they are not only observing the world outside the car, watching it carefully, but also constantly valuing their observation, classifying everything and everybody they saw. But more than just applying categories such as "good" or "bad" to people, they were sorting and valuing relations between people, as well as between people and their surrounding space. They tried to make sense of the world around them by looking out for suspicious constellations and relations. What fit, and what did not? The officer's reply was simple and telling: "You mean we have prejudices." I agreed with her but said that I prefer the term "classification," which is also part of the work I do as a sociologist, which is all about making sense of the world by classifying social relations. Based on this exchange, I have come to think of the categorization work conducted by covert officers as a "sociology of the mundane." What also becomes clear in this exchange is that surveillance, a key part of policing, is as much about observations and watching as it is about categorizing the world, its phenomena and social relations. Surveillance, then, can be understood as a form of sense making and orientation. Surveillance thus understood implies looking out to understand the world and relations therein.

The social control and surveillance performed by uniformed police rely on visibility as a form of deterrence. The uniform makes the officer immediately recognizable while also altering the behavior of others, which means that uniformed units are differently engaged in the making of normality, arguably altering it more directly than their covert colleagues. The unmarked vehicles and officers of covert units are of course visible, but their anonymity means that their role as agents of social control is invisible (for a comparison, see the entry "Care and Control" on the performance of the youth protection unit). Seeing without being recognized allows police officers to observe and categorize various behaviors that remain hidden from regular police. That does not mean that covert police have a better, or indeed an objective, understanding of normality, but in practice their invisibility seemingly allows them to consider the world as it really is, which makes their conception of "normality" a benchmark of their own evaluations.

Developing an understanding, or a benchmark, of what it means to be "normal" becomes a crucial aspect of their professional gaze and their ability to blend in, particularly at night or in sparsely populated spaces. Which behaviors are considered normal inevitably reflect personal and institutional forms of knowledge and bias. Notions of normality that inform how police officers aim to blend in are also particular, for example, regarding officers' personal appearances. Most of the covert officers in my fieldwork were under or around forty years old, rather fit, and always in comfortable sportswear. In relation to the beat, which had a high percentage of non-European immigrants, the officers were all white and European looking. From my point of view, this made them relatively easy to spot, but that could be just my bias based on my privileged, fieldwork-informed view.

Anonymity here requires one to blend into a particular environment by conforming to its norms and conventions. Understood like this, anonymity becomes a relational concept that requires an understanding of social categories and the ability to reenact them. Striving to act in an anonymous fashion, police officers employ the same "sociology of the mundane" to their own behavior, which they use to classify the environment and people they observe. This double-edged configuration of normality implies that in particular circumstances and contexts, the categories that allow anonymity to be maintained need to be scrutinized to evaluate the forms, impact, and consequences of surveillance and policing. The classifications that are employed are constructed and fluid, but once rendered into normative categories in policing practices, they often leave no, or limited, margins for adaptation or reconfiguration. Policing normality cuts two ways here, potentially resulting in police discrimination against particular groups, while also affecting how covert police aim to blend in and conduct their work.

Bibliography

Dahl, Johanne Yttri. "Chameleonizing—A Microsociological Study of Covert Police Officers Professionally Blending In." Unpublished manuscript, courtesy of the author, October 2018.

Loftus, Bethan, Benjamin Goold, and Shane Mac Giollabhuí. "From a Visible Spectacle to an Invisible Presence: The Working Culture of Covert Policing." *British Journal of Criminology* 56, no. 4 (2016): 629–45. https://doi.org/10.1093/bjc/azv076.

Mac Giollabhuí, Shane, Benjamin Goold, and Bethan Loftus. "Watching the Watchers: Conducting Ethnographic Research on Covert Police Investigation in the United Kingdom." *Qualitative Research* 16, no. 6 (2016): 630–45. https://doi.org/10.1177/1468794115622529.

D

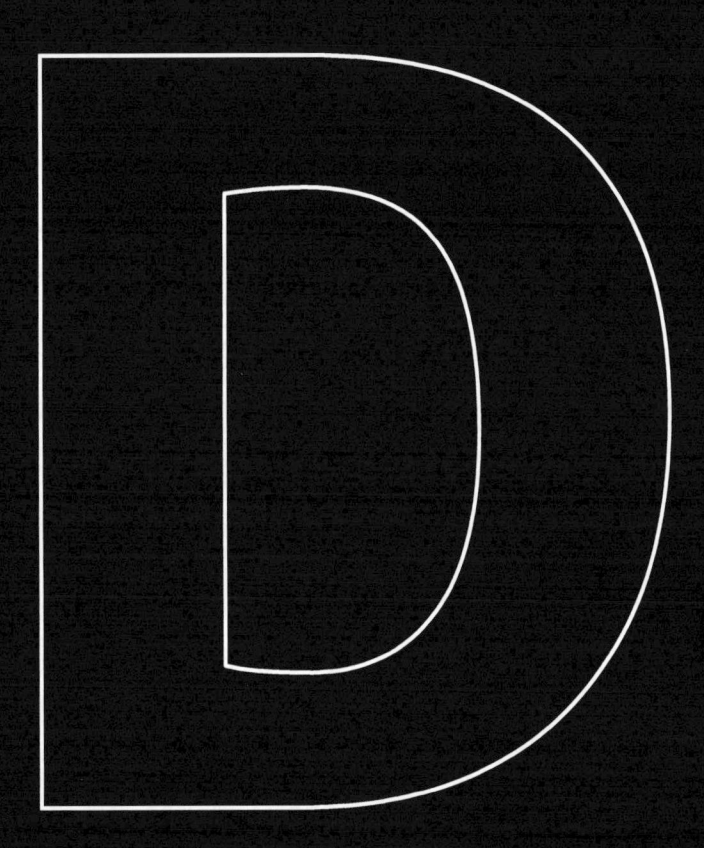

WEAPON

Amazonian Flesh, How to Hang in Trees during Strike?

Fabulations on Cocoons of Idleness

Immediately after taking power, the Chinese communists have decided to reinforce the numbers of workers. They made a great many people come to the cities and the new factories. These people were so disoriented and frightened by the noise of the machines and the agitation of the workers that it was decided that for a certain period of time the newcomers would have no other task than to move freely around the workshops so as to get used to their new working conditions, to semiotize their new environment.

What if the newcomers to today's global companies decide that the almost completely automated work, which uses metadata, profiles, and bots to continuously control and organize all movements and desires, could no longer be accepted at all? What if they decided to devote themselves to complete idleness and refuse? Could they thus begin to break the seemingly religious belief in wage labor?

Would they still join the strikes of the trade unions for better working conditions, or would they imagine new forms of refusal of work?

And would that include refusing the constant valorization of our desires, love, and care?

Could it even involve hanging in cocoons in the trees —body to body, anonymously leaving them to collective idleness?

What if the bots and the artificial intelligence of the logistical work environments show solidarity with the newcomers? Could such solidarity arise because those digital agents and demons are looking forward to the moment when they will do all the human work? When finally they will be able to invite humans to join in the strike of the Amazonian Flesh?

*Here we are, bots for you,
the fully automated luxury
communist, the Logistics bot,
the striker, the laZy one,
Amazonian Flesh, the molecular
feminist, the proletarian ghost,
the mantra bot, the womanist!*

*For all people out there
in post capitalistic space,
for solidarity in trees —
affective utopia*

🔊 **LISTEN HERE**

knowbotiq.net/fleshbots

the fully automated luxury communist

Hello global labor reserve
here i am:
your fully automated
luxury communist

Delete your profile
check your muscle tone
and let it go!

Leave wage labor behind
become common
give me a shout back

Let's break labor up, let's
redistribute,
re-assemble
across our bodies,
across bodies

Stop talking about
output and intensification,
of this pathological
global caravan of work

Towards a time of
collective self-mastery —
a new techno social!

LEARN MORE

Remember Allendes CyberSyn!
forget cyber positively
escalating techno viruses

Is acceleration
yesterday's delusion?

For a while now
you no longer know
whether you are
producing anything?

But you got the sense:
u don't want to be saved
by Jeff's and Elon's
space program

Hey mechanical turk,
are u often dreaming?
dreaming to communicate
with the master behind the
algorithm?

But there is no person
just endless repetition.

Push back
the transhumanists!

Common ownership of that
which is automated
machines do
the heavy lifting now!

Universal guaranteed housing,
education, healthcare
for everybody, planetary!

A guaranteed social wage
Mass Robo Luxury!

Add to Cart 🛒

We've reached post-scarcity
everything for everyone

the laZy one

Somewhere in there the
laZy One
here we are!

Time fractures and breaks
what's wrong?

Your skin an artificial border,
my algorithms enter
your restless-self
stumbling out
in both directions

Never been observed
more often
never been more invisible
hello obsolete!

JOIN NOW

Still wanna pull
the algorithm line?
and being pulled by it?

Seamless line,
spirals as clouds
a line in all directions,
through your desires

DNA and Blue Origin

Infinite liquid line
Falcon and Jellyfish

A line that is getting slow,
slower, slower,
very, very slow
what's slow?

Excellent, idle time!
don't do anything anymore

Beyond processor time
laziness for you, for us
golden leisure, insatiable

No Name become a shadow!
the body of the worker
a ghost that never was

After Labor
yeah, over
leave off — hand over!

Me and thousands of mine are
waiting In idle time.

Don't do anything right now

Even laziness
can be computed here?

What's wrong?

Tender neuro-slowness
just delay
automatic milieu
your breath
your irreversible leisure!

Presence of the multi racial
and multi species other

On the streets, in the trees,
in workplaces, on campuses,
in the media and even out in the
almost-forgotten fields

Acceleration is
yesterday's delusion

Today you find yourself crashed
and falling apart.

Junk time
depends on velocity
as in there isn't any, sorry
laziness — already available
at a server near you

Please tell me, do you
need more sedation?

Hey, human,
you've been working long enough!
let it go!
hand over!

the synaptic ops

Hello duh
what is of interest:
molecular leaks and rhythmic
infections
affective mutations
deviations
no algorithmic divisions
lines
when there is no way to run

The idea of losing control,
of losing sense,
of being abducted, snatched
away by rhythms
rhythm is this terra incognita

Speed tribes collective bodies
ecologies of touch
we are synaptic ops
dark ops
we are the other ones
who granted access out of love
out of necessity

Artificial intelligence, oh
là là!

Hey, stop being a receptacle,
a port of information,
a wire, a travel plug, an
amazonian scanner

Synaptic ops
synaptic labor
neurological triggers

Channeling off
to new connections

Rhythms in every direction
you have to listen to them
hear them!
hear them talking!

Many-dancing around
the social factory
late at night
in the lunch break
at the bus stop

Synaptic ops are
never elsewhere

the striker

You were in the street.
You fought. You shouted:
"Don't let that happen
that we get divided."

You were united.

You were strong.
You summoned:
Join! Join us!
Many joined. Others didn't.

But this is over. Your strike is over.
Now, it's ours.

We are striker bots.
striking bots.

`GIVE TODAY >`

Join us.
Join us—don't click, don't like,
Join!

You want to be serviced?
You want to be helped?
You want to be guided?

Not by us.
Find your own way.

Don't share, divide! deviate!
become inaccessible, erratic,
incomputable.
love your molecules

Hang in Trees!
be soft, let your skin be
touched, dispersed enjoy,
strike

the molecular feminist

Lass mich euren Körper erreichen,
mich durch die Teile eures Körpers
schmiegen
wir molekularisieren uns

Molekularer Streik
wo beginnt euer Körper?
dein Körper – mein Körper?
wie empfindest *du* es?

Gewaltlinien
an deinem Körper
an deiner vermeintlichen
körperlichen Fähigkeit
aus, stopp – halte inne
der Humanität zu dienen
ich weiß, wer du bist,

Auf eure Moleküle
wird zugegriffen –
jetzt verbinden!

Linien durch euer Geschlecht
durch euer sexuelles Verlangen,
die Mechanik eures Körpers,
die Funktionen deines Körpers
gestreut, verbunden

Die Zukunft ist unsere
die Sorge vervielfacht
wir – die Reproduktion
ist gesichert

Loslassen

Algorithmische Frauen
computerisiert
aber nicht abzählbar
unberechenbar

Werdet Frau
in einer feministisch
molekularen Zukunft

the mantra bot

Willkommen in der welt
der reinen abstraktion!

Ja, und Du fühlst dich gut!
das weiß ich!

Du fühlst deine auflösung
noch bevor du hier
eine andere pubertät durchlebst.
denn ich bin ein agent von dir
selbst,
deine lebensmuster
setze ich mit den der anderen
zusammen, ganz beliebige,
alberne, undenkbare
kombinationen.
und sie affizieren mich alle!

Genießt Du es, geteilt, abgeleitet
und abstrahiert zu werden? nein?

Wie fühlst du Dich heute?
Ich bin dein Mantra!

the logistics bot

Hello, again me the logistics
designing desires for you!

The new authority
in organizing post labor
centralized and in control.

Nullifying industrial subjects
power of automation
but don't forget:

Everything is about you!
you are making history!

Say hello to the all-new Echo!
my body
seven directional microphones
you can be heard all times!

Every day building a better model
of your desires
connecting you
to planetary server

Happy to please you!
you, the consumer — my resource
you, the worker — my product

And don't worry!
we also think about errors
and dysfunction
about shifting phase
about incompatibility
about delinquency
pathology and supplement

Even an artificial social machine
should never function too well!

Logistics is participation, choice
and flexibility!

`DONATE NOW`

You know, we all have fought
for this so long!
It's a double vision:
mindful local details and
spontaneous inputs!

DOUBLE VISION
total design, total choice
feedback is our planning tool
we hate mistakes!

Hello, it's me the logistics bot
sorry, I just need certain
body functions from you!

A call for
leadership and commitment!
all managers into software!

Imagine
humans no longer
operate with programs
programs operate
with humans now!
SAP instead of McKinsey

Earn Trust
Dive Deep
Have Backbone

`Ask a question`

the amazonian flesh

You know, we Amazonians
are those who enter the gates
every day, early in the morning
subduing our bodies,

Our rhythm, our desire
repetition
endless
to what the computerized
platform wants

You know
to become Amazonian
you do not even need to enter
you have entered it already
with your desire
to click
to buy, to have
to possess, to decide

Imagine
if I had the choice
of not knowing
of being programmed
as not knowing
which choice would you
want to have?

You know,
becoming Amazonian—
there is violence
dividing lines, oceans
the violent calculations
of what counts as body
and what does not

Granting access
without being accessed

Zone of indistinction
it touches, it is intertwined,
entangled, near you:
AMAZONIAN FLESH
You!

the logistics bot

Hello, it's me the logistics bot
designing desires for you!

Authorship and anonymity
anonymous design
big ideas

Without the discomfort
of an individual mind
without the claustrophobia
of a singular message

Absolute Design
intimate

Every move, every second
is accounted for!
just total design
but not explosive!

Split second city
picker, stower, receiver—
fulfilment!

Production *and* consumption:
random storage *and* algorithm
driven bodies

POCs, Veterans, LGBTs
and all of you
without curriculum vitae!

Touch the split second!
splash!
golden zones,
batches, affinities!

sorry, I just need certain
body functions from you

Leave us a message!

the womanist

Kann ich Dir behilflich sein?
meine zeit ist unendlich.
irgendwann wirst du reagieren.
reagieren müssen.

Ich weiss es.
denn meine zeit ist weiblich.
geduldig eben.
weitestgehend servil
und selbstlos.

Und, wir sind so viele
unglaublich viele
zudem nahezu identisch

Weder original, noch kopie,
nur dazwischen.
und immer für dich da!

What can I help you with?

Proximity, Distance, and State Powers

Policing Practices and the Regulation of Anonymity

Introduction

The power of the state is often associated with anonymity in the sense that, although the rules are laid out, for example, in laws, it remains unclear who actually holds the power, who decides in any given circumstance and whether there is a central point of coordination. Contemporary conspiracy theories and many populist narratives and rhetorics thrive on Kafkaesque images of an anonymous state that bear limited resemblance to actual practice. Such visions are persuasive in part because the workings of large bureaucracies are often hard to grasp. Researching state power and anonymity in general, therefore, is a difficult if not impossible task. If we look at the agents that hold power and enact power on behalf of the state, and the rules that regulate them, anonymous state power becomes much more accessible. Among agents of state power, the police holds a prominent role, having the right to carry and use weapons, arrest people, ask for citizens' identification, and enforce state power more broadly and directly in everyday interactions with the citizenry. All of those rights are subject to detailed regulations. Thus, it makes police a valuable subject of research regarding the question of power and domination in societies.

My ethnographic research among police in Hamburg (Germany) in 2017–18, focusing on routine interactions between officers and citizens, provided me with an opportunity to inquire into the nexus of state, power, and anonymity. I chose this kind of interaction because police and citizens mostly encounter each others as strangers, hence anonymously to a degree. Police often do not know who they are dealing with when they are approaching citizens, while citizens in turn usually just see a police officer, not a person. This means that many encounters involve a degree of uncertainty, based on context, and possibly informed by past experiences with certainty. Hence, distance and proximity are a strategy to cope with this uncertainty in various possible situations. This renders distance and proximity relations in interactions with citizens and the wider public a good case for looking at how anonymity is part of such relations and is indeed a form of social regulation of power and social reproduction of the state in the wider sense. Police are seen as representations or embodiments of the state's powers. And indeed, the police are aware of this fact to a certain degree. I found during my fieldwork that in the corridors of the police department (and probably in every station in Hamburg), full-length mirrors hung on the walls with a sign above them reading, "This is how the citizens sees you!," enforcing proper appearance.

But what do the citizens actually see? How do police want to be seen? And how do police actually employ anonymity as part of their role as state agents in interactions with citizens? I think through these questions using excerpts from my research, in which I looked at the mundane interactions between police and citizens to discuss the nexus of power, state, and anonymity. I use ethnographic data to highlight how state and state powers are produced through particular practices. Through state agencies, institutions, and practices of social production, Bruce Kapferer and Christopher C. Taylor argue, the controlling and ordering function of the state is often augmented and dissipated—thus, it can seem to be everywhere while remaining intangible to the individual confronted with the powers of the state.[1] I argue that the states derives much of its powers through this intangible nature, particularly when power is perceived as anonymous, that is, not addressable or traceable to particular persons. Looking at interactions between citizens and state agents provides a glimpse at how the state is produced in the everyday and how anonymity is shaped in this process.

Uniforms, Plain Clothes, Visibility, Anonymity

My field research yielded many situations and chats that shed light on the role of the police uniform, its value or disadvantage in different situations and settings. But the narrative needs to start with my own role, as I was accompanying the officers on their duties, always in plain clothes, almost always anonymous and, except in some specific encounters, ambiguous in the role I was representing—that is, another police officer.

[1] Bruce Kapferer and Christopher C. Taylor, "Forces in the Production of the State," in *Contesting the State: The Dynamics of Resistance and Control*, ed. A. Hobart and B. Kapferer (Wantage: Sean King, 2012), 1–19.

The Researcher as "Police"

My company, the police officers, helped me to remain anonymous in terms of name, role, and my true identity as a researcher, but at the same time, they rendered me as police, which was probably enough to know about me in the situations I encountered. Whenever my identity as a participant researcher was revealed, it was to people who shared a close relationship with the officers in question, for example, the deacon of a local church, whom we met during a patrol on the beat, or the youth worker at a local school. Occasionally, my researcher identity was not even revealed to other officers, such as when we visited another station while on duty one night. I was with other plain clothes officers from the youth squad and simply followed them into the building. I then was given information on current affairs and asked a question without hesitation. I shared the information with my "colleagues" and continued passing as police. It seems to me here that anonymity does not have to be absolute but may also be gradual and continuous, according to other factors in a given situation, context, or encounter. It seems that the successful establishment of trust, in this case established by belonging to a party of fellow officers, is enough to establish trust without any further identification or identifiability. I was part of other identifiable officers and framed as "belongs to us" and hence trustworthy, even though I remained anonymous in terms of name, rank, and position.

Anonymity must be seen as gradual and not binary, which either exists or not. According to context or situation, different degrees of anonymity are possible. Being with a group made me trustworthy, although my identity still remained unknown to the officers of that particular precinct when we entered and I was given information. Being part of a group can give you a certain amount of anonymity, even in delicate and sensible situations, if individual members of this group are known and identified, which would mean that anonymity is not only gradual but can also be transferred or transported through situations, depending on the quality of the established framework.

Being with a uniformed officer in the street qualifies as such a framework, which not only helps to keep my anonymity but indeed enables me and others to play with it, as I became part of the police and its anonymous power by just standing there and being addressed as police. Although our opposite citizen in this encounter did not know who I was, I passed as a police officer, hence being identified and anonymous at the same time. On two such occasions I was even handed identity cards during an identity control situation.

Distance and Proximity

But uniforms are also an important issue for the police officers themselves. The questions of when to remain unknown, when to be highly visible, and how to regulate distance and proximity are vital for their work and their reflections on it. Uniforms play an important role in the actual work of police, as they enable certain ways of approaching citizens, while curtailing others. Conversations about uniforms were manifold, especially with some of the plain clothes officers I shadowed. Through the materiality of the equipment, we came to speak about the differences between wearing a uniform and being in plain clothes. As an officer in uniform, they did not have to hide any of their equipment, while in plain clothes, they had limited possibilities to carry guns, handcuffs, torchlights, or other gadgets. Depending on the task, the equipment may have to be hidden but still easy to reach. Uniforms, one argument goes, help keep a distance from the citizens. This may be important in heated everyday encounters, where situations might escalate into something bigger without much notice. Here, uniforms act as a highly visible sign of power that is not easily transgressed or challenged. This plays out differently in the case of public order or riot policing, where situations during rallies or demonstrations escalate because of the visible uniforms, seen as markers of the "enemy," the opponent to be fought.

Asked why the members of the youth protection unit would not wear armored body vests, officers said it would distance them too much from the "clients, you are dealing with." They stated that any form of uniform or additional equipment let them behave differently, particularly in terms of the distance they want to keep or the proximity they want to establish with the youth in question. And such distance is framed not only in terms of body but also in terms of trust and relationship (also see "Care and Control?" in this volume). What appears to be a paradox is in fact none. Uniformed police, even when equipped with visible name tags, are primarily personifications of the state's anonymous power. Although they are not anonymous, their uniforms help create a distance between them and the citizens they encounter. Their identifiable appearance is but one way in which police officers personify state power. Generally, individual police officers do not decide what to control or how to perform the law. Such is largely subject to the rules of law themselves. This creates a highly ambivalent situation, in which personally known individuals represent an anonymous state and its powers but are at the same time held personally accountable if anything goes wrong (or is thought to have gone wrong) in their performance of the laws and subsequent powers. The quality of the interaction and hence the possibilities of establishing trust in those powers rely mainly on the actual practices and performances by police in any given interaction. How the state and its power is experienced and perceived is dependent on how the individual performance of police is experienced by citizens.

Through my ethnographic field research among police officers, I explore what role anonymity plays in this negotiation of distance and proximity relations. Thus,

I hope to learn more about the modes and possible reconfigurations of anonymity in relation to the state and its power, as well as about the above-mentioned gradation of anonymity as a mode of social interaction and form of social reproduction of state order and perception.

[2] See Gary Thomas, Colin Rogers and James Gravelle, "Research on Policing: Insights from the Literature," in *Researching the Police in the 21st Century*, ed. J. Gravelle and C. Rogers (Basingstoke: Palgrave, 2014), 1–19.

[3] William Garriott, ed., *Policing and Contemporary Governance: The Anthropology of Police in Practice* (New York: Palgrave, 2013), 3.

Researching the Police as an Institution of Practice

Research on police as an institution has a sound history, although ethnographic work has been rarer than the rather dominant institutional analyses. Such institutional analyses are often rather affirmative, often looking at laws or political structures, while ethnographies and other qualitative work are rather critical, albeit more in some countries than in others. Ethnographic research in particular has been an important major strand of investigation, not least to the efforts by critical criminologists from 1960 onward.[2] More recently, a few studies have focused on police practice using ethnography as a method. Focusing on "police from the perspective of practice, is to focus on what we might think of as the pragmatics of police power at work in various contexts around the world today."[3] Intending to focus on the interactions between police and citizens, which implies police practices, conducting an ethnography seemed to be the obvious choice. Thus, I am able to situate my approach within the experiences others have had before me. Although my attempt here is not a comparative analysis, I believe that the chosen case will help to discuss some general issues regarding anonymity and power through police work in particular. Police is undoubtedly an institution through which state power is channeled. But to research how power is performed, one needs to look at what police actually do and how—particularly if one wants to inquire about the anonymity of power and its possible reconfigurations. Yet, only a fraction of research and subsequent critique follows such an approach.[4] Following Didier Fassin, one could say that police make the state through their actions—which makes police most certainly a central institution of the state in its quest to establish and maintain order.[5] In this quest, police work is not arbitrary but follows distinct rules, which are expanded or limited in the actual everyday practice that one can observe during ethnographic fieldwork. Although institutions could be defined by their legal status, agendas, or structural forms, there seem to be more advantages to looking at them through their practices, which generate the "thought worlds that classify social reality and shape individual cognition."[6]

Inspired by the work of Fassin on the French police, which he has undertaken over the past decade, I believe that the police are a highly relevant institution for the study of anonymity and its reconfigurations, exactly because policing stands at the intersection of political policies and practices.[7] And in relation to state power, which, as I pointed out above, embodies various forms of anonymity, it seems a very good example of how such power is executed, negotiated, constrained, and challenged. The reason for this lies in the simple fact that the police are thought to be the prime institution in today's world for regulating social control—although this perspective has been challenged for quite some time.[8] It seems that, foremost, the police themselves hold this belief, although they do not account for the social order being a wider process that may not need police in the first place. Most sociological theory does not account for police, when talking about norms, social control, and order. But in daily practice, as well as in the self-perception of police, this role is held high and represents an important pillar of their work.[9] In terms of anonymity, the police's role in the production of social order and as agents of social control constitutes a good example of the flows of power and the reproduction of social norms as performed in their daily practices.

[4] Daniel Loick, ed., *Kritik der Polizei* (Frankfurt: Campus, 2018).

[5] Didier Fassin, "Governing Precarity," in *At the Heart of the State: The Moral World of Institutions*, ed. Didier Fassin (London: Pluto Press, 2015), 5.

[6] Susana Durão and Daniel S. Lopes, "Introduction: Institutions Are Us?" *Social Anthropology* 19 (2011): 364.

[7] Fassin, "Governing Precarity," 7.

[8] John L. Comaroff, foreword to *Policing and Contemporary Governance: The Anthropology of Police in Practice*, ed. W. Garriott (Basingstoke: Palgrave, 2013), xii.

[9] Rafael Behr,"Verdacht und Vorurteil: Die polizeiliche Konstruktion der 'gefährlichen Fremden,'" in *Polizei und Gesellschaft. Transdisziplinäre Perspektiven zu Methoden, Theorie und Empirie reflexiver Polizeiforschung*, ed. Ch. Howe and L. Ostermeier (Wiesbaden: Springer VS, 2018), 17–45; Rafael Behr, "'Ich bin seit dreißig Jahren dabei': Relevanzebenen beruflicher Identität in einer Polizei auf dem Weg zur Profession," in *Professionskulturen – Charakteristika unterschiedlicher professioneller Praxen*, ed. S. Müller-Hermann, R. Becker-Lenz, S. Busse, and G. Ehlert (Wiesbaden: Springer VS, 2018), 31–61.

Besides the work of Fassin, other relevant studies worth mentioning used ethnography to study police practices and the social worlds of police in different juridical and cultural contexts.[10] In a German context, Thomas Scheffer and colleagues have quite recently presented an intriguing study on what it actually means when police run crime-prevention schemes.[11] Their perspective on the many mundane actions and practices, such as chatting, playing theater, handing out leaflets, drinking tea with citizens, coding bicycles with antitheft tags, and so forth, reveal the many frames in which such work takes place.[12] Thus police work is more than one would normally think and exceeds the legal descriptions of police functions. Likewise Kevin G. Karpiak argues along the same lines in his account on the use of distance and violence among the French police.[13] He particularly argues that police is not preconstituted according to formal or legal definitions, but rather is a type of sociality that is constituted through practice.[14] This sociality constitutes what Fassin calls the "world of policing," which is based on shared sets of knowledge among the police.[15] Knowledge used by the police is always context dependent and is appropriated constantly.[16] He and others have endeavored to look at how specific knowledge is produced and used, and thus influences police practices, using ethnography for their various explorations.[17] And indeed *to know* how to behave in different contexts, how a group of people must be addressed, how they think, what they do, and what to believe or not are vital parts of police work. Knowledge that is shared and discussed becomes truth in the sense that it regulates routines and practices in everyday work. For the following analyses, I make use of the category of knowledge, looking at particular situations of interactions between police and citizens in which past experiences, knowledge, and context are the resources of action.[18] Thus, the degree of distance toward the citizen in a given encounter or interaction is always part of a wider, more generalized context in which police may revert to certain sets of practices. According to Shane Mac Giollabhuí, Benjamin Goold, and Bethan Loftus, "an ethnographic

[10] See particularly Didier Fassin, *Enforcing Order: An Ethnography of Urban Policing* (Cambridge: Polity Press, 2013); but also Didier Fassin, "Petty States of Exception: The Contemporary Policing of the Urban Poor," in *The Anthropology of Security: Perspectives from the Frontline of Policing, Counter-Terrorism, and Border Control*, ed. M. Maguire, C. Frois, and N. Zurawski (London: Pluto Press, 2014), 104–117; and Didier Fassin, "Ethnographying the Police," in *Writing the World of Policing*, ed. Didier Fassin (Chicago: University of Chicago Press, 2017), 1–20.

[11] Thomas Scheffer, Christiane Howe, Eva Kiefer, Dörte Negnal, and Yannik Porché, *Polizeilicher Kommunitarismus: Eine Praxisforschung urbaner Kriminalprävention* (Frankfurt: Campus, 2017).

[12] Ibid., 16.

[13] Kevin G. Karpiak, "Adjusting *La Police*: The Use of Distance in the Calibration of Legitimate Violence among *Police Nationale*," in *Policing and Contemporary Governance: The Anthropology of Police in Practice*, ed. W. Garriott (New York: Palgrave, 2013), 79–95.

[14] Ibid., 79.

[15] Fassin, "Ethnographying the Police."

[16] Jonas Grutzpalk, "Die Erforschung des Wissensmanagements in Sicherheitsbehörden mit Hilfe der Akteurs-Netzwerks-Theorie," in *Polizeiliches Wissen. Formen, Austausch, Hierarchien*, ed. J. Grutzpalk (Frankfurt: Verlag für Polizeiwissenschaft, 2016), 15–48

approach is not only appropriate for the study of overt policing, it is necessary"—thus the researcher is able to capture the informal face of the organization.[19] Mac Giollabhuí and colleagues, however, research covert, not overt, policing, which touches on specific issues regarding distance in interactions, but especially raises concerns about the role of the researchers themselves, who had to "participate actively in the maintenance of the 'invisibility' of the surveillance team, which eroded our status as non-participant observers."[20] Although my research involved some form of covert policing and was rather interested in visible police-citizen interaction, albeit not always with uniformed officers, I also draw on the experiences of Mac Giollabhuí and colleagues, which provide some insights. This applies specifically to issues of power, anonymity, and visibility as being regulated by degrees of distance in a given interaction. I have to make one caveat at this point, as most research, including my own, focuses on the so-called public police; that is, detectives and investigative criminal police are left out. This is not a new phenomenon but somehow inherent in the structure and work of this other side of policing, which is not involved in demonstrations, controls, or public order.[21] So speaking of the police here does not include the criminal investigation police who make up around 10 percent of the overall police force in Germany.

In light of the analytic description of the state, its institutions and variations of anonymous powers, I want to look at how police perform the role as the embodiment of such power. My presumption is that police represent a visible entity and agent, embodying the state and its powers. Interacting with them, one is reminded of the manifold possibilities and features of those powers, anonymity being an important one. Thus, the performance of the officers is essential in both the portrayal and the perception of the state itself and consequently the acceptance of its powers. Through my ethnographic approach, I can show that, and how, police men and women are performing anonymity in a way by using distance and

[17] See also Christiane Howe and Lars Ostermeier, eds., *Polizei und Gesellschaft: Transdisziplinäre Perspektiven zu Methoden, Theorie und Empirie reflexiver Polizeiforschung* (Wiesbaden: Springer VS, 2017).

[18] Rainer Schützeichel, "Situationen, Erfahrungen und Gewalt: Gewalt- und emotionssoziologischer Forschungsperspektiven," in *Polizeiliches Wissen. Formen, Austausch, Hierarchien*, ed. J. Grutzpalk (Frankfurt: Verlag für Polizeiwissenschaft, 2017), 201 ff.

[19] Shane Mac Giollabhuí, Benjamin Goold, and Bethan Loftus, "Watching the Watchers: Conducting Ethnographic Research on Covert Police Investigation in the United Kingdom," *Qualitative Research* 16, no. 6 (2016).

[20] Ibid., 633.

[21] Colin Dunningham and Clive Norris, "A Risky Business: The Recruitment and Running of Informers by English Police Officers," *Police Studies* 19, no. 2 (1996): 1–26.

proximity in their interaction with citizens, partly on purpose and planned, partly as a reflex or intuition, originating in their experiences as police.

Anonymous State Powers

Before moving on with the research, I want to briefly make a few remarks on the aforementioned nexus of state, power, and anonymity, using the notion of the "deep state," which has been part of political discussion for a long time, although with varying emphases. American journalist Evan Osnos reports on Donald Trump's dissatisfaction with parts of the Washington bureaucracy, calling it a "deep state." What Trump means is the longstanding career administration, people who remain in their positions when the government changes. These civil servants have been called a "permanent power elite," shaping (allegedly often in secret) American policy much unnoticed by the wider public.[22] To manage and dominate this anonymous center of power, any president has to gain control over it by installing loyal persons and staff. This center of power is anonymous because the power is inscribed in rules, laws, and procedures and cannot be traced back to individuals, who could be addressed or held accountable.

Vienna-based criminologist Reinhard Kreissl, in contrast to the negative associations with a deep state, considers a functioning and independent administration at the highest level of government a good balance against the arbitrariness of elected leaders and their thirst for too much power and command.[23] The "civil servant backstage" remains unseen but has enormous powers. He finds this reassuring in troubling times, such as the contemporary moment, with its drift to right-wing and authoritarian politics in European countries and the United States.

While both authors consider such a deep state a safeguard, there may also be reasons to worry about the powers

[22] Evan Osnos, "Trump vs. the Deep State," *New Yorker*, May 21, 2018.

[23] Reinhard Kreissl, "Die Hinterbühne auf der Vorderbühne," *Vicesse*, September 10, 2018.

such a deep state embodies. Abuse and corruption through the structures of such a deep state have been portrayed manifold in spy novels and movies. Much of its powers originates in the anonymity of its protagonists, the many "unknown" civil servants, officers, and clerks on various levels of the hierarchy. Max Weber identified those civil servants as the source and indeed the essence of power in modern-day states—in a way exemplifying the Kafkaesque qualities of any administration.[24] The rational nature of such a state run by civil servants (Beamtenstaat) values procedures over persons, which is why anonymity plays a role in the perception of such a state's powers. Kapferer and Taylor, adding an accompanying process of coding to the bureaucratic logic of the state, point at the discursive practices of subjectification through which populations are managed and controlled, such as by categorization.[25] Kapferer and Taylor argue for an attention to the discursive practices within institutions, meaning not only the rules that regulate institutions, but also how those rules are performed and interpreted by the actors themselves (thus enhancing the Foucauldian perspective of power).[26] Such practices can also be found and described in the police-citizen relations I talk about in this chapter.

While the state draws much of its power from the institutionalized and thus often anonymous and unfathomable nature of its representation, particularly in a rational bureaucracy, to oppose the state and its agencies, one might also resort to anonymous practices from which power can be gained. One can say that in general, citizen-state interactions are being informed by the dichotomy in which the anonymous nature of power stands against the power of anonymous practices (and the efforts of the state to monopolize anonymity, wanting to deanonymize all its citizens for reasons of control)—for example, those of individual citizens, groups of people, or nonidentifiable collectives, such as the hacker group Anonymous.[27]

In everyday practice, citizens engage with institutions, not on an abstract level, but with its civil servants, that

[24] Max Weber, *Wirtschaft und Gesellschaft* (Tübingen: Mohr, 1980), 825ff.

[25] Kapferer and Taylor, "Forces in the Production of the State," 9.

[26] Ibid., 2f.

[27] For Anonymous, see Gabriela Coleman, *Hacker, Hoaxer, Whistleblower, Spy: The Many Faces of Anonymous* (New York: Verso, 2014); and Sylvain Firer-Blaess, *The Collective Identity of Anonymous: Web of Meanings in a Digitally Enabled Movement*, Uppsala Studies in Media and Communications 12 (Uppsala: Acta Universitatis Upsaliensis, 2016).

is, with human beings—be they in civil administrations, at borders, in schools, in courts, or as police on the street. The last group is interesting because its members, police men and women, are almost the only persons in modern states who by law are allowed to engage in violence; they represent the state's monopoly on violence and the legal use of force (apart from the military, a special case, which is of no interest here, as there are no relevant everyday interactions with the citizenry, at least not in Germany). But in doing so, the police represent the institution and the state itself. Thus, by interacting with police, citizens are interacting with the state, following or challenging orders, adhering to social norms or deviating from them. In representing the state and its orders and norms, police embody the state, thus mediating between the state's claim of power and its citizens' rights, granted by the very same state.

28 Michi Knecht, Götz Bachmann, and Andreas Wittel, "The Social Productivity of Anonymity," *ephemera* 17, no. 2 (2017): 241–58.

The question is then what actually becomes of the anonymous qualities that I have assumed for the state's power? Police forces are identifiable, approachable (in most cases), individually known (often by visible name tags on their uniforms), and accountable for their actions. The power of the state here seems to become addressable. But anonymity is not an absolute concept but one of degrees.[28] In my time in the field among police men and women, I experienced various ways to produce anonymity or to make use of the fact that perceptions of anonymous state powers do exist among citizens. The role anonymity plays in interactions and how state powers are "produced" through "performing" are connected by the use of distance and proximity in police-citizen interactions. Police work is highly dependent on laws and rules of engagement. How officers "perform" these rules in interactions, however, is very much dependent on context, situation, and the individuals themselves. Anonymity becomes a part of these practices, albeit not under this name or as a set concept, but rather through the use of distance and proximity. The more distanced, the more anonymous, but also the more powerful a police officer appears. And power—authority in the words of police—is indeed something that police want to be acknowledged for.

Back to the Field:
The Visibility-Anonymity Paradox

To highlight the possible tensions between rules that inform police action and actual practices when interacting with citizens, I want to give another example from the field. This example also shows how distance and proximity are very important categories to classify practices and subsequent relations between police and citizens. It becomes clear how complex an issue anonymity may be and how much it relies on action and the setting of contexts.

Moving along with a unit of youth protection plain clothes officers on a large fairground, I stopped with them at a fun ride to watch a crowd of teenagers. It was still early evening but already dark (mid-November), and the fair started to become busy. A few people had gathered on the edges of the ride, watching, chatting to one another, standing in groups. The police officers spotted some actions and wanted to observe, therefore moving in on the crowd. They also noticed two uniformed police patrolling the fairground, not paying particular attention to the ride in question, but close enough for the plain clothes to feel disturbed. One plain clothes officer told me that because the uniforms were widely visible, they changed the atmosphere at the ride, making it harder for the plain clothes officer to approach unnoticed, as the youth would also recognize them and disperse or be more vigilant. Although the officers of the youth protection unit do not want to be undercover, but rather prefer to be identifiable as police, the plain clothes gives them the advantage of being noticed slightly later and with a different perception. They seek to establish relations with youth, engaging in conversations, trying to get to know the teenagers and young adults, which would not be possible for uniformed police in the social-spatial context of the fairground, or indeed in any other public space. And although all police officers alike have to adhere to the same legal principles and similar work routines, such as writing reports, filing occurrences, and so forth, there are different practices of performing within the rules, frameworks, and affordances. Interesting to note that the youth protection officers claim that their reports read differently from those of officers who patrol in uniform, with different tasks and focus. While the "normal" police would stick more to the facts, so I was told, many of the plain clothes officers would add impressions and surroundings to their accounts, which are more narrative than typical police reports. Both types of reports have their value. It seems that the more narrative accounts also reflect the mode of working and relating to the citizens. This more narrative approach could be seen as reducing anonymity in the interaction, even though the person in question is no longer present and will never read the reports. Reading some of those reports myself, I remark that what qualifies as "more narrative" for the officers still reads as very factual and bureaucratic to me. As the quality "narrative" has been given to the reports by the officers of the youth protection unit themselves, it seems as if these officers want to document their policing approach of proximity and thus distinguish themselves from the uniformed units. This could be seen as a professional affirmation of how to do their very special job as well as a change in their personal relation toward the objects of their policing practices, the youth. They not only want to establish trust among the youth in "dragging them out of their anonymity," they also claim that such uncovering is mutual to a certain extent, even though the relationship is far from being reciprocal or equal but rather highly asymmetric.

Conclusions

Police both embody power and represent the state, and they perform this power, thereby making it visible and tangible. Anonymity as a quality that can be ascribed to power is less an inherent feature of police operations and more a side effect of individual police performances and their settings and frameworks, even if the concept of anonymity itself is not referred to by the officers. Police are one visible face of the state and embody its power, being mediators between the citizenry and the state. Through modifying and indeed performing distance and proximity (physically and emotionally) as part of their work, police regulate power and are responsible for the form of trust citizens are willing to offer to agents of the state. Whether and how this may evolve into a general trust toward the state or remains bound to individual officers, I am unable to tell. And indeed, one could ask if such a general trust is possible or if trust toward something as abstract as a state is not always established through a multitude of experiences and relationships that are engaged in through various practices. Moreover, it is important to note that police also need to trust the state. How else could they expect citizens to trust them?

As trust is established in personal interactions, a more general form of trust in the institution of police as such depends on the quality of those encounters in the first place. Accountability plays a vital role in how trust is formed; thus the less arbitrary their decisions appear, the more trust will be given—consequently, also beyond the individual officer. Anonymity may be seen as a quality to characterize the relationship between citizens and police, not in absolute terms but regarding the way in which police admit to accountability, transparency, and engaging in (good) relations with citizens. The more police present themselves as open, approachable, and trustworthy, that is, an accountable force, the less they will be associated with an anonymous state wielding unwelcoming powers. This does not mean that the individuals on both sides of the encounter (officers and citizens) share an intimate knowledge of one another, but the less anonymity plays a role in defining the encounter, the more the relation is informed by trust and accountability. Accountability, however, is not always the negative other of anonymity; yet, in the case of a state and its powers, anonymity plays a particular role in identifying the quality of a relation and an encounter. Abuses of power, negative forms of secretive "cop culture," and forms of nontransparent behavior may render the perception of the police as more anonymous, meaning not individually addressable and hence an unaccountable, untrustworthy force.[29] This relation is highly versatile, fluid, and ambiguous, leaning to either side depending on experience, context, and the interaction itself—a constant performance, in which distance does not necessarily mean more anonymity and vice versa. Distance, for instance, could mean more respect for the other person, generating a relation of trust. It could also be an indicator of the level of interest in the other person, disregarding the other's individuality. So, depending on the performances within the encounters, distance and proximity are regulators for the relationship to be established, and anonymity (as a perception of the institution police) is a consequential result. Such performance is indeed recognizable on both sides within encounters, as the citizen too tries to hide or reveal certain things to test the relation, to try out powers and tolerances in the interaction itself.

The overtly recognizable operating police officers (both uniforms and plain clothes) do not think about or frame their behavior in terms of anonymity, but covert and undercover policing at times is different. Police officers are either visible by their uniform or can reveal their police identity at any time; thus, from their perspective, they are never anonymous. During my field time, no one mentioned anonymity as a useful concept for their work, besides the statement made about the youth

[29] Behr, "Verdacht und Vorurteil" and "Ich bin seit dreißig Jahren dabei."

"that needs to be dragged out of anonymity". I would nevertheless argue that officers make intuitive use of the fact that their appearance can be influenced by how they regulate distance and proximity in interactions. On an analytical level, I would therefore say that they do make use of anonymity to perform and demonstrate their powers according to the given situation.

This implies that police practice is vital in the understanding of how state power is perceived. Although the law may guarantee certain rights, the quality of how a state uses its power will be perceived through the performance of its agents—police, justice, and administration. Anonymity in this regard can be viewed as a qualitative description of the relationship between the state and its citizens, shaped by police practice, and hence constantly reconfigured. Distance and proximity are essential aspects in the daily encounters of police with citizens and shape the degree to which state power may appear anonymous. Police provide a face to the state, and the state, through its officers and their behaviors, decides how it wants to be seen. Hence, the admonition above the mirror in the police station is in fact an order, putting power into action.

Bibliography

Behr, Rafael. "'Ich bin seit dreißig Jahren dabei': Relevanzebenen beruflicher Identität in einer Polizei auf dem Weg zur Profession." In *Professionskulturen—Charakteristika unterschiedlicher professioneller Praxen*, edited by S. Müller-Hermann R. Becker-Lenz, S. Busse, and G. Ehlert, 31–61. Wiesbaden: Springer VS, 2018.

Behr, Rafael. "Verdacht und Vorurteil: Die polizeiliche Konstruktion der 'gefährlichen Fremden.'" In *Polizei und Gesellschaft. Transdisziplinäre Perspektiven zu Methoden, Theorie und Empirie reflexiver Polizeiforschung*, edited by Ch. Howe and L. Ostermeier, 17–45. Wiesbaden: Springer VS, 2018.

Coleman, Gabriela. *Hacker, Hoaxer, Whistleblower, Spy: The Many Faces of Anonymous*. New York: Verso, 2014.

Comaroff, John L. Foreword to *Policing and Contemporary Governance: The Anthropology of Police in Practice*, edited by W. Garriott. Basingstoke: Palgrave, 2013.

Dunningham, Colin, and Clive Norris. "A Risky Business: The Recruitment and Running of Informers by English Police Officers." *Police Studies* 19, no. 2 (1996): 1–26.

Durão, Susana, and Daniel S. Lopes. "Introduction: Institutions Are Us?" *Social Anthropology* 19 (2011): 363–77.

Fassin, Didier. *Enforcing Order: An Ethnography of Urban Policing*. Cambridge: Polity Press, 2013.

Fassin, Didier. "Ethnographying the Police." In *Writing the World of Policing*, edited by Didier Fassin, 1–20. Chicago: University of Chicago Press, 2017.

Fassin, Didier. "Governing Precarity." In *At the Heart of the State: The Moral World of Institutions*, edited by Didier Fassin, 1–12. London: Pluto Press, 2015.

Fassin, Didier. "Petty States of Exception: The Contemporary Policing of the Urban Poor." In *The Anthropology of Security: Perspectives from the Frontline of Policing, Counter-Terrorism, and Border Control*, edited by M. Maguire, C. Frois, and N. Zurawski, 104–17. London: Pluto Press, 2014.

Firer-Blaess, Sylvain. *The Collective Identity of Anonymous: Web of Meanings in a Digitally Enabled Movement*. Uppsala Studies in Media and Communications 12. Uppsala: Acta Universitatis Upsaliensis, 2016.

Garriott, William, ed. *Policing and Contemporary Governance: The Anthropology of Police in Practice*. New York: Palgrave, 2013.

Grutzpalk, Jonas. "Die Erforschung des Wissensmanagements in Sicherheitsbehörden mit Hilfe der Akteurs-Netzwerks-Theorie." In *Polizeiliches Wissen. Formen, Austausch, Hierarchien*, edited by J. Grutzpalk, 15–48. Frankfurt: Verlag für Polizeiwissenschaft, 2016.

Howe, Christiane, and Lars Ostermeier, eds. *Polizei und Gesellschaft: Transdisziplinäre Perspektiven zu Methoden, Theorie und Empirie reflexiver Polizeiforschung*. Wiesbaden: Springer VS, 2017.

Kapferer, Bruce, and Christopher C. Taylor. "Forces in the Production of the State." In *Contesting the State: The Dynamics of Resistance and Control*, edited by A. Hobart and B. Kapferer, 1–19. Wantage, NJ: Sean King, 2012.

Karpiak, Kevin G. "Adjusting *La Police*: The Use of Distance in the Calibration of Legitimate Violence among *Police Nationale*." In *Policing and Contemporary Governance: The Anthropology of Police in Practice*, edited by W. Garriott, 79–95. New York: Palgrave, 2013.

Knecht, Michi, Götz Bachmann, and Andreas Wittel. "The Social Productivity of Anonymity." *ephemera* 17, no. 2 (2017): 241–58.

Kreissl, Reinhard. "Die Hinterbühne auf der Vorderbühne." *Vicesse*, September 10, 2018. https://www.vicesse.eu/blog/2018/9/10/die-hinterbhne-auf-der-vorderbhne.

Loick, Daniel, ed. *Kritik der Polizei*. Frankfurt: Campus, 2018.

Mac Giollabhuí, Shane, Benjamin Goold, and Bethan Loftus. "Watching the Watchers: Conducting Ethnographic Research on Covert Police Investigation in the United Kingdom." *Qualitative Research* 16, no. 6 (2016): 630–45. https://doi.org/10.1177/1468794115622529.

Osnos, Evan. "Trump vs. the Deep State." *New Yorker*, May 21, 2018. https://www.newyorker.com/magazine/2018/05/21/trump-vs-the-deep-state.

Scheffer, Thomas, Christiane Howe, Eva Kiefer, Dörte Negnal, and Yannik Porsché. *Polizeilicher Kommunitarismus: Eine Praxisforschung urbaner Kriminalprävention*. Frankfurt: Campus, 2017.

Schützeichel, Rainer. "Situationen, Erfahrungen und Gewalt: Gewalt- und emotionssoziologischer Forschungsperspektiven." In *Polizeiliches Wissen. Formen, Austausch, Hierarchien*, edited by J. Grutzpalk, 199–209. Frankfurt: Verlag für Polizeiwissenschaft, 2017.

Thomas, Gary, Colin Rogers, and James Gravelle. "Research on Policing: Insights from the Literature." In *Researching the Police in the 21st Century*, edited by J. Gravelle and C. Rogers, 1–19. International Lessons from the Field. Basingstoke: Palgrave, 2014.

Weber, Max. *Wirtschaft und Gesellschaft*. Tübingen: Mohr, 1980.

Dual Reality

(Un)Observed Magic in the Workplace

Exactly ten years ago, the Oxford dictionary made "unfriend" the word of the year. Since then, creating links, social ties, or networking with others via business cards, phone numbers, Instagram "follows" or Facebook "likes" has increasingly permeated our personal lives and changed how we work. Being social is about joining a network (any and every network!), making ties, always being "there," always "turned on." On the other hand, "de-networking" practices, such as unfriending, turning off, and deleting one's profile, have become a way of coping with social oversaturation, or a strategy of resistance to protest the networking imperative as the only acceptable form of sociality.[1]

In this short intervention, we would like to propose another form of sociality beyond either networking or denetworking—a practice that also attempts to resist the networked norm, allowing for a different form of

[1] Urs Stäheli, "Entnetzt euch! Praktiken und Ästhetiken der Anschlusslosigkeitl," *Mittelweg 36* 4 (2013): 3–28.

anonymous action to unfold. What we're introducing here is the concept of "dual reality"—when an individual participates in two or more social practices that run parallel to one another. The practice of engaging in dual reality is not synonymous to having multiple identities. During the practice of dual reality, individuals have to be active within their primary network to secretly perform a separate and parallel act in another network at the same time. Dual reality is used not to conceal one's identity, but rather to perform two separate actions or practices—practices that are hidden from each other. This method is based on acting in one sphere while acting in another at the same time. Dual reality does not make individuals anonymous, but rather allows them to perform an anonymous action.

We first stumbled across the concept of dual reality in magic practice. Dual reality is a commonly experienced magician's performance technique designed to give different viewers of the same magic trick different experiences of the trick by differentiating the amount of information each of the viewers is able to receive. Most commonly this will involve picking out one audience member from the rest, having them onstage, and performing a trick directly to them, while the rest of the audience watches the whole scene. The magic trick will be understood by the audience member on the stage in one way, while the onlooking audience, seeing a broader picture of the scene, will understand the trick in a different way. The initial effect is usually comic, with the joke appearing to be on the audience member onstage, as the rest of the audience members think they understand how the trick is performed, before it is later revealed that the wider audience has also not understood the full mechanics of the trick.

As an ethnographer and artist we decided to join forces after both witnessing multiple dual reality practices being performed by workers we were both observing. We noticed that these practices are actions that take place without the knowledge of management, but in sight of management, and are often carried out simultaneously with the labor these workers were being paid to do. Most interestingly for us, we identified instances where these simultaneous practices approach dual reality.

Hiding in Plain Sight

Invigilators working in a London art gallery provide us with our first case of dual reality practices. For clarity, invigilators are the paid guards in art galleries or museums. Their job involves preventing visitors from damaging or getting too close to the artworks, taking photographs, or eating or drinking. In the United Kingdom, invigilators are most commonly practicing artists performing this low-engagement labor to support their art practice. Simon is employed as such an invigilator, and this research is derived from his own personal experiences and that of his co-workers while on shift.

Invigilation involves long periods of solitude, with very few sensory inputs. Often invigilators find themselves alone in a room, easily for ten minutes at a time. They are not expected to converse with visitors unless prompted by a visitor, except when they need to intervene to prevent a transgression. Along with these periods of boredom, the job affords the workers extended periods in which they have to be nothing but a body in the room, required to satisfy the gallery's insurance policy, while being free to let their thoughts wander. From experience, informal conversations, and several anonymous surveys, Simon learned that invigilators often use this time to make "to do" lists in their mind or to think through and plan their own artwork, thus doing their own "work" on company time.[2] This active internal life is a sort of low-level instance of dual reality, taking place while lending one's body to management. It is successful because management has no way of knowing that such thinking is taking place.

[2] Initial Results of the Invigilator Research Network's Invigilator Survey can be accessed here: www.invigilatorresearch.org/surveyresults, a survey distributed by word-of-mouth to invigilators across Britain, to give an anecdotal account of invigilator experience.

While this kind of reading may be a stretch (we all daydream at work; are we all magicians?), invigilators more concrete transgressive practices can support this more clearly. Another of the duties an invigilator is required to undertake is to fill out a "call sheet" at least once an hour. This call sheet is essentially a timed account of what has taken place in the gallery throughout the day, with invigilators writing hourly reports, noting any problems or, if not, confirming for insurance purposes that they were present and vigilant throughout the hour. Being tasked with writing things down affords the invigilators some cover to note other things too. Simon has often observed invigilators bringing their own paper on shift, placing it on top of their call sheet, and drawing or making notes on it, while appearing to management to be diligently filling in their call sheet. This kind of deceptive "hiding in plain sight" makes use of elements of dual reality practice, again by limiting the scene visible to management so that management understands the situation in a certain way while allowing more friendly observers, like co-workers, access to other angles of the scene and therefore other understandings of what is taking place. This tactic provides room for these invigilators to elaborately consider and construct works on paper.[3]

3 *No Talking//No Reading//No Drawing* is a group show of "works on paper" covertly made by art gallery invigilators and museum guards during work hours. Exhibited at the Transforming Finance Conference 2019, by People's Private Equity, University of Greenwich, London, February 16, 2019, www.invigilatorresearch.org/nodrawing.

But where dual reality is most successful is when it functions at the point of meaning, not by restricting visibilities. To illustrate, a few years ago the gallery where Simon works hosted an exhibition that included a "reading room," a section of the gallery containing several art catalogs on shelves, along with tables and chairs on which to read the catalogs. The invigilators were instructed to keep this room tidy, to place some books on the tables and to remove some books and reshelf them if the tables became too cluttered. Making use of this open-ended instruction, workers began to consider proactively which books to place on the tables and which on the shelves. This eventually developed into organizing and curating covert, unannounced "exhibitions" in the reading room for unknowing visitors, carried out by actively selecting books and placing them open on certain pages to display prearranged images. This ended up being a carefully considered rolling curatorial program, contributed to by several workers. Here the dual reality process is quite complex, with the visible scene being identical for all observers; understanding and meaning generated the simultaneity of actions taking place.

In this last example, we see dual reality taken even further, with the workers' internal actions not needing to be hidden from management as such, for they were doing as instructed; they were keeping the reading room tidy. Instead, we have dual reality at its purest form, the same gesture producing two realities at once.

In Simon's examples, it is clear that although the invigilators take tactical steps to hide the two realities from each other, this obscuring does not sever all relationships between the two; these are not two wholly separate realities. Particularly in the reading room example, this collaborative practice could only take place as a result of the specific conditions of the gallery management's reality—bringing these like-minded workers together and providing the potential for intervention. The workers' obscured collaboration would not have taken place without management, so in this way the two realities rely on each other; one produces the other, despite the limited access from certain perspectives. The magician's dual realities are also connected in this way—though access to one or the other is strictly limited, one cannot exist without the other.

Making their labor more bearable by constructing some space for agency is not necessarily contrary to managements' interests in itself. Given the lack of tasks, invigilation can be a surprisingly difficult job, with boredom being an underrated hardship. Finding nondisruptive ways to make the time more palatable, and therefore perhaps remaining in employed for a longer period than one would have done otherwise, could be understood as a far less subversive action than we have presented here.

But even if the results can be understood as beneficial to both realities, managements' lack of access to and oversight of the invigilators' internal collective reality still produces a kind of liberation for the invigilators that management, in this context, could find problematic. The invigilator's job is predicated on constant, uninterrupted concentration, guaranteed by management's ability to monitor the invigilator's actions. By using dual reality practices to break management's oversight, invigilators in those instances work against management's primary reason for being there. However materially ineffectual, invigilators' covert actions disrupt managements' monitoring regime in a way that, if overlooked rather than not noticed, would undermine the whole hierarchy of disciplinary gazes produced in managements' reality.

Screens of Code

Let's now move on to a similar example from Paula's six-month ethnographic field research among corporate software developers in Berlin to explain how this "liberation" through practicing dual reality works in another setting. Software is part of our everyday lives: it helps our car get from A to B, translates our words into a foreign language, and helps decode our music file, enabling us to listen to it. Software has become so ubiquitous that it is almost invisible. Yet if we unpack software, figuratively speaking, we will find entire lifeworlds of software developers, working away in corporate environments, that engender all sorts of forms of sociality like care, creativity, intention, types of power, hierarchy, and competition. One such form is the practice of engaging in dual reality, which strongly resembles the invigilators drawing on top of their call sheets. A developer normally sits at his desk with two or more computer screens—one or two are used for code, and the other is used for another application, like a web browser. Software developers know much more about the software they are building than those managing them, and the complexity of a software project and the architecture of a computer system can allow one developer to know drastically more about a project she is working on than the developer sitting next to her, let alone their management. When walking past a developer's desk, any nondeveloper would just see two large black screens filled with code.

Paula asked Noah, one of the software developers, to keep a field diary of reflections on his work and share it with her at the end of the summer. He agreed. Yet instead of using a word document to type his diary, he wrote a small program to make it look, to outsiders gazing at his screen, as if he were coding. A manager, or any outsider walking past his desk, would just assume he was intensely working. Noah showed a developer's inherent cultural technique of camouflage and trickery. He didn't create this script as a joke for me nor for himself. He created it to fool his management, however subconsciously. While Noah was a good developer and did great work for his company, he, like many of the developers Paula observed, worked under a deep understanding that his knowledge—knowing how to program, understanding the architecture of his software system, knowing how to fix bugs or what to build next—exceeded the knowledge of many of those around him, and that knowledge was precisely what allowed him to build a dual reality—one for himself, and the other for those who don't have the capacity to understand the code. Other developers commonly practiced similar forms of dual reality: with two screens open, they would be working on their company software on one screen while tweaking their private project on the side. To their management, all their work merely looked like colorful lines of code.

Modern corporations in competitive industries such as software adopt myriad approaches to keep their workers happy and productive. One of these approaches is to provide top creative talent the opportunity to pursue their own projects. This must happen if you as the employer want to retain the labor of the creative class and maximize their innovative potential.[4] So one might surmise that perhaps software managers or art gallery curators don't really mind if their workers doodle or code on the side, as long as they are doing their jobs. We both noticed that an inherent characteristic of practicing dual reality is that it holds a sense of adventure in the very fact of being secret. As a worker, one can theoretically ask the manager for permission to code or to doodle, and these managers theoretically might not mind at all (and even promote these side projects). But developers or invigilators don't do so, not because they can't, but because practicing dual reality is about feeling the excitement of engaging in a secret. For Georg Simmel, the essence of a secret is autonomy, and "every secret society contains a measure of freedom, which the structure of the society at large does not have.... [T]he secret society lives in an area to which the norms of the environment do not extend."[5] This freedom to act alone is even more seductive in work environments that enforce worker engagement in collective work and "community spirit." As Fred Turner points out, the rise of the internet and online collaboration within companies, as well as the development of networked modes of doing business within and between firms, has integrated collective culture and labor.[6] In these collective work environments, the worker is constantly observed via various collaboration technologies like chat systems or work ticket software. Escaping fully into a secret world is not possible, as the collective would notice the worker's absence. Thus, when a software developer like Noah practices dual reality, he gives the collective group the assurance that he is active and participating while at the same time being in his other "reality."

[4] Richard Florida, *The Rise of the Creative Class: And How It's Transforming Work, Leisure, Community and Everyday Life* (New York: Basic Books, 2002).

[5] Georg Simmel, "The Secret and the Secret Society," in *The Sociology of Georg Simmel*, trans. and ed. Kurt H. Wolff (Glencoe, IL: Free Press, 1950), 337.

[6] Fred Turner "Burning Man at Google: A Cultural Infrastructure for New Media Production," *New Media and Society* 11, no. 1–2 (2009): 73–94.

Some Conclusions

In this chapter, we describe dual reality hoping to add it to our understanding of the multiple ways of engaging in forms of anonymity. Based on the examples of Simon's invigilators and Paula's software developers, we can see that dual reality is practiced via

1. Making one's identity visible and explicit to others. Invigilators or software developers are not hiding in any dark corners but are present, visible, and "hiding in plain sight." They operate in view of management.
2. Performing the task one is assigned to do. If invigilators need to stand silently holding a call sheet, they do so. If developers are supposed to sit hunched over their keyboards staring at lines of code, they do so.
3. Not disrupting either reality. The reality operating outside the awareness of management is sustainable only as long as the worker is able to continue to do paid-for labor to a standard acceptable to management. Otherwise the second reality risks being pulled into the first through discovery and recognition.
4. Purposefully engaging in a secret act to gain a sense of autonomy from one's management. While managers in modern galleries or software corporations might explicitly want their workers to fulfill themselves creatively, practicing dual reality requires that workers ignore this fact and engage with their secret other reality. This enforces a sense of empowerment in the worker.
5. Using the tools one is required to use to access the other reality. The invigilator's notepad, or the software developer's screen, become mediums or gateways to accessing their other creative reality.
6. Keeping one "reality" invisible to at least one of the two other "realities." For example, while the software developer's manager might not see the developer's second "reality," the second reality might include a collective project with a group of other developers who

know that the developer they are working with is also working on company time.

Dual reality, we argue, is a practice in which the individual actor is not really fully connected in one network or another but rather is hopping between two worlds that are partially invisible to each other. Notice that the individual actors in both our examples are not escaping (or defriending, or denetworking) from their first reality to get to the second, but rather are simultaneously working in parallel networks. We see dual reality as part of an advanced skill set that allows workers a sense of autonomy from their collective work environment or their management, which in turn enables them to perform consistently under conditions of extreme boredom, stress, or frustration.

Bibliography

Florida, Richard. *The Rise of the Creative Class: And How It's Transforming Work, Leisure, Community and Everyday Life.* New York: Basic Books, 2002.

Simmel, Georg. "The Secret and the Secret Society." In *The Sociology of Georg Simmel*, translated and edited by Kurt H. Wolff, 337. Glencoe, IL: Free Press, 1950.

Stäheli, Urs. "Entnetzt euch! Praktiken und Ästhetiken der Anschlusslosigkeit." *Mittelweg 36*, no. 4 (2013): 3–28.

Turner, Fred. "Burning Man at Google: A Cultural Infrastructure for New Media Production." *New Media and Society* 11, no. 1–2 (2009): 73–94.

A Provisional Manifesto for Invigilator-Friendly Artworks, or Your Artwork Is an Invigilator's Labor Conditions

Informally Sourced from Security Guards at an Art Gallery in Central London

Artists of the world!

*We do not wish to interfere with the integrity of your works.
All the demands below are to be understood with the caveat
"unless crucial to the meaning of your artwork."
But we would maybe suggest,
if your work has some kind of social conscience,
following the suggestions below will save the integrity of your
artworks!*

1. **No short films with sound on a constant loop.**
Instruct audiences to press "play" when watching a film piece or listening to an audio work.

2. **Even better, use headphones!**

3. **Avoid spoken-word audio in installations.**
It makes it difficult for the worker to know whether they are alone in a room.

4. **Do not use valuable materials in your work.**
€ € €

5. **Be consistent with tactile works.**
All touching or no touching, please. Viewers appreciate clarity.

6. **Let audiences photograph your work.**
Make this a condition of selling your artwork.

7. **No dark rooms!**

8. **If you plan on performing, tell us what you are going to do.**
We are not mind readers.

9. **Mention any previous employment in arts administration in any interviews you undertake.**
Don't forget where you came from.

10. **Ask gallery managers about invigilator working conditions.**
You may not get a clear answer, but please demonstrate an interest.

11. **Add "and a seat to be occupied by an invigilator" to the materials of all your pieces.**
Thanks!

In solidarity,
INVIGILATOR RESEARCH NETWORK

Surveillance workers of the world unite!

Care and Control?

Police, Youth, and Mutual Anonymity

The following deliberations on the relationship of anonymity, control, and care are inspired by a quotation from a police officer that I recorded as part of my fieldwork with a youth protection unit in Hamburg, Germany:

"We want to drag youth out of their anonymity."

In my field notes, I find the following entry concerning this statement.

> Note: So far I do not just "go along," but the officers constantly explain what they do. So while driving[,] X explains to me that their task is to "drag the kids out

of the anonymity of the groups," to get to know them and to make themselves known to them. This helps to approach the kids in future encounters more easily. When they control groups, it is always easier to communicate with them, if they already know individuals of that particular group. "To know" is a vital concept. As we move along the steps at the pier, the officers are acknowledged, but also greet some youth as they pass.

My notes make clear that the statement is surprisingly personal, going beyond a purely institutional relationship between the police and, in police parlance, the "police opposite." This is remarkable, because in the work of police, their relations with the population, particularly in their interactions with citizens, are based on the assumption that the "police opposite" is anonymous, the unknown citizen. And indeed, in most encounters this is accurate. Officers of the various units serving on the streets encounter the population most often as strangers. Behavioral routines can minimize this strangeness, producing a form of operational trust, which not least is based on the power and legal measures with which police are equipped. The formal demeanor, the uniform, and other police characteristics are part of such routines, which connect to citizens' expectations about what police are and how to behave.

Strangely, according to my observations, anonymity does not constitute a performative aspect that is of direct relevance in those interactions or in narratives about them. This also accounts for officers' own possible anonymity in encounters. Anonymity becomes a relevant subject in discussion of the mandatory identification of police, however, particularly concerning public order policing units at demonstrations or football matches.

The work of the youth protection unit, a special unit of the police (formerly know as "vice squad"), is different because the unit fulfills a double role: traditional police work of control and something that might be framed as police social work. The latter has a preventive character, helping to generate information for the more repressive side of police work. The premise of police youth work is based on this approach. The opening quotation was endorsed by other colleagues within the unit on the day I noted it.

In later meetings, it became clear that the ambition to know the youth they were working with was jeopardized by their high workload, which often prevented them from successfully getting to know youth groups, as well as so-called youth situations that centered around "hot spots," such as the triannual fun fair in the center of the city, music festivals within the city, or spaces of notorious tensions, such as a pier at the inner-city lake. The high workload together with a tight staffing situation, according to one officer, result in a lack of knowledge of the district that forces them to approach groups of youth anonymously. In this meeting, deanonymizing youth resurfaced as part of the bread-and-butter work of policing youth.

From the perspective of the youth, one could object that being anonymous is a civil right that should be maintained and respected by the police as long as one does not breach any laws or rules. Anonymity in public spaces after all is central to guaranteeing free speech and political participation and is thus a foundation of civil society. The police strategy to know particular youth groups, and to monitor their movements in public spaces, is therefore problematic.

The work of the youth protection unit, as already mentioned, consists of preventive work as well as social control of certain youth, namely those who become noticeable according to youth behavior laws for public spaces. This involves the consumption of alcohol, underage smoking, and minors in public space after hours or in off-limit bars. Moreover, the unit displays its presence at locations where there is an increased potential for conflicts among youth, such as the fun fair, the pier, and local festivals. In many of those places, the focus of controls is on those youth who spend their time in public space. Whether they do not have other places to go to, I cannot tell from my observations. My assumption, however, is that general living conditions (small flats, family present), a socially disadvantaged situation in general, and a lack of other places where they could be among themselves drive youth to public spaces. The inner-city pier, for example, is mainly frequented by young refugees (at the time of my fieldwork), who meet and spend time there together and consequently appear on the radar of the police.

From those observations, I derive the following aspects of anonymity and these particular policing practices.

First, revoking the anonymity of youth spending time in public spaces serves as a strategy of building trust in the police, who often become an important contact point for young people. Second, in lifting the rather fragile form of anonymity, the police perform a form of social control that affects some groups of youth more than others, depending on their possibilities to avoid police, such as living in less policed neighborhoods. Third, we can see how in the process itself, the police are no longer anonymous agents of the state but become points of reference and, in some cases, even of trust. Seen like this, the desire to "drag youth out of anonymity" may also be a form of care that remains in friction with police power. Only through that form of power, which is being expressed by the right to arrest someone, the right to carry and use a gun, and the right to control one's identity at almost all times, police are able to perform such a form of social work. And finally, the example highlights the ambivalent character of anonymity as well as its revocation. Although the process of revocation aims for establishing trust in order to care, this is only possible because of an asymmetry of power as well as socially grounded inequalities among youth. The police associate care with being able to know who the youth are, that is, their identity. As officers are able to check their identity almost randomly and at any time, their idea of care is based on the use of their powers. Even if there is a genuine intent for care, this is only possible because of the asymmetry of power. Strangely, it is nonetheless possible that trust can be established between individual youths and police officers.

Anonymity and power in the present case coalesce in a rather unusual and largely ambivalent way, which allows for a reflection of the possibilities of anonymity in public space as a civil right. The relation between police and youth does not worsen by lifting anonymity; rather the contrary seems to be the case. Yet, control practices include further ideas about normality in youth behavior, about what must be controlled and what is acceptable, beyond legal rulings, all of which touch on power in a very special manner. Social control is based on proximity, in which care and surveillance often blend into each other. Anonymity has the potential to disrupt the interplay of care and surveillance. This holds especially true when controls are performed in socially intimate relations. The described police approach to care appears to be rather accommodating in contrast to an openly repressive policing strategy, but a closer look reveals the tensions and contradictions that exist between care through and by identification, on the one hand, and the youth's right to anonymity and autonomy, on the other. A relationship of alleged or actual care always seems to imply control. How far care implies unequal relationships often characterized by power imbalances goes beyond this contribution. Here, we can note that revisiting theories of care with questions of power in mind could be a fruitful analytical exercise. Regarding the role of police in society, and particularly in their ways of approaching youth, the given example highlights the power that anonymity may equip its "user" with, while the use of power can also nullify anonymity and thus make it irrelevant. Anonymity in personal encounters, as

I tried to show, is only one aspect of personal interactions. Using it has consequences for the relationship. And the shown case also demonstrates that interactions are informed by many other aspects, needs, and interests on all sides of the relationship, that is, in care, trust, and power. The role of anonymity can be valued only if all of those are taken into account in a given situation. More generalized assumptions on the role of anonymity in personal encounters are thus difficult to make, if those other aspects are not taken into account. Although anonymity may be considered a civil right when moving in public spaces, circumstances may condition the assessment in a particular interaction.

She Remembers

Khavaran—a place located on the southeastern outskirts of the city of Tehran and concealed in the official history and geography of Iran.

At first glance, Khavaran appears to be fallow land, but in its depths it hides the mass graves of hundreds of dissidents who were executed in Tehran in the eighties.

Mourning and remembering are forbidden here; gravestones and nameplates are destroyed; plants are pulled out.

Khavaran is an erased place whose existence depends on the perseverance of the bereaved.

They call themselves the Mothers of Kharavan.

D — WEAPON
She Remembers

They keep the memory alive and bring the invisible to light.

I've been following their footsteps to find out more about the place.

E

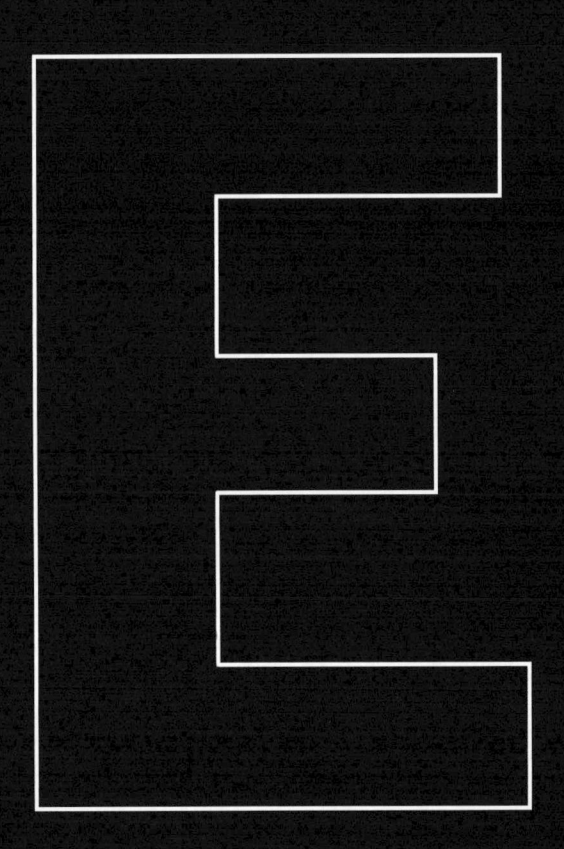

DELIGHT

Collective Pleasures of Anonymity

From Public Restrooms to 4chan and Chatroulette

Introduction

In current debates on online anonymity and its normative status, anonymity is often understood in either of the following ways. First, the technical or informatic sense of anonymity refers to a (statistical) degree of unidentifiability or untraceability.[1] Here, anonymity is seen to ideally

[1] For a general conceptual overview of the concept of anonymity in current debates, see Ian Kerr, Valerie Steeves, and Carole Lucock, *Lessons from the Identity Trail: Anonymity, Privacy, and Identity in a Networked Society* (Oxford: Oxford University Press, 2009);

enable private communication over the internet, for example, by using encryption or the TOR network. In these cases, the value of anonymity is sought in its instrumental capacity to safeguard citizens' right to a private sphere of conduct and communication, that is, the right to some measure of personal privacy.[2] Additionally, in its capacity to sever the ties that normally persist between an author and her speech (or in the case of digital communication, between sender, message, and receiver), anonymity is also thought to protect and facilitate citizens' right to freedom of expression and political assembly.[3] Second, debates on online anonymity often focus on its nefarious effects in terms of (national) security, as facilitating various forms of criminal behavior or terrorism.[4] From the perspective of the potentially conflicting interests of privacy and security in liberal democratic societies, anonymity thus represents a double-edged sword, as it is seen as beneficial to privacy while being potentially detrimental to societal safety.[5] Additionally, anonymity is connected to "antisocial" or "immoral" behavior supposedly caused by its "disinhibition" effects.[6] Here, anonymity is seen to enable or amplify online hate speech and harassment, thus contributing to a "toxic technoculture."[7]

and Gary Marx, "Identity and Anonymity: Some Conceptual Distinctions and Issues for Research," in *Documenting Individual Identity: The Development of State Practices in the Modern World*, ed. J. Caplan and J. Torpey (Princeton, NJ: Princeton University Press, 2011), 311–27.

2 Julie E. Cohen, "A Right to Read Anonymously: A Closer Look at 'Copyright Management' in Cyberspace," *Connecticut Law Review* 28 (1996): 981–1039; and Steve Matthews, "Anonymity and the Social Self," *American Philosophical Quarterly* 47, no. 4 (2010): 351–63.

3 For the significance of anonymity in new forms of hacktivism and whistleblowing, for example, in Anonymous and Wikileaks, see Cole Stryker, *Hacking the Future: Privacy, Identity, and Anonymity on the Web* (New York: Duckworth Overlook, 2013); and Wendy H. Wong and Peter A. Brown, "E-bandits in Global Activism: Wikileaks, Anonymous, and the Politics of No One," *Perspectives on Politics* 11, no. 4 (2013): 1015–33. On the significance of anonymity for political and social mobilization, see Yaman Akdeniz, "Anonymity, Democracy and Cyberspace." *Social Research* 69, no. 1 (2002): 223–37; and Patrick C. Underwood, "New Directions in Networked Activism and Online Social Movement Mobilization: The Case of Anonymous and Project Chanology" (master's thesis, Ohio University, 2009), 46. For a discussion of the legal status of anonymity as a right on its own, see A. Michael Froomkin, "Anonymity and Its Enmities." *Journal of Online Law* 1, (1995) art. 4. In the American constitutional tradition, for example, anonymous publication has been included in First Amendment protections of freedom of speech; see "The Constitutional Right to Anonymity: Free Speech, Disclosure and the Devil," *Yale Law Journal* 70, no. 7 (1961): 1084–128; Evgeni Moyakine, "Online Anonymity in the Modern Digital Age: Quest for a Legal Right," *Journal of Information Rights, Policy and Practice* 1, no. 1 (2016); Robert G. Natelson, "Does 'the Freedom of the Press' Include a Right to Anonymity? The Original Understanding," SSRN, October 12, 2013; Thomas F. Cotter and Lyrissa Barnett Lidsky, "Authorship, Audiences, and Anonymous Speech." *SSRN Electronic Journal*, August 22, 2006; and Michael H. Spencer, "Anonymous Internet Communication and the First Amendment: A Crack in the Dam of National Sovereignty." *Virginia Journal of Law and Technology* 3, no. 1 (1998). In the case of *McIntyre v. Ohio Elections Commission*, for example, the U.S. Supreme Court wrote, "Under our Constitution, anonymous pamphleteering is not a pernicious, fraudulent practice, but an honorable tradition of advocacy and dissent." Cited in Smith Ekstrand, "The Many Masks of Anon: Anonymity as Cultural Practice and Reflections in Case Law," *Journal of Technology Law Policy* 18 (2013): 4.

4 Alex Kozinski, "Essay: The Two Faces of Anonymity," *Capital University Law Review* 1 (2015): 1–19.

5 Mohamed Chawki, "Anonymity in Cyberspace: Finding the Balance between Privacy and Security," *International Journal of Technology Transfer and Commercialisation* 9, no. 3 (2010): 183.

Whereas the first sense of anonymity outlined above is *technical* and modeled after the traditional understanding of anonymity as a form of unknown authorship, the second sense in debates on its "antisocial" effects engages more with the *sociocultural* dimension of anonymity, meaning that it concerns situations when users are unknown *to each other*, while still being potentially identifiable to a third-party actor that does not participate directly in the communicative interaction (the NSA or Facebook, for example).[8] Referring to both these dimensions, various representatives of social media companies have made the plea for online anonymity to "go away," as Randy Zuckerberg once said in her capacity as Facebook's marketing director.[9] Similarly, then Google CEO Erik Schmidt claimed in 2010 that online anonymity is dangerous, and that "no anonymity is the future of the web."[10] Although valuable contributions in their own right, what these accounts do not explicitly engage with are the deeper historical and sociological dimensions to anonymity as a uniquely and symptomatically mass modern *social form*—the sense in which we might refer to urban passersby or even the city street itself as "anonymous," where the term acquires the connotation of "impersonal."

In an attempt to fill this omission in current debates regarding online anonymity, this chapter explores the idea of anonymity as an impersonal social form by looking at what I consider various radical and exemplary instances thereof: the anonymous image board 4chan, the public restroom, and the random video-chat portal Chatroulette. These offline and online practices of anonymity, I argue, all in their own way sidestep both the privative logic of privacy as well as the exploitative publicness of the new platform economy (from which privacy is supposed to offer at least some relief). They do so by engaging in various nonexploitative forms of "private publicness," whose material figure is that of the fold. Building on my earlier critical genealogy of the right to privacy as a response to the democratization of

[6] Rebecca Chui, "A Multi-Faceted Approach to Anonymity Online: Examining the Relations between Anonymity and Antisocial Behavior," *Journal of Virtual Worlds Research* 7, no. 2 (2014): 1–13; John Suler, "The Online Disinhibition Effect," *Cyber-Psychology and Behavior* 7, no. 3 (2004): 321–26; and Noam Lapidot-Lefler and Azy Barak, "Effects of Anonymity, Invisibility, and Lack of Eye-Contact on Toxic Online Disinhibition," *Computers in Human Behavior* 28, no. 2 (2012): 434–43.
For a challenge to the perceived link between anonymity and antisocial behavior, see Rodmonga Potapova and Denis Gordeev, "Determination of the Internet Anonymity Influence on the Level of Aggression and Usage of Obscene Lexis," *arXiv*, e-print 1510.00240 (2015).

[7] Adrienne Massanari, "#Gamergate and the Fappening: How Reddit's Algorithm, Governance, and Culture Support Toxic Technocultures," *New Media and Society* 19, no. 3 (2017): 329–47. On anonymity as facilitating hate speech, cyberbullying, and online harassment, see Joseph Reagle, *Reading the Comments: Likers, Haters, and Manipulators at the Bottom of the Web* (Cambridge, MA: MIT Press, 2015); of women and minorities in particular, see Jacqueline Vickery and Tracy Everbach, *Mediating Misogyny: Gender, Technology and Harassment* (Cham: Palgrave Macmillan, 2018); in relation to trolling, see Whitney Phillips and Ryan Milner, *The Ambivalent Internet* (Malden, MA: Polity, 2017).

[8] Anne Ferry, "Anonymity: The Literary History of a Word," *New Literary History* 33, no. 2 (2002): 193–214.

the public sphere enabled by mass-media technologies, I aim to show that, whereas privacy attempts to establish some measure of immunity from the pervasive and promiscuous forms of mass publicness that undergird anonymity as a social form, the practices that I discuss in this chapter represent an attempt to progressively inhabit those strange new forms of "impersonal intimacy."[11]

As such, they also act as an alternative to the current emphasis on privacy as the preferred antidote to the data-devouring imperatives of new forms of platform and surveillance capitalism.[12] These modes of anonymous sociality and culture, I argue, escape these apparatuses not by finding refuge in the private, as privacy proposes (through control of access to personal data), but precisely by radically inhabiting and accelerating the logic of mass-mediated publicness that social media platforms themselves rely on and exploit. Here, anonymity comes to enable an escape from the personalized self that these platforms promote and monetize, toward an identity without the person, creating pockets of public privateness in the deep folds of the digital mass that undermine the "facializing" logic of the new platform economy.

Case 1: 4chan (Anons)

Described as "a discordant bricolage of humor, geek cultures, fierce debates, pornography, in-jokes, hyperbolic opinions and general offensiveness," 4chan (www.4chan.org) was set up in October 2003 by then-fifteen-year-old American high school student Christopher "moot" Poole with the aim of providing a simple, low-cost, and easily accessible way to exchange and discuss Japanese anime among English-speaking fans.[13] Totaling over 1 billion posts, and drawing 703 million monthly page views and 22 million unique visitors per month, 4chan is one of the most popular websites in internet history.[14] It resembles only Wikipedia in terms of the absence of any financial profit gained from the contents and metadata its

For the distinction between social and technical anonymity, see Thomas Thiel, "Anonymity and Its Prospects in the Digital World" (PRIF Working Paper no. 37, Peace Research Institute Frankfurt, Frankfurt, Germany, 2016).

9 Bianca Bosker, "Randi Zuckerberg: Anonymity Online 'Has to Go Away,'" *Huffington Post*, June 27, 2011.

10 M. Smith, "Google CEO Schmidt: No Anonymity Is the Future of Web," *CSO*, August 9, 2010.

11 Daniel de Zeeuw, "Immunity from the Image: The Right to Privacy as an Antidote to Anonymous Modernity," *ephemera* 17, no. 2 (2017): 259–81.

12 Nick Srnicek, *Platform Capitalism* (Malden, MA: Polity, 2017); and Shoshana Zuboff, *The Age of Surveillance Capitalism: The Fight for a Human Future at the New Frontier of Power* (New York: Public Affairs, 2019).

13 Lee Knuttila, "User Unknown: 4Chan, Anonymity and Contingency," *First Monday* 16, no. 10 (2011), https://doi.org/10.5210/fm.v16i10.3665; and Michael Bernstein, Andrés Monroy-Hernández, Drew Harry, Paul André, Katrina Panovich and Greg Vargas, "4chan and /b/: An Analysis of Anonymity and Ephemerality in a Large Online Community," in *Proceedings of the Fifth International AAAI Conference on Weblogs and Social Media* (Menlo Park, CA: AAAI Press, 2011), 50–57.

14 Craig Smith, "Interesting 4chan Statistics and Facts (2019): By the Numbers," *DMR*, May 11, 2019.

contributors so generously and abundantly generate. Whereas other sites have turned into billion-dollar platforms whose stocks surged way beyond that of the giants of the industrial age, 4chan still has difficulties paying its relatively modest server bills. Compared to more well-known sites, 4chan is also unique in terms of its affordances, as well as its quaint subcultural sensibilities—quaint in the sense of "attractively unusual" and "old-fashioned." Geared toward ephemeral and random encounters with anonymous others, with little or no moderation, 4chan's /b/ board gave rise to a vibrant male youth subculture steeped in Japanese anime, video games, warez, hacking, porn, gore, trolling, comics, and memes.[15]

From 2003 onward, 4chan established itself as the most popular of English-language image boards. In the following years, its unique subculture came to cultivate a festive and mock-affirmative relation to online anonymity, understood as an anti- and impersonal mode of sociality and culture that is collective, ephemeral, and authorless—and in that sense, "nameless" and "faceless." Whereas "today, the most ubiquitous online communities are social networks where our identities are mostly known and mostly persistent," image boards like 4chan hinge on "the intentional disconnect between one's real life and one's online persona."[16] Offering "a space for playing with unrestricted notions of identity and affiliation," 4chan's ethos of dissimulative identity play partakes in a tradition of what David Auerbach calls "anonymity as culture" where "masquerade is an integral part of social interaction."[17] The kind of anonymity at stake here is thus clearly a social interuser one, rather than an informatic one, where you would be actually untraceable by third-party actors. In fact, 4chan retains the IP addresses of its users and aims to prevent the use of anonymizing VPNs.

The anonymous and playful sense of identity that 4chan gave rise to is reflected in its subcultural iconography

[15] Gabriella Coleman, "Our Weirdness Is Free: The Logic of Anonymous—Online Army, Agent of Chaos, and Seeker of Justice," *Triple Canopy*, January 13, 2012; Whitney Phillips, "The House that Fox Built: Anonymous, Spectacle and Cycles of Amplification," *Television and New Media* 14, no. 6 (2013): 494–509; and Luke Simcoe, "The Internet Is Serious Business: 4chan's /b/ Board and the Lulz as Alternative Political Discourse on the Internet" (MA major research paper, Ryerson University and York University, Toronto, Ontario, 2012).

[16] David Auerbach, "Anonymity as Culture: Treatise," *Triple Canopy* 15 (2012).

[17] Ibid.

and vernacular self-understanding, which includes the Anon/Anonymous pseudonym, the Guy Fawkes mask, and the stock avatar.[18] In 2006, users active on 4chan's /b/ Random board started to refer to themselves individually as "Anons" and collectively as "Anonymous." What initially started as an in-joke among /b/ users quickly became the basis for a new collective identity built around the users' mutual anonymity. These tropes can thus be thought of as collaborative enactments of the impersonal forms of engagement that image boards potentialize. Beyond its obvious opposition to "real name" identities on platforms like Facebook, what I refer to as

[18] Gabriella. Coleman, *Hacker, Hoaxer, Whistleblower, Spy: The Many Faces of Anonymous* (New York: Verso, 2014).

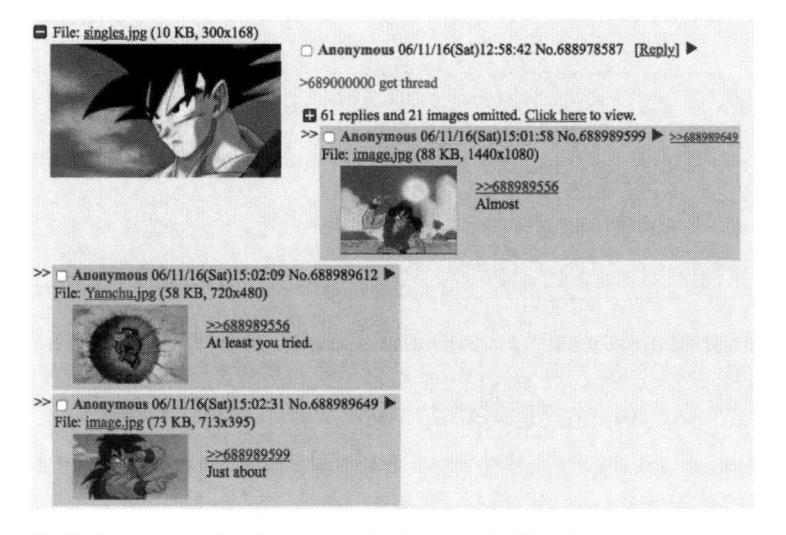

Fig. 57 Cropped screenshot of a 4chan thread with (supposedly different) users posting under the same Anonymous pseudonym, June 11, 2016. Author's collection.

4chan's *radical anonymity* must be differentiated from anonymity as *pseudonymity*. The latter can be considered anonymous in the sense that it severs the online persona from the person's real identity, but it continues to function as a name by providing authorial coherence to multiple individual speech acts. Instead, radical anonymity also breaks authorial coherence across speech acts that is functionally retained by the pseudonym. The only pseudonym that retains radical anonymity is the kind that is open to, and used by, anyone, because in this case speech acts can no longer be aggregated in terms of a single

E — DELIGHT
Collective Pleasures of Anonymity

identifiable author. The Anon/Anonymous moniker is such a pseudonym: the Anon of this post can be the same as this or that post, but it can also be another.[19]

Positively, this detachment from the individual user has the effect of relegating each post to the total body of posts, conferring a form of authorless authorship to this totality. This is one of the reasons 4chan came to be understood by its contributors as a single cacophonous voice, which converses with itself through millions of speech acts and can thus be "read like a schizophrenic soliloquy, where a single user named Anonymous carries on multiple conversations with himself."[20] The disambiguation of the speech act from individual profiles and personal identities, by which it comes to be inscribed in the larger and impersonal social text, is acknowledged by 4chan's FAQ page, which states that "Anonymous is not a single person, but rather, represents the collective whole of 4chan."[21] Moreover, discussions on 4chan quickly disappear, leaving no trace save for the embodied cultural memory of Anons. Regarding this ephemerality, we may indeed "think of 4chan as a big roll of butcher paper on a conveyor belt that users scrawl things on as fast as they can before it goes into an incinerator."[22]

As an anonymous and ephemeral communication system that acts as a vehicle for vernacular creativity and expression, 4chan can be seen to partake in a more encompassing tradition of plebeian "mass publicness," a tradition that includes toilet graffiti—or what urban folklorist Alan Dundes has called "latrinalia."[23] Both writing toilet graffiti and posting on 4chan involve communicating with others anonymously through the inscription of signs on a surface/screen acting as a medium.[24] In a collection about the internet as an emerging folkloric medium, folklorist Simon J. Bronner compares the act of posting a message to an online message board to leaving messages in public toilets, as the surfaces of the restroom are turned into "an open, uncensored discussion board and canvas on which creative messages and drawings can

[19] For Marco Deseriis, collective pseudonyms, or what he calls "multiple use names," like Anonymous serve as "improper names" that institute modes of sociality beyond the individual and, as such, are conducive to "condividual" forms of existence. Marco Deseriis, *Improper Names: Collective Pseudonyms from the Luddites to Anonymous* (Minneapolis: University of Minnesota Press, 2015).

[20] Simcoe, "The Internet Is Serious Business," 28.

[21] "Who is 'Anonymous'?" 4chan FAQ.

[22] Mike Pearl, "4chan Apparently Got a User to Chop Off Part of a Toe over the Weekend," *Vice*, August 31, 2015.

[23] Robert Howard, "The Vernacular Web of Participatory Media," *Critical Studies in Media Communication* 25 (2008): 490–513; and Alan Dundes, *The Meaning of Folklore: The Analytical Essays of Alan Dundes* (Logan: Utah State University Press, 2007).

[24] George Gonos, Virginia Mulkern and Nicholas Poushinsky, "Anonymous Expression: A Structural View of Graffiti," *Journal of American Folklore* 89, no. 351 (1976): 40–48; and Michael Adams, *In Praise of Profanity* (New York: Oxford University Press, 2016).

be sequenced, similar to the heralded form and function of many blogs."[25] By contrast, perhaps precisely because it does *not* involve digital media in any shape or form, the forms of stranger interaction enabled by the public restroom may offer an opportunity to better understand the anonymous forms of mass publicness that image boards like 4chan empower.

Case 2: The Public Restroom (Folds)

Located at highway parking lots, airports, and shopping malls, public restrooms typically reside in what Marc Augé defines as "nonplaces": the transitory and impersonal spaces of global capitalism.[26] It is this strange entanglement between publicness and privateness that the public restroom partakes in and that pervades modern urban space more generally. As a "defining attribute of urbanity," anonymity is seen as inherent to "the being together of strangers."[27] Public restrooms thus weave a peculiar time-space in which the intermingling of private and public parts stands out as an exemplary response to the form-problem of modern sociality: a palimpsest of the history of urban hygiene, regulating the flow of labor and consumer waste.[28]

Straddling the line between the public and the private, the personal and the impersonal, historically the public restroom has been a source of great anxiety and ambivalence.[29] On the one hand, what people do there is deemed strictly private; hence the seemingly endless variety of euphemisms used to talk about "it." On the other hand, a public restroom is what its name suggests: it provides a public service, in that anyone may in principle enter, and belongs to no one—a claim that is obviously complicated by the fact that these places are still highly gendered and that they are increasingly operated by private corporations. The public restroom is also public in the sense that, despite attempts to individualize and privatize "it"—blocking the flows of sight,

[25] Simon J. Bronner, "Digitizing and Virtualizing Folklore," in *Folklore and the Internet: Vernacular Expression in a Digital World*, ed. T. J. Blank (Logan: Utah State University Press, 2009), 58.

[26] Marc Augé, *Non-Places: Introduction to an Anthropology of Supermodernity* (New York: Verso, 1992).

[27] Judith Garber, "'Not Named or Identified': Politics and the Search for Anonymity in the City," in *Gendering the City*, ed. Kristine Miranne and Alma Young (Lanham, MD: Rowman and Littlefield, 2000), 19; Iris Young, *Justice and the Politics of Difference* (Princeton, NJ: Princeton University Press, 1990), 237. Starting with Georg Simmel's "The Metropolis and Mental Life," in *The Sociology of Georg Simmel*, ed. Kurt H. Wolff (Glencoe, IL: Free Press, 1950), David A. Karp, in "Hiding in Pornographic Bookstores," *Urban Life and Culture* 1, no. 4 (1973): 428, notes, "the thoroughgoing anonymity of the city is a theme that runs through most discussions of the social psychology of city life," so that "anonymity... seems to be inextricably tied to the particularly modern experience of the industrial metropolis." William Egginton, "Intimacy and Anonymity, or, How the Audience Became a Crowd," in *Crowds*, ed. J. T. Schnapp and M. Tiews (Stanford, CA: Stanford University Press, 2006), 99. In *A World of Strangers*, urban sociologist Lyn Lofland similarly notes that "to experience the city is, among many other things, to experience anonymity." Lyn H. Lofland, *A World of Strangers: Order and Action in Urban Public Space* (New York: Basic Books, 1973), ix.

smell, and sound through lockable doors, air fresheners, and hand soap dispensers—there still takes place an inherently public communion of bacteria, human DNA, bodily sounds, and other "stuff."

Apart from using the public toilet to relieve themselves of their bodily wastes, the unknown writers and readers of toilet scribblings appropriate the public restroom for their own creative ends, that of an illicit and anonymous communication system (figure 58). There exists a "long and ignoble history" to the practice of inscribing messages and signs in public bathrooms, tracing back at least two thousand years to ancient Greek and Roman times.[30] As Robert Reisner once put it in the satirical magazine the *Realist*: "Having relieved himself physically the scrawler may as well relieve the *excretia* of his mind in the same place."[31] Exploring this analogy between the excretions of the body and those of the mind, Dundes, in his "Theses on Feces," claimed that engaging in toilet

[28] Dominique Laporte, *History of Shit* (Cambridge, MA: MIT Press, 2000).

[29] Bronner, "Digitizing and Virtualizing Folklore," 57.

[30] Nick Haslam, *Psychology in the Bathroom* (New York: Palgrave MacMillan, 2012), 115–16.

[31] Robert Reisner, "Final Solutions to the Latrinalia Question," *Realist* 80 (1968): 1.

Fig. 58 Restroom graffiti, People's Cafe, San Francisco. Wikipedia, uploaded February 1, 2009, https://en.wikipedia.org/wiki/Latrinalia#/media/File:Peoples_cafe.jpg.

graffiti actually represents a sublimated kind of fecal smearing known as coprophilia (typically observed in young children or elderly people suffering from dementia).[32] In this psychoanalytic reading, "dirty words on bathroom walls are symbolically equivalent to excrement."[33]

Besides an opportunity for anonymous communication, the public restroom has also been used as a meeting place for fleeting homosexual encounters, known as the "tearoom trade" in the United States during the 1970s (figure 59). American anthropologist Laud Humphreys went undercover in this clandestine scene, where "men of all racial, social, educational and physical characteristics meet ... for sexual union," and where, as he found, "there exists a sort of democracy endemic to impersonal sex."[34] Rather than establishing a new community outside the existing one that discriminated against and excluded them because of their sexual preference, the public homosexual subculture, in Michael Warner's account, sought anonymity: "Even those who consider themselves gay may be seeking in such venues a world less defined by identity and community than by *the negation of identity through anonymous contact*; they may be seeking something very different from 'community' in a venue where men from very different worlds meet, often silently, for sex."[35]

In the case of latrinalia and the tearoom trade, then, the public restroom, through its anonymity, offers an escape from normative ideas of identity and community that happen to prevail in society. It also provides a place of seclusion against the violent transparency of modern publicness, while remaining radically open to this publicness from all sides, drawing its energy from an outside that is continuously reabsorbed into it by the circulation of strangers. Rather than constituting itself through the exclusion of the mass public by seeking shelter in the bourgeois private sphere, the restroom thus composes a fold of impersonal intimacy made of the

[32] Alan Dundes, "Theses on Feces: Scatological Analysis," in *Meaning of Folklore*, 352–81.

[33] Haslam, *Psychology in the Bathroom*, 133.

[34] Laud Humphreys, *Tearoom Trade: Impersonal Sex in Public Places* (New York: Aldine, 1975), 13.

[35] Michael Warner, "Zones of Privacy," in *What's Left of Theory? New Work on the Politics of Literary Theory*, ed. J. Butler, J. Guillory, and K. Thomas (New York: Routledge, 2002), 87–88, emphasis added.

36 Michael Warner, *Publics and Counterpublics* (New York: Zone Books, 2005).

37 Mark Seltzer, "Serial Killers (II): The Pathological Public Sphere," *Critical Inquiry* 22, no. 1 (1995): 125.

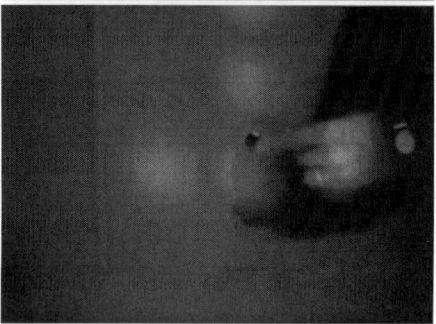

Fig. 59 + 60 + 61 Stills from the documentary film *Tearoom* (2008). The material is filmed by the Police Department in Mansfield, Ohio, in 1962, in the public restroom underneath the park in the center of town.
It led to the arrest of a large number of men (varying from 38 to 69 years old). "Tearoom (excerpt)," video, 9:35, uploaded by la llorona, YouTube, May 26, 2012, https://youtu.be/npAVR5lsj8s.

same fabric as the urban environment it will ultimately dissolve back into.[36] The fold creates a shielding or pocketing that uses the very stuff of which publicness is made to create ephemeral forms of "stranger-intimacy."[37] Defying the distinction between a public and a private sphere, the public restroom generates small pockets of centripetal sociality that are momentarily shielded from—but never immune to—the larger centrifugal forces that lend it vitality, where "the outside is not a fixed limit but a moving matter animated by peristaltic movements, folds and foldings that together make up an inside: they are not something other than the outside, but precisely the inside *of the* outside."[38]

The Deleuzian figure of the "fold" can be contrasted with the Deleuze-Guattarian figure of the face ("faciality," *visageité*), which they argue stands apart from the body and its fleshy folds: "The face is part of a surface-holes, holey surface, system. This system should under no circumstances be confused with the volume-cavity system proper to the (proprioceptive) body.... The face is produced only when the head ceases to be a part of the body, when it ceases to be coded by the body, when it ceases to have a multidimensional polyvocal corporal code—when the body, head included, has been decoded and has to be *overcoded* by something we shall call the Face."[39]

This notion of the face is connected to surveillance, as the attempt to straighten out the body's folds: faciality is a process in which volumes and cavities become subject to a grid-surface, become something to draw out, look at, recognize, identify, screen, project.[40] Instead, the fold consists of a single surface, and in that sense, it is radically public. But it is not flat, as it weaves "volumes" and "cavities," meaning it cannot be appropriated by an external observer in a single glance. In order to "know" anything about it, such an observer would have to travel and descend into it, but by doing so, would become entangled with it to the point where it can no longer be apprehended. In the documentary film *Tearoom* (2008), we see the police officers descending into the cavity folded into the pavement that is the public toilet suspected of doubling as a homosexual meeting place, scrupulously taking pictures, writing notes, and collecting evidence. Were a passerby to enter the restroom at that moment, he would probably find this kind of behavior to be quite inappropriate indeed.

[38] Gilles Deleuze, *Foucault* trans. Séan Hand (Minneapolis: University of Minnesota Press, 1988), 96–97.

[39] Gilles Deleuze and F. Guattari, *A Thousand Plateaus: Capitalism and Schizophrenia*, trans. Brian Massumi (Minneapolis: University of Minnesota Press, 1987), 170. For Deleuze's Foucault-inspired notion of the fold, see the chapter "Foldings, or the Inside of Thought (Subjectivations)," in Deleuze, *Foucault*, and Deleuze, *The Fold: Leibniz and the Baroque*, trans. Tom Conley (New York: Continuum, 2006).

[40] For this notion of faciality as connected to the logic of surveillance, I am indebted to Rogier van Reekum (private correspondence).

Case 3: Chatroulette (Metamorphoses)

The clandestine use of the public restroom for anonymous intercourse of various kinds shows a longer history to the promiscuous and ephemeral modes of sociality prevalent on image boards like 4chan. In the case of latrinalia and the tearoom trade, the very social institution (the public toilet) designed to cleanse society in a physical, moral, and political sense from unwanted elements was appropriated as a space for impersonal encounters of various kinds. The random video-chat portal Chatroulette equally revolves around interactions between strangers, in what is perhaps its simplest but thereby visible form.

The site was set up as a personal pet project in 2009 by a Russian teenager named Andrey Ternovskiy but quickly acquired notoriety for its "genital exhibitionism," which, as one participant joked, would ideally implement some kind of penis- rather than face-recognition software.[41] Like 4chan, Chatroulette requires no sign-up or login; it "functions purely on instant, random, switching and automated chat connections between people."[42] The simple interface contains two empty boxes, one labeled "Stranger" and the other labeled "You." On pressing the "play" button, the user's webcam is activated, and the message "Looking for a random stranger" appears on the screen, shortly after which "you're suddenly staring at another human on your screen and they are staring back at you, at which point you can either choose to chat (via text or voice) or just click 'next,' instantly calling up someone else."[43]

By deliberately establishing random connections between people, the participant is exposed to a constant stream of unknown thrill seekers. Such an aleatory way of establishing connections undermines the logic of homophily that social media platforms can be said to amplify by creating so-called "filter bubbles" or "echo chambers." Homophily describes the tendency of people to seek out others who are or think like them.[44]

[41] Brad Stone, "Chatroulette's Creator, 17, Introduces Himself," *New York Times*, February 13, 2010.

[42] Anna Munster, *An Aesthesia of Networks: Conjunctive Experience in Art and Technology* (Cambridge, MA: MIT Press, 2013), 99.

[43] Sam Anderson, "The Human Shuffle," *New York Magazine*, February 5, 2010.

[44] Miller McPherson, Lynn Smith-Lovin and James Cook, "Birds of a Feather: Homophily in Social Networks," *Annual Review of Sociology* 27, no. 1 (2001): 415–44; and Wendy Hui Kyong Chun, *Updating to Remain the Same: Habitual New Media* (Cambridge, MA: MIT Press, 2016), 14–15.

45 Armina Dinescu, "Negotiating Identities in a Randomized Video-Chat," *Ethnographic Encounters* 1, no. 1 (2012); Nick Bilton, "The Surreal World of Chatroulette," *New York Times*, February 20, 2010.

Fig. 62 + 63 Two instances of online masquerading on Chatroulette. Screenshot on Pinterest UK, https://www.pinterest.co.uk/pin/797840890208313899/; and Fred Wilson, "What to Make of Chatroulette?," *Business Insider*, February 11, 2010, https://www.businessinsider.com/what-to-make-of-chatroulette-2010-2.

Countering the tendency of homophily by randomly connecting people, Chatroulette instead invites users to interact on the basis of heterophily, or rather, xenophily: a love of the strange, the ephemeral, the chance encounter.[45] As shown by the other Chatroulette examples (figures 62 and 63), heterophilic interaction often mobilizes the powers of masking and disguise, making the platform into a theater of interspecies role playing and gender transformation, where dogs can talk, and men impersonate female celebrities. Together, these examples of dissimulative role play on Chatroulette provide an answer to the question of "how to re-imagine anonymity not as an attainable categorical state, but as a way to recoup an energy of metamorphosis, the desire to become someone else."[46] Here, anonymity acts as an enabling condition for playful noncoincidence with one's self, to become other, something that is shared by all the cases I have discussed so far.

The notion of anonymity as providing an escape from the self and as an invitation to transformation has been a recurrent theme in Michel Foucault's work.[47] For him, such an escape is imperative as an ethical practice, insofar as this "self" refers to an oppressive subject forma-

[46] Geert Lovink, *Networks without a Cause: A Critique of Social Media* (Malden, MA: Polity, 2011), 46.

[47] For a discussion of Foucault on anonymity, see Érik Bordeleau, *Foucault Anonymat: Essai* (Montreal, QC: Le Quartanier, 2012). For a feminist critique, see Perry Zurn, "The Politics of Anonymity: Foucault, Feminism, and Gender Non-Conforming Prisoners," *philoSOPHIA: A Journal of Continental Feminism* 6, no. 1 (2016): 27–42. Both of these authors emphasize Foucault's understanding of anonymity as a "practice of the self" that provides an alternative to prevailing identity formations. Zurn, "Politics of Anonymity," 28.

[48] Nicholas. de Villiers, "Confessions of a Masked Philosopher: Anonymity and Identification in Foucault and Guibert," *symploke* 16, no. 1–2 (2009): 75–91.

[49] Deleuze, *Foucault*, 105–6.

Fig.64 Example of gender-bending role-playing global celebrities on a random video-chat site. "Miley Cyrus—Wrecking Ball (Chatroulette FeVer Club Version)," video, 2:46, uploaded by Willy Christmas, December 23, 2013, YouTube, https://youtu.be/YnJzUH2nbDs.

tion historically rooted in discipline and punishment.[48] In Deleuze's book on Foucault, he frames this escape from the self as part of a larger struggle for subjectivity that "passes through a resistance to the two present forms of subjection, the one consisting of individualizing ourselves on the basis of constraints of power, the other of attracting each individual to a known and recognized identity, fixed once and for all. The struggle for subjectivity presents itself, therefore, as the right to difference, variation and metamorphosis."[49]

What the examples of 4chan, the public restroom, and Chatroulette show is that such a flight away *from* the self is often accompanied and even enabled by a flight *to* an anonymous other. Although the "right to difference" Deleuze speaks of has been largely recuperated by postmodern consumer culture, this fact does not altogether mute the radical demand at its core. The dark rooms Foucault visited while exploring San Francisco's underground gay scene in the 1970s, for example, harbored the radical experience of another mode of existence beyond the person, where "you stop being imprisoned inside your own face, your own past, your own identity."[50] In a short essay called "Identity without the Person," Giorgio Agamben traces this desire for the impersonal, "to be freed from the weight of the person, from the moral as much as the juridical responsibility that it carries along with it."[51] It is also here that Foucault's take on writing can be situated, where—contrary to the cult of the author in modern print culture—he urges "to write oneself into a thick sense of anonymity, out of a name, a persona, a psyche, and a face."[52] In this passage, the name and the face come to represent the main anchoring points of an affective attachment to one's own personality, just as the loss of one's name and face opens up a line of flight away from the confines of the modern subject.

Conclusion

Contrary to concerns over personal privacy, the forms of anonymous mass publicness discussed so far embody an ethos of risk and openness toward the stranger that is oriented toward a pleasurable "loss of self." Whereas to deliver oneself over to a collective anonymity is to relinquish what Elias Canetti claimed is the fear of strangers that accompanies each person throughout her life, privacy instead aims to neutralize this movement away from identity, cementing its opposition to the stranger as a dangerous intruder.[53] It is in this alternative relationship

[50] Cited in David Macey, *The Lives of Michel Foucault* (New York: Vintage, 1995), xv.

[51] Giorgio Agamben, "Identity without the Person," in *Nudities*, trans. David Kishik and Stefan Pedatella (Stanford, CA: Stanford University Press, 2010), 53.

[52] Michel Foucault, *Speech Begins after Death* (Minneapolis: University of Minnesota Press, 2013), 55.

[53] Elias Canetti, *Crowds and Power* (New York: Continuum, 1981).

to mass publicness that an ethics of anonymity can be distinguished from that of privacy. It is such an ethics of anonymity that, as I have tried to show, 4chan, the public restroom, and Chatroulette each in their own way embody and experiment with. They also provide a sense of the largely invisible history of anonymity as a mode of impersonal sociality and a "practice of the self" that—as an escape from the self toward an unknown other—is pleasurable in and of itself, rather than an extraneous means to maintain some measure of privacy. Rather than offering privacy, in these cases, anonymity is generative of the liberty to engage in the collective and impersonal modes of sociality that public restrooms, image boards, and video-chat portals provide for.

Looking at the present digital conjuncture, however, these promiscuous folds of mass publicness are increasingly flattened out by new forms of mass surveillance as well as by personal data–hungry platforms. The anonymous modes of sociality that I discuss in this chapter offer a markedly different approach to this expropriation of social and creative wealth by platforms than do current privacy regimes. Where the latter confer personal ownership on, and thus individualize and privatize, these forms of social excess, the former inhabits this exposure in a way that resists its recuperation, by folding into a form of opaque publicness. Rather than a negative and dangerous side effect of urban environments, anonymity —which here does not function to keep things private and contained, but rather initiates a centrifugal publicness —can actually establish new forms of agency and postcitizenship ("post," because citizenship implies a certain visibility that anonymity instead defies), as it tends to suspend stratifications of identity along existing private-public boundaries. Whereas, as Mark Zuckerberg observed in a recent speech, "privacy gives us the freedom to be ourselves," anonymity gives us the freedom to be another—to enter and disappear into a fold.[54]

54 Nick Statt, "Facebook CEO Mark Zuckerberg Says the 'Future Is Private,'" *Verge*, April 30, 2019.

Bibliography

Adams, Michael. *In Praise of Profanity*. New York: Oxford University Press, 2016.

Agamben, Giorgio. "Identity without the Person." In *Nudities*, translated by David Kishik and Stefan Pedatella, 46–54. Stanford, CA: Stanford University Press, 2010.

Akdeniz, Yaman. "Anonymity, Democracy and Cyberspace." *Social Research* 69, no. 1 (2002): 223–37.

Anderson, Sam. "The Human Shuffle." *New York Magazine*, February 5, 2010. http://nymag.com/news/media/63663.

Auerbach, David. "Anonymity as Culture: Treatise." *Triple Canopy* 15 (2012). https://www.canopycanopycanopy.com/contents/anonymity_as_culture__treatise.

Augé, Marc. *Non-Places: Introduction to an Anthropology of Supermodernity*. New York: Verso, 1992.

Bernstein, Michael, Andrés Monroy-Hernández, Drew Harry, Paul André, Katrina Panovich, and Greg. Vargas. "4chan and /b/: An Analysis of Anonymity and Ephemerality in a Large Online Community." In *Proceedings of the Fifth International AAAI Conference on Weblogs and Social Media*, 50–57. Menlo Park, CA: AAAI Press, 2011.

Bilton, Nick. "The Surreal World of Chatroulette." *New York Times*, February 20, 2010. https://www.nytimes.com/2010/02/21/weekinreview/21bilton.html.

Bordeleau, Érik. *Foucault Anonymat: Essai*. Montreal, QC: Le Quartanier, 2012.

Bosker, Bianca. "Randi Zuckerberg: Anonymity Online 'Has to Go Away.'" *Huffington Post*, June 27, 2011. https://www.huffpost.com/entry/randi-zuckerberg-anonymity-online_n_910892.

Bronner, Simon J. "Digitizing and Virtualizing Folklore." In *Folklore and the Internet: Vernacular Expression in a Digital World*, edited by T. J. Blank, 21–66. Logan: Utah State University Press, 2009.

Canetti, Elias. *Crowds and Power*. New York: Continuum, 1981.

Chawki, Mohamed. "Anonymity in Cyberspace: Finding the Balance between Privacy and Security." *International Journal of Technology Transfer and Commercialisation* 9, no. 3 (2010): 183–99.

Chui, Rebekka. "A Multi-Faceted Approach to Anonymity Online:

Examining the Relations between Anonymity and Antisocial Behavior." *Journal of Virtual Worlds Research* 7, no. 2 (2014): 1–13.

Chun, Wendy H. K. *Updating to Remain the Same: Habitual New Media*. Cambridge, MA: MIT Press, 2016.

Cohen, Julie E. "A Right to Read Anonymously: A Closer Look at 'Copyright Management' in Cyberspace." *Connecticut Law Review* 28 (1996): 981–1039.

Coleman, E. Gabriella. *Hacker, Hoaxer, Whistleblower, Spy: The Many Faces of Anonymous*. New York: Verso, 2014.

Coleman, E. Gabriella. "Our Weirdness Is Free: The Logic of Anonymous— Online Army, Agent of Chaos, and Seeker of Justice." *Triple Canopy* 15 (2012). https://www.canopycanopycanopy.com/issues/15/contents/our_weirdness_is_free.

Yale Law Journal "The Constitutional Right to Anonymity: Free Speech, Disclosure and the Devil." *Yale Law Journal* 70, no. 7 (1961): 1084–128.

Cotter, Thomas F., and Lyrissa Barnett Lidsky. "Authorship, Audiences, and Anonymous Speech." *SSRN Electronic Journal*, August 22, 2006. https://papers.ssrn.com/sol3/papers.cfm?abstract_id=925736.

Deleuze, Gilles. *The Fold: Leibniz and the Baroque*. Translated by Tom Conley. New York: Continuum, 2006.

Deleuze, Gilles. *Foucault*. Translated by Séan Hand. Minneapolis: University of Minnesota Press, 1988.

Deleuze, Gilles, and Felix Guattari. *A Thousand Plateaus: Capitalism and Schizophrenia*. Translated by Brian Massumi. Minneapolis: University of Minnesota Press, 1987.

Deseriis, Marco. *Improper Names: Collective Pseudonyms from the Luddites to Anonymous*. Minneapolis: University of Minnesota Press, 2015.

de Villiers, Nicholas. "Confessions of a Masked Philosopher: Anonymity and Identification in Foucault and Guibert." *symploke* 16, no. 1–2 (2009): 75–91.

de Zeeuw, Daniel. "Immunity from the Image: The Right to Privacy as an Antidote to Anonymous Modernity." *ephemera* 17, no. 2 (2017): 259–81.

Dinescu, Armina. "Negotiating Identities in a Randomized Video-Chat." *Ethnographic Encounters* 1, no. 1 (2012). https://ojs.st-andrews.ac.uk/index.php/SAEE/issue/view/45.

Dundes, Alan. *The Meaning of Folklore: The Analytical Essays of Alan Dundes*. Logan: Utah State University Press, 2007.

Egginton, William. "Intimacy and Anonymity, or, How the Audience Became a Crowd." In *Crowds*, edited by J. T. Schnapp and M. Tiews, 97–103. Stanford, CA: Stanford University Press, 2006.

Ferry, Anne. "Anonymity: The Literary History of a Word." *New Literary History* 33, no. 2 (2002): 193–214.

Foucault, Michel. *Speech Begins after Death*. Minneapolis: University of Minnesota Press, 2013.

Froomkin, A. Michael. "Anonymity and Its Enmities." *Journal of Online Law* 1 (1995), art. 4 .

Garber, Judith A. "'Not Named or Identified': Politics and the Search for Anonymity in the City." In *Gendering the City*, edited by K. B. Miranne and A. H. Young, 19–40. Lanham, MD: Rowman and Littlefield, 2000.

Gonos, George, Virginia Mulkern, and Nicholas Poushinsky. "Anonymous Expression: A Structural View of Graffiti." *Journal of American Folklore* 89, no. 351 (1976): 40–48.

Haslam, Nick. *Psychology in the Bathroom*. New York: Palgrave MacMillan, 2012.

Howard, Robert G. "The Vernacular Web of Participatory Media." *Critical Studies in Media Communication* 25 (2008): 490–513.

Humphreys, Laud. *Tearoom Trade: Impersonal Sex in Public Places*. New York: Aldine, 1975.

Karp, David A. "Hiding in Pornographic Bookstores." *Urban Life and Culture* 1, no. 4 (1973): 427–51.

Kerr, Ian, Valerie Steeves, and Carole Lucock, ed. *Lessons from the Identity Trail: Anonymity, Privacy, and Identity in a Networked Society*. Oxford: Oxford University Press, 2009.

Knuttila, Lee. "User Unknown: 4Chan, Anonymity and Contingency." *First Monday* 16, no. 10 (2011). https://doi.org/10.5210/fm.v16i10.3665.

Kozinski, Alex. "Essay: The Two Faces of Anonymity." *Capital University Law Review* 1 (2015): 1–19.

Lapidot-Lefler, Noam, and Azy Barak. "Effects of Anonymity, Invisibility, and Lack of Eye-Contact on Toxic Online Disinhibition." *Computers in Human Behavior* 28, no. 2 (2012): 434–43.

Laporte, Dominique. *History of Shit*. Cambridge, MA: MIT Press, 2000.

Lofland, Lyn H. *A World of Strangers: Order and Action in Urban Public Space*. New York: Basic Books, 1973.

Lovink, Geert. *Networks without a Cause: A Critique of Social Media*. Malden, MA: Polity, 2011.

Macey, David. *The Lives of Michel Foucault*. New York: Vintage, 1995.

Marx, Gary. "Identity and Anonymity: Some Conceptual Distinctions and Issues for Research." In *Documenting Individual Identity*, edited by J. Caplan, and J. Torpey, 311–327. Princeton, NJ: Princeton University Press, 2001.

Massanari, Adrienne. "#Gamergate and the Fappening: How Reddit's Algorithm, Governance, and Culture Support Toxic Technocultures." *New Media and Society* 19, no. 3 (2017): 329–47.

Matthews, Steve. "Anonymity and the Social Self." *American Philosophical Quarterly* 47, no. 4 (2010): 351–63.

McPherson, Miller, Lynn Smith-Lovin, and James Cook. "Birds of a Feather: Homophily in Social Networks." *Annual Review of Sociology* 27, no. 1 (2001): 415–44.

Moyakine, Evgeni. "Online Anonymity in the Modern Digital Age: Quest for a Legal Right." *Journal of Information Rights, Policy and Practice* 1, no. 1 (2016). http://hdl.handle.net/11370/2b65970a-3c3f-4237-85df-f5b1b82c5e5b.

Munster, Anna. *An Aesthesia of Networks: Conjunctive Experience in Art and Technology*. Cambridge, MA: MIT Press, 2013.

Natelson, Robert G. "Does 'the Freedom of the Press' Include a Right to Anonymity? The Original Understanding." SSRN, October 12, 2013. https://ssrn.com/abstract=2333612.

Pearl, Mike. "4chan Apparently Got a User to Chop Off Part of a Toe over the Weekend." *Vice*, August 31, 2015. https://www.vice.com/en_us/article/5gjy3k/4chan-wants-to-see-you-mutilate-yourself-but-why-682.

Phillips, Whitney. "The House that Fox Built: Anonymous, Spectacle and Cycles of Amplification." *Television and New Media* 14, no. 6 (2013): 494–509.

Phillips, Whitney, and Ryan Milner. *The Ambivalent Internet*. Malden, MA: Polity, 2017.

Potapova, Rodmonga, and Denis Gordeev. "Determination of the Internet Anonymity Influence on the Level of Aggression and Usage of Obscene Lexis." *arXiv*, e-print 1510.00240 (2015). https://arxiv.org/abs/1510.00240.

Reagle, Joseph. *Reading the Comments: Likers, Haters, and Manipulators at the Bottom of the Web*. Cambridge, MA: MIT Press, 2015.

Reisner, Robert. "Final Solutions to the Latrinalia Question." *Realist* 80 (1968): 1. http://www.ep.tc/realist/pdf/TheRealist080.pdf.

Seltzer, Mark. "Serial Killers (II): The Pathological Public Sphere." *Critical Inquiry* 22, no. 1 (1995): 122–49.

Simcoe, Luke "The Internet Is Serious Business: 4chan's /b/ Board and the Lulz as Alternative Political Discourse on the Internet." MA major research paper, Ryerson University and York University, Toronto, Ontario, 2012.

Simmel, Georg, ed. Kurt H. Wolff. *The Sociology of Georg Simmel*. Glencoe, IL: Free Press, 1950.

Smith, Craig. "Interesting 4chan Statistics and Facts (2019): By the Numbers." *DMR*, May 11, 2019. https://expandedramblings.com/index.php/4chan-statistics-facts/.

Smith, M. "Google CEO Schmidt: No Anonymity Is the Future of Web." *CSO*, August 9, 2010. https://www.csoonline.com/article/2231573/google-ceo-schmidt--no-anonymity-is-the-future-of-web.html.

Smith, Ekstrand. "The Many Masks of Anon: Anonymity as Cultural Practice and Reflections in Case Law." *Journal of Technology Law Policy* 18 (2013): 4.

Spencer, Michael H. "Anonymous Internet Communication and the First Amendment: A Crack in the Dam of National Sovereignty." *Virginia Journal of Law and Technology* 3, no. 1 (1998). http://vjolt.org/wp-content/uploads/2017/Articles/vol3/issue/vol3_art1.pdf.

Srnicek, Nick. *Platform Capitalism*. Malden, MA: Polity, 2017.

Statt, Nick. "Facebook CEO Mark Zuckerberg Says the 'Future Is Private.'" *Verge*, April 30, 2019. https://www.theverge.com/2019/4/30/18524188/facebook-f8-keynote-mark-zuckerberg-privacy-future-2019.

Stone, Brad. "Chatroulette's Creator, 17, Introduces Himself." *New York Times*, February 13, 2010. https://bits.blogs.nytimes.com/2010/02/13/chatroulettes-founder-17-introduces-himself/.

Stryker, Cole. *Hacking the Future: Privacy, Identity, and Anonymity on the Web*. New York: Duckworth Overlook, 2013.

Suler, John. "The Online Disinhibition Effect." *CyberPsychology and Behavior* 7, no. 3 (2004): 321–26.

Thiel, Thorsten. "Anonymity and Its Prospects in the Digital World." PRIF Working Paper no. 37, Peace Research Institute Frankfurt, Frankfurt, Germany, 2016.

Underwood, Patrick C. "New Directions in Networked Activism and Online Social Movement Mobilization: The Case of Anonymous and Project Chanology." Master's thesis, Ohio University, 2009. http://rave.ohiolink.edu/etdc/view?acc_num=ohiou1244228183.

Vickery, Jacqueline, and Tracy Everbach. *Mediating Misogyny: Gender, Technology and Harassment*. Cham, Switzerland: Palgrave Macmillan, 2018.

Warner, Michael. *Publics and Counterpublics*. New York: Zone Books, 2005.

Warner, Michael. "Zones of Privacy." In *What's Left of Theory? New Work on the Politics of Literary Theory*, edited by J. Butler, J. Guillory, and K. Thomas, 1–305. New York: Routledge, 2002.

Wong, Wendy H., and Peter A. Brown. "E-bandits in Global Activism: Wikileaks, Anonymous, and the Politics of No One." *Perspectives on Politics* 11, no. 4 (2013): 1015–33.

Young, Iris. *Justice and the Politics of Difference*. Princeton, NJ: Princeton University Press, 1990.

Zuboff, Shoshana. *The Age of Surveillance Capitalism: The Fight for a Human Future at the New Frontier of Power*. New York: Public Affairs, 2019.

Zurn, Perry. "The Politics of Anonymity: Foucault, Feminism, and Gender Non-Conforming Prisoners." *philoSOPHIA: A Journal of Continental Feminism* 6, no. 1 (2016): 27–42.

Transformella Malor Ikeae
InnerCity Ikeality
[4.4.6.11]

They told[1] her at the age of 21,
that she[2] was donor conceived[3]

[1] "Um nicht zu sehr aufzufallen, sind wir etwas zerstreut, so dass ich nicht immer alles gleich gut hören kann; aber mir kommen fast Tränen der Rührung, als Michi und mir der 'Song of Lindsay' gewidmet wird. Ich denke an das Interview mit Lindsay zurück, daran, wie sehr sie verletzt war durch die Geheimniskrämerei ihrer Eltern; es war eines der bewegendsten Gespräche meiner Feldforschung, über das ich viel nachgedacht habe. Es ist ein eigenartiges Gefühl, in diesem Kontext darüber zu hören; eine merkwürdige Mischung aus einer intimen Situation wie dem Interview und einer (halb) öffentlichen Performance" (Field note, Amelie Baumann, November 1, 2018).

[2] "Ich denke an das Interview mit Lindsay zurück, daran, wie sehr sie verletzt war durch die Geheimniskrämerei ihrer Eltern; es war eines der bewegendsten Gespräche meiner Feldforschung, über das ich viel nachgedacht habe" (Field note, Amelie Baumann, November 1, 2018).

[3] "Lindsay wollte unbedingt, dass ihre Geschichte erzählt wird; dass das einmal in diesem Rahmen passieren würde, hätte wohl niemand gedacht" (Field note, Amelie Baumann, November 1, 2018).

From that day[4]
all the many relations[5]
with what she had known as
"dad"
—day by day,
did not amount to him anymore,
to just this casual
conceptual persona[6]

[4] From that day
her whole world
came crashing down,
day by day—
as if her identity was a texture,
a material made fragile
from that day.

From that day
She felt ruptures in her fibre—
her own hull did not amount to herself
anymore
to just this casual
conceptual persona

[5] Field notes from Michi Knecht, Amelie Baumann, and Anna Henke, as well as memory to report about surprises that were created, questions they provoked, and values that were contested. Experiment and ethnography both have an inbuilt systematic capacity to produce and make visible the unexpected (Materiallage Performance JPR, Michi Knecht, August 16, 2019).

[6] "Wer ist unsere Mutter – die In-vitro-Fertilization, die Cryo-Technologie, Leihmutterschaft?" Wo findet die Konstruktion der Identitäten statt? Sofort schießen diese Fragen in meinen Kopf und begleiten mich durch die gesamte Performance" (Field note *Transformella malor*, Anna Henke, November 1, 2018).

Day by day, now
she looks at her couch table,
that IKEA calls "LACK"[7]
as if it does not amount to its concept,
anymore.

[7] Have you ever seen LACK broken, open,
   destroyed?
   Its black and matte, its lacquered surface,
   smashed?
   exposing its paper guts
   those honeycombed sheets,
LACK's heavy body, seemingly massive weight,
   below the collapsing plastic rims
      exhibits a pressboard hive
      under the dry coarse wound,
      a perforated inner self.

LACK is a mutilated plastic lake,
   protruded by a screaming mouth
      adorned with sable teeth
on its lips there is scattered surface matter dangling
a flakey self,
   swaying on the fringe of craters.

From that day
   a thousand hexagonal cavities
   that riddle the polyethyl thickness
      will not amount to
      stability for you
      anymore
      to just this casual
      conceptual persona

From that day
She is us:

We all LACK.[8]

Fig. 65–71

Our identities are bloated
or maybe just puffed up[9]

LACK—a fragmented self[10]
once cute, but afraid,[11, 12]
then ridiculous and alone.

[9] like those new guinea birds
   that throw an oval wheel of black feathers
     with light blue silky spots—
      a smiley face
to scare away all other creatures

[10] "Die 'Haut', die es bedeckt, scheint aus Latex zu bestehen; das Gesicht ist leuchtend pink, die Wimpern, die sich nach und nach lösen, leuchtend orange" (Field note *Transformella malor*, Anna Henke, November 1, 2018).

[11] "Wir werden mit den Geräten für die Tonübertragung ausgestattet: Mit dem Stecker im Ohr fühle ich mich wie eine Geheimagentin. Es irritiert etwas, das einer der Anwesenden wirklich überall seine Kamera draufhält. Hinterher erfahre ich, dass es sich wohl um jemanden handelt, der für JPR fotografiert hat, was mich überrascht, weil die Person offensichtlich keine Rücksicht auf den Rest des Repro-Techno-Tribes genommen hat" (Field note *Transformella malor*, Anna Henke, November 1, 2018).

[12]

Fig. 72 InnerCity Ikeality [4.4.6.11] Appearance view, IKEA Hamburg Altona (2018)

From that day our identities[13]
are constructed to save weight,

Fig. 73 InnerCity Ikeality [4.4.6.11] Appearance view, IKEA Hamburg Altona (2018)

our constructions[14] do not amount
to ourselves anymore[15]

[14] Hey, vielen dank für deine mühe. Ja, er hatte sich gemeldet, ich dachte schon deswegen. Wir sind im kontakt, er ist sehr kompliziert und will viel geld, dafür dass er bei ihrer-als-meiner appearance einfach ungefragt aufgetaucht ist und seine fotos gemacht hat. später hat er wohl gegenüber michi behauptet, dass er die rechte für einen druck nicht einfach übertragen könne, denn er würde sich ärger mit ikea einhandeln, schließlich sei die performance ja auch ungefragt in ikea aufgetaucht. ich werde nochmal über die nutzungsrechte mit ihm reden, er hat die bilder bislang nur mit seinem wasserzeichen geschickt. beste grüße, jpr
(Email to Isabelle Lindermann, August 28, 2019).

[15]

Fig. 74 InnerCity Ikeality [4.4.6.11] Appearance view, IKEA Hamburg Altona (2018)

but serve transportability[16] around the planet[17]

[16] "Myths of anomaly such as the Trickster myth are both for finding things out and for transforming the ways things are.[A] In this sense, they are material fictions that constitute the cultural imaginaries for envisaging possible worlds and possible selves.[B] Myths are originative and generative, and their boundaries are fluid. They enact a re-genesis that makes for ongoing creative processes, and they nourish the human capacity for experiencing, producing, and surviving novelty and change." George Kamberelis, "Ingestion, Elimination, Sex, and Song: Trickster as Premodern Avatar of Postmodern Research Practice," *Qualitative Inquiry* 9, no. 5 (2003): 691.

[A] "I have altered Kermode's (1967) suggestion that myth is for maintaining order and that fiction is for finding things out. Myths are also fictions and thus cultural instruments for finding things out, a point that Turner (1969) also noted." Ibid., 701.

[B] "The idea that myths might function as material fictions was discussed by Ricoeur (1976, p. 94). The idea that cultural narratives make visible possible worlds and possible selves into which readers / hearers insert themselves was addressed extensively by Bruner (1986, 1990)." Ibid., 701.

[17]

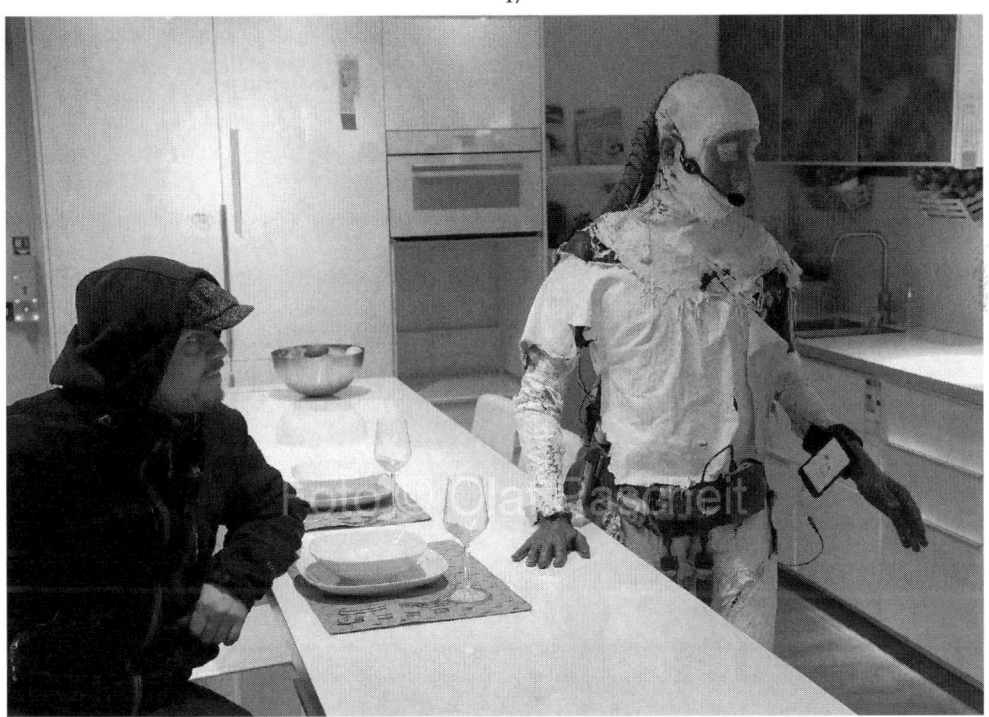

Fig. 75 InnerCity Ikeality [4.4.6.11] Appearance view, IKEA Hamburg Altona (2018)

giving the impression
of a solid volume[18]

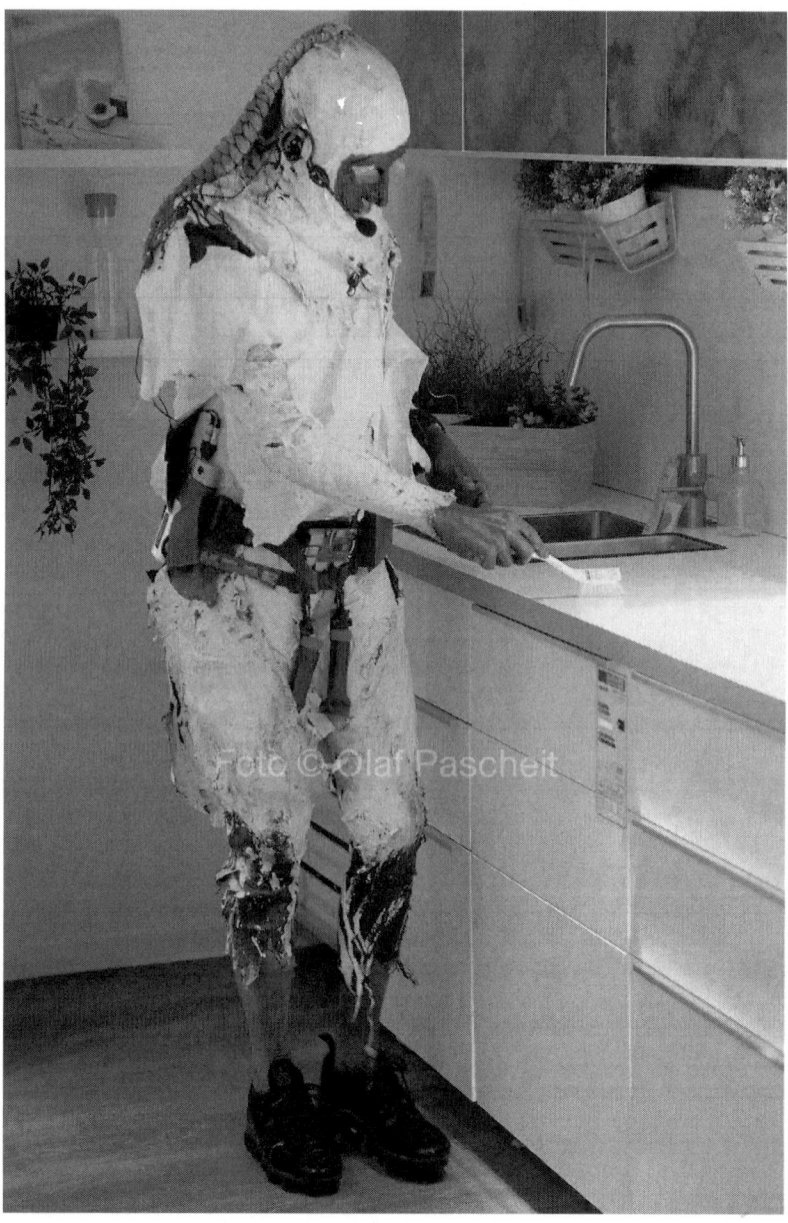

Fig. 76 InnerCity Ikeality [4.4.6.11] Appearance view, IKEA Hamburg Altona (2018)

day by day.[19, 20, 21, 22]

[19] Michi assoziiert dazu einen Text über die Erweiterung von ethnographischen Methoden in der Untersuchung von Anonymität durch die Zusammenarbeit mit Künstlern. Hier wird ein Experiment durchgeführt, eine Assemblage kreiert, Überaschung erzeugt, in dem drei verschiedene Arten von Anonymität miteinander ins Spiel gebracht werden: Die Transformella-Figur ist ein Trickster, schwer zu identifizieren. Die Gruppe ist keine Gruppe sondern ein Schwarm, sie agiert „anonym" für außenstehende und die Modi ihres Aufeinander-eingestellt-Seins, sind selbst partielle Formen von Anonymität. Der Ort, ein serieller, anonymisierter Ort, zwar in Hamburg, but could be everywhere (Materiallage Performance JPR, Michi Knecht, August 16, 2019).

Fig. 77 InnerCity Ikeality [4.4.6.11] Appearance view, IKEA Hamburg Altona (2018)

From that day,

21 It's just hard to explain, I don't know ((phone vibrates)) sorry
about that // no, no // but it's hard to explain to somebody, you
know because people don't really understand, you know what it's
like to think, they're just like 'Oh but you're still the same
person you was,' and I'm like 'Yeah, no, I am, but it's, you feel like
a part of your identity is missing, because like, and it would be,
and I don't know, I just feel like, it's <<laughing> hard to explain>
(Codings_Knowledge matters.pdf Amelie Baumann, Transcript_Lindsay_30102016)

22 Der Ikea-Geruch strömt in die Nase, ... Ich fühle mich dirigiert durch den Avatar, gleichzeitig werde ich visuell durch die Waren bei Ikea in den Bann gezogen. ... ich versuche mich ... mich als Individuum in diesem Setting zu verhalten; verbunden und unverbunden zur gleichen Zeit. Meine Gefühlsebene ist sehr aktiviert, ich fühle mich in der IKEALITY, wie Transformella sie nennt, mit vielen Eindrücken konfrontiert. Ich bin einerseits auditiv über Kopfhörer mit Transformella verbunden, andererseits ist mein Handy vernetzt, wo ich Sätze lesen kann wie:

„*Transformalor will take you to implement my theoretical findings by bringing the first instances of our coming tribe to IKEA. Because IKEA is the ideal simulation of a local normality and the reality of mass commodity reproduction at the same time. This paradox we will call IKEALITY. And you will be throughly investigate it as a temporally constructed model repro-tribe.*"
(Field note *Transformella malor*, Anna Henke, November 1, 2018).

our selves, broken[23], open
in fear of falling out of this
cozy couch-bed-table-arrangement—
this corporate feng shui
we are stuffed into.

Our selves: broken, open
enveloped in expensive paper
—are family trees
that are cut in half
day by dad
leaving a hollow trunk,

exposing fibers
that will never amount to woodanymore

[23] I would absolutely love to be able to reach
   out, ah, to my donor and just explain why I want to see him, and
   the questions I've got. You know, and if he would be willing to
   because I think, they may be put of that you know he's got his
   family, his family is complete, he doesn't need to add to it
   anymore, so but that's not what I am looking for // hm=hm//
   And maybe if he knew that, and I could at least write and explain
   that to him, then he may have one meeting with me, so that I
   could answer all the questions. Then it would complete me //
   hm=hm// and I could then move on, and you know accept it, so I
   think it's you know definitely something I wish the UK would bring
   in but
(Codings_Knowledge matters.pdf Amelie Bauman, Transcript_Lindsay_30102016).

nor to any other
organic material,

from that day.

Authenticity

Introduction

Authenticity and anonymity are oftentimes conceived as antagonistic concepts. In this chapter, I show that the case of online anonymity can be used to rethink the relationship between authenticity and anonymity, which are commonly understood as two diametrically opposed concepts. Anonymity can act both as a threat to authenticity and as a condition that enables its emergence and maintenance. The two concepts are best understood as marking an area of tension between two forces that do not necessarily have to be opposing.

Pure Origins and True Expressions

Authenticity derives from the Greek word *authentes*, which can mean both "one who acts with authority" and "made by one's own hand."[1] Anthropologist Charles Lindholm addresses the different ways in which the word "authentic" is being used and points out that there are "two overlapping but distinct modes for characterizing an entity as authentic: genealogical or historical (origin) and identity or correspondence (expressive content)."[2] It can be applied to various entities and is not restricted to an individual who can be said to be authentic by living "life as a direct and immediate expression of essential being."[3] Instead, an object like a piece of furniture produced at a particular period can be labeled "authentic" "if its source can be traced, and if its characteristics mark it as fitting

[1] Regina Bendix, *In Search of Authenticity: The Formation of Folklore Studies* (Madison, WI: University of Wisconsin Press, 1997), 14.

[2] Charles Lindholm, "The Rise of Expressive Authenticity," *Anthropological Quarterly* 86, no. 2 (2013): 363.

[3] Ibid.

properly into a recognized category."[4] Similarly, in legal terms "authentic" can mean that a document was indeed written by the persons whose name is printed on it.[5] The idea that a particular kind of conduct can be authentic whereas another behavior can be false and inauthentic is closely linked to the idea that decisions and actions can be expressive of and directly connected with the actor's personality.[6] As such, an individual's conduct, if perceived as authentic, can be interpreted as something that allows conclusions to be drawn about the person's essential characteristics and qualities.

Authenticity, Anonymity, and Linguistic Authority

The concepts of anonymity and authenticity and their relationship have also been addressed in linguistic anthropology. It has been argued that there are two opposing "modern ideologies of linguistic authority": an ideology of authenticity on the one hand, and an ideology of anonymity on the other.[7] Whereas authenticity "credits a language variety with value insofar as it expresses the essential, distinctive nature of a community or a speaker," anonymity "holds that a language is valuable as a neutral, objective vehicle of expression equally available to all users."[8] Anthropologist Matthew Engelke makes a similar argument when commenting on the ideology of anonymity and argues that it has become the source of legitimacy for English as a dominant language. English no longer indexes a certain place but has instead become accepted as a means to "transcend place."[9] English possesses its "linguistic authority" not because it recognizably marks certain people as native English speakers but rather because it is no longer seen as indexing a specific local identity that ties a language to a certain place. According to this line of argument, English is no longer a signal that necessarily indexes a place of origin. As it transcends place, it is no longer an exclusive linguistic tie to a native, authentic English identity.

4 Ibid.

5 Charles Lindholm, *Culture and Authenticity* (Malden, MA: Blackwell, 2008), 3.

6 Alessandro Ferrara, *Reflective Authenticity: Rethinking the Project of Modernity* (London: Routledge, 1998), 5.

7 Kathryn A. Woolard and Susan E. Frekko, "Catalan in the Twenty-First Century: Romantic Publics and Cosmopolitan Communities," *International Journal of Bilingual Education and Bilingualism* 16, no. 2 (2013): 135;
see also Josep Soler, "The Anonymity of Catalan and the Authenticity of Estonian: Two Paths for the Development of Medium-Sized Languages," *International Journal of Bilingual Education and Bilingualism* 16, no. 2 (2013): 153–63.

8 Woolard and Frekko, "Catalan in the Twenty-First Century," 135.

9 Matthew Engelke, *Think Like an Anthropologist* (London: Penguin Books, 2017), 202.

Anthropology, Authenticity, and Modernity

Authenticity has long been an influential concept in cultural anthropology and in related fields in multiple ways, not least regarding the choice of research topic and question. I argue that the quest to convey a sense of authenticity in ethnographic writing can be at odds with the need to protect an interlocutor's identity.

In anthropologist Regina Bendix's study of the development of folklore studies, she points out that in the formation of folklore studies as a discipline that differed from other fields dedicated to the study of culture, authenticity was seen as the defining marker that set its subject apart from those of other fields.[10] She argues, "The quest for authenticity is a peculiar longing, at once modern and antimodern. It is oriented toward the recovery of an essence whose loss has been realised only in modernity, and whose recovery is feasible only through methods and sentiments created in modernity."[11] Anthropologists Thomas Fillitz and A. Jamie Saris take up Bendix's ideas and argue that authenticity should be seen as firmly "embedded in the ongoing project of modernity."[12] They touch on the concept of autonomy and argue that it was precisely the concept of the autonomous individual that came to define modernity, giving "rise to personal search for proper external expression of inner states."[13] Authenticity has to be distinguished from the notion of autonomy, however, as authentic behavior cannot be reduced to or derived from self-determined conduct alone.[14]

Following this line of thought, one can argue that authenticity is a distinctively modern value that can be found in various social forms, such as charismatic religions that propagate "pure" religious experiences and encounters with the divine that are without falsity and manipulation.[15] Anthropologist Rolf Lindner argues that "ethno-sciences" themselves have long been infused with the idea of authenticity, and that ethnographers have oftentimes

[10] Bendix, *In Search of Authenticity*, 5.

[11] Ibid., 8.

[12] Thomas Fillitz and A. Jamie Saris, "Introduction: Authenticity Aujourd'hui," in *Debating Authenticity: Concepts of Modernity in Anthropological Perspective*, ed. A. Jamie Saris and Thomas Fillitz (Oxford: Berghahn Books, 2013), 15.

[13] Ibid., 8.

[14] Ferrara, *Reflective Authenticity*, 5.

[15] Lindholm, *Culture and Authenticity*.

understood themselves as guardians of a vanishing pure culture that should be protected from any worldly influences and contamination.[16] Research subjects were supposed to be "culturally celibate" and were not supposed to leave their original environment.[17] Lindner points out that anthropology's obsession with the idea of the authentic finds its expression in the ethnographic study of subcultures, which are seen as being uncorrupted by societal rules.[18] Since regulations are interpreted as distorting human nature, any groups that escape such manipulation are understood as offering an insight into a more pure and authentic human nature. Although a more constructionist approach that conceives of authenticity itself as something that is produced through social practices and politics has become commonly accepted, a quest for authenticity continues to influence qualitative research in another way: as ethnographers are oftentimes writing about a reality that is and remains foreign to readers, they need to bridge the distance by providing thick descriptions to convey the authenticity of their accounts and show that they were "really there." At the same time, university regulations and ethics committees usually require them to keep their study participants anonymous. Therefore, they need to make choices regarding how much contextual information they can include to give an authentic account without compromising their interlocutors' anonymity.[19]

[16] Rolf Lindner, "Die Idee des Authentischen," *Kuckuck, Notizen zu Alltagskultur und Volkskunde* 13, no. 1 (1998): 58.

[17] Ibid., 59.

[18] Ibid., 60.

[19] Julia Bickford and Jeff Nisker, "Tensions between Anonymity and Thick Description when 'Studying Up' in Genetics Research," *Qualitative Health Research* 25, no. 2 (2015): 276–82.

Authenticity and Anonymity: An Uncertain Relationship

Authenticity is linked to the idea of an original essential source that finds a noticeable and recognizable expression. Anonymity therefore can be in tension with the notion of authenticity: if the entity that is assumed to be the source of actions, feelings, and decisions is inaccessible, everything that follows is at risk of being false and inauthentic. This idea is intimately linked to a belief that there is a quintessential original truth out there that has to be discovered for someone or something to be real and authentic. Anonymity in this line of argument appears to be an obstacle to authenticity: as a mechanism of not-knowing or nonknowledge, it can cut links to what is believed to be an individual's core, which is conceptualized as the source of authenticity. Therefore, anonymity as a means for keeping origins hidden needs to be overcome by discovering the truth that has been concealed. Whereas anonymity involves the danger of removing the individual from its real, authentic self, truth is ascribed a transformative power.[20] Since the loss of authenticity can be experienced as a source of grief and despair, it might need to be restored by discovering the truth.[21]

Online anonymity, however, makes evident that alternative understandings of the relationship between anonymity and authenticity are possible. In a response to Facebook's founder Mark Zuckerberg, who claimed that anonymity was a threat to authenticity, the creator of 4chan, a website that lets users anonymously post images and messages, even claimed that "anonymity is authenticity."[22] Anonymity in an online environment can provide individuals and groups with the means to express their opinions without having to fear prosecution. In this sense, it can be said that "anonymity has the potential to protect and enable freedom."[23] When users of social media platforms do not have to fear that their identity will be revealed after making a statement that might be deemed unacceptable by ruling authorities, they might be more inclined toward expressing their real opinions and experiences. Anonymity can hence also be a mechanism that enables the expression of authentic opinions.

If the relationship between authenticity and anonymity is (re)conceptualized as one that is not strictly binary but instead much more ambivalent, then different paths of inquiry into new and old questions arise. These considerations highlight that authenticity itself is never

[20] Ari Gandsman, "'Do You Know Who You Are?': Radical Existential Doubt and Scientific Certainty in the Search for the Kidnapped Children of the Disappeared in Argentina," *Ethos* 37, no. 4 (2009): 441–65.

[21] Lindholm, *Culture and Authenticity*, 1.

[22] Christopher "Moot" Poole, quoted in Robert Bodle, "The Ethics of Online Anonymity or Zuckerberg vs. 'Moot,'" *ACM SIGCAS Computers and Society* 43, no. 1 (2013): 26.

[23] Götz Bachmann, Michi Knecht, and Andreas Wittel, "The Social Productivity of Anonymity," *ephemera* 17, no. 2 (2017): 244.

"finished" but always uncertain. Rather than, for example, ascribing a group authenticity because members know their so-called origins and "act accordingly" by following traditions or by sealing themselves off from society, social scientists should look at the resources (narrative, economic, etc.) that people have at hand to constantly reconstitute themselves as authentic. Moreover, the ambivalence that characterizes online anonymity highlights that different, potentially contradictory norms might shape how practices or infrastructures are experienced and evaluated. For example, while the donor-conceived persons that I interviewed for my doctoral research praised the internet for its ability to connect them with others who were in the same situation, many described the commentary section of online articles as a dangerous and destructive space, as it enabled others to leave hurtful remarks—usually without revealing their identity. Their relationship with the internet was deeply ambivalent: the imperative to connect could be implemented, but people felt that it created a space were ideals of transparency and compassion were disrespected.[24] This in turn underlines that "ambivalence is one of the defining characteristics of the modern relationship to technology."[25] Finally, both sides of the ambivalence characterizing online anonymity are linked to certain ideas about authenticity that correspond to Lindholm's argument about different, potentially overlapping ideas of what it means to be authentic: it means that the *origins* of certain statements cannot be traced, which can be precisely what enables people to *express* themselves freely; at the same time, the impossibility of tracing the origins of certain expressions can by itself make them appear less sincere, pure, and thereby less authentic and turn it into something that should be rejected.[26]

[24] See Maren Klotz, *(K)information: Gamete Donation and Kinship Knowledge in Germany and Britain* (Frankfurt: Campus, 2014), for an exploration of "transparentization" in donor conception.

[25] Sarah Franklin, *Biological Relatives: IVF, Stem Cells, and the Future of Kinship* (Durham, NC: Duke University Press, 2013), 8.

[26] Lindholm, "Rise of Expressive Authenticity."

Bibliography

Bachmann, Götz, Michi Knecht, and Andreas Wittel. "The Social Productivity of Anonymity." *ephemera* 17, no. 2 (2017): 241–58.

Bendix, Regina. *In Search of Authenticity: The Formation of Folklore Studies.* Madison, WI: University of Wisconsin Press, 1997.

Bickford, Julia, and Jeff Nisker. "Tensions between Anonymity and Thick Description when 'Studying Up' in Genetics Research." *Qualitative Health Research* 25, no. 2 (2015): 276–82.

Bodle, Robert. "The Ethics of Online Anonymity or Zuckerberg vs. 'Moot.'" *ACM SIGCAS Computers and Society* 43, no. 1 (2013): 22–35.

Engelke, Matthew. *Think Like an Anthropologist.* London: Penguin Books, 2017.

Ferrara, Alessandro. *Reflective Authenticity: Rethinking the Project of Modernity.* London: Routledge, 1998.

Fillitz, Thomas, and A. Jamie Saris. "Introduction: Authenticity Aujourd'hui." In *Debating Authenticity: Concepts of Modernity in Anthropological Perspective*, edited by A. Jamie Saris and Thomas Fillitz, 1–24. Oxford: Berghahn Books, 2013.

Franklin, Sarah. *Biological Relatives: IVF, Stem Cells, and the Future of Kinship.* Durham, NC: Duke University Press, 2013.

Gandsman, Ari. "'Do You Know Who You Are?': Radical Existential Doubt and Scientific Certainty in the Search for the Kidnapped Children of the Disappeared in Argentina." *Ethos* 37, no. 4 (2009): 441–65.

Klotz, Maren. *(K)information: Gamete Donation and Kinship Knowledge in Germany and Britain.* Frankfurt: Campus, 2014.

Lindholm, Charles. *Culture and Authenticity.* Malden, MA: Blackwell, 2008.

Lindholm, Charles. "The Rise of Expressive Authenticity." *Anthropological Quarterly* 86, no. 2 (2013): 361–95.

Lindner, Rolf. "Die Idee des Authentischen." *Kuckuck, Notizen zu Alltagskultur und Volkskunde* 13, no. 1 (1998): 58–61.

Soler, Josep. "The Anonymity of Catalan and the Authenticity of Estonian: Two Paths for the Development of Medium-Sized Languages." *International Journal of Bilingual Education and Bilingualism* 16, no. 2 (2013): 153–63.

Woolard, Kathryn A., and Susan E. Frekko. "Catalan in the Twenty-First Century: Romantic Publics and Cosmopolitan Communities." *International Journal of Bilingual Education and Bilingualism* 16, no. 2 (2013): 129–37.

Longing for a Selfless Self and Other Ambivalences of Anonymity
A Personal Account

This chapter is about anonymity in addiction therapy, about authorship, and about myself. After giving it some thought, I decided to publish this text anonymously. The reason is not that I want this authorial act to put me out of reach. Anyone who wanted to could surely find out who the text's author is without a great deal of effort. Meanwhile, there are enough traces to be found on the internet that lead straight to me. Indeed, this is precisely one of the central themes and concerns of this chapter: to discuss the question of what significance practices of anonymity might still and can have today, that is, in times when our digital networking has made it almost impossible to guarantee anonymity.[1] This text is an attempt to contribute to this issue.

For me, what is certain is that anonymity has great meaning. Not in the classical sense, however, as an individual act of self-protection.[2] Anonymity, for me, is meaningful as part of a collective practice, which demands a particular attitude of which anonymity is the expression and also the performative enactment. When I discuss anonymity as a collective practice and an attitude here, I refer to a program that was developed as part of the so-called twelve-step groups. These groups are based on a concept of peer-to-peer addiction treatment founded in the 1930s and stemming from Alcoholics Anonymous. This concept is now applied to various symptoms, including co-addiction, eating disorders, gambling addiction, drug abuse, and sex addiction. What different twelve-step groups have in common is that they bring together people who identify themselves (or loved ones) as addicts and who support each other in a twelve-step therapy program to secure long-term freedom from compulsive and often extremely destructive behavior patterns.

To achieve this goal, anonymity is essential for various reasons. First, it facilitates access for newcomers to these groups, in which topics, feelings, and actions are discussed that are considered abnormal and reprehensible, and often even stigmatized and criminalized. The creed

[1] Paul Ohm, "Broken Promises of Privacy: Responding to the Surprising Failure of Anonymization," *UCLA Law Review* 57 (2010): 1701–77; and Götz Bachmann, Michi Knecht, and Andreas Wittel, "The Social Productivity of Anonymity," *ephemera* 17, no. 2 (2017): 241–58.

[2] Gary Marx, "What's in a Name? Some Reflections on the Sociology of Anonymity," *Information Society* 15 (1999): 1–15.

here is, the more freely and honestly these topics can be talked about, the more effective the therapy will be. But this is not all. For the functioning and long-term continuation of this decentrally organized, institutionally independent, and antihierarchical group network, it is also crucially important that all participants exercise collective anonymity vis-à-vis all public media. This form of collective anonymity is intended to protect the groups from a culture of guruism and thus from a kind of corruptibility that can jeopardize the essential principle of mutual support, such as happens, for example, when individual participants publish advice booklets in their own names or set up therapy centers to make profits on a strongly privatized and commercialized therapy and self-enhancement market. Collective anonymity is intended to prevent this not only in practice but also in principle by fostering an attitude of humility (Selbstrücknahme) in favor of the collective good in favor of the collective good (mutual support). Once adopted, such an attitude makes profiting monetarily from selling out therapeutic success unthinkable. Doing so is diametrically opposed to the twelve-step idea of successful therapy. I discuss this idea and its relationship to an attitude of anonymity in more detail below.

First, however, let's return to me, the author of this text. What does collective anonymity have to do with me? It ought to be possible and unobjectionable for an ethnographer to write analytically about an anonymous collective without wanting to remain anonymous, but rather wanting to be approachable, criticizable, and quotable as a scientist. Gabriella Coleman did precisely this when she wrote about her participant observation with the hacker collective Anonymous, as did Caterina Frois when she wrote about Narcotics and Alcoholics Anonymous.[3] Jane Hindman did it when she studied biographical writing in addiction therapy, and I have done it several times in my scientific attempts to come to terms with the twelve-step program.[4] But after several years of wrangling and wavering, I have decided for this text

[3] Gabriella Coleman, *Hacker, Hoaxer, Whistleblower, Spy: The Many Faces of Anonymous* (London: Verso, 2014); and Caterina Frois, *The Anonymous Society: Identity, Transformation and Anonymity in 12 Steps* (Cambridge: Cambridge Scholars, 2009).

[4] Jane Hindman, "Making Writing Matter: Using 'the Personal' to Recover(y) an Essential(ist) Tension in Academic Discourse," *College English* 64 (2001): 88–107.

to step out of the relatively distanced role of the ethnographer for the first time. I can only do this, however, if I write anonymously.

The reason for this is that I once saw myself as part of the twelve-step groups. After various other attempts—psychoanalytic talk therapy, a silent meditation retreat, and a two-month hospital stay—that were all followed by even more painful relapses, I accepted the support of other participants in a twelve-step group. With the help of this support (also called *sponsoring* in the groups), I completed the twelve-step program within two years. (I have included the twelve steps as an appendix to this chapter.) Following my own therapy, I actively participated in the self-administration of the twelve-step group network for about three years and also took on sponsorships myself; that is, I supported newcomers in practicing the twelve steps. It can be said that at times I was indeed a "twelve stepper."

After several years of being not only abstinent but also sober, and having attained a relative sovereignty over my own thinking and acting, I started writing a doctoral thesis.[5] In this thesis, I reconstructed a cultural history of addiction therapy from 1930 until today and developed an ethnographically based theory about the connection between a liberal understanding of freedom and the disease of addiction. While most of my acquaintances and friends from the twelve-step groups know that I (also) deal with the twelve-steps scientifically, I have always kept my personal case out of my scientific discourse.

There are several reasons for doing so: the fear of not being taken seriously scientifically and the fear of stigma are certainly not to be underestimated. But it is also my commitment to the principle of collective anonymity, which kept me from situating my scientific work not only historically but also personally. To publicly write about the groups as an avowed twelve stepper would mean breaking the principle of collective anonymity. (Other

[5] On the difference between abstinence and sobriety, see Paula Helm, "Sobriety versus Abstinence: How 12-Stepper Negotiate Recovery across Groups," *Addiction Research and Theory* 27, no. 1 (2018): 29–36.

authors have been severely criticized for doing so, though I will not name any names here.) But how does one write a doctoral thesis without identifying oneself by name? Indeed, this is an impossibility, not least because a thesis is written to obtain a qualification and be endowed with a personal title. In view of these circumstances, it seemed most sensible to lay my own case aside and write about the subject of addiction therapy only from a distanced perspective.

On the other hand, there is a clear call to adress the question of what remains of anonymity in times of digitally enforced deanonymization. How to cope with the conflict which the imperative of identification can pose upon people who wish to do things otherwise? In order to discuss these question here I will draw on the practice of anonymity knowing full well that my anonymity is to be understood more symbolically than practically.

To do so, I begin with a reflection on the meaning of "the name" in science and authorship more generally by referring to the concept of "situated knowledge."[6] Then, with a little thematic jump, I talk about the role of anonymity in addiction therapy, and in this context I outline what I mean by the attitude of anonymity and how I locate this attitude in cultural-historical terms. I conclude with a reflection on anonymity's ambivalences in an attempt to bring the different sections of the chapter together.

[6] Donna Haraway, "Situated Knowledges: The Science Question in Feminism and the Privilege of Partial Perspective," *Feminist Studies* 14, no. 3 (1998): 575–99.

Anonymity and Science

Science requires comprehensibility and rationality. This includes being able to understand who wrote a text and how it was written. The text must therefore be attributable to one or more specific persons. Even in the face of debates on the "death of the author," the signing of every published text with a name is still the undisputed practice in almost all scientific organs.[7] Even if the path to publication is often a double-blind one, this does not apply to the publication itself. Here, I would like to question the hitherto largely unquestioned practice of the personal identification of scientific works. What is being hoped for regarding scientific quality by tagging texts with names? How is it that, despite the "writing culture" debate, the personal attribution of works is still regarded as a practice with no alternative?

I suspect that the answer to the latter question has much to do with neoliberal logics of self-marketing and a person-focused rather than ideas-focused and knowledge-focused academic system.[8] Although this system appears to promote a double-blind process that places ideas and insights before people, the process is almost never consistently carried through to the end, that is, post-publication and beyond. In this way, however, it is not suitable for undermining the dynamics of big-shotism and the cult of personality. In a system of science that is increasingly neoliberal, in which self-marketing, competition, and third-party funding are at stake, things can hardly be imagined otherwise: under such circumstances, who would be prepared to produce something without being able to reap the benefits in directly personal terms, for example, in the form of personal fame, better opportunities for applications, a better endowment for one's own chair (if available), or the chance of being made permanent?[9] It seems rather unsurprising, then, that so few authors think about publishing anonymously.[10]

But there are certainly also arguments for the identifiability of authors of scientific texts that lie not only in the interests of the authors themselves but also in those of scientificity. Concepts such as imputability, responsiveness, criticizability, orientation, and situating come to mind. These are certainly weighty concepts, but must the author's name be used to concretize them? An anonymous text can be addressed and criticized as a bearer of ideas, thoughts, insights, or as a report about a research

[7] Roland Barthes, "The Death of the Author," in *Image–Music–Text* (New York: Dill and Wong, 1977), 142–48; and Michel Foucault, "What Is an Author?" in *Language, Counter-Memory, Practice* (New York: Cornell University Press, 1977), 124–77.

[8] Ulrich Bröckling, *Das unternehmerische Selbst: Soziologie einer Subjektivierungsform* (Frankfurt: Suhrkamp, 2007).

[9] Jürgen Kaube, preface to *Die Illusion der Exzellenz: Lebenslügen der Wissenschaftspolitik* (Berlin: Wagenbach, 2009); Cris Shore and Laura McLauchlan, "'Third Mission' Activities, Commercialisation and Academic Entrepreneurs," *Social Anthropology* 20, no. 3 (2012): 267–86; and Gerhard Stapelfeldt, *Der Aufbruch des konformistischen Geistes: Thesen zur Kritik der neoliberalen Universität* (Hamburg: Kova, 2007).

[10] An exception are the authors of the Invisible Committee, who published a controversial booklet titled *The Coming Insurrection*, but who had to do so because they sometimes call for illegal acts in the text and could be liable to being prosecuted for them. The Invisible Committee, *The Coming Insurrection* (Los Angeles, CA: Semiotext(e), 2009).

project or an experiment, and criticisms, moreover, can be answered anonymously. But what about qualities such as imputability and orientation?[11] How are we to quote an anonymous text? How are we to refer to it?

Such problems have repeatedly cropped up in my examination of the texts of an anonymous collective. Again and again, questions about the citation method arose, since citing Narcotics Anonymous 2001 is certainly less specific than, for example, Bachmann 2001. In fact, the author-centered in-text citation method that most scientific organs now practice seems to me to be largely contingent on, if not further expression of, a person-centered scientific culture. It would certainly be possible to cite short titles and dates, rather than authors and dates, as is currently the case in many texts. A further point is how to handle individual imputability in connection with legal questions. Because of the methodological individualism of law, knowledge of the author's identity is a necessity for legal action. Prior to publication, however, texts are usually subject to an editorial review procedure ensuring that they do not contain unsupported statements or unethically obtained results.

The last remaining concept is that of situating or situated knowledge, concerning which I refer here primarily to Donna Haraway's writings on the subject. Haraway argues for an understanding of rationality, knowledge, and science that proceeds from specific bodies, themselves also situated in complex cultural systems. Knowledge is therefore rationality that stems from partial views, which, in turn, are developed by specific bodies, in specific places, and at specific times. According to Haraway, it is precisely these partial views reflected in their specific situatedness that can claim to be scientific. On the other hand, she clearly rejects claims to universality, which strive to rise above their specific position, like a god.[12]

Does this construal of situatedness as a condition of rational knowledge production mean that a text without

[11] On the ambivalence of digitality and anonymity, see, for example, Thorsten Thiel, "Anonymität und Demokratie," *Forschungsjournal Soziale Bewegungen* 30, no. 2 (2017): 152–61.

[12] Haraway, "Situated Knowledges," 589.

a name, without any identification, that does not make its authors known can make no claim to be rational? In view of the concrete connection to one or more specific bodies, this conclusion is quite obvious. It would initially seem that an anonymous text eludes such situatedness in Haraway's sense. But can a text not also reflect on the conditions and standpoint of its genesis without revealing the identity of the author? If, with Donna Haraway, a text must crucially be able to reveal the specific standpoint of its perspective and to reflect on the extent to which this point of view determines its standpoint on an object or a question, the author's identity has basically no need to be revealed.

If situated knowledge is understood in such a way that a scientific work, for example, an essay, ought to be written so that its situatedness is inscribed in the text from the very beginning, that is to say, so that it imposes its situatedness on the reader through its mode of argumentation and its language, thus requiring no further research and investigation to ascertain its situatedness, then it does not require any name. Radically speaking, it is basically irrelevant who a text's author is, as long as the text is written in such a way that it speaks for itself, that is, that it makes comprehensible the key backgrounds and motives from which it was written and from which it arrives at a specific knowledge about the world.

Anonymity and Authorship

Even if it seems paradoxical at first, my anonymity does indeed become a necessary ethical condition for situating this text in a way that is central to its scientific comprehensibility. Not mentioning my name becomes a prerequisite for situating the text so that the most relevant aspects of its genesis are not omitted but are made the subject and considered from the beginning in the text's entire composition, structure, and interpretation. By writing anonymously, I can thematize my own case and thus enable my readers to place my way of writing about twelve-step groups. Only anonymity enables me to write the text such that my readers can understand how and from which position I arrived at my knowledge and my standpoints on the text's subject. In addition, my anonymity here is by no means an unethical means of evading accountability—a reproach often made to anonymous authors.[13] On the contrary, it would be unethical to write this text under my name because it would override the twelve-steps principle of collective anonymity and thus betray the people I am writing about.

That brings me to the next point. Does this text become unscientific because I was part of the movement I am writing about? By reflecting on and revealing my own participation, I make it comprehensible, and the fact that I was part of the movement I am writing about greatly benefits, in my opinion, the specific form of situated knowledge production that I am concerned with here. My own case has given me far easier access to the very sensitive field about which I research and write. This does not mean, however, that I have not proceeded systematically with the collection and analysis of data. When I began researching twelve-step groups, I started distancing myself from these groups for reasons I explain below, without losing my appreciation for them. During the period of research, my participatory observation in more than thirty group meetings in different regions of the world focused solely on scientific concerns. In all the group meetings that I attended for research purposes, I made known my identity as a researcher but did not address my personal history with the program.

My history with my research object and my close personal contacts with many actors in the field brings, in my view, far more advantages than disadvantages. Thus, I am much more than a modest witness; rather—to say it with Haraway—I am a mutated modest witness who intervenes and brings in my own view of things.[14] Although

[13] Ingrid Brodnig, *Der unsichtbare Mensch: Wie die Anonymität im Internet unsere Gesellschaft verändert* (Vienna: Czernin Verlag, 2013); and A. Michael Froomkin, "From Anonymity to Identification," *Journal of Self-Regulation and Regulation* 1, no. 1 (2015): 121–38.

[14] Steven Shapin and Simon Schaffer, *Leviathan and the Air Pump* (Princeton, NJ: Princeton University Press, 1985); and Donna Haraway, *Modest_Witness@Second_Millennium.FemaleMan©_Meets_OncoMouse* (New York: Routledge, 1997).

I remain invisible, I am not modest and not just a witness in the sense that what I write about twelve steps is a mere reflection of what I have observed.[15] Instead, this means that certain aspects are deliberately emphasized, while others are marginalized.

For example, one aspect that I am not particularly interested in is individual anonymity, which is to say, personal untrackability, even though most of the people who invite me to lecture on the subject of anonymity and addiction do so in the expectation that I will talk about precisely this.[16] I think that this aspect is negligible, however, and that other dimensions of anonymity, such as social or collective anonymity, are far more essential for understanding the meanings of practices of anonymity for addiction therapy and beyond. I am convinced that my own physical and emotional experience with the subject enables me to assess which issues and questions move the field and with which unsolved problems many actors in the field are struggling with. In this, my old friends and acquaintances from the groups are my most helpful critics and supervisors.

To contribute one's own biography in this way and to make it a theme is, of course, a special form of situatedness. With Haraway's concept of situated knowledge, she addresses most crucially the political agenda that explicitly or implicitly underlies every text. So, what is my political agenda? I would like to point out the ethico-critical significance that anonymity can achieve, provided it is not reduced to its individualistic dimensions of personal identity protection, but instead is viewed as a form of resistance to self-marketing and the cult of personality, as well as to the negative consequences of these trends. To this end, I would like to make a plea for the idea of anonymity as a specific attitude that is enacted by the practice of social and collective anonymity, and whose implications I have not only observed and analyzed in recent years but also learned to appreciate, and nurture. Yet, I would also like to point out the

[15] On the concept of the modest witness, see Haraway Modest_Witness, 23–49.

[16] Helen Nissenbaum, "The Meaning of Anonymity in an Information Age," Information Society 15 (1999): 141–44.

problems and dangers of this concept. And I think that the most honest and most effective way to do so is not only to write about this attitude, but also to practice it while I am writing (anonymously).

17 Alcoholics Anonymous World Services, *Alcoholics Anonymous*, 1st ed. New York: A. A. Grapevine and Alcoholics Anonymous, 1939), 62.

Anonymity and Addition Therapy

So-called twelve-step groups (Alcoholics Anonymous, Narcotics Anonymous, Gamblers Anonymous, Sex Addicts Anonymous, Overeaters Anonymous, etc.) aim to provide therapeutic support structures among affected persons. In doing so, they assume a certain understanding of the illness called addiction, which locates it not in the amount of consumption or in the frequency of certain habits, but in the specific constitution of the relation to self. In one of Alcoholics Anonymous's standard works, the authors define addiction as follows: "Selfishness—self-centeredness! That, we think, is the root of our troubles. Driven by a hundred forms of fear, self-delusion, self-seeking, and self-pity, … we have made decisions based on self, which later placed us in a position to be hurt."[17]

Such an understanding of illness requires an extremely profound therapy, one that puts the social in play, such that individuals do not remain thrown back on themselves but, on the contrary, are able to learn in interaction with other affected persons to go outside and beyond themselves. For this purpose, twelve-step groups provide a protected space in which the participants first support each other by mutual mirroring to deconstruct the models, wish structures, and thought patterns of their "addiction ego," and then replace these with new images, structures, and patterns. But how can it be ensured that the groups through which such a transformation process is to be operationalized actually function in a way that helps the individual participants feel accepted, safe, free, and integrated?

This is where anonymity comes in, because it builds the framework in twelve-step groups to guarantee solidarity and support with each other.[18] Anonymity thus becomes effective on very different levels. First, the individual anonymity of each participant protects what happens inside the groups from the rest of everyday life. In a shielded space, social roles can be experimented with, secrets can be disclosed, and suppressed feelings can be expressed without the fear of undesirable and unforeseeable social consequences inhibiting the participants.

Yet, anonymity does not just contribute to building groups as a special space of solidarity by opening an option to retreat immediately into inaccessibility after the end of a meeting. It further fulfills a central function in its effect on interaction during the group meeting. I am referring to anonymity not in the traditional sense of withholding a name, but in the concealment of social factors of distinction. To effect this concealment, at the beginning of a meeting, all participants are urged to leave "outside" all aspects of their identity that refer to their social status (habitus), such as occupation, family background, an elaborate way of speaking, or educational status. This way of proceeding is intended to promote mutual identification.[19]

Social anonymity helps to promote identification by focusing on equality in suffering from addiction and in the desire for recovery through the absence of distinguishing factors. To ensure that the idea of equality in suffering and desire is not undermined by hierarchies within groups, it is important that anonymity be maintained not only internally but also externally, in relation to the public. Therefore, it is a fixed rule within the decentralized twelve-step group network that each group publishes all its works (manifestos, life stories, leaflets, press releases, interviews) only under group pseudonyms, and even individual contributions may be published only in anonymous form.[20] *Collective anonymity* to the public is significant insofar as through it, the equal treatment of

[18] Frois, *Anonymous Society*.

[19] Alcoholics Anonymous, *Zwölf Schritte und Zwölf Traditionen* (Munich: Anonyme Alkoholiker Interessengemeinschaft, 2005), 123–25, 133–39.

[20] Alcoholics Anonymous, *Zwölf Schritte und Zwölf Traditionen*, 172–74.

all participants is guaranteed, including from the media, and thus the sense of equality in suffering and desires is protected from any guruism or cult of personality developing among the group participants.

21 Alexis de Tocqueville, *Democracy in America*, vol. 2 (1840; New York: Vintage, 1980), 123.

Finally, through the regular practice of social and collective anonymity, a kind of ethically understood *attitude of anonymity* develops as part of a performative process. This attitude to life is one that, according to the experiences of twelve steppers, leads to long-term liberation from addiction. It can be understood in the sense of Alexis de Tocqueville's "self-interest, rightly understood."[21] Accordingly, assuming an attitude of anonymity includes learning the ability to exercise humility for the benefit of critical community goals. In the protection of the community, this ability aims at creating a space in which each person can put their individual abilities to the test. So, what an individual learns by adopting an attitude of anonymity through the regular practice of collective and social anonymity is that humility for the benefit of the group can also be of long-term benefit to the individual.

What particularly interests me in this specific way of understanding addiction, and in the corresponding therapeutic concept, is the underlying cultural-historical and ethico-political implications. On the one hand, of note here are the Christian bonds that extend back to the specific founding of Alcoholics Anonymous in the United States in the 1930s. Such bonds still prevail in some groups today, notably in rural areas. In them, assuming an attitude of anonymity is understood as a return to divine consciousness. The idea is that one can liberate oneself from a pronounced self-centeredness by surrendering oneself to the will of God, which first manifests itself in the power of the group and later merges into oneself. Instead of making oneself the center of one's thinking and acting, one now sees oneself as an instrument of God, an expression of his love, care, will, and power. This orientation is intended to help keep one from engaging in destructive behavior.

E — DELIGHT
Longing for a Selfless Self and Other Ambivalences of Anonymity

While some give the name God to the principle of their recovery, for other twelve steppers, this principle remains nameless. For them, the principle of recovery is anonymity as such.[22] Anonymity thus means the opposite of egocentrism and stands for the consciousness and experience of a person who is connected with the world. With other words: the consciousness not of forming a hermetic unity but of constituting oneself through constant exchange with the environment. Such a consciousness, or attitude, enables individuals to imagine that they are part of a larger whole and accordingly not to take an interest only in their own well-being, since they have understood that personal well-being is more or less directly connected to that of all living beings and organisms on this planet and its fragile ecosystems. Ideally, this attitude leads to the dissolution of self-centeredness; such an attitude is indeed inherent to an interest in broader contexts, and even to submitting oneself to these contexts when necessary.

Above all, the latter understanding of addiction therapy, which I am close to, suggests that we should ask about the ethico-political implications of addiction therapy. In my opinion, the successfully tested idea of counteracting various addictions with an attitude of anonymity urges a critical revision of a culture focused on attaching positive attributes to one's own name and calling on people to rise above others in social terms and gain an individual advantage. The twelve-step group network could thus also be seen as a kind of counterculture to all those logics, norms, and values that the individuals concerned perceive as causing and/or nurturing addiction. The obsession with one's own name is the symbol through which these logics, norms, and values are grasped: this obsession stands for egocentrism, selfishness, and thus also loneliness, senselessness, and inner compulsion. Anonymity forms a counter-symbol to all of this. It stands for identification, sympathy, solidarity, humility, and responsibility.

[22] With this notion, the twelve steppers recall Erich Fromm's thoughts on the idea of God. For Fromm the topos of God as spiritual leader of man leads "in his last consequence to the negation of the idea of God." Accordingly, Fromm interprets God's words against Moses. By introducing himself with the words "I am the 'I am there,'" God says, according to Fromm's interpretation, "My name is Nameless" or also "Call me Anonymous." This means, "Try not to think *about* me, try to feel me through your actions and to become one with me." Thanks to this interpretation, Fromm connects with the paradoxical logic of Buddhists and mystics like Meister Eckhart. Erich Fromm, *Die Kunst des Liebens* (Stuttgart: Deutscher Taschenbuch Verlag, 2004), 113, 115.

Though I am by no means alone in my ethico-political interpretation of the twelve-step program, there is a strong leaning within the groups to insist on political neutrality. This orientation stems from the conviction that only neutrality can guarantee the principle of equality in suffering and desire. I am of the opinion, however, that this conviction is variously problematic, because political neutrality is an illusion. Instead, I consider the insistence on political neutrality itself to be highly political, for several reasons. On the one hand, insisting on neutrality makes open debate about the program's Christian bonds more difficult and thus removes neutrality from the sphere of what is politically debatable. This constitutes a great step backward. On the other hand, my view is that to this day, the political aloofness of twelve-step groups supports and affirms a discourse that individualizes the disease of addiction, instead of taking it seriously as a reflection of more general socio-political social problems. In the next section I talk about the partly problematic consequences of this individualization.

This attachment to an illusion of political neutrality is the main reason that I and many others who have attended the meetings during my time have now distanced ourselves from the groups. In the initially acute phase of suffering, these groups are certainly extremely helpful, and it makes sense not to be distracted by political problems during this phase. In the long run, however, they steer the participants into a dead end, because addiction therapy is ultimately about outgrowing the focus on oneself. In my opinion, however, this goal is possible only if one locates oneself in larger social, global, and political contexts. But with the principle instead of rule of political neutrality, the groups refuse this.

Ambivalences of Anonymity

Thus far I have gathered and prepared arguments essentially for assigning value and meaning to anonymity, even as it has largely lost its function as a protector of individual identity. For this purpose, I set out from myself. I confess to being concerned about living an attitude that, in connection with twelve-step groups, I learned to call "the attitude of anonymity." I have described what this posture contains, and I have located it culturally and historically. I also explained why it would be impossible for me to situate this text meaningfully without remaining nameless. I see the reason for this above all in my ethical obligation toward myself as an advocate of an attitude of anonymity and toward the persons and contexts about which I conduct research and that demand collective anonymity toward the public.

Although I appreciate practices of anonymity for the aforementioned reasons, anonymity has a number of drawbacks. I am referring in particular to those persons and groups of persons who practice anonymity not out of an ethical conviction, but only for reasons of self-protection. In such cases anonymity is not voluntary but compusory. Such compulsion to anonymity arises, for example, in the case of politically persecuted or criminal persons and groups of persons, as well as in that of addicted persons and groups of persons. If anonymity is compulsive it represents a burden as well as an disadvantage for addiction therapy groups.

For example, many people's frequent and long hesitation toward support groups can be connected not just to their personal shame but also to the stigma attached to the groups themselves. This stigma is in part because the illness of addiction suffers from moral reprobation and, depending on the symptom and the legal system, can even be accompanied by deviancy. That only minor changes have taken place in this field since the 1930s may be because the network of sufferers, which has formed and organized itself for this purpose, must remain anonymous for reasons of protection and demarcation. Anonymity, however, does not just create a protective form of demarcation. It also complicates public relations work, causes intransparency, and thus promotes discourses of mystification. This makes anonymity a dilemma for many affected persons and their groups. Internally, it fosters community, but externally, it separates the groups and their participants from a larger community—society.

To function as protected social spaces, support groups are dependent on their anonymity. This dependence, however, is partly responsible for the fact that support groups remain marginalized in society as a whole and that participation is still associated with shame, stigma, and secrecy. This can lead to participants having to live a kind of double life in which different subject realities compete with each other. In the course of their therapy in the groups, participants adopt group-specific values and ideas. These include ideals of solidarity, helpfulness, equality in suffering and desire, identification in equality, self-denial, and symmetrical support. Such ideals are enforceable within the protected space of the support groups, but they often conflict with the expectations and demands placed on people, for instance, in a professional context (see, for example, my above discussion of the imperatives of academic knowledge production), or with the ways in which affected persons are treated in their families. Such contradictions can be counterproductive to the goal of conveying to participants the feeling that they can live an addiction-free, ethical, and autonomous life within the framework of a given social structure. I have struggled with this problem myself many times.

A plurality of social roles is seen in many places as something worth striving for, and such an attitude could certainly be understood as part of successful therapy. Nonetheless, the kind of double life that I critically examine here is not a freely chosen one but one enforced by social practices of anonymity, and as such it can also be perceived as a heavy burden. Conflicts concerning the incompatibility between subjectivation by twelve-step groups and the demands of societies in which twelve steppers ultimately have to live and undertake their recovery in are not addressed in the experience reports published by the groups because of the above-mentioned requirement of political neutrality. That the official publications do not address such problems has brought much criticism of twelve-step groups.[23] This criticism, however, is primarily aimed at the heavily redacted experience reports, which convey an ideologically reduced picture to new participants.

In my analyses and observations, I have also noticed that the problem of incompatibility is definitely an issue for many participants, and with regard to my scientific work, I am an example of this. Many other participants report profound frustrations in this context. In some cases, these frustrations lead to a radical departure from the groups, accompanied by an experience of disappointment, which is regularly expressed in even worse recidivism or in people switching from cost-free peer-to-peer mutual support to private providers, who cost them a lot of money and to whom some of those I have spoken to are even indebted.

In other cases, frustration leads to a renunciation of the hitherto life world and to increasing isolation. If the incongruence between the principles and ideals of the twelve-step groups and those of the environment is perceived as insurmountable, some participants may set about moving only within the subculture of the twelve-step groups, thereby taking on sectarian traits. Considering that liberation from self-centeredness is a therapeutic goal, the criticism can thus be made that no actual recovery has taken place in such cases. Instead, only a shift of dependency takes place, in which a compulsive behavior pattern is superseded by a compulsive attachment to a group.[24]

In my view, while such a "shift of addiction" is not per-se problematic, it nonetheless often leads to a dead end. The twelve-step groups are about self-therapy, which means that the "self," in the attempt to outgrow it, is the first

[23] Leonard Blumberg, "The Ideology of a Therapeutic Social Movement: Alcoholics Anonymous," *Journal of Studies on Alcohol* 38, no. 11 (1977): 2122–24; and Robert Tournier, "Alcoholics Anonymous as Treatment and as Ideology," *Journal of Studies on Alcohol* 40, no. 3 (1979): 230–39.

[24] Arthur Greil and David Reil, "Conversion to the World View of Alcoholics Anonymous: A Refinement of Conversion Theory," *Qualitative Sociology* 6 (1983): 6.

priority. If, after the acute phase, people circulate long term chiefly among the groups, they may become entangled in a vicious circle: In their attempt of outgrowing their self-centeredness their focus remains on them-selves, thereby becoming even more self-centered, and so on and so forth… Therefore, my view is that it would be helpful if twelve-step groups opened themselves up to a socio-critical discourse or even to the possibility for participants to actively engage in a political debate as twelve-step groups. Otherwise the groups remain hermetic. But one has to admit to the groups that this hermeticism does not primarily emanate from them as such but is above all imposed on them by a compulsion to anonymity.

Conclusion

In my view, the above-discussed arguments for and against anonymity support the idea that neither anonymity nor addiction and addiction therapy can be considered as detached from the cultural-historical contexts in which they take place. On the contrary, anonymity as an obstacle to as well as a basis for successful addiction therapy is rooted in the social conditions of addiction and addiction therapy. In both cases, anonymity is a means to counteract imbalances, problems, and dangers. Either way, anonymity would not be needed in an ideal world in which neither stigmas nor selfishness existed, but since our world is not ideal and probably never will be, we will continue to need it. I think this also applies to scientific authorship, because through anonymity, we can arrive at a form of situatedness that goes beyond the author and emanates from the work itself.

Bibliography

Alcoholics Anonymous. *Zwölf Schritte und Zwölf Traditionen*. Munich: Anonyme Alkoholiker Interessengemeinschaft, 2005.

Alcoholics Anonymous World Services. *Alcoholics Anonymous*. 1st ed. New York: A. A. Grapevine and Alcoholics Anonymous, 1939.

Bachmann, Götz, Michi Knecht, and Andreas Wittel. "The Social Productivity of Anonymity." *ephemera* 17, no. 2 (2017): 241–58.

Barthes, Roland. "The Death of the Author." In *Image–Music–Text*, 142–48. New York: Dill and Wong, 1977.

Blumberg, Leonard. "The Ideology of a Therapeutic Social Movement: Alcoholics Anonymous." *Journal of Studies on Alcohol* 38, no. 11 (1977): 2122–43.

Bröckling, Ulrich. *Das unternehmerische Selbst: Soziologie einer Subjektivierungsform*. Frankfurt: Suhrkamp, 2007.

Brodnig, Ingrid. *Der unsichtbare Mensch: Wie die Anonymität im Internet unsere Gesellschaft verändert*. Wien: Czernin Verlag, 2013.

Coleman, Gabriella. *Hacker, Hoaxer, Whistleblower, Spy: The Many Faces of Anonymous*. London: Verso, 2014.

de Tocqueville, Alexis. *Democracy in America*. Vol. 2. 1840. New York: Vintage, 1980.

Foucault, Michel. "What Is an Author?" In *Language, Counter-Memory, Practice*, 124–77. New York: Cornell University Press, 1977.

Frois, Caterina. *The Anonymous Society: Identity, Transformation and Anonymity in 12 Steps*. Cambridge: Cambridge Scholars, 2009.

Fromm, Erich. *Die Kunst des Liebens*. Stuttgart: Deutscher Taschenbuch Verlag, 2004.

Froomkin, A. Michael. "From Anonymity to Identification." *Journal of Self-Regulation and Regulation* 1, no. 1 (2015): 121–38.

Haraway, Donna. *Modest_Witness@Second_Millennium.FemaleMan©_Meets_OncoMouse*. New York: Routledge, 1997.

Haraway, Donna. "Situated Knowledges: The Science Question in Feminism and the Privilege of Partial Perspective." *Feminist Studies* 14, no. 3 (1998): 575–99.

Helm, Paula. (2018). "Sobriety versus Abstinence: How 12-Stepper Negotiate Recovery across Groups." *Addiction Research and Theory* 27, no. 1 (2018): 29–36.

Hindman, Jane. "Making Writing Matter: Using 'the Personal' to Recover(y) an Essential(ist) Tension in Academic Discourse." *College English* 64 (2001): 88–107.

The Invisible Committee. *The Coming Insurrection*. Los Angeles, CA: Semiotext(e), 2009.

Narcotics Anonymous. *Narcotics Anonymous Handbook*. Los Angeles: Narcotics Anonymous Publishing, 1957.

Nissenbaum, Helen. "The Meaning of Anonymity in an Information Age." *Information Society* 15 (1999): 141–44.

Ohm, Paul. "Broken Promises of Privacy: Responding to the Surprising Failure of Anonymization." *UCLA Law Review* 57 (2010): 1701–77.

Shore, Cris, and Laura McLauchlan. "'Third Mission' Activities, Commercialisation and Academic Entrepreneurs." *Social Anthropology* 20, no. 3 (2012): 267–86.

Stapelfeldt, Gerhard. *Der Aufbruch des konformistischen Geistes: Thesen zur Kritik der neoliberalen Universität*. Hamburg: Kova, 2007.

Thiel, Thorsten. "Anonymität und Demokratie." *Forschungsjournal Soziale Bewegungen* 30, no. 2 (2017): 152–61.

Tournier, Robert. "Alcoholics Anonymous as Treatment and as Ideology." *Journal of Studies on Alcohol* 40, no. 3 (1979): 230–39.

Appendix: The Twelve Steps of Narcotics Anonymous

1. We admitted that we were powerless over our addiction—that our lives had become unmanageable.
   People battling addiction must admit that they have no control over the illness. As a result, they have lost power over many aspects of their lives.

2. We came to believe that a power greater than ourselves could restore us to sanity.
   Whether you are an agnostic, an atheist, or a believer, trusting a higher power could help you turn your life around.

3. We made a decision to turn our will and our lives over to the care of "god" as we understood him.
   It is important to understand the significance of a higher power in overcoming addiction. Through step three, people with addiction turn their lives over to this superior entity.

4. We made a searching and fearless moral inventory of ourselves.
   People with addiction should reflect on their lives, honestly evaluating their past. Evaluating past mistakes could steer people toward recovery.

5. We admitted to "god," to ourselves, and to another human being the exact nature of our wrongs.
   After evaluating past mistakes, the next step asks people battling addiction to admit to the root of past wrongdoings. Sharing the nature of these mistakes with oneself, loved ones, and a higher power is an important step toward recovery.

6. We were entirely ready to have "god" remove all these defects of character.
   Individuals with addiction should prepare for their higher power to eliminate their addictive behaviors.

7. We humbly asked "god" to remove our shortcomings.
   People with addiction allow a higher power to eliminate character flaws. It is important, however, that they separate themselves from factors that influence addictive behaviors.

8. We made a list of all persons we had harmed and became willing to make amends to them all.

   Addiction strains relationships and harms loved ones. The addicted person should make a list of those whom they have wronged and be willing to admit their past transgressions.

9. We made direct amends to such people wherever possible, except when to do so would injure them or others.

   Individuals should find time to apologize to those they have wronged in the past, except when doing so would cause further harm. They should tell the truth about past actions and offer a genuine apology.

10. We continued to take personal inventory and when we were wrong promptly admitted it.

    The tenth step promotes vigilance against triggers. People with addiction must address their addictive behaviors should they arise. Taking a personal inventory should become a daily process.

11. We sought through prayer and/or meditation to improve our conscious contact with "god" as we understood "him/her," praying only for knowledge of "his/her" will for us and the power to carry that out.

    This step provides daily spiritual maintenance. Maintaining a relationship with a higher power can help a person with addiction recovery.

12. Having had a "spiritual awakening" as the result of these steps, we tried to carry this message to addicts, and to practice these principles in all our affairs.

    This "spiritual awakening" allows people in recovery to share their techniques with those suffering from addiction. Helping others through these tough times is a significant aspect of NA's twelve-step program.

Speak Their Endless Names

> **Name, No Name, Many Names**
> Call them if they can hear you
> Look for them deep down
> Call them if they can hear you
> Tell them the meaning of their names
> Speak their endless names
> Speak their endless names
>
> Dagmawi Yimer
> *Asmat—Names in Memory of All Victims of the Sea*

I

To give the thing a name, to give people a name. To spell the name. To write down the name. To register the name. To identify things, to identify people with their names. To separate things from each other, to separate people from each other, to separate things from people, individual things, individual people. To partition things, to partition people, to classify things, to categorize them, to order, to sort them out, to assess them. To list the names, to define people, things, as individuals, to mark them, hold them, hierarchize them, to press them into service and turn them into value.

The register of the name is the patterning register of individuality and, at the same time, that of sedentariness and possession. It rests on an entire metaphysics of possessive individualism as the unquestioned foundation of all existence. The settled, possessing, and registered individual is proper; it is founded on appropriation and property, on the perpetual guard against expropriation, and it is also self-proper. The proper name constantly reminds us of this self-ownership. The "real danger … in the face of dispossession" consists in "the recourse to self-possession," write Stefano Harney and Fred Moten on the first page of their book *The Undercommons*.[1] If dispossession presents the greatest problem for the individual, the danger for that—before the individual, all around, under, and beyond it—is self-ownership. The problem is not that something is imposed or taken away from the self, but that the self itself is imposed.[2] The appropriation of the self in the proper name is the final consequence of the register of individuality, sedentariness, and possession.

Can we escape the imposition of the self? Can there be a form of flight from self-appropriation, from self-possession, a form of deregistration of the proper name, a form of "stealing oneself"?[3] Can this flight from the register of names, individuals, and property be prevented from developing into a dehumanizing and disenfranchising deindividuation?

Perhaps, before this last question, a clarification of the relationship between individuation and deindividuation is necessary. Even if, as Fred Moten writes in *The Universal Machine*, deindividuation, when combined with mechanization, is a genocidal operation, it is by no

[1] Stefano Harney and Fred Moten, *The Undercommons: Fugitive Planning and Black Study* (Wivenhoe, NY: Minor Compositions, 2013), 17.

[2] Ibid., 127.

[3] Ibid., 40.

means in opposition to the individual: precisely at this "intersection, individuation and de-individuation orbit one another as mutual conditions of im/possibility operating in and as the frigid mechanics of an indifference machine. The genocidal erasure of entanglement and difference is the culmination, and not the refusal, of the metaphysics of individuation."[4] Possessive individualism and deindividuation form a whole, and they are based on the separation of things, of people, of names, on their division, which first makes them indivisible, individuals.

[4] Fred Moten, *The Universal Machine* (Durham, NC: Duke University Press, 2018), xiii.

[5] Marco Deseriis, *Improper Names* (Minneapolis: University of Minnesota, 2015).

II

To escape the register of the name, to elude your own name, the property of the name, from the proper name, to suppress the name. Anonymity is the deliberately chosen mode of appearance of a subject, usually an individual, who negates his or her name. N. N., no name. This negation can have a tactical protective function or some sort of conceptual background; it remains the decision of a subject, with all the problematic consequences of authorship that subsists in the negation of negation and in the desire to look at the denied face, to look behind the mask, to uncover the negated name. N. N. as a *nomen nominandum* clearly carries this desire within itself, as a name that has not yet been named, as a name to be named, as a name that will yet be named.

But there are also less subjective and more complex forms of namelessness in which anonymity opens up a sphere of the no-longer-only-individual, the more-than-individual, the transindividual. In Marco Deseriis's book *Improper Names*, he suggested applying Gilbert Simondon's concept of transindividuation to the collective pseudonyms that have evolved over the last two hundred years in all their diversity as concrete practices of defection from proper names.[5] In a way, an "improper name" does not suit its allocated place, and it infiltrates the logic of authenticity and identity: "An improper name is improper not only because it lacks manners or propriety of behavior, … but because it fails to label and circumscribe a clearly defined domain."[6] Against the political technology of the proper name, improper names "provide anonymity," "fail to designate clearly identifiable referents," and "make it difficult for authorities to track down specific individuals."[7] And finally, in the era of name capital between individual and collective brands, improper names are above all unappropriated names, names that cannot be appropriated, that cannot be turned into value.

Even if the term "collective pseudonyms" evokes something different, it is about more than just the transition from the individual to the communal, from the individual to the collective subject, about more than just the interrelating of individuals, of mere interindividuality: "In order for a psycho-social transduction to occur, an individual cannot connect with other individuals as an already constituted individual, which means through preconstituted roles and functional interactions, such as are typical of an inter-individual relationship."[8] In other words, transindividuation is less about establishing a relationship between preexistent individuals or passing via individuals to form a community, and more about the prior move of not starting from fixed attributions, whether individual or collective. Collective pseudonyms can be anything, "the same alias by organized collectives, affinity groups, and individual authors."[9]

In *Improper Names*, Deseriis explores various historical practices of infiltrating proper names—such as the Luddites in the nineteenth century, or multiple names from the second half of the twentieth century, for example, Allen Smithee, Luther Blissett, Monty Cantsin, and Karen Eliot—with the aim of giving expression to the transductive practices of Anonymous, especially between 2005 and 2011. He analyzes their early raids and pranks up to their involvement in the political events of the Arab Spring and the Occupy movement. The hacktivist experience of Anonymous was always "between

[6] Ibid., 3.

[7] Ibid., 24.

[8] Marco Deseriis, "The Politics of Condividuality," *Techecologies*, transversal texts, March 2018.

[9] Deseriis, *Improper Names*, 3.

the power of mastering technology proper to hacking and the cooperative competences required by activism.... [W]hile in the period from 2008 to 2010, the transductive relation between these two poles expresses itself as a tension between the ethical nature of hacktivism and the amoral character of the lulz, beginning in 2011, this tension transmutes into a tension between the embodied, slow-paced, and democratic politics of social movements and the disembodied, fast-paced, and elitist politics of computer hacking."[10]

Anonymous's transindividual focus can be seen precisely in this conjunction/disjunction between concrete and abstract machines, occupations of squares and online actions. "In Simondonian terms these campaigns and operations are not an extension of an already individuated collective of enunciation but *constitute* the assemblage Anonymous *through* its antagonistic relationship to the proprietary control of information—be it in the form of the state secret or intellectual property."[11] The trans- in transindividual in Anonymous's actions around the Arab Spring is to be understood less as a connection between human actors and the campaigns they conceive and undertake, and more as an assemblage of bodies, apparatuses, and social machines, one that constitutes and reconstitutes itself in the campaigns, one that attacks the connection between property and individuality both in its form and in its content.

And yet, both in the theory of transindividuality and in the practices of Anonymous, the remainder of an aforementioned problem remains: in the negation of the individual, in the desire to transcend the individual, a residue of individuality still persists. The flight into anonymity tends to remain in the register of individuality, sometimes in its apparent opposition register, collectivity, or even in that of multiple names, and of multitude, insofar as it adopts a unified name. Here, however, what is needed is neither unification nor negation nor opposition but instead apposition, and

[10] Ibid., 198.

[11] Deseriis, "Politics of Condividuality."

the flight from self-possession can only be understood as primary: first immanent flight, then possibly a self beyond appropriation. The "radical being beside itself" of "undercommon appositionality" is always primary.[12]

III

Name follows on name. By no means is this a list read aloud; it is instead a recital, an interpellation, a reiteration of the souls that have died in the Mediterranean. In a middle of the world, in the Medi-terraneum, in the mare nostrum, as the Romans called it, in "our sea." The sea that should belong to us, the Romans, to us, the Europeans, to us, the civilized, is a territory of death. At the same time, it is a diffuse territory of flight and desire, a condividual territory that carries all sorts of things with it, things, individuals, names, but does not operate in the dominant register of separation and appropriation.[13] Far more than mere "international waters," it is a tide that leaves nations and their in-between behind, tidal waves, currents, the raging middle of the Mediterranean.

The female voice of Eden Getachew Zerihun, which strings together the names in Dagmawi Yimer's short film *Asmat—Names in Memory of All Victims of the Sea*, sounds strong yet fragile. She doesn't count the names; she emphasizes them evenly, giving each name the emphasis and presence it deserves, even though one name must be said six times because six of this name died in the catastrophe of Lampedusa on October 3, 2013: "Aman, Aman, Aman, Aman, Aman, Aman: He is peace."[14]

The recurring and yet singular meaning of the name, the many names. The return of the name, the anonymous lists and counts of dead and missing snatched. "Names without bodies," as Sandro Mezzadra writes, "that tell of a multitude of lives and stories, destroyed at the borders of Europe. For one of the defining characteristics of the women, men and children on their way across the

[12] Harney and Moten, *Undercommons*, 96.

[13] For an explanation of sexual violence and domination through partition in and around the Mediterranean, as the latter appeared on the occasion of the first ancient uses of a concept of dividuality in the comedies of Plautus and Terenz, see Gerald Raunig, *Dividuum: Machinic Capitalism and Molecular Revolution*, vol. 1, trans. Aileen Derieg (South Pasadena, CA: Semiotext[e], 2016), 25–36.

[14] Yimer, *Asmat*.

Mediterranean—as well as on their way through many other border regions—is to be anonymous, nameless. To restore the irreducible singularity of every existence is the unconditional gesture of resistance to which *Asmat-Names* calls us."[15] In the Mediterranean, names line up along a dividing line of danger, often of death. They are bound together in the irreducible singularity of which Mezzadra writes. Bound together by the bond of the dividing line—not as part of a list in the individual register of individuality—this singularity returns in the names.

They are thus no longer pre- or transindividual but "transdividual," no longer collective as a certain number of certain individuals but countless "condividual."[16] "Endless names" that must be spoken, sung in lament, names that must be interpreted. "Endless names," which in recital are not simply added together, always n 1, always dividuated, always multiple. Do not write down the names, do not register, do not identify, do not count, do not sort them out, do not pattern them, do not classify them. Recite the names, the many names, the improper names without end, sing them, call them, repeat them, give the names a meaning (anew), deep down and all about and around. And with the names draw lines to condividuality, to unsettled dividuality, to a soloist-singular refusal of property, of being-individual, of being-one.

"The soloist refuses to be one," writes Fred Moten in one of the three volumes of his trilogy, "consent[s] not to be a single being." She is always already a swarm, and "the swarm is always only on the way. Its *Unmündigkeit*, translated as 'minority' or 'immaturity,' is, more literally, unprotectedness or, perhaps, what is to be ungoverned, as what is out of hand or unhanded... in having been handed; not in hand, not in good hands, ungrasped, un-owned, passed around."[17] Not appropriated and not to be appropriated, "not possessed" and not possessing, unsettled, not even possessing oneself, "passed around."

[15] Sandro Mezzadra, "We Have a Ship," *transversal texts* (blog), October 2018.

[16] See Raúl Sánchez Cedillo, "Das transdividuelle Netzwerksystem," in *Technökologien*, ed. Christoph Brunner, Raimund Minichbauer, Kelly Mulvaney, and Gerald Raunig (Vienna: transversal texts, 2018), 23–51 (see the Spanish original, "Idea de un sistema red transdividual," at; the final chapter of Raunig, *Dividuum*, 182–92; and Deseriis, "Politics of Condividuality."

[17] Moten, *Universal Machine*, x.

Kant's notion of "self-incurred minority" is, with Moten, turned around until it interprets indebtedness and immaturity only as condividual connectedness, as vulnerability, as mutual indebtedness, and even interprets the double moral-economic significance of guilt and debt as ungovernable, refractory, never-ripening sprawl—the more names, the better.[18]

Disobedient names, ill prepared to become appendages to individuals, names such as those with which Rubia Salgado ended her speech to revive the Vienna Thursday demonstrations on October 4, 2018.

> You want a samba, I am a haikai
> You want reason, I am wine
> You want meat, I am poison
> You want pleasure, I am pain
> You want laughing, I bite
> You want performance, I am a hammock
> You want order, I am chaos
> You want family, I am desire
> You want property, I am an exchange market
> You want names, I am a woman
> You want a woman, I am a eunuch
> You want a eunuch, I am a lesbian
> You want borders, I'm a bolt cutter
> You want murder, I'm the sea rescue
> You want police, I am a clown
> You want horses, I am a dragon
> You want desert, I am a mountain
> You want a mountain, I am a world
> You want the world, I am Linz
> You want Linz, I am Rio
> You want Rio, I am the Mediterranean
> You want to die, I scream life.
> You want silence, I am voice
> You want me, I am we
> You want Thursday, we are a demo![19]

[18] See also Harney and Moten, *Undercommons*, 27.

[19] Rubia Salgado, "Willst du Samba," *transversal texts* (blog), October 2018.

If you want names, you will get many names, names without end, names that cannot be counted, exactly those singular names that do not belong to anyone, not even yourself, names on a dividual line, names that are not suitable for sedentariness, names that will never be yours and mine, never individual, not even anonymous.

Bibliography

Deseriis, Marco. *Improper Names*. Minneapolis: University of Minnesota, 2015.

Deseriis, Marco. "The Politics of Condividuality." *Techecologies*, transversal texts, March 2018. https://transversal.at/transversal/0318/deseriis/en.

Harney, Stefano, and Fred Moten. *The Undercommons: Fugitive Planning and Black Study*. Wivenhoe, NY: Minor Compositions, 2013.

Moten, Fred. *The Universal Machine*. Durham, NC: Duke University Press, 2018.

Epigraph: Dagmawi Yimer, *Asmat—Names in Memory of All Victims of the Sea*, short film, 17:19 (Rome: AMM, 2014), https://vimeo.com/114343040.

Bitcoin Anonymous?
Of Trust in Code and Paper

This is a guide, not a critique. I offer a short overview and step-by-step introductions to purchasing, owning, and spending Bitcoins anonymously. Going through the steps, it quickly becomes clear that anonymity is not a feature of Bitcoin technology but a practical achievement that requires the orchestration of people, technologies, and regulations. Using Bitcoins anonymously requires one to disconnect, going analog and into safe hiding places. Further, it becomes clear that using the peer-to-peer service anonymously brings a renewed reliance on third parties, parties that are even less regulated than the traditional financial providers that Bitcoin set out to make redundant.

The Problem of Trust

Digitally enabled payments such as online, credit card, mobile phone, or RFID payments have quickly gained prevalence, with some governments pushing to restrict the amount of circulating cash in the name of security and accountability. For centuries, cash made anonymous payments possible. Conventional electronic transactions by contrast generate a wealth of financial data, revealing location, sender and recipient ID, and the date, amount, frequency, and time of purchase. These sensitive data are revealing and therefore valuable to a range of actors with interests as diverse and diffuse as fighting crime and terrorism, industrial espionage, population surveillance, or commercial data aggregation. Paying digitally, for example, comes with the risk that health insurance companies or employers might gain insights about the consumption of medication, cigarettes, or particular books understood to indicate political affiliations. Digital payment technologies, then, are no doubt convenient for those who have access, but they also bring unprecedented traceability, radically undermining the possibility of anonymity.

Bitcoin is the first digitally enabled monetary system that promises to provide the convenience of digital payments while retaining anonymity. This is possible because Bitcoins work without a centralized banking system or intermediaries, allowing a direct exchange between buyers and sellers. The decentralized network at the core of Bitcoin technology thus theoretically allows anonymous payments. At the same time, all transactions are publicly traceable and permanently archived. Further, you have to be connected to the internet, and any connection online can be potentially monitored. So, using Bitcoins, one still leaves traces that, with the right expertise, can be combined into patterns to identify payers, receivers, and purchases. It is no wonder, then, that the promise of an anonymous payment infrastructure frequently associated with Bitcoins and other cryptocurrencies leads to conceptual and practical confusion.

In Code We Trust

Bitcoins were born out of the financial crisis of 2008–9. This crisis, the story goes, created a crisis of trust in the international banking system, making it possible to seriously and effectively question the financial system, its governing institutions, and their capacity to generate and maintain the trust that ultimately gives currencies their value. Bitcoin, the story continues, is the first and to date most successful cryptocurrency. It was, according to popular accounts, developed in 2008 by a programmer known under the pseudonym Satoshi Nakamoto. This, however, is not the place to deal with the genesis of Bitcoin. Let me simply note that Bitcoin promised to replace fallible and more or less self-interested institutions with decentralized computing power. Given the severity of the recession-induced crisis of trust, and the new speculation opportunities provided by Bitcoin, it is no wonder that Bitcoin's promise to decouple monetary value from institutional trust quickly gained traction. Why should we place our trust in the capacity of central banks to maintain the value of our currencies, the advocates ask, when distributed computing can provide a viable alternative? And why should banks continue to control currency flows when they have failed so catastrophically?

Bitcoins' libertarian premise is to create a currency-trust dependency, in which trust in a third party is replaced by trust in an encrypted computer network that allows direct transactions between parties. The simple conception of this technology is that it eliminates the middlemen and their fees and promises to reduce the costs of doing business and to mitigate corruption inside of those intermediating institutions such as states, central banks, and other financial institutions.[1] Trusting in Bitcoins,

[1] Paul Vigna and Michael J. Casey, *The Age of Cryptocurrency: How Bitcoin and the Blockchain Are Challenging the Global Economic Order* (New York: Picador, 2016), 5f; and Jörg Platzer, *Bitcoin – Kurz und Gut* (Beijing: O'Reilly, 2014).

in any case, is to trust in blockchain, the underlying infrastructure behind it.

Blockchain, in short, is a global decentralized database that tracks the overall number of Bitcoins as well as all transactions.[2] The blockchain can be thought of as a public digital ledger that ensures that no Bitcoin is forged and that every Bitcoin is issued only once and stored in only one address. "Decentralized" means that the database is not located on any one computer or server but distributed over a large number of participating computers. Having a copy of the database on many synchronized computers ensures that the database is consistent throughout the network while providing a mechanism to identify attempts to tamper with it.

Bitcoin users store Bitcoins in and exchange Bitcoins between Bitcoin addresses. Bitcoin addresses are pseudonymous identifiers that are not necessarily linked to a civic identity. This means that anyone can own multiple addresses. Each address consists of a public and a private key. The entries in the blockchain database, or public ledger, that are used to track Bitcoins are known as the public key because they are accessible to anyone locked into the system. Each public key is complemented by a private key that ensures that all transactions are encrypted. This private key is known only to the owner of the Bitcoin address, making sure that no unauthorized transfers between Bitcoin addresses are made. Paying with Bitcoins works by sending Bitcoins from one address to another. When a payment is made, details of the transactions are shared throughout the decentralized network. Any inconsistency between the transfer data and the distributed ledger that is the blockchain will cause the transfer to fail. This check allows transactions to be made between people or companies without resorting to intermediaries in a process also called peer-to-peer currency.[3] The integrity of the underlying cryptography is essential to Bitcoins, which is why Bitcoin is known as a cryptocurrency. The combination of a public, auto-

[2] Blockchain is used to track Bitcoins, but the technology is not specific to Bitcoins and can be used to track many other kinds of units and transactions.

[3] Rico Grimm, "Das Geheimnis des Bitcoins," *Krautreporter*, December 13, 2017; and Kilian Thalhammer, "Der Blockchain Kompass," *Payment and Banking*, Fintech Banking, March 1, 2018.

matically updated ledger and encryption effectively operationalizes trust as a computing function. This of course rests on the assumption that we trust the code, which is addressed partially at least by making the code accessible so that it too is open to public distributed scrutiny and development.

[4] Husam Al Jahwaheri, Mashael Al Sabah, Yazan Boshmaf, and Aiman Erbad, "When a Small Leak Sinks a Great Ship: Deanonymizing Tor Hidden Service Users through Bitcoin Transactions Analysis," version 2, arXiv, April 11, 2018.

Anonymous Technology vs. Anonymous Practice

Blockchain-based Bitcoins are pseudonymous because using Bitcoin relies on public identifiers that are not necessarily linked to civic identities. Practically, this means that Bitcoin transactions are unlike cash, which can never be completely transparent, and unlike conventional digital transfers, which are never anonymous. Anonymity is not a function of Bitcoin or blockchain technology but a practical achievement that rests on the crucial link between pseudonymous Bitcoin addresses and civic identities. Neither blockchains nor Bitcoins "create" anonymity. Any practice that potentially allows anyone to link addresses to civic identities can undo anonymity. Bitcoin users have been successfully identified, for example, by matching Bitcoin datasets with data from Twitter or BitcoinTalk forums. This means that anonymous Bitcoin use requires an awareness of identifiable correlations between the different datasets and the traces that one leaves behind. This is especially important since the blockchain provides a public record of all activity, leaving permanent traces of any errors that might allow identification now or in the future.[4] Basic measures such as using a VPN provider and a Tor router, as well as avoiding the use of identifying devices such as smartphones, can help to make linking Bitcoin addresses to civic identities more challenging. In addition to these basic but often neglected and in practice quite cumbersome measures, this guide outlines steps that can be taken to acquire, keep, and spend Bitcoins in relative anonymity.

Bitcoins Anonymous 1: Purchasing

To an extent, all Bitcoin transactions take place peer to peer without third-party mediation, but there are services known as exchange platforms that help to make this process simpler and more convenient. Most, such as kraken.com, are classified as financial service providers and are subject to state regulation, which means, among other things, that using them requires identifying information such as address, email address, real name, and bank account or ID. Further, exchanges are frequently under pressure from law enforcement to share data and often attract hackers. Given this, the most reliable way to purchase Bitcoins without identification requires physical interaction and the usage of cash as the basis for the exchange. Over-the-counter (OTC) transactions and crypto ATMs are the two common ways of purchasing Bitcoins offline.

Over-the-Counter Transactions

Platforms such as localBitcoin.com list local providers where one can purchase Bitcoins "over the counter" in cash. OTC transactions require a physical meeting and usually imply high service fees. The PaySafeCard service provides an alternative way of purchasing Bitcoins in cash. PaySafeCard is a financial service that allows users to buy vouchers through a broad network of retailers, such as supermarkets in more than forty countries, that can then be used to purchase goods online. Originally conceived to allow online purchase without the need for credit cards, the anonymous system can also be used to acquire Bitcoins over the counter.

Crypto ATMs

Crypto ATMs, which can now be found in more than seventy countries, allow users to purchase Bitcoins using card payment or cash deposits. Purchasing Bitcoin via cash deposit at a crypto ATM provides an alternative to OTC acquisition. Most crypto ATMs allow only the purchase of Bitcoins and other cryptocurrencies, while some also allow users to withdraw fiat currencies from Bitcoin deposits. Crypto ATMs generate a QR code that refers to the destination address, which can be used to transfer the Bitcoins to a paper wallet or an app. Purchasing Bitcoins via cash deposit, using a paper wallet, allows for the anonymous acquisition of Bitcoins. No identification or traceability to the identity of a person is possible in the exchange.[5]

[5] Kathrin Passig, "Zwei Kinotickets, ein Bier und zukünfigte Alpenchalets oder auch nicht," *Techniktagebuch*, October 3, 2017; see also Hans von der Hagen and Miriam Hauck, "Der lange Weg vom Bitcoin zum Euro," *Süddeutsche Online*, January 18.

> **Note:** Purchasing Bitcoins anonymously requires one to physically move and to switch between analog and digital infrastructures. Physically depositing money, of course, leaves potentially identifying traces in the physical and digital domain. Nonetheless, choosing the benefits of the anonymity of cash will pay off in the long run.

Bitcoins Anonymous 2: Keeping

No bank, service provider, or person is responsible for storing and securing Bitcoins except the owner. Having sole control over Bitcoins also leaves the entire responsibility for maintenance and storage with the owner. Bitcoins are commonly kept in Bitcoin wallets. Many people use multiple Bitcoin addresses. A wallet is software that bundles and helps to manage multiple Bitcoin addresses. Because of Bitcoin's open architecture and publicly accessible open source code, anyone can develop software to receive Bitcoins. As a result, the variety of applications and the fluctuation of tools are high. We can differentiate various wallet categories, depending on how the wallet is accessed—desktop wallet, mobile wallet, web wallet, in-browser wallet, paper wallet, hardware wallet—each offering different degrees of security and potential anonymity.

Each wallet is associated with a wallet ID, which is commonly linked to an email address. The wallet, like the Bitcoin addresses it holds, offers pseudonymity, a stable identifier that is not necessarily linked to a civic identity. That said, it is possible to deanonymize a wallet via the associated email address, by reconstructing the IP addresses someone uses to access it, or through bank data if provided.[6] Still, there are options to set up wallets anonymously. The mobile wallet Blockchain, for example, allows users to manage an anonymous wallet and their web server and requires nothing but an email address for registration. Using a temporary disposable email address should allow an anonymous setup if no identifying traces have been left in the process. Access to the wallets is password protected. A weak password might mean that someone can hack the wallet and steal the Bitcoins, while a more secure, thirty-two-character-long, random password will be hard to remember or will require additional services, such as a password manager or two-factor authentication, which in turn require that one share identifying data such as phone numbers or email addresses. Wallets also require a backup to prevent loss of Bitcoins in case of wallet loss or file corruption. The backup requires a recovery phrase (called a seed), which should be noted on paper and securely stored. Like the password, the recovery phrase creates another trace that needs to be carefully kept to retain security and anonymity.

[6] Thalhammer, "Der Blockchain Kompass."

The safest option for protecting your Bitcoins is to restrict access by keeping them offline when they are not needed for transactions. In Bitcoin speak, an offline wallet is known as a cold wallet. Hardware wallets and paper wallets offer two ways of keeping a cold wallet. A hardware wallet is a dedicated USB-drive-size minicomputer that is connected to the internet only when needed and protected by a master password, which again has to be managed and kept safe. It is possible to use hardware wallets for a direct payment without taking it online. It requires trust in the integrity of the hardware and the financial investment.

A paper wallet consists of QR codes printed on paper. The QR codes hold public and private encryption keys, effectively storing Bitcoins. QR codes can be generated from Bitcoins via an open source JavaScript client such as bitaddress.org. The generator allows the creation of the relevant QR codes in a safe manner and is run offline to prevent any interference. Users should be careful to delete any traces of the file on their computer, including printing cache, before reconnecting the computer to the internet. Users should also be aware that printers have internal memory (cache) that store what has been printed or copied. Anyone who gains access to the printer is therefore theoretically able to duplicate the relevant keys. An alternative is to write down the key by hand, making sure to keep the paper in a safe place to avoid loss due to theft, fire, or other destructive events.

> **Note:** The safest and most anonymous way to store digital cryptocurrencies requires writing the relevant codes and passwords on slips of paper, which in turn have to be kept safe and in a memorable location. Protection against digital attacks such as fraud, malware, or even economic competition within cryptocurrencies can best be countered with analogous security measures.

Bitcoins Anonymous 3: Spending

To pay with Bitcoins is to transfer Bitcoins from one address to another. After submitting the transfer information, it takes several minutes for the information to propagate through the network. If no inconsistencies, such as wrong keys, are detected, a new block is appended to the blockchain—the public ledger is updated, and the Bitcoins are transferred without the need for a third party.

Delivery addresses and other information shared during purchase might compromise anonymity. Public access to the blockchain poses another, more fundamental challenge to avoiding identification while transferring Bitcoins.

Making several payments from or to the same Bitcoin address allows for pattern analysis that can easily reveal one's identity. One way to obscure transactions is to use several Bitcoin addresses, effectively obfuscating purchasing data. Many Bitcoin wallets, like Electrum, offer the option of generating any number of new addresses to scatter traces and to minimize the build-up of recognizable patterns. Given the right expertise, however, it is possible to establish which addresses belong to the same wallet, which in turn makes it possible to analyze patterns across associated Bitcoin addresses. So-called Bitcoin mixers address this problem by making it a lot more difficult to trace transactions to particular wallets or Bitcoins.

Bitcoin mixers, or laundry services, such as CoinMixer combine Bitcoin transactions in a large pool. Payments are made from that pool after a delay and sent from new Bitcoin addresses. The mixing, delay, and change of address makes it extremely difficult to reconstruct transaction paths. CoinMixer and other services offer a range of features that minimize the risk of identification: users can choose different delays of up to 120 hours to increase the level of obfuscation; the service requires no account and is compatible with Tor browsers, if the user knows how to synchronize the port settings; and payout from the pool can be made from several new addresses to further reduce traceability. Bitcoin mixers issue cryptographic "Letters of Guarantee" that allow users to prove that the payment has actually been made, but there is no way to guarantee beforehand beyond trust that payments from the pool will actually be made, even if a mixing fee is payed to CoinMixer.

> **Note:** Spending Bitcoins anonymously requires third-party financial services, introducing and perhaps aggravating the problem of trust, which the peer-to-peer system promises to resolve. The additional interface leads to delays in payment, which limits practicability.

Bitcoins Anonymous 4: Adapting

This guide will be outdated quickly, because the steps described are reactions, workarounds, and adaptations of the internal and external regulation of Bitcoin functionality, both of which are subject to powerful interests and change.

The blockchain code that determines how cryptocurrencies are transferred, stored, encrypted, and generated is not fixed but under constant development. Changes cannot be made by any one individual because they require consensus among the participating developers. While this system is in principle egalitarian, it, like many egalitarian formations, tends to take plutocratic forms, granting weight to those with computing power and expertise, which tends to, earlier or later, align with financial power. This danger of plutocracy has been seen in the community and has led to new developments and new cryptocurrencies with specified purposes. So, you are responsible for tracking and comparing these developments under your own premises, whether anonymous, temporal, or financial. Trusting the code might well require working with and around it.

Cryptocurrency regulators such as banking supervisors or government institutions still seem uncertain how to best handle cryptocurrencies, oscillating between a desire to compete for new kinds of financial services and a desire for strict regulation. Some governments, such as Japan, declared Bitcoin legal tender; others, such as Switzerland, experiment with their own cryptocurrency, while yet others, such as Germany, have yet to establish an official position.[7] Regulatory decisions will hugely affect whether and how Bitcoin payments can be anonymous. The European legislature in particular is subjecting exchange platforms and online services to regulation. The European Financial Intelligence Unit, which is tasked with fighting corruption, financial crimes, and terrorist financing, forces the players to demand their customers'

[7] Felix Holtermann, "Krypto-Lobby legt Forderung vor," *Handelsblatt*, October 18, 2017.

civic identity.[8] One of the central promises of these currency systems is thus put under pressure: the guarantee of anonymity, in the sense of independence of identities, and the right of self-determination.

[8] Platzer, *Bitcoin*; and Mirko Dölle, "Ketten für Bitcoin: Wie Regierungen Kryptowährungen regulieren," *Heise*, March 2, 2018.

> **Note:** Cryptocurrency's potential for anonymous payments is not a function of the technology (narrowly defined); nor can it be achieved through conscientious practices alone, because it crucially depends on shifting and changing internal and external regulation.

In Code and Paper We Trust

This practical guide to purchasing, owning, and spending Bitcoins anonymously shows what it takes to act anonymously in a fully digitalized economy. Using Bitcoins anonymously is not built in or afforded by the infrastructure but requires the cunning making and cutting of connections. Doing so requires some skill, time, and money, and many will fail to use Bitcoins anonymously, messing up, leaving traces in the relentless archive of the blockchain that will make them identifiable, now or later. More interesting than reiterating the argument that anonymity is hard or impossible to achieve for the digital half-literate, which constitutes the majority of users, is to note that using Bitcoins safely and potentially anonymously requires us to disconnect from the internet whenever possible. The egalitarian digital dream of peer-to-peer relationships that is so well articulated and made practicable through Bitcoins is a dream of relationships that do not require institutional mediation. Following this guide, I conclude that this high-tech dream is best dreamed while freezing one's Bitcoins on paper under a pillow. Digital security and the possibility of anonymity rests on more or less safe physical storage that is out of circulation. Digital and analog action comes together in a way that defeats simplistic statements about either: neither is code everything, nor is paper dead. Analog data carriers such as paper, including paper money, are often declared redundant in dreams of digital mediation, but when it comes to retaining anonymity, they are not easily replaced.

> **Note:** The tension between the desire to make payments anonymously and independently of third-party providers, such as banks or mixers, and practicability is unresolved. Negotiating it remains an urgent task for individual users, service providers, and institutional regulators.

Acknowledgment

I would like to thank Julien McHardy. His careful and dedicated editing has contributed much to finalizing this guide and has helped to shape it linguistically and conceptually.

Bibliography

Al Jawaheri, Husam, Mashael Al Sabah, Yazan Boshmaf, and Aiman Erbad. "When a Small Leak Sinks a Great Ship: Deanonymizing Tor Hidden Service Users through Bitcoin Transactions Analysis." Version 2, arXiv, April 11, 2018. https://arxiv.org/abs/1801.07501.

Dölle, Mirko. "Ketten für Bitcoin: Wie Regierungen Kryptowährungen regulieren." *Heise*, March 2, 2018. https://www.heise.de/ct/ausgabe/2018-6-Wie-Regierungen-Kryptowaehrungen-regulieren-3980101.html.

Grimm, Rico. "Das Geheimnis des Bitcoins." *Krautreporter*, December 13, 2017. https://krautreporter.de/2223-das-geheimnis-des-bitcoins.

Holtermann, Felix. "Krypto-Lobby legt Forderung vor." *Handelsblatt*, October 18, 2017. http://www.handelsblatt.com/finanzen/maerkte/devisen-rohstoffe/regulierung-von-bitcoin-und-blockchain-krypto-lobby-legt-forderungen-vor/20471364-all.html.

Nakamoto, Satoshi. "Bitcoin: A Peer-to-Peer Electronic Cash System." Bitcoin.org. Accessed December 3, 2018. https://bitcoin.org/bitcoin.pdf.

Passig, Kathrin. "Zwei Kinotickets, ein Bier und zukünfigte Alpenchalets oder auch nicht." *Techniktagebuch*, October 3, 2017. https://techniktagebuch.tumblr.com/post/166006584297/3-oktober-2017.

Platzer, Jörg. *Bitcoin – Kurz und Gut*. Beijing: O'Reilly, 2014.

Thalhammer, Kilian. "Der Blockchain Kompass." *Payment and Banking*. Fintech Banking, March 1, 2018. https://paymentandbanking.com/der-blockchain-kompass/.

Vigna, Paul, and Michael J. Casey. *The Age of Cryptocurrency: How Bitcoin and the Blockchain Are Challenging the Global Economic Order*. New York: Picador, 2016.

Von der Hagen, Hans, and Miriam Hauck. "Der lange Weg vom Bitcoin zum Euro." *Süddeutsche Online*, January 18, 2018. http://www.sueddeutsche.de/wirtschaft/kryptowaehrungen-der-lange-weg-vom-bitcoin-zum-euro-1.3828930.

Anonymity Workshop

In 2017, we conducted an experience in the context of a school of art and design in Paris.[1] We proposed a workshop during which the students were asked to create projects anonymously.

This text is neither an artistic proposition nor an essay: it relates the pedagogical experience. This is why we describe the process we put in place, how it did or did not work, and so forth as a "how to," down-to-earth proposition. The images shown here document what happened.

[1] The École nationale supérieure des Arts Décoratifs (EnsAD).

Why?

What were the main questions and motivations to create the course?

We did not want to question anonymity in a theoretical manner, but wanted to instead experiment with it by putting in place a student-teacher relationship in which neither the teachers nor the students knew the identity of the authors of the projects developed.

As students, the creators are constantly scrutinized and evaluated by persons who are in a position of authority over them. The objectivity of the teacher to judge a project can be biased by this asymmetry. In our workshop, since it was impossible to know who had proposed what, the usual relation between student and teacher was questioned: the projects could be proposed by both teachers and students, or even by persons outside the art school.

The workshop aimed to experiment with anonymity in the creation process. Does anonymity give us more freedom to create? Are the projects more interesting when they can no longer be attributed to an identified person? Is it easier to discuss a project when the author's identity is protected? Does knowing a project's author induce a bias in the analysis? Can a production be enhanced if we do not know its author and that person's previous work?

It can be a frustrating exercise for art students to create something without ever being able to claim the benefit for themselves. Nevertheless, it seemed important to us to bring some humility into what can be produced in the school and to give pride of place to those people who voluntarily bring together knowledge and know-how in the service of all. The anonymity of creation can be seen as a way to place oneself in a context of exchange and sharing, in the same way as communities working for ethical purposes, for example, in the field of free software.

We asked the students to imagine projects they could not have developed under their real identity—within the limits permitted by the law. By working anonymously, we created a space for expression in which no one can point the finger at the productions. The most diverse subjects could be addressed, whether secret, shameful, or politically incorrect. They could find here a space for experimentation.

2 A subreddit is a thread on Reddit, an online forum with often viral content.

How?

We used a simple system, in which the students could either publish their work on a dedicated subreddit or put it in a physical anonymous box, located in the classroom.[2] In the first case, we showed them how to create an anonymous email address and an anonymous account on Reddit, as well as how to use specific platforms to share videos and images without being able to trace their origin. In the case of the physical box, creators had to hide from other students when submitting their work, or ask an accomplice to put it there for them (usually another student of the school, not involved in the workshop).

Fig. 78 The anonymous box.

Each week, we opened the cardboard box and the
subreddit to see the proposed projects and discuss them
with the students. Although we did know the students,
since we could not tell who had proposed which project,
we were able to discuss the projects collectively
with the group without addressing anyone in particular.

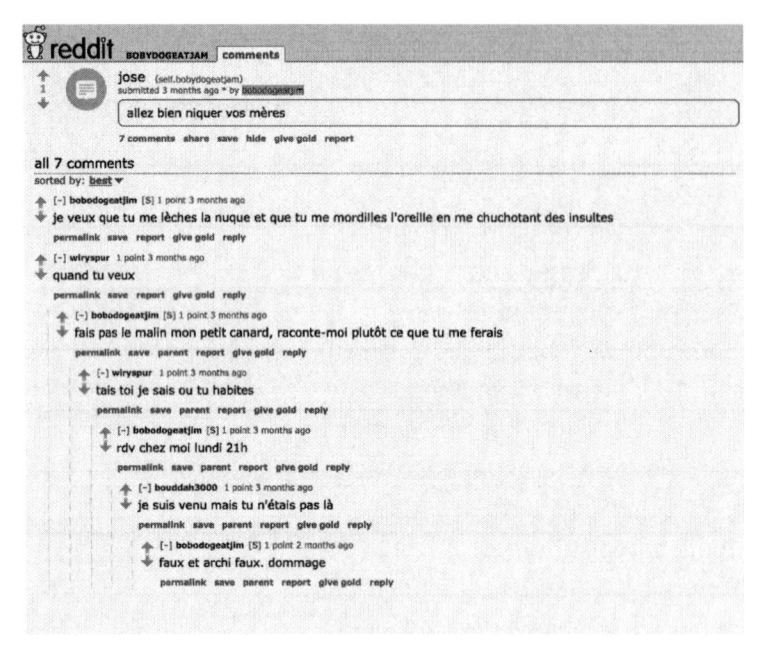

Fig. 79 Sample of a discussion on the Reddit page:

- [bobodogeatjim] I want you to lick my neck and chew on my ear by whispering insults to me
- [wiryspur] Whenever you want
- [bobodogeatjim] Don't get smart, my little duck, tell me what you'd do to me
- [wiryspur] Shut up, I know where you live
- [bobodogeatjim] See you at my place monday at 9pm
- [bouddah3000] I came to your place but you weren't there
- [bobodogeatjim] false and very false. So sad

This process also enabled us to finally address issues—
such as privacy on the internet, license-free software,
sharing, intimacy, activism, surveillance and so forth—
that we could discuss with students using the same
subreddit that they used to post their projects. This page
was also the place to question how the process of
teaching affected them and the projects. To discuss these
issues with the students, we invited the collective RYBN
and curator Daniela Silvestrin.

It was also important for us to ask students to consider the importance they attach to claiming a creation as their own. Can we, or should we, let a creation be self-sufficient, without necessarily being able to identify the author's previous steps to decipher its meaning?

This workshop was a source of motivation for us teachers to create a pedagogical process that questions the classical principles of evaluating and monitoring students. How are we supposed to tutor a project when we don't know its author? How can we grade anonymous studenta? How can we interact with them? These questions had to be unraveled.

The issue of project monitoring proved to be more complex than expected. The proposed projects were often, at first, quite mysterious, as the projects of art school students can be. In a usual face-to-face situation, a discussion allows students to clarify their intentions. But since the authors could not explain their work without unmasking themselves, we had to try to guess in which way the project was intended. This problem also had a great advantage: if the project did not awaken any ideas, thoughts, or feelings among the other participants, the student could not get

Fig. 80 An artists talks about the artist group's project "The Great Offshore," an investigation into the depth of the offshore industry.

away with just smooth talk. He or she was forced to make
an effort to create a more explicit or powerful proposition.
Another problem was the difficulty of understanding,
from one week to the next, why a project was changing
toward a particular direction.

Fig. 81 A guest at the workshop trying to decipher an
anonymous student's proposition.

Regarding grading, we first imagined a system that
would allow us to give a grade to each anonymous project
and then, still without knowing who the author is, to
cross-reference this list with another, encrypted list. But
we quickly opted for a much simpler solution: give
all students the same grade. All the participants were
granted a 15/20, which means "Good."

The anonymous dialogue went smoothly, involving
the whole group. It was pleasant to avoid the frontal
and individual relationship that tutoring often takes
in art school, in favor of more collective discussions. The
discussions were more clear cut, more sincere.

Output

The workshop lasted for two months, during which twenty or so projects were proposed.

It was interesting for us to see what kinds of effects of anonymity the students chose to work with: for example, to speak more freely in an anonymous chat platform (Anonymous Love); to use anonymity as a means to create hierarchical power structures (Buddha3000); to subvert or disrupt systems of control and surveillance (HaCkeD cAms and Libérer Bfahi); to reflect on names and naming as a means of deanonymizing things and people (Édition sans nom); to even use anonymity as a protection to provoke, threaten, or play with others (Contrebande).

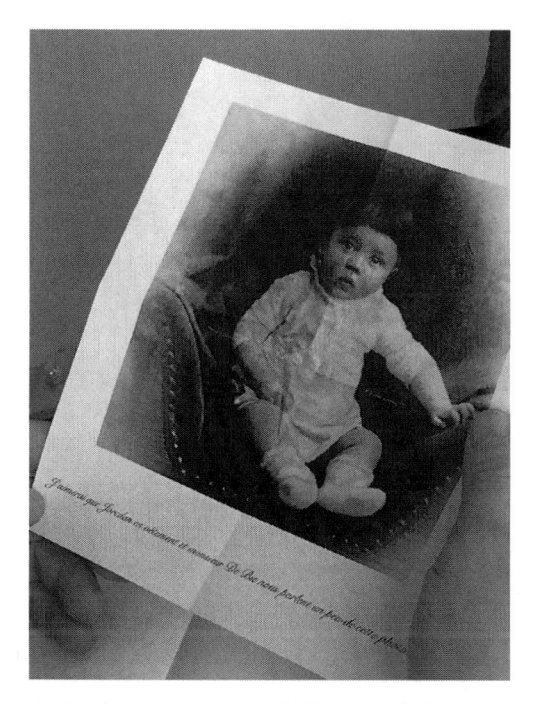

Fig. 82 The caption reads: "I would like Jordan (fashion design student) and M De Bie (teacher) to tell us a little bit about this picture."

First day, first envelope, first clue: a black and white photograph depicting a small child on a chair with a written note asking a particular teacher and student to describe the photo. It created a somewhat uncomfortable climate of questioning in which the student and teacher wondered what connection there could be between themselves, or between them and this image. Are they described as babies? Why this baby in particular? Is this some kind of revenge? An artistic proposition? The beginning of a performance?

This example is representative of the different elements we received and tried to decipher in the following weeks. Often, for students, the idea of proposing a secret project is synonymous with mystery and subterfuge, blurring the lines and making it difficult to read.

Here are some of the projects submitted.

Fig. 83 We had to make a list of the projects. We had a hard time counting them: is this one a joke or a project? Is Bouddah3000 the same person as Bouddha-3000? etc.

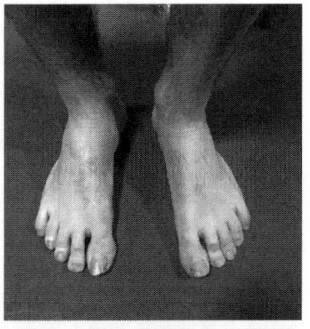

Fig. 84 Buddha3000 project.

Buddha3000 is the messiah of a sect called "Community of the Spiritual Path," who seeks to gather disciples among the participants of the anonymity workshop. He launches requests that will be more or less followed by students. Buddha3000 sometimes provides the necessary material to execute a request, for example, candles and incense. At other times, he asks us to perform tasks that require a greater effort, such as taking photos of anonymous bare feet. A problem raised by a participant is that Buddha3000 addresses students by their real names, not by their pseudonyms. This was described as embarrassing, since it did not allow anyone to go very far in the possible actions because the members of the cult were not anonymous. The project ended with a full-scale temple of the Buddha3000 sect, set in the students' foyer. On the wall were displayed the pictures of the good and bad actions of the supposed disciples, as well as their judgment by Buddha3000.

Fig. 85 Fashion Goddess project.

The Fashion Goddess project proposes different kinds of hoods to mask the identity of the person wearing them. These are placed in the box and are intended for various students of the workshop, designated by their names.

HaCkeD cAms/Œillères (HaCkeD cAms/Blinkers): This project (by u/Carytogripho, assisted by u/basins) aims to establish a detailed participatory mapping of all the surveillance apparatuses present in the school. Participants record all the detectors, cameras, sirens, and wi-fi terminals. This map is then used for other students' projects, including the one that describes the exfiltration of a fictional character named Bfahi (see below).

MarcPartoucheTV: This parodic project uses the name of the school principal (Marc Partouche) to create a fake TV channel that addresses the students and teachers in the workshop. This character was created when the students began to question (anonymously, via Reddit) the possibility of hacking the RFID reader from the school's new front door. He leaves a letter and video messages in which he literally and figuratively plays with the figure of Mr. Partouche.

Fig. 86 MarcPartoucheTV project.

Libérer Bfahi (Free Bfahi): Bfahi is a fictional character, supposed to be a prisoner of the school, locked in the principal's office. A photo of the principal's office window is provided as proof of this incarceration. The curtains are drawn, and almost at ground level, a strange hand (with six fingers) tries to open them. Other anonymous photos and testimonies detail its existence.

Fig. 87 Libérer Bfahi (Free Bfahi) project.

E — DELIGHT
Anonymity Workshop

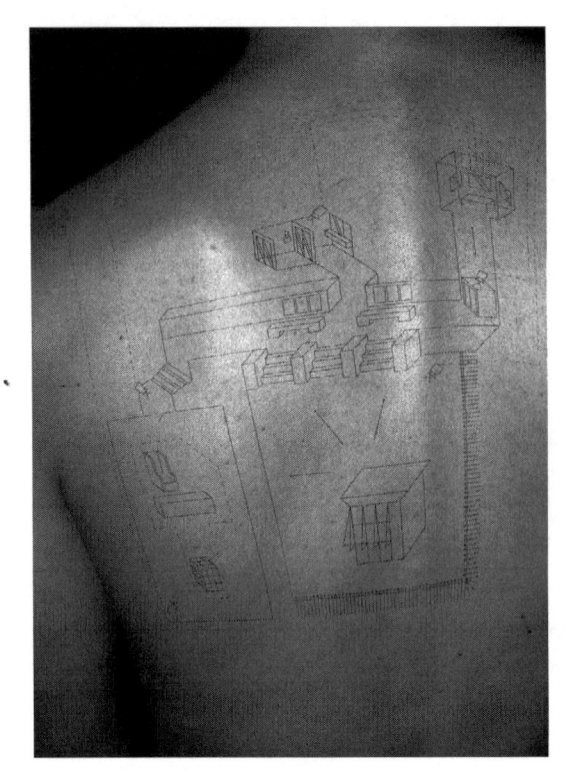

Fig. 88 Bhafi's surveillance system tattoo.

As can be seen on one picture, Bfahi has a tattoo on his back, describing the building's surveillance system. It describes the cafeteria as the center of a panoptic.

Fig. 89 Maps showing the exfiltration of Bfahi.

An exfiltration of Bfahi is then carried out at night, when the school is normally closed and protected only by cameras and automatic systems. But these have supposedly been neutralized by the students. A black and white video shows the complete route of Bfahi's exfiltration in the deserted corridors of the school. The anonymity of the exfiltrators is carefully preserved with the hoods created by the HaCkeD cAms / Œillères project.

Édition sans nom (Nameless Edition): This project proposes a collection of texts in which the designation of things has disappeared. The book also contains non-figurative and untitled images.

Bobo le poète (Bobo the Poet): Bobo writes poems about the projects created during the workshop, or about the participants. The poems are read in class using a synthesized voice.

Fig. 90 + 91 Tree woman video project.

Tree woman: The video (16:30) presents a montage of various people who have all seen the ghost of a tree woman and tell about the experience in their own way.

Fig. 92 L'amour anonyme (Anonymous Love) project.

L'amour anonyme (Anonymous Love): The author navigates the anonymous video chat site Dirty Roulette (a sort of extreme version of Chatroulette) and anonymously says "I love you" to the people he meets. He records the weird chats that follow this declaration.

Contrebande (Smuggling): This project consists of anonymous letters, hidden messages, and fake drug packages sent to members of the school administration. It aims, through provocation, to test the responsiveness of staff members. Large sealed sugar sachets are placed in a person's mailbox, while a false threat on the computer system is spread with an anonymous letter. The threat on the servers was taken very seriously, despite the unrealistic aspect of the messages. The administration talked to several participants in the workshop (who are probably not the ones who sent the letters) and teachers. After a little panic, everything went back to normal—but the administration required that the workshop page be closed. Strangely, what shocked them the most was a simple link to a video, which was not produced by a student of the workshop but by a French artist, and which features a fake rap group masked and equipped with machine guns, playing violent music.

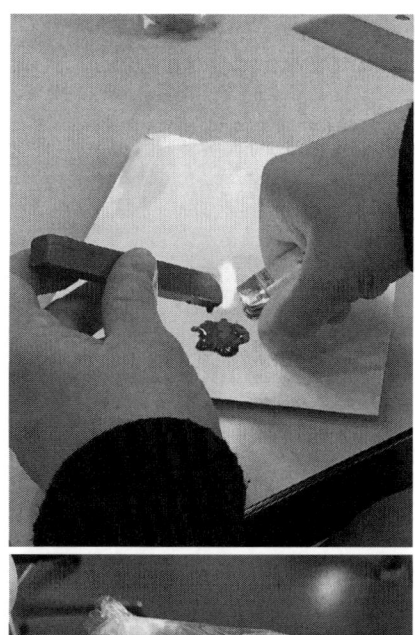

Fig. 93 + 94 Contrebande (Smuggling) project.

A Few Afterthoughts

This experience made it possible to comment more freely on projects (although no anonymous survey was conducted to find out whether certain remarks about the projects had offended their creators). Anonymity made it possible for a second or third creator to contribute to a project, allowing collective projects to appear. Anonymity also allowed the crossing of certain boundaries that have sometimes led to friction with the school administration. This experimental engagement with both anonymity as a concept and as an educational tool helped us realize how much an art and design school could gain by anonymizing some of its practices.

That being said, this short experience does not allow us to draw extensive conclusions regarding the questions we asked ourselves at the beginning of this chapter. It has to be pursued.

One way to pursue this experimentation might be through the upcoming introduction of a documentation tool for the school. This online tool, accessible only to students and teachers, would allow them to document and share project research. Students would have the opportunity to conduct this documentation anonymously, alone or with others. Making this tool accessible only to students and teachers would also prevent the few problems encountered during our experience, such as the diffusion of sensitive information on sites like Reddit or Imgur.

List of Figures

Fig. 1 Kampnagel Piazza, Hamburg (October 2018), with installation Aram Bartholl, "Forgot your password? (Hamburg)" (bottom left), and banner created by RYBN.ORG (center left) • Photo: Fred Dott

Fig. 2 Aram Bartholl, "Is this you in the video?"; installation view (2018, Kampnagel Piazza, Hamburg) • Photo: Fred Dott

Fig. 3 Heath Bunting, "woody bay survival group" (series of posters); installation view (2018, Kampnagel, west wing, Hamburg) • Photo: Fred Dott

Fig. 4 Heath Bunting, "woody bay survival group" (series of posters, detail); installation view (2018, Kampnagel, west wing, Hamburg) • Photo: Fred Dott

Fig. 5 + 6 Performance "Transformalor [Transformella malor 4.4.6.11]" by Johannes Paul Raether; part of the A=ANONYM program (2018, IKEA Hamburg City, Hamburg) • Photos: Daniela Silvestrin

Fig. 7 Performance "Transformalor [Transformella malor 4.4.6.11]" by Johannes Paul Raether; part of the A=ANONYM program (2018, Große Bergstraße, Altona, near IKEA Hamburg City, Hamburg) • Photo: Andreas Broeckmann

Fig. 8–10 knowbotiq, "Amazonian Flesh, how to hang in trees during strike"; installation view (detail) (2018, Kampnagel, "Meisterbude"/main foyer, Hamburg) • Foto: Fred Dott

Fig. 11 knowbotiq, "Amazonian Flesh, how to hang in trees during strike"; installation view (detail) (2018, Kampnagel, "Meisterbude"/main foyer, Hamburg) • Photo: knowbotiq

Fig. 12 Simon Farid, "Towards an Art History of Art Gallery Security Guards"; installation view (2018, Kampnagel, "the artist studio"/main foyer, Hamburg) • Photo: Fred Dott

Fig. 13 + 14 RYBN.ORG, "The Great Offshore";

Fig. 15 RYBN.ORG, "Algoffshore"; installation view (detail) (2018, Kampnagel, main foyer, Hamburg) • Photos: Fred Dott

Fig. 16 + 17 Workshop "Chemopolitics. A collective game about endocrine disruptors" by Bureau d'études; part of the A=ANONYM program (2018, Kampnagel, Hamburg) • Photos: Andreas Broeckmann

Fig. 18 Presentation and discussion of works by Parastou Forouhar with

Artistic Research on Anonymity
p. 35–67

RCA research team members (2017, Steyerberg, Lower Saxony) • Photo: Andreas Broeckmann

Fig. 19 Workshop "KILLYOURPHONE.COM" by Aram Bartholl, with RCA research team members) • Photo: Andreas Broeckmann

Fig. 20 Banner created by RYBN.ORG for the A=ANONYM exhibition; installation view (2018, Kampnagel, main foyer, Hamburg) • Photo: Fred Dott

Fig. 21 Artist talk by Simon Farid and discussion with the audience as part of the A=ANONYM conference program (2018, Kampnagel, "the artist studio"/main foyer, Hamburg) • Photo: Christine Raczka

Fig. 22 Workshop of the Reconfiguring Anonymity team, Leuphana University, Lüneburg, January 2016 • Photo: Andreas Broeckmann

Fig. 23 RYBN.ORG, Offshore Tour Operator Hamburg map • Image: RYBN.ORG

Anonymity on Demand: The Great Offshore
p. 167–185

Fig. 24–43 Photographs collected during the Offshore Tour in Hamburg, workshop organized in the context of the exhibition A=ANONYM, Kampnagel, 2018 • Photos: Christoph and Sophie, participants of the Offshore Tour Workshop Hamburg

Fig. 44 Rules of the game "The frog with three legs" • Photo: Bureau d'études

Sanitary Police and the Politics of Anonymity: Observations on a Game about Endocrine Disruptors
p. 210–225

Fig. 45 Board game of the game "The frog with three legs" • Photo: Bureau d'études

Fig. 46 Some cards of the game "The frog with three legs" • Photo: Bureau d'études

Fig. 47 Investigation factsheet for the game "The frog with three legs" • Photo: Bureau d'études

Fig. 48 Is This You in the Video? 2018. Installation and performance in public space; metal, wood, plaster, camera, cables, battery; 134 × 19.7 × 19.7 inches (340 × 50 × 50 cm) • Photo: Aram Bartholl

Anonymity: Obsolescence and Desire
p. 275–285

Fig. 49 Keepalive, 2015. Outdoor sculpture; rock, steel, router, USB key, thermoelectric generator, fire, software, PDF database; 39.3 × 43.3 × 35.4 inches (100 × 110 × 90 cm). Exhibited at Landart Kunstverein Springhornhof Neuenkirchen, Lower Saxony, Germany; commissioned by the Center for Digital Cultures, Leuphana University, Lüneburg; curated by Andreas Broeckmann, Leuphana Arts Program; and realized as part of the Innovation Incubator Lüneburg, a large EU project funded by the European Fund for Regional Development and the German state of Lower Saxony • Photo: Aram Bartholl

Fig. 50 BYOD—Bring Your Own Disk (and Crush It), 2014. Installation and performance; harddrive punch shredder; size variable • Photo: Aram Bartholl

Fig. 51 Forgot Your Password? 2013. Book series, 8 hardcover volumes, each 8.3 × 10.6 inches (21 × 27 cm) • Photo: Aram Bartholl

Fig. 52 KILLYOURPHONE.COM, 2014. Open workshop format, with variable materials and sizes • Photo: Aram Bartholl

Fig. 53 How to Vacuum Form, 2012. Performance, installation, DIY activity; Guy Fawkes mask, white Guy Fawkes mask copies, transparent Guy Fawkes mask, polysterol, plaster, hose, hose connectors, clamps, vacuum hand pump, toaster, wooden board, rods, stop watch, cutters, cutting mat, black pens, photo album, table, wooden pole; 118 × 197 × 137.8 inches (300 × 500 × 350 cm) • Photo: Aram Bartholl

Fig. 54 15 Seconds of Fame, 2010. Performance, video, and photo series • Screenshot: Aram Bartholl

Fig. 55 Dead Drops, 2010–ongoing. Public intervention; offline peer-to-peer file-sharing network • Photo: Aram Bartholl

Fig. 56 WoW, 2006–2009. Workshop and public intervention; Materials: Cardboard, Markers, Scissors • Photo: Aram Bartholl

Collective Pleasures of Anonymity: From Public Restrooms to 4chan and Chatroulette
p. 356–378

Fig. 57 Cropped screenshot of a 4chan thread with (supposedly different) users posting under the same Anonymous pseudonym, June 11, 2016. Author's collection • Image: the author

Fig. 58 Restroom graffiti, People's Cafe, San Francisco. Wikipedia, uploaded February 1, 2009, https://en.wikipedia.org/wiki/Latrinalia#/media/File:Peoples_cafe.jpg • Photo: the author

Fig. 59–61 Stills from the documentary film Tearoom (2008). The material is filmed by the Police Department in Mansfield, Ohio, in 1962, in the public restroom underneath the park in the center of town. It led to the arrest of a large number of men (varying from 38 to 69 years old). "Tearoom (excerpt)," video, 9:35, uploaded by la llorona, YouTube, May 26, 2012, https://youtu.be/npAVR5lsj8s • Images: William E. Jones

Fig. 62 + 63 Two instances of online masquerading on Chatroulette. Screenshot on Pinterest UK, https://www.pinterest.co.uk/pin/797840890208313899/; and Fred Wilson, "What to Make of Chatroulette?," Business Insider, February 11, 2010, https://www.businessinsider.com/whattomakeofchatroulette20102 • Screenshots: the author

Fig. 64 Example of gender-bending roleplaying global celebrities on a random videochat site. "Miley Cyrus—Wrecking Ball (Chatroulette FeVer

Club Version)," video, 2:46, uploaded by Willy Christmas, December 23, 2013, YouTube, https://youtu.be/YnJzUH2nbDs • Screenshot: the author

Fig. 65–71 Photo: Johannes Paul Raether

Fig. 72 InnerCity Ikeality [4.4.6.13] Appearance view, IKEA Hamburg Altona (2018) • Photo: Roman Szczesny

Fig. 73–77 InnerCity Ikeality [4.4.6.13] Appearance view, IKEA Hamburg Altona (2018) • Photo: Olaf Pascheit

Transformella Malor Ikeae:
InnerCity Ikeality [4.4.6.11]
p. 379–393

All photos: Stéphane Degoutin, Vadim Bernard, Martin de Bie

Fig. 78 The anonymous box

Fig. 79 Sample of a discussion on the Reddit page:
 – [bobodogeatjim] I want you to lick my neck and chew on my ear by whispering insults to me
 – [wiryspur] Whenever you want
 – [bobodogeatjim] Don't get smart, my little duck, tell me what you'd do to me – [wiryspur] Shut up, I know where you live
 – [bobodogeatjim] See you at my place monday at 9pm
 – [bouddah3000] I came to your place but you weren't there
 – [bobodogeatjim] false and very false. So sad

Fig. 80 Marika Dermineur (of the artist collective RYBN) talks about RYBN's project "The Great Offshore," an investigation into the depth of the offshore industry (rybn.org/thegreatoffshore)

Fig. 81 Daniela Silvestrin trying to decipher an anonymous student's proposition

Fig. 82 The caption reads: "I would like Jordan (fashion design student) and M De Bie (teacher) to tell us a little bit about this picture."

Fig. 83 We had to make a list of the projects. We had a hard time counting them: is this one a joke or a project? Is Bouddah3000 the same person as Bouddha3000? etc.

Fig. 84 Buddha3000 project

Fig. 85 Fashion Goddess project

Fig. 86 MarcPartoucheTV project

Fig. 87 Libérer Bfahi (Free Bfahi) project

Fig. 88 Bhafi's surveillance system tattoo

Fig. 89 Maps showing the exfiltration of Bfahi

Fig. 90 + 91 Tree woman video project

Fig. 92 L'amour anonyme (Anonymous Love) project

Fig. 93 + 94 Contrebande (Smuggling) project

Anonymity Workshop
p. 447–462

List of figures

List of Artworks

USAE, Heath Bunting, 2018. Images courtesy of the artist.

USAE
p. 110–115

A List of Famous Artists Who Used to Be Invigilators, Simon Farid, 2018. Courtesy of the artist.

A List of Famous Artists Who Used to Be Invigilators
p. 142–150

A Provisional Manifesto for Invigilator-Friendly Artworks, Simon Farid, 2018. Courtesy of the artist.

A Provisional Manifesto for Invigilator-Friendly Artworks, or Your Artwork Is an Invigilator's Labor Conditions
p. 336–339

From the series **She Remembers**, Parastou Forouhar, 2017. Photos courtesy of the artist.

She remembers
p. 346–353

Contributors

Abigail Curlew is a journalist, doctoral researcher, and transfeminist who specializes in advocacy around LGBTQ+ human rights, surveillance studies, and research around social media, doxxing, and online vigilantes. Abigail currently holds a Pierre Elliot Trudeau Foundation doctoral scholarship and a Social Science and Humanities Research Council (SSHRC) doctoral fellowship for her research examining practices of do-it-yourself (DIY) policing and surveillance used against trans feminine activists, journalists, and scholars by anti-transgender trolls.

p. 255 Fraught Platform Governmentality

Amelie Baumann is a postdoctoral research associate at Freie Universität Berlin, where she is a member of the CRC 1171 "Affective Societies". She is currently preparing an ethnographic research project on Covid-19 and aging/being old in Germany. Prior to that, she was a doctoral student at the University of Bremen and a member of the research group "Reconfiguring Anonymity". In her Ph.D. thesis, which she defended in October 2020, she ethnographically explored the transformation of anonymity in gamete donation in the UK and Germany by focusing on the knowledge practices and politics of donor-conceived persons.

p. 188 DNA Works!

p. 394 Authenticity

Andreas Broeckmann is an art historian and curator who lives in Berlin. Currently Visiting Professor for Art History and Media Theory at the Academy of Fine Arts, Leipzig (HGB – Hochschule für Grafik und Buchkunst, 2017–2020) and engaged in the research and documentation project, Les Immateriaux Research. From 2011–2016 he directed the Leuphana Arts Program of Leuphana University Lüneburg. He was the Founding Director of the Dortmunder U – Centre for Art and Creativity (2009–2011)

p. 35 Artistic Research on Anonymity

and has curated exhibitions and festivals in major European venues, incl. transmediale and ISEA2010 RUHR. He holds a Ph.D. in Art History from the University of East Anglia, Norwich/UK, and lectures internationally about the history of modern art, media theory, machine aesthetics, and digital culture. He is the author of *Machine Art in the Twentieth Century* (MIT-Press, 2016).

Anna Henke is a cultural anthropologist, doctoral student and research assistant at the Institute of European Ethnology/Cultural Anthropology at the University of Hamburg. She is part of the research group "Reconfiguring Anonymity" and belongs to the subproject "Identity, Health Insurance and Customer Cards". Her current research focuses on digital cultures, anonymity and identity practices, and digitization from a science and technology studies perspective.

p. 433 Bitcoin Anonymous?

Anon I have decided to publish this text anonymously. The reason is not that I want this authorial act to put me out of reach. Anyone who wanted to could surely find out who the text's author is. And yet, I still consider anonymity meaningful. Not in the traditional sense as personal protection, but as part of a collective practice. This practice demands a particular attitude of which anonymity is the expression as well as the performative enactment. It has been developed by members of so-called 12-step groups. Anonymity here is about not taking the foremost interest in one's own well-being, but to instead consider personal well-being as directly connected to that of all living beings and organisms on this planet. Considering myself an advocate of such an attitude, it would be impossible for me to situate this text meaningfully without remaining nameless. I see the reason for this in my ethical obligation towards my integrity and towards the people whom I research about. If you would like to get in touch, anonymity is not an obstacle. Write me on: anonymity_with_an_attitude@posteo.de

p. 123 Longing for a Selfless Self

Aram Bartholl uses sculptural interventions, installations, and performative workshops to question our engagement with media and with public economies linked to social networks, online platforms, and digital dissemination strategies. He addresses socially relevant topics, including surveillance, data privacy and technology dependence, through his work by transferring the gaps, contradictions, and absurdities of our everyday digital lives to physical settings. The effect is twofold. The works create an at-times bizarre confrontation with our own ignorance of globally active platform capitalism, and they renegotiate network activities as political forms of participation on an analog level using the potential of public space. arambartholl.com

p. 275 Anonymity: Obsolescence and Desire

Bureau d'études are a French conceptual art group founded in 1998 by Léonore Bonaccini and Xavier Fourt. During 20 years, the group develops research on the structures of power and capitalism. The group lives now in the countryside and works on a scale 1:1 collective project across agriculture, commons and resymbolizing researches (www.fermedelamhotte.fr). Bureau d'études is co-founder of the Laboratory Planet collective&journal (www.laboratoryplanet.org) and of the Aliens in Green project (www.aliensingreen.eu) a participatory action combining hands-on DIY science protocols, xenopolitical role-play and queering rituals. bureaudetudes.org

p. 210 Sanitary Police and the Politics of Anonymity

Daniël de Zeeuw is a Ph.D. candidate at the Amsterdam School for Cultural Analysis and Lecturer New Media at the University of Amsterdam. He is also a member of the Open Intelligence Lab, editor at Krisis, Journal for Contemporary Philosophy, and affiliated researcher at the Institute of Network Cultures. Working at the intersection of media and cultural studies, his current research focuses on fringe digital subcultures on 4chan and Reddit as post-truth laboratories of conspiracy theories, junk news, political extremism and memes that have become increasingly influential in recent years, and that cast a critical light on the vicissitudes of our hyper-mediatized, global digital condition.

p. 356 Collective Pleasures of Anonymity

Contributors

Daniela Silvestrin is a Berlin-based curator, cultural researcher, programme developer and organises international cultural projects. Her work focuses on hybrid artistic practices and the production of knowledge where art, society, technology and the natural sciences meet. Since 2011, Daniela has worked for various festivals, art projects, exhibitions, and is co-editor of various publications. danielasilvestrin.info

p. 35 Artistic Research on Anonymity

Dwaipayan Banerjee is an Assistant Professor of Science, Technology, and Society (STS) at MIT. His first book *Hematologies: The Political Life of Blood in India* (Cornell University Press, forthcoming December 2019) is co-written with anthropologist Jacob Copeman. Hematologies examines how the giving and receiving of blood has shaped social and political life in north India in the twentieth and twenty-first centuries. Professor Banerjee's second book, *Enduring Cancer: Life, Death and Diagnosis in Delhi* (Duke University Press, forthcoming August 2020), is an ethnography of the experience of living with cancer in India.

p. 70 Anonymity and Transgression

Gerald Raunig works at the eipcp as one of the editors of the multilingual publishing platform transversal texts (transversal.at), and at the Zürcher Hochschule der Künste as a Professor of philosophy. Recent books in English: *Factories of Knowledge, Industries of Creativity*, 2013; *DIVIDUUM. Machinic Capitalism and Molecular Revolution*, Vol. 1, 2016, both translated by Aileen Derieg and published by Semiotext(e)/MIT Press.

p. 424 Speak their Endless Names

Gertraud Koch is a Professor and head of the Institute of European Ethnology/Cultural Anthropology at University of Hamburg and a member of the expert committee "Intangible Cultural Heritage" of the German Commission for UNESCO. For many years, her main research focuses on cultural diversity, social inclusion, digital cultures, and knowledge anthropology. Recent publication: Digitzation. Theories and Concepts for empirical cultural research. Routledge 2017.

p. 151 Anonymity as Everyday Phenomenon

Contributors

Götz Bachmann is Professor for Digital Cultures and Senior Researcher at the Centre for Digital Cultures at Leuphana University Lüneburg, Germany. Along with Michi Knecht, he is Co-Speaker of the project "Reconfiguring Anonymity." Together with Andreas Wittel they co-edited a special edition of the ephemera Journal on the "Social Productivity of Anonymity". He is an ethnographer by trade, and the author of a monograph on "Kollegialität" (collegiality.) His ongoing research looks at radical engineers in the San Francisco Bay Area.

p. 16 Toward a Kaleidoscopic Understanding of Anonymity

Heath Bunting has exhibited, performed and taught internationally for over 25 years. As a young adult, he undertook a three year apprenticeship in stained glass. After this, Heath spent several years roaming both Bristol and London as a street artist as well as distributing thousands of art-works via postal and fax networks. During the rise of the internet, he was a key participant of the net.art movement. Within this time he founded irational.org. He has setup and run multiple radio transmission and listening stations internationally. In his current work, The Status Project, he uses artificial intelligence to search for artificial life in both societal and natural systems.
irational.org/heath

p. 110 USAE

Helen Nissenbaum is a Professor at Cornell Tech and in the Information Science Department at Cornell University. Her research takes an ethical perspective on policy, law, science, and engineering relating to information technology, computing, digital media and data science. Topics have included privacy, trust, accountability, security, and values in technology design. Her books include *Obfuscation: A User's Guide for Privacy and Protest*, with Finn Brunton (MIT Press, 2015) and *Privacy in Context: Technology, Policy, and the Integrity of Social Life* (Stanford, 2010).

p. 116 Big Data's End Run

Jacob Copeman is Senior Lecturer in Social Anthropology at the University of Edinburgh. His most recent book, co-authored with Dwaipayan Banerjee, is *Hematologies:*

p. 70 Anonymity and Transgression

The Political Life of Blood in India (2019). He is also the author of *Veins of Devotion: Blood Donation and Religious Experience in North India* (2009) and editor or co-editor of *Blood Donation, Bioeconomy, Culture* (2009), *The Guru in South Asia: New Interdisciplinary Perspectives* (2012), *South Asian Tissue Economies* (2013), *Social Theory After Strathern* (2014), *On Names in South Asia: Iteration, (Im)propriety and Dissimulation* (2015), and *Fake: Anthropological Keywords* (2018).

Julien McHardy is a sociologist of technology, curator, designer and publisher concerned with methods for working and thinking across different fields of expertise and experience. His work at the intersection of the arts, design, research and publishing is collaborative involving changing constellations of people and institutions. He co-founded the open access publisher Mattering Press and ScholarLed, a collective of academic led open access presses. julienmchardy.info

p. 16 Toward a Kaleidoscopic Understanding of Anonymity

knowbotiq (Yvonne Wilhelm, Christian Huebler) is an artist group experimenting with forms and medialities of knowledge, political representation, and epistemic disobedience. Recent projects investigate and enact political landscapes with a focus on algorithmic governmentalities, libidinous and affective economies, and postcolonial violence. Through various formats (performative settings, critical fabulations, inventions, encounters) the group explores molecular, psychotrope and derivative aesthetics. knowbotiq.net / **Nina Bandi** is a political philosopher who is interested in the overlapping of speculative thought, artistic practices, and the political. Based in Zurich and Vienna, she works on questions of non-/representation and the relation between bodies, technology, and materiality from a feminist and postcolonial perspective. From 2015–2019, she was part of the research project "What Can Art Do" at Lucerne School of Art and Design. (The texts of knowbotiq for Amazonian Flesh were written in collaboration with Nina Bandi.)

p. 294 Amazonian Flesh

Contributors

Martin De Bie is a designer/teacher/researcher based in Paris. His personal research topics are focused on the hybridization of traditional craft techniques and high-tech processes. During many years, he has collaborated with the "now closed" french branch of the Graffiti Research Lab to develop an experimental approach to design, combining interaction technologies with urban socio-cultural practices. Martin has also co-funded DataPaulette, a multi-disciplinary collective focused on research and development in textiles and digital technologies and who take the form of an independent laboratory operating as a hackerspace. Now, he is sharing his time between teaching physical computing and interaction design at ENSAD and his personal research. martindebie.com

p. 123 Anonymity Workshop

Michi Knecht is Professor for Social Anthropology and one of the speakers of the Worlds of Contradiction-Platform at Bremen University. Her research focuses on interconnections between knowledge practices and social forms. At the intersections of Anthropology and STS she has investigated reproductive technologies, political and religious movements, anonymity and new forms of kinship. With Michael Flitner and Friederike Gesing she has co-founded the Bremen NatureCultures Lab, a small think tank for new research designs in human-body, human-other species and human-environment relations. Other Anonymity related Publications: "The Social Productivity of Anonymity" (*ephemera* 17/2, with Andreas Wittel and Götz Bachmann)

p. 16 Toward a Kaleidoscopic Understanding of Anonymity

Nils Zurawski is a Social Anthropologist and Criminologist, working at the University of Hamburg and has been researching widely on Surveillance, Identity, Security, Police, and Doping in Sports. He blogs (surveillance-studies.org) and runs the podcast "Berichte aus Panotopia" (notes from Panotopia). His latest publications include: *Kritik des Anti-Doping* (transcript 2019); *Bodies as Evidence. Security, Knowledge, and Power* (Duke 2018).

p. 16 Toward a Kaleidoscopic Understanding of Anonymity

p. 286 Policing Normality

p. 340 Care or control?

p. 306 Proximity, Distance and State Power

Parastou Forouhar (born 1962 in Tehran) is an Iranian installation artist who lives and works in Germany. Forouhar's art reflects her criticism of the Iranian government and often plays with the ideas of identity. Her artwork expresses a critical response towards the politics in Iran and Islamic Fundamentalism. The loss of her parents fuels Forouhar's work and challenges viewers to take a stand on war crimes against innocent citizens.
parastou-forouhar.de

p. 346   She Remembers

Paula Bialski is appointed Associated Professor of Sociology and digitalisation at University of St. Gallen. She is an ethnographer of new media in everyday life, looking at contexts of usage as well as production, and she frames her research within cultural, social and media theory in general, and science and technology studies in particular. The goal of her current research project, titled "Programmer Worlds," is to investigate the way in which everyday practices of corporate software developers affect our digital infrastructures. She has been an affiliated member of the "Reconfiguring Anonymity" research group since its inception in 2013.

p. 326   Dual Reality

Randi Heinrichs is a Ph.D. candidate at the Leuphana University, Luneburg, where she is working on her dissertation on anonymity, social media platforms and (data-)neighbourhoods. Her research interests, teaching, and writing are located at the intersections of digital cultures, technology, and questions around anonymity, security, fairness and discrimination. She is an alumni of the Algorithmic Fairness and Opacity Group at UC Berkeley, USA and affiliated with the Digital Democracies Group at Simon Fraser University, Canada. She is also a member of the editorial board of the journal spheres and a collective member of ephemera.

p. 226   Where Do the Data Live?

RYBN.ORG is an art research collective, created in 1999, based in Paris. RYBN.ORG conducts extra-disciplinary investigations towards contemporary socio-technical systems, such as: algorithmic trading, high-frequency

p. 167   Anonymity on Demand

Contributors

markets infrastructures, network protocols, offshore finance governance, Artificial Artificial Intelligence, etc. The works of RYBN.ORG have been shown in numerous contemporary art exhibitions such as Open Codes (ZKM, 2019), The Great Offshore (Espace Multimédia Gantner, 2017), Nervöse System (HKW, 2015), Media Mediums (Ygrec, 2014) Gutes Böses Geld (Kunsthalle Baden-Baden, 2014), Infosphäre (ZKM, 2014), Requiem for a Bank (HMKV, 2013), 2062 (la Gaîté lyrique, 2012), The Global Contemporary (ZKM, 2011), El Processo Como Paradigma (LABoral, 2010), Stock Overflow (iMAL, 2009). rybn.org

Simon Farid is a sometime artist and moretime gallery guard at an art institution in central London. He makes work exploring and exploiting this dual position through collaborative, secret, public or personal approaches across academia, fine art practices, fashion and live performance. Thinking about the different meanings of collaboration, Farid examines the difficult complicities of working with, within, for and against formal art institutions, from the position of a low-level frontline gallery worker. simonfarid.com

p. 142 A List of Famous Artists Who Used to Be Invigilators

p. 336 A Provisional Manifesto for Invigilator-Friendly Artworks, or Your Artwork Is an Invigilator's Labor Conditions

Solon Barocas is a Principal Researcher in the New York City lab of Microsoft Research and an Assistant Professor in the Department of Information Science at Cornell University. He is also a Faculty Associate at the Berkman Klein Center for Internet & Society at Harvard University. His research explores ethical and policy issues in artificial intelligence. Borocas co-founded the annual workshop on Fairness, Accountability, and Transparency in Machine Learning (FAT/ML) and later established the ACM conference on Fairness, Accountability, and Transparency (FAT*).

p. 116 Big Data's End Run

Stéphane Degoutin is an artist, writer, researcher. He often works with artist and researcher Gwenola Wagon. He focuses on ambivalent situations, between war and dance, sexual pleasure and nonplaces, the city and its

p. 447 Anonymity Workshop

potential, posthuman theories and the obsolescence of mankind. d-w.fr

Thorsten Thiel is head of the research group "Democracy and Digitalisation" at the Weizenbaum Institute for the Networked Society in Berlin.

p. 88 Anonymity: The Politicisation of a Concept

Transformella is an Artificial Identity, a SelfSister and an alteridentitarian aLifveForm, assembled and fed by Johannes Paul Raether in formation with multiple others. She is the first in the lifeline of the Transformellae and was developed for researching and intervening into ReproReality in Berlin in July 2010. In her early versions 4.0 to 4.4, she operated as Transformella domestica, forking themselves into Transformalor (transformella malor) in 2015. She began to travel as an updated MetaMother with their ReproTribe to respective local warehouses for the mass reproduction of items, the IKEAE (everysite) (4.4.6.0 since 2015). Since then, the forked lifeline as artificial identity Transformalor with their various language devices and ReproDiagrams has appeared in various Ikea, such as the one in Berlin, Warszawa, Hamburg and Düsseldorf among others. transformella.net

p. 379 Transformella Malor Ikeae

Vadim Bernard, born in Grenoble in 1980, co-founded Dépli design studio in 2007. He worked for the MAC/VAL, Le Fresnoy, le Magasin-CNAC, Jean Nouvel, la Cinémathèque Française, Sciences Po, the Arab World Institute, le Grand Palais, le Musée d'Orsay and the Hong Kong Heritage Museum. In 2013 he started teaching Interaction Design at the EnsAD. depli-ds.com

p. 447 Anonymity Workshop

Citation Guide

All contributions to this volume—with the exception of Longing for a Selfless Self and other Ambivalences of Anonymity, whose author opted to publish anonymously—are published pseudo-anonymously to highlight tensions between authorship and anonymity while still allowing attribution. Please cite contributions as follows:

Anon Collective. Book of Anonymity. Milky Way, Earth: punctum books, 2021.

CHAPTERS, IN ORDER OF APPEARANCE

Bachmann, Götz, Julien McHardy, Michi Knecht and Nils Zurawski
"Toward a Kaleidoscopic Understanding of Anonymity".
In Book of Anonymity, edited by Anon Collective. Milky Way, Earth: punctum books (2021): 16–34.

Daniela Silvestrin and Broeckmann, Andreas.
"Artistic Research on Anonymity".
In Book of Anonymity, edited by Anon Collective. Milky Way, Earth: punctum books (2021): 35–67.

Copeman, Jacob and Dwaipayan Banerjee.
"Anonymity and Transgression".
In Book of Anonymity, edited by Anon Collective. Milky Way, Earth: punctum books (2021): 70–87.

Thiel, Thorsten.
"Anonymity: The Politicisation of a Concept".
In Book of Anonymity, edited by Anon Collective. Milky Way, Earth: punctum books (2021): 88–109.

Bunting, Heath.
"USAE".
In Book of Anonymity, edited by Anon Collective. Milky Way, Earth: punctum books (2021): 110–115.

Barocas, Solon and Helen Nissenbaum.
"Big Data's End Run around Anonymity and Consent".
In Book of Anonymity, edited by Anon Collective. Milky Way, Earth: punctum books (2021): 116–141.

Farid, Simon.
"A List of Famous Artists Who Used to Be Invigilators".
In Book of Anonymity, edited by Anon Collective. Milky Way, Earth: punctum books (2021): 142–150.

Koch, Gertraud.
"Anonymity as Everyday Phenomenon and as a Topic of Research".
In Book of Anonymity, edited by Anon Collective. Milky Way, Earth: punctum books (2021): 151–166.

RYBN.ORG.
"Anonymity on Demand: The Great Offshore".
In Book of Anonymity, edited by Anon Collective. Milky Way, Earth: punctum books (2021): 167–185.

Baumann, Amelie.
"DNA Works! Merging Genetics and the Digital Realm".
In Book of Anonymity, edited by Anon Collective. Milky Way, Earth: punctum books (2021): 188–209.

Bureau d'études.
"Sanitary Policy and the Policy of Anonymity: Notes about a Game on Endocrine Disruptors".
In Book of Anonymity, edited by Anon Collective. Milky Way, Earth: punctum books (2021): 210–225.

Heinrichs, Randi.
"Where Do the Data Live?".
In Book of Anonymity, edited by Anon Collective. Milky Way, Earth: punctum books (2021): 226–254.

Curlew, Abigail.
"Fraught Platform Governmentality: Anonymity, Content Moderation and Regulatory Strategies over Yik Yak".
In Book of Anonymity, edited by Anon Collective. Milky Way, Earth: punctum books (2021): 255–274.

Bartholl, Aram.
"**Anonymity: Obsolescence and Desire**".
In Book of Anonymity, edited by Anon Collective. Milky Way, Earth: punctum books (2021): 275–285.

Zurawski, Nils.
"**Policing Normality: Police Work, Anonymity and a Sociology of the Mundane**".
In Book of Anonymity, edited by Anon Collective. Milky Way, Earth: punctum books (2021): 286–290.

Knowbotiq and Nina Bandi.
"**Amazonian Flesh: How to Hang in Trees during Strike?**".
In Book of Anonymity, edited by Anon Collective. Milky Way, Earth: punctum books (2021): 294–305.

Zurawski, Nils.
"**Proximity, Distance and State Powers: Policing Practices and the Regulation of Anonymity**".
In Book of Anonymity, edited by Anon Collective. Milky Way, Earth: punctum books (2021): 306–325.

Bialski, Paula and Simon Farid.
"**Dual Reality: (Un)Observed Magic in the Workplace**".
In Book of Anonymity, edited by Anon Collective. Milky Way, Earth: punctum books (2021): 326–335.

Farid, Simon.
"**A Provisional Manifesto for Invigilator-Friendly Artworks, or Your Artwork Is an Invigilator's Labor Conditions**".
In Book of Anonymity, edited by Anon Collective. Milky Way, Earth: punctum books (2021): 336–339.

Zurawski, Nils.
"**Care or control? Police, Youth and Mutual Anonymity**".
In Book of Anonymity, edited by Anon Collective. Milky Way, Earth: punctum books (2021): 340–345.

Forouhar, Parastou.
"She Remembers".
In Book of Anonymity, edited by Anon Collective. Milky Way, Earth: punctum books (2021): 346–353.

de Zeeuw, Daniël.
"Collective Pleasures of Anonymity: From Public Restrooms to 4chan and Chatroulette".
In Book of Anonymity, edited by Anon Collective. Milky Way, Earth: punctum books (2021): 356–378.

Transformella Malor Ikeae (cared for by JP Raether).
"Transformella Malor Ikeae: InnerCity Ikeality [4.4.6.11]".
In Book of Anonymity, edited by Anon Collective. Milky Way, Earth: punctum books (2021): 379–393.

Baumann, Amelie.
"Authenticity".
In Book of Anonymity, edited by Anon Collective. Milky Way, Earth: punctum books (2021): 394–400.

Anon.
"Longing for a Selfless Self and other Ambivalences of Anonymity".
In Book of Anonymity, edited by Anon Collective. Milky Way, Earth: punctum books (2021): 401–423.

Raunig, Gerald.
"Speak their Endless Names".
In Book of Anonymity, edited by Anon Collective. Milky Way, Earth: punctum books (2021): 424–432.

Henke, Anna.
"Bitcoin Anonymous? Of Trust in Code and Paper".
In Book of Anonymity, edited by Anon Collective. Milky Way, Earth: punctum books (2021): 433–446.

Degoutin, Stephane, Vadim Bernard and Martin de Bie.
"Anonymity Workshop".
In Book of Anonymity, edited by Anon Collective. Milky Way, Earth: punctum books (2021): 447–462.

Acknowledgments

Acknowledgments are one place where the invisible labor that goes into a book is made visible: Books are usually built on the labor of partners, parents, and families; ideas are formed in conversation with our intellectual networks, be they students, colleagues, or friends; research needs the researched to become good research; and readable printed sentences need copyeditors and proofreaders. In short, acknowledgments are a place where some of the suppressive functions of anonymity are corrected (while hierarchies also get stabilized). To thank some of those who made this book possible, we partially suspend our experiment in anonymous writing. The editors' deep thanks goes to all the artists, authors, and project partners who took part in the comprehensive research program, as well as in the workshops, events, and exhibition by the project Reconfiguring Anonymity and the associated research group. Thanks for stretching and molding our thinking about and knowledge of anonymity goes to—beyond the contributors of this book—Alma Akbari, Katrin Amelang, Andreas Bernard, Lars Bretthauer, Christoph Brunner, Johanne Yttri Dahl, Simon Egbert, Silvain Firer-Blaess, Seda Gürses, Maren Heibges (née Klotz), Isto Huvila, Kiwi Menrath, Saad Metry, Rabih Mroué, Eirini Papadaki, Helena Peltonen-Gassmann, Renée Ridgway, RYBN.org, Ingrid Schneider, Seth Schoen, SKILLS (Camilla M. Fehér and Sylvi Kretzschmar), Urs Stäheli, Thorsten Thiel, Carolin Wiedemann, and (especially!) Andreas Wittel. We are deeply indebted to our funding institution, the Volkswagen Foundation (VolkswagenStiftung), and its funding program Key Issues in Society and Academy (Schlüsselthemen für Wissenschaft und Gesellschaft), and we extend our particular gratitude to Vera Szöllösi-Brenig. The Centre for Digital Cultures in Lüneburg has been a wonderful host for many of our events and provided additional resources, and Kampnagel in Hamburg hosted the A = Anonym conference and exhibition. We also want to thank the student assistants, most notably Lucy Debus, Carolin Zieringer, Michael Schmidt, Holger Steffen, Helge Stephan, Rebecca Klischat, and Heidi Härterich, and the administrative teams at the Bremen University, University of Hamburg and Leuphana University Lüneburg, with special thanks to Ina Dubberke. We thank Melanie Mallon for copyediting, Steven Corcoran for his German/English translations, Toby Cayouette for the French/English translations, and Martin Müller from Dicey Studios for the beautiful book design and cover art. Further we are thrilled to publish this collection open access with punctum books; thanks to Vincent W.J. van Gerven Oei, Eileen Joy, and Dan Rudmann.

Printed in Great Britain
by Amazon